AF225195

CONTENTS

PORK RECIPES **100**

VEGETABLES RECIPES 130

POULTRY RECIPES

APPETIZERS AND SNACKS 184

BEEF LAMB AND GAME RECIPES 194

INTRODUCTION

Traeger Wood Pellet Grill is a fascinating type of wood Grills that burns wood in the grill using the firewood pellets. Traeger Wood Pellet grill is one of the most common among the top 10 wood pellet grills. It is a perfect match for the warm seasons because they grill any kind of meat, fish, vegetables, chocolate, and fruit to be delicious. For meat lovers, it is a perfect option to turn on the grill to enjoy their favorite meat on the grill. The way to enjoy the grill in any weather with grillers is truly amazing. While using it, all the greasy, smoky, and meat smell will vanish away. It is an open grill, clean, and environment friendly. Using the white oak wood pellets, you can make your favorite meal truly delicious. Every day, you will definitely enjoy your food with the grillers.

Traeger grill and smoker cookbook is your complete guide to use your Traeger grill and smoker to make your home cooking masterpieces, from appetizers to desserts. Traeger grills feature a wood flavoring system that makes the invisible air around you taste as good as if you were eating in a log cabin. This book is a guide to take full advantage of using your Traeger grill or smoker.

We have put this book together with the intent to make you knowledgeable on how to use your Traeger grill to the maximum. We want everything in this book to be as easy as possible for you to achieve. That's why Jack has included her recipes and cooking techniques for you to learn from.

Working:

As it is an electronic grill, so it has several features for us. It has surprising features that are not found in any other product. It has wood pellets. These wood pellets are the main feature of this grill. It has inbuilt fans in it, and it does not need a man to operate. You can easily experience this grill while sitting or standing in your drawing-room. Little efforts are required from your side such as controlling the temperature. It is truly applicable to you because you are the only person who controls the temperature. The fan filter system will automatically seal the air inside the grill so it will never smell of food or any other odor. The controlled temperature is the most unique feature of the grill that will give you the best result at the end of the meal.

ESSENTIALS OF TRAGER WOOD PELLET GRILL

It is not necessary for anyone to say how important an easy griller is. Anyone can use it without much involvement along with professional help. It is a convenient, compact, and comfortable griller. It is very versatile and can be used for creating a BBQ Menu in a relatively short time. You don't require any freestanding gas or propane tanks which makes it very friendly to the environment. It requires very little effort for light, temperature, and comfort. It is the best answer for easy grilling and it is the appetizing kind of grill.

Here are some essentials for every grill owner's tool kit.

1. Gourmet Rubs & Spices

If you've ever slathered a pork roast in a grocery-store BBQ sauce and stuck your meat with a bunch of flavorless, loaded with sugar, trade-name spikes, then you instantly understand the importance of making your rubs and sauces.

While it's awesome to have access to the authentic, high-quality ingredients (and cheap, too!), you don't have to give up your everyday cheat list either.

2. Premium Wood Pellets

There are two big reasons why wood pellets are at the top of the food chain: A) They have zero additives, and B) they smoke up like a pro. It might look like hard work, but woods like hickory, oak, apple, cherry, and maple are the best breeds of trees for the tastier grilling you can get. Never settle for convenience store chips again!

3. Pink Butcher Paper

The light-colored surface of Signature pink butcher paper acts as a natural pad for protecting the meat from the direct heat source. It has a low permeability, dissolves quickly, and can reflect infrared rays to prevent excessive drying. The difference is that you'll eat more of the meat you paid for instead of throwing away a dry crusty surface.

4. Flexible Stainless-Steel Skewers

Looking to master your kebab game? Then your grill shouldn't be without stainless-steel skewers. They're almost odorless, won't scratch your grill like wooden ones, and the flavor-converting ability is way better than regular metal skewers. Plus, building your own kebabs will allow you to master your creative side.

5. Stainless Steel Meat Shredding Claw

Get that juicy pulled chicken and pork meat you've been dreaming about, every time. The meat claw is the ultimate bathroom staple, making it easy to use your hands (and fingers) to finish shredding a huge amount of meat, veggies, cheese, noodles or whatever else the situation calls for.

6. Drip Tray Liners

When it comes to charcoal or wood grilling, you can't go wrong with a drip tray liner. It's not like you have to be a genius to know it helps a lot. It's basically like a mini, removable grill rack for easy cleanup. These liners are great for any grill that doesn't have a removable rack, whether it's a huge monster offset BBQ or a small, compact tabletop electric grill.

7. Stuffed Burger Press

You're barbecuing sick burgers, but have you tried to make bacon-stuffed burgers? Wait-there are hamburgers stuffed with blue cheese? Burger stuffing options are limitless, and they're delicious! But, whether you're a meatloaf-stuffer, a taco-stuffing-whiz, or a burger-ball-flinger, the Ball Stuffer Burger Press makes it easy to add all the deliciousness that's already inside the meat.

8. Dexter Large Cut Slicing Knife

So, carving up a brisket is no easy task -especially if you opt for a single-point blade. More than likely, you'll end up sawing from side to side and hacking up your meat wherever you see fit. That's why we love Dexter's Large Cut Slicing Knife. It's got a serrated edge and a comfortable grip that will make the toughest cuts look like a piece of cake.

9. Barbecue, Smoking & Grilling Cookbooks

Barbecue cookbooks are not one-size-fits-all, but we rounded up a list of the best barbecuing titles out there. Whether you're a smoker-meister or a rotisserie-rager, you'll find something that suits your preferences for how you like your meat to be cooked.

10. Spray Bottles

If you want value-added to your food, then you need a spray bottle. Whether you're spraying a fresh burst or a light mist of flavor, these bottles are the perfect tools for nailing your perfect meal.

11. Vacuum Sealer

Vacuum sealers keep your food wholesome and tasty. It locks in all the juices that are lost when wrapped in plastic wrap or aluminum foil and makes keeping meats, veggies, and snacks fresh and delicious.

12. Magnetic & Clamp Grill Light

If you're a grill-master, then you're a daytime grill-master. This explains why you need a clamp light.

13. Food Saver Jar Sealer

If you vacuum seal your food, then you're also a day-time vacuum sealer. The Food Saver Jar Sealer lets you expand the shelf life of your meats, veggies, and snacks with an airtight, watertight seal. It locks deep flavors in and keeps air, bacteria, and other contaminants out.

14. High Heat Baking Pans + Lids

Bring out the grill master in you. High heat baking pans and lids are two tools that work great for grilling food indoors. You can even stack your pans for a unique presentation.

15. Grill-Shaped Cake Pan

Cake for dinner anyone? A grill-shaped cake pan is perfect for sweeping up all the flavors of your favorite grilled meats.

What Is Traeger Wood Pellet Grill

Traeger Wood Pellet Grill is a wood pellet grill that has a set of manual controls that allows the user to control the cooking temperature. It differs from other smoker grills such as the Traeger electric smoker and the pellet grills that use a digital control to adjust the temperature. The grill uses a wood pellet fuel that causes it to smoke. The different types of wood pellets that the grill uses to smoke food are Apple wood pellets, Hickory wood pellets, Mesquite wood pellets, Cherry wood pellets, and Alder wood pellets. The wood pellets can be used to smoke chicken, turkey, fish, oysters, cow beef, and many other types of poultry.

The wood pellets can be used to smoke other foods such as pizza, vegetables, and other foods. The wood pellets are made using recycled wood materials. The wood pellet grill can also be used to grill foods and bake foods. The grill is easy to use because it's made of a simple design and it doesn't have any complicated elements. The Traeger wood pellet grill is easy to use and can be used indoors as well as outdoors. The user can check the temperature to make sure that the food is cooked perfectly. Most types of grill can be used both as gas grills and charcoal grills.

One of the popular features of the Traeger wood pellet grill is the result of its smoke from the wood pellet. Many customers are amazed by the wood pellet smoker. There are hundreds of positive and amazing testimonials about the grill. The grill allows users to smoke and grill their food and the meat can be smoked for up to 15 hours. The grill is easy to use, functional, and reliable. The Traeger grill is also very durable because of its body. The body of the grill is made of cast iron. The BBQ grill is easy to install and is easy to maintain.

The grill can create smoke by using wood pellets and it can be adjusted to a temperature of about 225 degrees Fahrenheit. The food cooked on the grill has a consistent smoky flavor because of the wood pellets. The grill is an automatic cooker, meaning it conserves the heat that it produces and doesn't lose it.

Components of Traeger Wood Pellet Grill

Traeger makes a few additions to most of their models including the firebox, heat exchanger, side shelf, and cabinet. Each model has a specific focus the allows the customer to decide which grill will fit their needs. Below is a brief description of what makes each model different. Some components are shared among the models. The firebox and heat exchanger are shared among Traeger's entire line of grills.

The firebox is the heart of every Traeger grill. The wood pellets are loaded into the firebox from the front of the grill. The firebox is a rectangular box with the fires for the grill in it. After the wood pellets are loaded in, the lid is closed, igniting the pellets. First, as the wood pellets ignite, they begin to release smoke. As the fire burns, smoke carries the heat to the heating element inside the grill where it is turned into heat that is used to cook the meat, and then convection that distributes the heat evenly throughout the grill.

The heating element is what does most of the work. It is made of aluminum blocks stacked to create a column and is covered in Therma-cast which is insulation that prevents heat from exiting the grill too much. When a customer grills on the Traeger Pellet grill, they are grilling on the heating element, which slowly cooks the meat evenly.

The side shelf is where most of the tools and wood pellets are kept on the Traeger Pellet grill. It has a coated surface to prevent the tool and pellets from damaging the finish of the grill. Tools are kept on the side shelf while the grill is in use don't need quick access. If a tool does need to be used in mid grilling, it can be placed in the warming drawer with the wood pellets.

The warming drawer is found on all of Traeger's grills except for one. On all of Traeger's grills except for the RecTec, the warming drawer can be found on the side table on the front of the grill. The warming drawer is more of a compartment than a drawer. It provides a place where the tools that need to be kept hot can stay warm while their job is being finished. It also provides a place where novices can keep wood pellets until they are ready to be put into the firebox.

The secondary cooking chamber is used on the 4-burner grill and the 4-burner grill with the side burner. The extra space on the firebox is left open for maximum heat exposure. The customer can place their meat on the exposed grates in the secondary cooking chamber to give them more options in how to cook their food.

The cabinet holds accessories for Traeger Pellet grills. Every Traeger pellet grill has its specific accessories that can be purchased from Traeger's website and applied to the grill. The accessories are ranging from back up wire to protect and insulate the electronics to the cabinet, allowing more accessories and attachments to be added. The cabinet on Traeger's pellet grill is offered for extra smoke when cooks desire more smoke or if the grill is in an outdoor environment where the temperature fluctuates a lot, waterproofing the firebox can add protection to the grill.

The rear-mounted fill tray is unique to Traeger Pellet grills. It can be folded and used as a table or can be set up in the back of the grill. The rear-mounted fill tray is equipped with a Velcro latch that can hold the tray in an upright position. The rear-mounted fill tray allows for easier and more accessible adding of wood pellets.

A general purpose of Traeger, from inception, was to cook food with the wood pellets. Almost all Traeger models have the capability of smoking and grilling. However, all of Traeger's grills are capable of grilling and smoking except for the smaller Traeger Junior Elite.

How It Works

Many people try to grill using real firewood methods while grilling in the Traeger grill. But they do not know how to use Traeger grill with wood pellets. Let's first see how Traeger pellet grill works.

To start with Traeger grill, the user has to open the lid and set the temperature at 250 and make the grill smoke by turning it on. It has to be set as 250 for the first 30 mins. The user also has to turn on the heat of the grill and grill meat or food, which you want to use. The smoke has to be essential for cooking with pellets. If Traeger grill is not important to work with, then the user can also set the smoker for working with the Traeger pellets.

It will not work without smoke. So, the first thing to do is get the griller hot and the smoker working. The temperature will rise up to 260. The grill grates are placed on the grill to let the smoke pass through the meat while cooking. The temperature will rise up to 260, if one is not able to control it, be sure to turn off the barbecue grill. The Traeger grill is very simple to use and it is quite easy to control the temperature. Once you want to know how to use Traeger grill and smoke, you will be able to find it quite easy and all you need to do is to open the lid and then set the temperature. Switch on the smoke for the first time so that smoke can come out and cook the food.

It is the same as the way how to use Traeger pellet grill for smoking

So, if you want to do BBQs for your family, then Traeger grill is the best choice to use. It has the capacity to hold about seventeen burgers. So, one can easily do a party or BBQ night for a quite large crowd. The food will be very tasty, once it is ready with Traeger pellet grill.

Traeger Wood Pellet Grill Vs. Charcoal and Wood Grills

Traeger wood pallets have numerous benefits that other charcoal and gas grill cannot provide. Barbecuing is a great gathering excuse and outdoor activity, but it is a hassle to set. In this day and age where everything is becoming more convenient, this activity should also become easier to deal with as well.

It is easy to start:

To get a charcoal or gas grill to ignite is a hassle, but the fire inside the firepot is easy to turn on. It also is much safer as you don't have to stick your hands inside the grill to start the fire.

It's versatile

This grill is not only used for grilling but can be used for different processes of cooking as well. You can bake, roast, smoke, and braise using this device. This also increases the menu at your barbecue gathering.

No burnt areas

Because the cooking process happens by convection mechanism, the entire piece of meat, or whatever, your cooking gets cooked evenly. There is also no need to flip around the meat constantly. Also, the drip tray prevents direct fire from hitting your food, so no charring occurs.

More flavor in your dishes

In grilling, nothing beats all-natural hardwood flavor. Professional chefs use them, and now, with ease, so could you. It is not hard to produce a much more delicious juicy meat steak at your home anymore.

Pellets to Use

The dark charcoal type of wood pellets is used to cook food. They are burned to cook food inside it. It is made of a variety of woods like beech, maple, and cherry that has a composition of 15 - 20 percent mesquite, it burns at 1400 degrees. The process to burn wood pellets is very simple. You need to pour it into a box, add in the grill, and light it with a matchstick, then it will burn to give you the best flavor. The burning wood pellets will provide you the warmth and keep you surrounded by the great and the best natural flavor.

This is the burning pellets or the logs that make the grills unique.

Wood Pellet Reference Chart

Wood	Flavor Profile	Use With
Apple	Mild, subtle sweet and fruity flavor	Pork, Poultry, Lamb, Wild Game, Beef, Some Seafood
Cherry	Light and sweet. Delicate, not overpowering	Pork, Poultry, Wild Game, Beef, Some Seafood
Hickory	Sweet, yet strong flavor. Not overpowering. Versatile	Pork, Poultry, Wild Game, Beef, Fish
Alder	Delicate, earthy, with a hint of sweetness	Fish, Shellfish, Pork, Beef, Lamb, Poultry, Veggies
Maple	Mild and slightly sweet flavor	Pork, Poultry, Beef, Small Game Birds, Cheese, Veggies
Oak	Medium smoky flavor. Versatile. Milder than Hickory, stronger than Cherry	Pork, Poultry, Beef, Some Wild Game, Fish
Mesquite	Strong and earthy flavor. One of the hottest burning woods	Red Meats, Dark Meats, Wild Game
Peach	Sweet, fruity flavor	Pork, Poultry, Small Game Birds
Pecan	Stronger than most fruitwoods, but milder than Hickory and Mesquite	Pork, Poultry, Beef

Most Popular Pellet Blends

Wood	Brand(s)	Flavor Profile	Use With
BBQ Blend	Pit Boss	Sweet, savory, and tart blend of maple, hickory, and cherry	All foods
Apple Mash Blend	CookinPellets	Lightly sweet blend of apple mash and hard maple	Chicken, Pork, Muffins, Cold-Smoked Dishes
Bourbon Brown Sugar	Cabela's	Seasoned oak blend of bourbon, smoke flavor, and sweetness	Chicken, Beef, Pork
Competition Blend	Traeger	Blend of sweet, savory, and tart (maple, hickory, cherry)	Chicken, Beef, Pork
Pellet Pro Exclusive Charcoal Blend	Smoke Daddy Inc.	Charcoal blended with red oak.Mix with any flavor of wood pellets and use to enhance smoke ring	All meats
Perfect Mix Blend	CookinPellets	Blend of cherry, hickory, maple, and hard maple	Short cooks for any foods
Texas Blend	Green Mountain	Blend of oak, mesquite and hickory	All meats
Turkey Pellet Blend with Brine Kit	Traeger	Hickory, oak, maple, and rosemary	Turkey
Realtree Big Game Blend	Traeger	Blend of hickory, rosemary, red and white oak	Venison, Pheasant, Game Meats
Tennessee Whiskey Barrel	Big Poppa Smokers	Aged oak from Jack Daniel's Whiskey	Most meats

TIPS AND TRICKS

It's been two years since we bought our Traeger grill, and I have a few suggestions to help new users with pellet smokers avoid any issues—usually due to inexperience or negligence. Let's start on the right foot.

Pellet Storage

You have to be vigilant in storing your pellets, especially if you live in a humid climate. Damp or wet pellets will not lead to the best grilling experience—you won't be able to get a fire going. What's worse, damp or wet pellets will damage the auger since it won't be able to rotate and will burn out the motor.

I bought some 5-gallon pails, and my husband went on the hunt for sealing lids, since storing your pellets in an open container is counterproductive. We found that screw-on covers work best to keep moisture out, and they're convenient—you won't have to break your fingers trying to pry them open.

Temperature Readings

After using your grill a few times, you may notice that the temperature starts to fluctuate quite a bit. This is because of grease and soot build-up on the temperature probe used to regulate the temperature. An effortless way to stop this from happening is to clean the probe and cover it with foil. Consequently, cooking temperature readings will be more accurate.

Cover Your Grill

You may think a grill cover isn't necessary, but believe me, it's crucial. Your Traeger grill is an appliance and one with electronics inside to boot! If you want to ensure your pellet smoker's durability, protect it from the elements. If you can, move your grill under a rooftop after having a barbeque and use a grill cover. You don't want your pellet smoker to stop working suddenly due to water damage.

Clean Your Grill

A lot of people fail at keeping their grill clean. This step is crucial to guard against overfilling the firepot and protect against flare-ups. Not to mention that your grill will look brand-new for longer if you care for it in this simple way. I recommend cleaning your Traeger grill after cooking something for an extended period, or after you're done using it for the weekend. If you love cooking greasier foods, you'll have to clean your grill more often. Here are the steps you should follow:

1. Use an all-natural degreaser/cleaner to spray the grill grate and the inside of the chimney.
2. Remove and clean the sides of the grill grates.
3. Throw away the old foil and drip tray liners.
4. Remove the drip tray and heat baffle.
5. Use a vacuum inside the grill and firepot to remove any food particles.
6. Clean the inside of the chimney.

7.	Again, use an all-natural degreaser/cleaner to spray the inside and outside of the grill. Wait a few minutes before wiping clean.

8.	Put all components back in their place, including the heat baffle, drip tray, and foil liners. You're all set for your next barbeque!

Tip: Avoid using wire brushes as it will scratch your Traeger grill. Heavy-duty paper towels or a cleaning cloth will work nicely.

Be Adventurous

This is vital to your grilling success—you won't enjoy your Traeger grill for long if you have to make the same recipes over and over. What's more, you own a 6-in-1 appliance, and you can't let that versatility go unused. In the beginning, as you get used to a pellet grill, you may end up cooking simple meals, but once you feel confident in your grilling abilities, try new things! Don't limit yourself to cook only traditional barbeque foods—what about making a smoky bean stew in your Traeger grill? Don't worry, later on in this cookbook, you'll see recipes that will spark your adventurous side.

These aren't the only elements that will contribute to your grilling success, but they cover some of the rookie mistakes many people, myself included, make. It put a real downer on my grilling plans!

HOW TO CLEAN YOUR TRAEGER WOOD PELLET GRILL

You will have to give your Trager grill a deep clean every few months. Think of it as spring cleaning your pellet smoker. You should give your Traeger grill a fairly good cleaning before firing it up for the first time in the spring. The manufacturer recommends cleaning the water pan and the firepot. Depending on how much you use the grill, you may want to give it a good cleaning before the season ends in the fall. A good cleaning before the first fire-up in the spring or a cleaning before you store it in the fall will ensure that your Traeger grill starts the season or the next season with a clean slate. Cleaning the interior of the smoker is fairly close to cleaning your oven. It's a bit messy, and it will probably leave you smelling like a campfire, but it's fairly easy to do, and it's the only way to maintain a perfectly clean pellet smoker. Here is a step-by-step instruction on how to clean your Traeger wood pellet grill. Tools and Supplies Needed: Clean your Traeger pellet grill thoroughly.

Cleaning the Water Pan

1. Empty the water tray and dump the water down the drain. Be sure not to fill up the drain with water.
2. Wash the water pan with warm, soapy water. Be sure to check for burnt-on stuff. Use a sponge or a soft-bristled brush, and make sure to soak into all corners of the pan.
3. Dry with a towel. This is very important.
4. If you have a pellet grill with a solid water pan, you will have to add water to the pan after cleaning it. You don't want a large gap between the bottom of the pan and the base of firepot.
5. If you have a pellet grill with a slotted water pan, you will be fine as is, or instead of adding water to the pan, fill the empty space with the unused pellets.

Cleaning the Firepot

1. Remove all of the grates and the heat deflector.
2. Empty the ash pan and remove all of the ashes.
3. Spray the ash pan with a degreaser and scrub with a brush. Rinse and dry.
4. Spray the firepot with a degreaser and scrub with a brush. Rinse and dry.
5. If you have a pellet grill with a hopper, empty the hopper and clean it.
6. Be sure to clean all of the areas around and under the pellet hopper and the firepot with a degreaser. Run water through the pellet hopper and firepot. This is especially important if you use a lot of pellets. Be sure all traces of the degreaser and water are out.

7. Clean the burner compartment and the chimney using a brush. Don't forget to clean the drip plate above the firepot.

8. Inspect all hardware before proceeding. If necessary, tighten the screws.

9. Reinstall the burners, heat deflector, and water pan. Make certain you have a tight connection between the burners and the water pan.

10. Fill the grill with pellets.

Cleaning Your Traeger Grill Oven Without a Clean Panel

1. Remove the cooking racks and place them in the sink.

2. Spray the racks, the interior of the grill, and the inside of the screened vents with a degreaser. This is very important. You don't want residual grease and ash on the cooking racks.

3. Scrub the cooking racks with a brush and rinse.

4. Scrub the interior of the grill and the inside of the screened vents with a brush and rinse.

5. Scrub the interior of the grill and the inside of the screened vents with a brush and rinse.

6. Scrub the interior of the grill and the inside of the screened vents with a brush and rinse.

7. Repeat until the racks are completely clean.

8. Be certain not to get the grill overheated with open flames.

9. Inspect all hardware before proceeding. If necessary, tighten the screws.

10. Fill the grill with pellets.

Cleaning your Traeger Pellet Grill Oven with a Clean Panel

1. Remove all the racks and the cooking grates. Place them in the sink.

2. Spray the racks, the interior of the grill, and the inside of the screened vents with a degreaser.

3. After using the cleaner, wipe the grill with a cloth to remove any stains or streaks. Dry with a clean cloth.

4. Spray the interior of the grill and the inside of the grilled vents with a degreaser.

5. Scrub the racks and the interior of the grill with a brush and rinse.

6. Spray the interior of the grill and the inside of the screened vents with a degreaser.

7. Scrub the racks and the interior of the grill with a brush and rinse.

8. Scrub the interior of the grill and the inside of the screened vents with a brush and rinse.

9. Scrub the interior of the grill and the inside of the screened vents with a brush and rinse.

After cleaning, you may want to season your new Traeger grill with a fresh coat.

TROUBLESHOOTING

Troubleshooting a Traeger grill is not an easy task. Most of the time unless you are well-versed with the internal workings of the grill, you will not be able to fix it yourself. Here is a troubleshooting guide for your Traeger pellet grill:

Problems caused by food:

1) Pellets are not igniting

Solution:

1) Clean the grill.

2) Change the pellets to another brand.

3) Replace the drip tray.

4) Check the settings and adjust the temperature.

5) Reset the grill (press the program button).

6) Check the grease tray.

If your Traeger grill has a problem igniting, do not panic. Just remember to keep calm and try the above solutions one by one. You may find that a single solution will do the trick.

2) Grill is not warm enough

Solution:

1) Clean the grill.

3) Check the location of the grill, make sure it is getting sufficient radiant heat from the sun, the room, nearby furniture, etc.

4) Check the nuts on the wheels.

5) Check the foil covering, chicken wire, and the lid.

6) Replace the drip pan.

7) Check the air intake.

8) Low Fuel

6) Food is not browning

7) Smoke is coming out of the exhaust

8) Weak flame

9) Smoky, bitter taste to food

Problem: Heat is not sufficient

1) Check location of the grill, scorched food, etc.

2) Loose or damaged cord.

3) Press the PROGRAM button on the grill outbox to reset the unit (press the button a couple of times longer than you normally would).

4) Check the grease tray and clean it.

5) Check the Set-It and forget-it box, lid, food temp, air intake tube, meat scoop, and the steps.

6) Make sure the cord is undamaged and connected to the light inside the grill.

7) Clean the wires and check for loose nuts.

8) Clean the coils and the air intake valve.

9) Clean off the food.

10) Replace the drip pan.

12) Turn the air intake valve several times to remove the burned insulation.

13) Check the lid to see if it is making good contact with the flame.

The Traeger Pellet Grill can be a great tool for anyone who is fond of grilling. It is perfect for people who spend a lot of time outside. It is indeed the best way to cook your food when you are on a camping trip or preparing yourself for a barbecue party. Troubleshooting these problems may be a bit frustrating but it can also be very enjoyable because you can save yourself the trouble of calling for repairmen.

COCKTAILS RECIPES

Smoked Berry Cocktail

Servings: 2
Cooking Time: 15 Minutes

Ingredients:

- 1/2 Cup strawberries, stemmed
- 1/2 Cup blackberries
- 1/2 Cup blueberries
- 8 Ounce bourbon or iced tea
- 2 Ounce lime juice
- 3 Ounce simple syrup
- soda water
- fresh mint, for garnish

Directions:

1. Supply your smoker with wood pellets and follow the start-up procedure. Preheat the grill, with the lid closed, to 180° F.

2. Wash berries well, spread them on a clean cookie sheet and place on the grill. Smoke berries for 15 minutes. Grill: 180 °F

3. Remove berries from grill and transfer to a blender. Puree berries until smooth then pass through a fine mesh strainer to remove seeds.

4. To create a layered cocktail, pour 2 ounces of berry puree in the bottom of a glass. Next, pour 2 ounces of bourbon or iced tea over the back of a spoon into the glass, then 1/2 ounce lime juice and 1/2 ounce simple syrup, top with soda water and ice. Finish with mint or extra berries for garnish.

5. Repeat the same process for 3 more servings. Enjoy!

Smoking Gun Cocktail

Servings: 2
Cooking Time: 45 Minutes

Ingredients:

- 2 Jar vermouth soaked cocktail onions
- 3 Ounce vodka
- 1 Ounce dry vermouth

Directions:

1. Supply your smoker with wood pellets and follow the start-up procedure. Preheat the grill, with the lid closed, to 180° F.

2. To make the smoked onion vermouth: Pour jar of vermouth soaked cocktail onions onto a shallow sheet pan. Smoke for 45 minutes. Remove from grill and set aside to chill. Grill: 180 °F

3. To make the cocktail: Add vodka, 1 teaspoon liquid from the smoked onions and dry vermouth to a mixing glass. Shake and strain into a chilled martini glass.

4. Garnish with smoked cocktail onions on a skewer. Enjoy!

Traeger Smoked Daiquiri

Servings: 2
Cooking Time: 25 Minutes

Ingredients:

- 2 limes, sliced
- 2 Tablespoon granulated sugar
- 3 Ounce Rum
- 1 Ounce Smoked Simple Syrup
- 1 1/2 Ounce lime juice

Directions:

1. Supply your smoker with wood pellets and follow the start-up procedure. Preheat the grill, with the lid closed, to 350° F.

2. Toss the lime slices with granulated sugar and place directly on the grill grate. Cook 20-25 minutes or until grill marks form. Remove from grill and cool. Grill: 350 °F

3. In a mixing glass add rum, Traeger Simple Syrup, and fresh lime juice. Add ice to the mixing glass and shake. Strain contents into a chilled glass.

4. Garnish with a grilled lime wheel. Enjoy!

In Traeger Fashion Cocktail

Servings: 2
Cooking Time: 20 Minutes

Ingredients:

- 2 Whole orange peel
- 2 Whole lemon peel

- 3 Ounce bourbon
- 1 Ounce Smoked Simple Syrup
- 6 Dash Bitters Lab Charred Cedar & Currant Bitters

Directions:

1. Supply your smoker with wood pellets and follow the start-up procedure. Preheat the grill, with the lid closed, to 350° F.

2. Place the lemon and orange peel directly on the grill grate and cook 20 to 25 minutes or until lightly browned. Grill: 350 ˚F

3. Add bourbon, Traeger Smoked Simple Syrup and bitters to a mixing glass and stir over ice. Stir until glass is chilled and contents are well diluted.

4. Strain into a new glass over fresh ice and garnish with grilled lemon and orange peel. Enjoy!

Smoked Apple Cider

Servings: 2
Cooking Time: 30 Minutes

Ingredients:

- 32 Ounce apple cider
- 2 cinnamon sticks
- 4 whole cloves
- 3 star anise
- 2 Pieces orange peel
- 2 Pieces lemon peel

Directions:

1. Supply your smoker with wood pellets and follow the start-up procedure. Preheat the grill, with the lid closed, to 225° F.

2. Combine the cider, cinnamon stick, star anise, clove, lemon and orange peel in a shallow baking dish.

3. Place directly on the grill grate and smoke for 30 minutes. Remove from grill, strain and transfer to four mugs. Grill: 225 ˚F

4. Finish with a slice of apple and a cinnamon stick to serve. Enjoy!

Grilled Blood Orange Mimosa

Servings: 4
Cooking Time: 15 Minutes

Ingredients:

- 3 blood orange, halved
- 2 Tablespoon granulated sugar
- 1 Bottle sparkling wine
- thyme sprigs, for garnish

Directions:

1. Supply your smoker with wood pellets and follow the start-up procedure. Preheat the grill, with the lid closed, to 375° F.

2. When the grill is hot, dip the cut side of the orange halves in sugar and place cut side down directly on the grill grate. Grill: 375 ˚F

3. Grill the oranges for 10-15 minutes or until grill marks develop. Grill: 375 ˚F

4. Remove from the grill and let cool at room temperature.

5. When cool enough to handle, juice the oranges and strain through a fine strainer removing any pulp.

6. Pour 5 oz of sparkling wine into each glass and top with 1 oz blood orange juice.

7. Garnish with a sprig of thyme. Enjoy!

Sunset Margarita

Servings: 2
Cooking Time: 55 Minutes

Ingredients:

- 4 oranges
- 2 Cup plus 1 teaspoon agave
- 1/2 Cup water
- 1 Ounce burnt orange agave
- 3 Ounce reposado tequila
- 1 1/2 Ounce fresh squeezed lime juice
- Jacobsen Salt Co. Cherrywood Smoked Salt

Directions:

1. Supply your smoker with wood pellets and follow the start-up procedure. Preheat the grill, with the lid closed, to 350° F.

2. For the Burnt Orange Agave Syrup: Cut one orange in half and brush cut side with agave. Place cut side down directly on the grill grate and grill for 15 minutes or until grill marks develop. Grill: 350 ˚F

3. While the orange halves are grilling, slice the other orange and brush both sides of the slices with agave.

Place slices directly on the grill grate next to the halves and cook for 15 minutes or until grill marks develop. Grill: 350 °F

4.   Remove orange halves from grill grate and let cool. After they have cooled, juice halves and strain. Set aside.

5.   Combine 1/4 cup water and agave in a shallow dish and mix well. Remove orange slices from the grill and place in the agave mixture, reserving a few for garnish.

6.   Reduce the grill temperature to 180 degrees F and place the shallow dish with agave and oranges directly on the grill grate. Smoke for 40 minutes. Remove from heat and strain. Set aside. Grill: 180 °F

7.   To Mix Drink: Rim glass with Jacobsen Smoked Salt. Combine tequila, fresh lime juice, grilled orange juice and burnt orange agave syrup in a glass. Add ice and shake well.

8.   Strain into a rimmed glass over clean ice. Garnish with a grilled orange slice. Enjoy!

Ryes And Shine Cocktail

Servings: 2

Cooking Time: 30 Minutes

Ingredients:

- 2 lemon, cut into wheels for garnish
- 6 Tablespoon granulated sugar
- 2 Ounce rye
- 1 Ounce bourbon
- 3 Ounce lemon juice
- 1 Ounce Smoked Simple Syrup
- 6 Dash Fernet-Branca

Directions:

1.   Supply your smoker with wood pellets and follow the start-up procedure. Preheat the grill, with the lid closed, to 325° F.

2.   Toss lemon wheels with granulated sugar to coat on both sides. Place wheels directly on the grill grate and cook for 15 minutes on each side or until grill marks form. Grill: 325 °F

3.   Add rye, bourbon, lemon juice, Traeger Smoked Simple Syrup and Fernet-Branca to a shaker and shake until slightly diluted (about 10 to 15 seconds).

4.   Pour into a fresh glass, serve neat and garnish with a grilled lemon wheel. Enjoy!

Grilled Peach Sour Cocktail

Servings: 2

Cooking Time: 15 Minutes

Ingredients:

- 2 peach, sliced
- 2 Tablespoon sugar
- 1 1/2 Ounce Smoked Simple Syrup
- 4 Ounce bourbon
- 6 Dash Bitters Lab Apricot Vanilla Bitters
- 2 Sprig fresh thyme, for garnish

Directions:

1.   Supply your smoker with wood pellets and follow the start-up procedure. Preheat the grill, with the lid closed, to 325° F.

2.   Toss peach slices with granulated sugar and place directly on grill grate. Cook for 20 minutes or until grill marks form. Remove from grill and let cool. Grill: 325 °F

3.   Place peaches and Traeger Smoked Simple Syrup into tin and muddle. Peaches should form about an ounce of juice during the muddling. Once completed, add remaining ingredients and shake.

4.   Pour contents into glass over fresh ice and garnish with fresh thyme. Enjoy!

Zombie Cocktail Recipe

Servings: 2

Cooking Time: 45 Minutes

Ingredients:

- fresh squeezed orange juice
- pineapple juice
- 2 Ounce light rum
- 2 Ounce dark rum
- 2 Ounce lime juice
- 1 Ounce Smoked Simple Syrup
- 6 Ounce smoked orange and pineapple juice
- 2 grilled orange peel, for garnish
- 2 grilled pineapple chunks, for garnish

Directions:

1.   Supply your smoker with wood pellets and follow the start-up procedure. Preheat the grill, with the lid closed, to 180° F.

2. Smoked Orange and Pineapple Juice: Pour equal parts fresh squeezed orange juice and pineapple juice into a shallow sheet pan and smoke for 45 minutes. Remove and let cool. Measure out 3 ounces of juice and reserve any remaining juice in the refrigerator for future use. Grill: 180 °F

3. Add dark and light rums, 3 ounces smoked orange and pineapple juice, lime juice and Traeger Smoked Simple Syrup to a mixing glass.

4. Add ice, shake and strain over clean ice into a Tiki glass.

5. Garnish with a grilled orange peel and grilled pineapple. Enjoy!

Smoked Hot Buttered Rum

Servings: 4
Cooking Time: 30 Minutes

Ingredients:
- 2 Cup water
- 1/4 Cup brown sugar
- 1/2 Stick butter, melted
- 1 Teaspoon ground cinnamon
- 1/4 Teaspoon ground nutmeg
- ground cloves
- salt
- 6 Ounce Rum

Directions:
1. Supply your smoker with wood pellets and follow the start-up procedure. Preheat the grill, with the lid closed, to 180° F.

2. In a shallow baking dish, combine 2 cups water with all ingredients except for the rum and place directly on the grill grate. Smoke for 30 minutes. Grill: 180 °F

3. Remove from the grill and pour into the pitcher of a blender. Process until somewhat frothy.

4. Pour 1.5 ounces of rum each into 4 glasses. Split hot butter mixture evenly between the four glasses.

5. Garnish with a cinnamon stick and freshly grated nutmeg. Enjoy!

Strawberry Mule Cocktail

Servings: 2
Cooking Time: 15 Minutes

Ingredients:
- 8 grilled strawberries, plus more for serving
- 3 Ounce vodka
- 1 Ounce Smoked Simple Syrup
- 1 Ounce lemon juice
- 6 Ounce ginger beer
- fresh mint leaves

Directions:
1. Supply your smoker with wood pellets and follow the start-up procedure. Preheat the grill, with the lid closed, to 400° F.

2. Place strawberries directly on the grill grate and cook 15 minutes or until grill marks appear. Grill: 400 °F

3. For the cocktail: Add vodka, grilled strawberries, Traeger Smoked Simple Syrup and lemon juice to a shaker. Shake vigorously.

4. Double strain into a fresh glass or copper mug with crushed ice.

5. Top with ginger beer and garnish with extra grilled strawberries and fresh mint. Enjoy!

Garden Gimlet Cocktail

Servings: 2
Cooking Time: 45 Minutes

Ingredients:
- 2 Cup honey
- 4 lemons, zested
- 4 Sprig rosemary, plus more for garnish
- 1/2 Cup water
- 4 Slices cucumber
- 1 1/2 Ounce lime juice
- 3 Ounce vodka

Directions:
1. Supply your smoker with wood pellets and follow the start-up procedure. Preheat the grill, with the lid closed, to 180° F.

2. To make smoked lemon and rosemary honey syrup, thin 1 cup honey by adding 1/4 cup water to a shallow pan. Add lemon zest and 2 sprigs rosemary.

3. Place the pan directly on the grill grate and smoke 45 minutes to an hour. Remove from heat, strain and cool. Grill: 180 °F

4. In a cocktail shaker, muddle the cucumbers and 1oz of the smoked lemon and rosemary honey syrup.

5. After muddling, add lime juice, vodka, and ice. Shake and double strain into a coup glass.

6. Garnish with a sprig of rosemary. Enjoy!

Grilled Hawaiian Sour

Servings: 2
Cooking Time: 15 Minutes

Ingredients:
- 2 Whole pineapple, trimmed and sliced
- 1/2 Cup palm sugar
- 3 Ounce bourbon
- 2 Ounce grilled pineapple juice
- 2 Ounce Smoked Simple Syrup
- 10 Ounce lemon juice
- 2 grilled pineapple chunk, for garnish
- 2 pineapple leaf, for garnish

Directions:
1. Supply your smoker with wood pellets and follow the start-up procedure. Preheat the grill, with the lid closed, to 350° F.

2. For the Grilled Pineapple Juice: Dust pineapple slices with palm sugar. Place directly on the grill grate and cook for 8 minutes per side. Grill: 350 °F

3. Remove from grill and let cool. Reserve a few pieces for garnish. Run remaining pineapple pieces through centrifugal juicer to extract juice.

4. To Make the Drink: Add bourbon, grilled pineapple juice, simple syrup and lemon juice to a cocktail strainer with ice. Shake vigorously. Double strain into a chilled coupe glass. Garnish with grilled pineapple chunk and pineapple leaf. Enjoy!

Smoked Pomegranate Lemonade Cocktail

Servings: 2
Cooking Time: 45 Minutes

Ingredients:
- 32 Ounce POM Juice
- 2 Cup pomegranate seeds
- 3 Ounce vodka
- 8 Ounce lemonade
- lemon wheel, for garnish
- fresh mint, for garnish

Directions:
1. Supply your smoker with wood pellets and follow the start-up procedure. Preheat the grill, with the lid closed, to 225° F.

2. For the Smoked Pomegranate Ice Cubes: Pour one small container of POM juice and 1 cup of pomegranate seeds into a shallow sheet pan. Smoke on the Traeger for 45 minutes. Pull off grill and let sit until cooled. Grill: 180 °F

3. Pour smoked POM juice into ice molds of your choice and put into freezer.

4. When ready to serve, place the frozen pomegranate cubes into a mason jar. Pour vodka and lemonade over the ice cubes.

5. Garnish with a lemon wheel and fresh mint. Enjoy!

Smoked Mulled Wine

Servings: 10
Cooking Time: 60 Minutes

Ingredients:
- 2 Bottle red wine
- 1/2 Cup whiskey
- 1/2 Cup white rum
- 1/2 Cup honey
- 1 cinnamon stick
- 2 pods star anise
- 4 whole cloves
- 1 (3 in) orange peel

Directions:
1. Supply your smoker with wood pellets and follow the start-up procedure. Preheat the grill, with the lid closed, to 180° F.

2. In a shallow baking dish, combine wine, whiskey, rum, honey, cinnamon stick, star anise, cloves and orange peel. Stir well until combined.

3. Place the dish directly on the grill grate and smoke for one hour until the mixture is warm. Grill: 180 °F

4. Remove from grill and ladle into mugs leaving the mulling spices behind. Garnish with fresh cinnamon sticks, anise, orange zest or a combination. Enjoy!

Batter Up Cocktail

Servings: 2
Cooking Time: 60 Minutes

Ingredients:

- 2 whole nutmeg
- 4 Ounce Michter's Bourbon
- 3 Teaspoon pumpkin puree
- 1 Ounce Smoked Simple Syrup
- 2 Large egg

Directions:

1. Supply your smoker with wood pellets and follow the start-up procedure. Preheat the grill, with the lid closed, to 180° F.
2. Place whole nutmeg on a sheet tray and place in the grill. Smoke 1 hour. Remove from grill and let cool. Grill: 180 °F
3. Add everything to a shaker and shake without ice. Add ice, then shake and strain into a chilled highball glass.
4. Garnish with grated, smoked nutmeg. Enjoy!

Smoked Ice Mojito Slurpee

Servings: 2
Cooking Time: 30 Minutes

Ingredients:

- water
- 1 Cup white rum
- 1/2 Cup lime juice
- 1/4 Cup Smoked Simple Syrup
- 12 Whole fresh mint leaves
- 4 Sprig mint
- 4 Whole lime wedge, for garnish

Directions:

1. Supply your smoker with wood pellets and follow the start-up procedure. Preheat the grill, with the lid closed, to 180° F.
2. For optimal flavor, use Super Smoke if available. Grill: 180 °F
3. Remove water from grill and pour smoked water into ice cube trays. Place in freezer until frozen.
4. Add rum, lime juice, Traeger Smoked Simple Syrup, mint and smoked ice to a blender.

5. Blend until a slushy consistency and pour into glasses.
6. Garnish with a mint sprig and lime wedge. Enjoy!

Grilled Frozen Strawberry Lemonade

Servings: 4
Cooking Time: 15 Minutes

Ingredients:

- 1 Pound fresh strawberries
- 1/2 Cup turbinado sugar
- 8 lemon, halved
- 1/4 Cup Cointreau
- 1/4 Cup simple syrup
- 2 Cup ice
- 1 Cup Titos Vodka

Directions:

1. Supply your smoker with wood pellets and follow the start-up procedure. Preheat the grill, with the lid closed, to High heat.
2. Dip the lemon halves in turbinado sugar and place directly on the grill grate. Toss the strawberries with remaining sugar and place next to the lemons.
3. Cook until grill marks develop on both, about 15 min for lemons and 10 min for strawberries.
4. Remove from heat and let cool.
5. Juice grilled lemons straining out any seeds or pulp. Pour into a blender pitcher.
6. Remove stems from grilled strawberries and place in blender pitcher with lemon juice. Add simple syrup, vodka, cointreau, and 2 cups of ice.
7. Puree until smooth and transfer to 4-6 glasses. Garnish with grilled strawberries and grilled lemon slices if desired. Enjoy!

Smoked Sangria

Servings: 6
Cooking Time: 45 Minutes

Ingredients:

- 1 (750 ml) medium-bodied red wine
- 1/4 Cup Grand Marnier
- 1/4 Cup Smoked Simple Syrup
- 1 Cup fresh cranberries
- 1 Whole apple, sliced

- 2 Whole limes, sliced
- 4 cinnamon stick
- soda water

Directions:

1. Supply your smoker with wood pellets and follow the start-up procedure. Preheat the grill, with the lid closed, to 180° F.

2. In a shallow dish, combine red wine, Grand Marnier, Traeger Smoked Simple Syrup and cranberries, and place directly on the grill grate.

3. Smoke for 30 to 45 minutes or until the liquid picks up desired amount of smoke. Remove from grill and place in the fridge to cool. Grill: 180 °F

4. When the mixture has cooled, place in a large pitcher. Add sliced apples, limes, cinnamon sticks and ice to pitcher.

5. Top with soda water, if desired. Enjoy!

Smoked Pumpkin Spice Latte

Servings: 4
Cooking Time: 45 Minutes

Ingredients:
- 1 Small sugar pumpkin
- olive oil
- 1 Can sweetened condensed milk
- 1 Cup whole milk
- 2 Tablespoon Smoked Simple Syrup
- 1 Teaspoon pumpkin pie spice
- pinch of salt
- cinnamon
- whipped cream
- shaved nutmeg
- 8 Ounce smoked cold brew coffee

Directions:

1. Supply your smoker with wood pellets and follow the start-up procedure. Preheat the grill, with the lid closed, to 325° F.

2. Cut the sugar pumpkin in half, scoop out the seeds and discard. Place the pumpkin halves cut side up on a baking sheet and brush lightly with olive oil.

3. Place the sheet tray directly on the grill grate and cook 45 minutes or until the flesh is tender. Remove from heat and place on the counter to cool. Grill: 325 °F

4. When the pumpkin is cool enough to handle, scoop out the flesh and mash until smooth.

5. Place 3 Tbsp of the pumpkin puree in a separate bowl and reserve the remaining for another use.

6. Add the sweetened condensed milk, whole milk, Traeger Smoked Simple Syrup, pumpkin pie seasoning and salt to the pumpkin puree. Whisk to combine.

7. Pour the cold brew over ice, add desired amount of pumpkin spice creamer and top with whipped cream, cinnamon, and shaved nutmeg if desired. Enjoy!

Fig Slider Cocktail

Servings: 2
Cooking Time: 15 Minutes

Ingredients:
- 2 peach, halved
- 4 oranges
- honey
- sugar
- 2 Teaspoon orange fig spread
- 1 Ounce fresh lemon juice
- 4 Ounce bourbon
- 3 Ounce honey glazed grilled orange juice

Directions:

1. Supply your smoker with wood pellets and follow the start-up procedure. Preheat the grill, with the lid closed, to 325° F.

2. Pit the peach and cut in half. Cut one of the oranges in half. Glaze the peach and orange cut sides with honey and set directly on the grill grate until the honey caramelizes and fruit has grill marks. Grill: 325 °F

3. Cut the second orange into wheels and coat with granulated sugar on both sides. Place directly on the grill grate and cook 15 minutes each side or until grill marks form. Grill: 325 °F

4. In a mixing tin, add grilled peaches, bourbon, orange fig spread, fresh lemon juice and honey glazed orange juice.

5. Shake vigorously to blend the juices and fig spread. Strain over clean ice. Garnish with grilled orange wheel. Enjoy!

Bacon Old-fashioned Cocktail

Servings: 2

Cooking Time: 20 Minutes

Ingredients:

- 16 Slices bacon
- 1/2 Cup warm water (110°F to 115°F)
- 1500 mL bourbon
- 1/2 Fluid Ounce maple syrup
- 4 Dash Angostura bitters
- 2 fresh orange peel

Directions:

1. Smoke bacon prior to making Old Fashioned using this recipe for Applewood Smoked Bacon.

2. To Make Bacon: Supply your smoker with wood pellets and follow the start-up procedure. Preheat the grill, with the lid closed, to 325° F.

3. Place bacon in a single layer on a cooling rack that fits inside a baking sheet pan. Cook in Traeger for 15-20 minutes or until bacon is browned and crispy. Reserve bacon for later. Let the fat cool slightly; you'll use the fat to infuse the bourbon. Grill: 325 °F

4. Combine 1/4 cup of warm (not hot) liquid bacon fat with the entire contents of a 750ml bottle of bourbon in a glass or heavy plastic container.

5. Use a fork to stir well. Let it sit on the counter for a few hours, stirring every so often.

6. After about four hours, put bourbon fat mixture into the freezer. After about an hour, the fat will congeal and you can simply scoop it out with a spoon. You can fine-strain the mixture through a sieve to remove all fat if desired.

7. Combine ingredients with ice and stir until cold. Strain over fresh ice in an Old Fashioned glass and garnish with reserved bacon and orange peel. Enjoy!

Smoked Salted Caramel White Russian

Servings: 4

Cooking Time: 20 Minutes

Ingredients:

- 16 Ounce half-and-half
- salted caramel sauce
- 6 Ounce vodka
- 6 Ounce Kahlúa

Directions:

1. Supply your smoker with wood pellets and follow the start-up procedure. Preheat the grill, with the lid closed, to 180° F.

2. Pour the half-and-half in a shallow baking dish and place directly on the grill grate. In another shallow baking dish, pour 2 to 3 cups of water and place on the grill next to the half-and-half.

3. Smoke both the half-and-half and water for 20 minutes. Remove from the grill and let cool. Grill: 180 °F

4. Place the half-and-half in the fridge until ready to use. Pour the smoked water into ice cube trays and transfer to the freezer until completely frozen.

5. Separate the smoked ice cubes into four glasses. Drizzle the salted caramel sauce around the inside of the glass.

6. Pour 1-1/2 ounce vodka and 1-1/2 ounce Kahlúa into each of the glasses and top with the smoked half-and-half. Enjoy!

Smoky Scotch & Ginger Cocktail

Servings: 2

Cooking Time: 60 Minutes

Ingredients:

- 1 Ounce ginger syrup
- 1/2 Ounce brandied cherry juice
- 1/2 Ounce agave nectar
- 4 Ounce scotch
- 1 1/2 Ounce lemon juice
- 2 Slices grilled lemon, for garnish
- 2 cherry, for garnish

Directions:

1. Supply your smoker with wood pellets and follow the start-up procedure. Preheat the grill, with the lid closed, to 180° F.

2. For the smoked ginger cherry syrup: Place ginger syrup, cherry juice and agave nectar in a shallow dish and place the dish directly on the grill grate.

3. Smoke for 60 minutes, or until the mixture has picked up the smoke flavor. Remove from grill and allow to cool for 30 minutes. Grill: 180 °F

4. Place smoked ginger cherry syrup, scotch and lemon juice into a shaker tin and shake with ice. Strain into a glass over fresh ice and garnish with a grilled lemon wheel and cherry. Enjoy!

A Smoking Classic Cocktail

Servings: 2
Cooking Time: 60 Minutes

Ingredients:
- 2 Bottle Angostura orange bitters
- 10 sugar cubes
- 8 Ounce Champagne
- lemon twist

Directions:
1. Supply your smoker with wood pellets and follow the start-up procedure. Preheat the grill, with the lid closed, to 180° F.
2. For the Smoked Orange Bitters: In a small skillet, combine 1 bottle of Angostura orange bitters with a splash of water and 4 sugar cubes.
3. Place skillet on the grill grate and smoke for 60 minutes. Cool the smoked bitters and put back into the bottle. Grill: 180 °F
4. Add a sugar cube to each Champagne flute and soak the sugar cubes with the smoked bitters.
5. Add champagne and a lemon twist in a flute glass. Enjoy!

Cran-apple Tequila Punch With Smoked Oranges

Servings: 2
Cooking Time: 15 Minutes

Ingredients:
- 6 Cup apple juice, chilled
- 6 Cup light cranberry cocktail
- 1 Cup cranberries, fresh or thawed
- 3 Large oranges, halved
- 1 Cup sugar, for rimming glasses
- 2 Tablespoon lemon juice
- 2 Cup reposado tequila
- 1 Cup orange-flavored liqueur, such as Grand Marnier or Cointreau
- 2 Bottle sparkling wine (such as prosecco) or sparkling water

Directions:
1. Combine 1 cup each of the apple and cranberry juices, then pour into ice cube trays. If the cube molds are big enough, place a few cranberries into each cube. Freeze for 6 hours to overnight.
2. Supply your smoker with wood pellets and follow the start-up procedure. Preheat the grill, with the lid closed, to 180° F.
3. Place the orange halves cut-side down on the grill and smoke for 15 minutes. Remove from the grill and juice oranges. Reserve smoked orange juice. Grill: 180 °F
4. When ready to serve, place the sugar on a flat plate. Pour the lemon juice into a bowl that will fit the rim of each glass.
5. Carefully dip the rim of each glass in the lemon juice, then dip in the sugar to create a 1/8" sugar rim. Turn the glass right-side up and allow to dry for a few minutes before using.
6. Just before serving, mix the remaining apple juice, cranberry cocktail and smoked orange juice with the tequila, orange liqueur, and sparkling wine in a large bowl or pitcher. Taste, adding more of any ingredient to meet your preference.
7. When ready to serve, place a few ice cubes in each glass, then pour a cup of the punch over the top. Alternatively, place all of the ice cubes in the punch bowl and allow guests to help themselves. Enjoy!

Smoked Cold Brew Coffee

Servings: 8
Cooking Time: 120 Minutes

Ingredients:
- 12 Ounce coarse ground coffee
- heavy cream or milk
- sugar

Directions:

1. Place half the coffee grounds in a plastic container and slowly pour 3-1/2 cups water over the top of the grounds. Add remaining grounds and pour another 3-1/2 cups water over the top in a circular motion.

2. Press the grounds down into the water using the back of a spoon. Cover and transfer to the refrigerator and let sit for 18 to 24 hours.

3. Remove from refrigerator and strain into a clean container through a fine mesh strainer or double layer of cheese cloth.

4. Supply your smoker with wood pellets and follow the start-up procedure. Preheat the grill, with the lid closed, to 180° F.

5. Pour cold brew into a shallow baking dish and place directly on the grill grate. Smoke for 1 to 2 hours depending on desired level of smoke. Grill: 180 °F

6. Remove from grill and place over an ice bath to cool. Drink as is over ice, with cream or sugar or use in your favorite coffee recipes. Enjoy!

Smoked Hibiscus Sparkler

Servings: 4
Cooking Time: 30 Minutes

Ingredients:
- 1/2 Cup sugar
- 2 Tablespoon dried hibiscus flowers
- 1 Bottle sparkling wine
- crystallized ginger, for garnish

Directions:
1. Supply your smoker with wood pellets and follow the start-up procedure. Preheat the grill, with the lid closed, to 180° F.

2. Place water in a shallow baking dish and place directly on the grill grate. Smoke the water for 30 minutes or until desired smoke flavor is achieved. Grill: 180 °F

3. Pour water into a small saucepan and add sugar and hibiscus flowers. Bring to a simmer over medium heat and cook until sugar is dissolved.

4. Strain out the hibiscus flowers and transfer your simple syrup to a small container and refrigerate until chilled.

5. Pour 1/2 ounce smoked hibiscus simple syrup in the bottom of a champagne glass and top with sparkling wine.

6. Drop in a few pieces of crystallized ginger to garnish. Enjoy!

Smoked Jacobsen Salt Margarita

Servings: 2
Cooking Time: 1 Day

Ingredients:
- kosher sea salt
- 3 Cup Jacobsen Co. Honey
- 6 Ounce tequila
- 4 Ounce fresh squeezed lime juice
- 1/2 Cup Jacobsen Salt Co. Cherrywood Smoked Salt or smoked kosher salt
- 2 Ounce simple syrup
- 2 Teaspoon orange liqueur

Directions:
1. If making your own smoked salt, take kosher sea salt (however much you want to smoke) and spread it out on a tray.

2. Supply your smoker with wood pellets and follow the start-up procedure. Preheat the grill, with the lid closed, to 165° F.

3. Place tray of salt directly on the grill grate and smoke for about 24 hours, stirring the salt every 8 hours. Once it has smoked for 24 hours, take off grill and use in all your favorite dishes. Note: If you want to skip the long smoke session, use Jacobsen Salt Co. Cherrywood Smoked Salt. Grill: 165 °F

4. Simple Syrup: Put the honey and 1 cup water in a small saucepan. Cook over low heat, stirring, for about 20 min.

5. Fill a cocktail shaker with ice. Add tequila, lime juice, simple syrup and orange liqueur. Cover and shake until mixed and chilled, about 30 seconds.

6. Place smoked salt on a plate. Press the rim of a chilled rocks glass into the salt to rim the edge. Strain margarita into the glass. Enjoy!

Smoked Barnburner Cocktail

Servings: 2

Cooking Time: 45 Minutes

Ingredients:

- 16 Ounce fresh raspberries
- 1/2 Cup Smoked Simple Syrup
- 1 1/2 Ounce smoked raspberry syrup
- 3 Ounce reposado tequila
- 1 Ounce lime juice
- 1 Ounce lemon juice
- 2 grilled lime wheel, for garnish

Directions:

1. Supply your smoker with wood pellets and follow the start-up procedure. Preheat the grill, with the lid closed, to 180° F.

2. For Smoked Raspberry Syrup: Place fresh raspberries on a grill mat and smoke for 30 minutes. After the raspberries have been smoked, reserve a few for garnish and place the remainder into a shallow sheet pan with Traeger Smoked Simple Syrup. Grill: 180 ˚F

3. Place sheet pan on the grill grate and smoke for 45 minutes. Remove from grill and let cool. Strain through a fine mesh sieve discarding solids. Transfer the syrup to the refrigerator until ready to use. Makes about 1/2 cup of smoked raspberry syrup. Grill: 180 ˚F

4. For cocktail: Add 3/4 ounce smoked raspberry syrup, tequila, lime juice and lemon juice with ice into a mixing glass. Shake and pour over clean ice. Garnish with smoked raspberries and a grilled lime wheel. Enjoy!

Smoked Pineapple Hotel Nacional Cocktail

Servings: 2

Cooking Time: 20 Minutes

Ingredients:

- 2 pineapple
- 1/2 Cup water
- 1/2 Cup sugar
- 3 Fluid Ounce white rum
- 1 1/2 Fluid Ounce lime juice
- 1 1/2 Fluid Ounce Pineapple Syrup
- 1 Fluid Ounce apricot brandy
- 2 Dash Angostura bitters

Directions:

1. For the Syrup: Supply your smoker with wood pellets and follow the start-up procedure. Preheat the grill, with the lid closed, to 180° F.

2. Trim both ends of the pineapple, discard the ends. Cut the pineapple into slices about 3/4" thick. Don't worry about the skin, it doesn't hurt to leave it on. Place the pineapple slices on the grill and smoke for about 15 minutes on each sideTrim both ends of the pineapple and discard the ends. Cut the pineapple into slices about 3/4 inch thick. Don't worry about the skin, it doesn't hurt to leave it on. Place the pineapple slices on the grill and smoke for about 15 minutes per side. Grill: 180 ˚F

3. While the pineapple is smoking, combine 1/4 cup water and sugar in a saucepan over low heat, stirring constantly, until sugar is dissolved. Pour syrup into a large bowl and set aside.

4. When the pineapple is done cooking, cut each slice into eight or so wedges and add the wedges to the bowl with the simple syrup, tossing to coat and cover.

5. Leave the mixture to macerate for at least 4 hours (or up to 24) in the refrigerator, stirring from time to time.

6. Strain the syrup into a clean bowl through a fine-mesh strainer and press on the pineapple with a ladle to extract as much liquid as possible. You can bottle and refrigerate the syrup for up to 4 days.

7. To make the cocktail: Combine the rum, lime juice, pineapple syrup, apricot brandy, and bitters in a cocktail shaker or mixing glass. Fill with ice cubes and shake until cold.

8. Strain into a chilled cocktail glass. Garnish with a lime wheel and serve. Enjoy!

Dublin Delight Cocktail

Servings: 2

Cooking Time: 20 Minutes

Ingredients:

- 2 orange, sliced
- 3 Fluid Ounce Teeling Whiskey
- 1 1/2 Fluid Ounce Smoked Simple Syrup
- 6 Dash aromatic bitters

- 6 Fluid Ounce Guinness beer
- 2 Amarena cherry, for garnish

Directions:

1. Supply your smoker with wood pellets and follow the start-up procedure. Preheat the grill, with the lid closed, to 450° F.

2. Place orange slices directly on the grill grate and cook 20 to 25 minutes. Remove from grill and let cool. Grill: 450 °F

3. In a mixing glass, add whiskey, Traeger Smoked Simple Syrup and bitters. Add ice and shake. Pour over a beer glass filled with ice and top off with cold Guinness.

4. Garnish with a grilled orange slice and Amarena cherry. Enjoy!

Grilled Peach Mint Julep

Servings: 2
Cooking Time: 45 Minutes

Ingredients:

- 2 Whole peach
- 4 Ounce whiskey
- 2 Cup sugar
- 4 Tablespoon pink peppercorns
- 20 Whole fresh mint leaves, plus more for garnish
- 2 lime wedge, for garnish
- 4 Ounce bourbon

Directions:

1. For the Grilled Whiskey Peaches: cut peach into slices, then soak peach slices in whiskey in the refrigerator for 4 to 6 hours.

2. For the Pink Peppercorn Simple Syrup: In a shallow pan, combine sugar, 1 cup water and pink peppercorns.

3. Supply your smoker with wood pellets and follow the start-up procedure. Preheat the grill, with the lid closed, to 180° F.

4. Cook syrup down on the grill for 30 minutes, or until desired smoke flavor has been reached. Remove from the grill. Grill: 180 °F

5. Increase Traeger temperature to 350°F and preheat. Place the whiskey peach slices directly on the grill grate and cook 10 to 12 minutes or until peaches soften and get grill marks. Grill: 350 °F

6. To make the Julep: Muddle 1/2 ounce Pink Peppercorn Simple Syrup with 10 fresh mint leaves and 4 slices of grilled whiskey peaches.

7. Add crushed ice over the rim of the glass. Pour bourbon over the crushed ice and stir. Garnish with 1 large sprig of mint and fresh lime. Enjoy!

Smoked Irish Coffee

Servings: 2
Cooking Time: 15 Minutes

Ingredients:

- 10 Ounce hot coffee
- 1/2 Cup heavy cream
- 1 Tablespoon sugar
- 2 Ounce Irish whiskey
- freshly grated nutmeg, for garnish (optional)

Directions:

1. Supply your smoker with wood pellets and follow the start-up procedure. Preheat the grill, with the lid closed, to 180° F.

2. Place the coffee and cream in separate shallow baking dishes and place both directly on the grill grate. Smoke for 10 to 15 minutes until the liquids pick up a slight smoke flavor. Grill: 180 °F

3. Remove from the grill and cool the cream. When the cream is cool, add sugar and whip in a stand mixer or by hand to soft peaks.

4. Pour the hot coffee into two mugs then add 2 ounces of whiskey to each.

5. Top with smoked whipped cream and finish with freshly grated nutmeg, if desired. Enjoy!

Smoked Texas Ranch Water

Servings: 4
Cooking Time: 60 Minutes

Ingredients:

- 3 Whole limes
- 1 Tablespoon Blackened Saskatchewan Rub
- 12 Ounce blanco tequila
- 24 Ounce Topo Chico or other sparkling mineral water
- 8 Slices jalapeño, optional

Directions:

1. Supply your smoker with wood pellets and follow the start-up procedure. Preheat the grill, with the lid closed, to 225° F.

2. Cut two of the limes in half and sprinkle with Traeger Blackened Saskatchewan Rub. Place the four lime halves on the edge of the grill grate and smoke for 1 hour. Remove from grill and set aside to cool. Grill: 225 °F

3. Pour some of the rub onto a small plate. Cut the third lime into 1/4 wedges and use the lime to rub the rim of 4 cocktail glasses, turn the glasses upside down, and into the rub to salt the rim.

4. Place several ice cubes into your rimmed glasses and pour 3 ounces tequila, 6 ounces Topo Chico, squeeze the juice of one smoked lime (discard after squeezing), and add one fresh lime wedge to each. If using the jalapeño, add one or two slices to each glass (muddle if desired).

5. Stir to combine and enjoy!

Traeger Old Fashioned

Servings: 2

Cooking Time: 60 Minutes

Ingredients:

- 2 orange
- 2 Cup cherries
- 3 Ounce bourbon
- 1 Ounce Smoked Simple Syrup
- 8 Dash Bitters Lab Apricot Vanilla Bitters

Directions:

1. Supply your smoker with wood pellets and follow the start-up procedure. Preheat the grill, with the lid closed, to 180° F.

2. While Traeger preheats, slice whole orange into wheels.

3. Place cherries on a small sheet pan and place in the Traeger. Place orange slices directly on the grill grate.

4. Smoke cherries for 1 hour and oranges for 25 minutes, depending on taste, before removing from the grill. Let oranges and cherries cool. Grill: 180 °F

5. Pour bourbon into glass, followed by Traeger Smoked Simple Syrup and bitters. Add ice and stir for 45 seconds or until drink is well-diluted.

6. Strain contents into new glass over fresh ice. Skewer orange wheel and add cherry for garnish. Enjoy!

Traeger Boulevardier Cocktail

Servings: 2

Cooking Time: 60 Minutes

Ingredients:

- 4 oranges
- 1/2 Cup honey
- 1500 mL rye whiskey
- 1 1/2 Ounce Campari
- 1 1/2 Ounce sweet vermouth
- 2 Tablespoon granulated sugar
- 3 Ounce grilled orange infused rye

Directions:

1. Supply your smoker with wood pellets and follow the start-up procedure. Preheat the grill, with the lid closed, to 350° F.

2. Slice 2 oranges in half and coat cut side with honey. Peel remaining orange and place peels on the grill. Cook 20 to 25 minutes. Grill: 350 °F

3. Remove from grill and let cool. Place orange halves cut side down directly on the grill grate and cook 20 to 30 minutes or until dark grill marks appear. Remove orange halves and allow to cool. Grill: 350 °F

4. Place orange halves into a bottle of rye whiskey and let steep for 10 to 12 hours. The longer they steep, the sweeter and more pronounced the orange flavor will be.

5. Add all ingredients into a mixing glass and stir until diluted. Strain into a fresh coupe glass and serve neat.

6. Garnish with grilled orange peel. Enjoy!

Grilled Rabbit Tail Cocktail

Servings: 2

Cooking Time: 25 Minutes

Ingredients:

- 1 1/2 Ounce lemon juice
- 4 Ounce Apple Brandy
- 1 Ounce orange juice
- 1 Ounce Smoked Simple Syrup

Directions:

1. Supply your smoker with wood pellets and follow the start-up procedure. Preheat the grill, with the lid closed, to 350° F.

2. Place lemon halves directly on the grill grate and cook for 20-25 minutes or until grill marks appear. Remove from grill and let cool. Once cool enough to handle, juice the lemons then chill and reserve the juice. Grill: 350 °F

3. Using the proportions listed above and considering the size and consumption rate of your tailgate crew or party, mix all the above ingredients in a large thermos and top with a bit of ice.

4. Using 6-8 oz glasses or cups, guests can serve themselves from the thermos and garnish each drink with a grilled apple slice. Enjoy!

Traeger Paloma Cocktail

Servings: 2
Cooking Time: 25 Minutes

Ingredients:

- 4 grapefruit, halved
- Smoked Simple Syrup
- 10 Stick cinnamon
- 3 Ounce reposado tequila
- 1 Ounce lime juice
- 1 Ounce Smoked Simple Syrup
- grilled lime, for garnish
- cinnamon stick, for garnish

Directions:

1. Supply your smoker with wood pellets and follow the start-up procedure. Preheat the grill, with the lid closed, to 350° F.

2. Grilled Grapefruit Juice: Cut 2 grapefruits in half. Place a cinnamon stick in each grapefruit half and glaze with Traeger Smoked Simple Syrup. Place on grill grate and cook for 20 minutes or until edges start to burn and it acquires grill marks. Remove from heat and let cool. Grill: 350 °F

3. After grapefruits have cooled, squeeze and strain juice. It should yield 10 to 12 ounces of juice.

4. In a mixing glass, add tequila, lime juice, Traeger Smoked Simple Syrup and 2 ounces of the grilled grapefruit juice.

5. Add ice and shake. Strain over ice in an old fashioned glass.

6. Add a grilled lime slice and cinnamon stick to garnish. Enjoy!

Smoked Grape Lime Rickey

Servings: 4
Cooking Time: 45 Minutes

Ingredients:

- 1/2 Pound red grapes
- 1/2 Cup plus 1 tablespoon sugar
- 1/2 Cup water
- 1 limes, sliced
- 2 limes, halved
- 1 Tablespoon sugar
- 1 L lemon lime soda

Directions:

1. Supply your smoker with wood pellets and follow the start-up procedure. Preheat the grill, with the lid closed, to 180° F.

2. Rinse grapes well and place in a shallow baking dish. Combine 1/2 cup sugar and water and stir until sugar dissolves. Pour over grapes.

3. Place the baking dish directly on the grill grate and smoke for 30 to 40 minutes until grapes are tender. Grill: 180 °F

4. Remove from the grill and pour entire contents of the baking dish in a blender. Puree on high until smooth then pass the mixture through a fine mesh strainer.

5. Increase Traeger temperature to 350°F. Grill: 350 °F

6. Toss the lime slices and lime halves with 1 tablespoon sugar and place directly on the grill grate. Cook for 15 to 20 minutes or until grill marks develop. Remove from grill and set slices aside. When cool enough to handle, juice grilled lime halves. Grill: 350 °F

7. To build the drink, fill a pint glass with ice. Pour in 1-1/2 ounce grilled lime juice, 1-1/2 ounce smoked grape syrup and top off with soda. Garnish with grilled lime slice. Enjoy!

Honey Glazed Grapefruit Shandy Cocktail

Servings: 2
Cooking Time: 20 Minutes

Ingredients:
- 4 grapefruits
- 4 Tablespoon honey
- granulated sugar
- 2 Ounce bourbon
- 1 Ounce Smoked Simple Syrup
- 4 Ounce honey glazed grilled grapefruit, juiced
- 2 Bottle Ballast Point Grapefruit Sculpin

Directions:
1. Supply your smoker with wood pellets and follow the start-up procedure. Preheat the grill, with the lid closed, to 375° F.
2. For the honey glazed grapefruit: Slice one grapefruit in half and coat with 2 tablespoons honey.
3. Take the other grapefruit and slice into wheels. Toss the wheels in granulated sugar until well coated.
4. Place the grapefruit halves and wheels directly on the grill grate, cut side down, and cook for 20 to 30 minutes. Remove from grill and set the wheels aside. Grill: 375 ˚F
5. Squeeze the grapefruit halves into a measuring cup. It should yield about 2 oz juice.
6. Pour the grapefruit juice into a shaker and add bourbon and Traeger Smoked Simple Syrup then top with ice. Shake for 10-15 seconds.
7. Strain into glass, add ice and fill with beer. Garnish with the grilled grapefruit wheel. Enjoy!

Smoked Plum And Thyme Fizz Cocktail

Servings: 2
Cooking Time: 60 Minutes

Ingredients:
- 6 fresh plums
- 4 Fluid Ounce vodka
- 1 1/2 Fluid Ounce fresh lemon juice
- 2 Ounce smoked plum and thyme simple syrup
- 4 Fluid Ounce club soda
- 2 Slices smoked plum, for garnish
- 2 Sprig fresh thyme, for garnish
- 8 Sprig thyme
- 2 Cup Smoked Simple Syrup

Directions:
1. Supply your smoker with wood pellets and follow the start-up procedure. Preheat the grill, with the lid closed, to 180° F.
2. Cut plums in half and remove the pit. Place the plum halves directly on the grill grate and smoke for 25 minutes. Grill: 180 ˚F
3. For the Plum and Thyme Simple Syrup: After 25 minutes, remove plums from the grill and cut into quarters. Add plums and thyme sprigs to 1 cup of Traeger Smoked Simple Syrup. Smoke the mixture for 45 minutes. Remove from grill, strain and let cool. Grill: 180 ˚F
4. Add vodka, fresh lemon juice and smoked plum and thyme simple syrup to a mixing glass.
5. Add ice and shake. Strain over clean ice, top off with club soda and garnish with a piece of thyme and slice of smoked plum. Enjoy!

Grilled Peach Smash Cocktail

Servings: 2
Cooking Time: 10 Minutes

Ingredients:
- 2 peach, sliced and grilled
- 10 fresh mint leaves
- 1 1/2 Ounce Smoked Simple Syrup
- 4 Ounce bourbon
- 2 mint sprig, for garnish

Directions:
1. Supply your smoker with wood pellets and follow the start-up procedure. Preheat the grill, with the lid closed, to 375° F.
2. Cut the peach into 6 slices and brush with Traeger Smoked Simple Syrup. Place directly on the grill grate and cook 10 to 12 minutes or until peaches soften and get grill marks. Grill: 375 ˚F
3. In a mixing glass, add 3 slices of grilled peaches, 5 mint leaves and Traeger Smoked Simple Syrup.

4. Muddle ingredients to release oils of the mint and juices from the grilled peaches. Add bourbon and crushed ice.

5. Shake and pour into a stemless wine glass. Top off with more crushed ice. Garnish with a grilled peach and mint sprig. Enjoy!

Smoked Eggnog

Servings: 4
Cooking Time: 60 Minutes

Ingredients:
- 2 Cup whole milk
- 1 Cup heavy cream
- 4 egg yolk
- Cup sugar
- 3 Ounce bourbon
- 1 Teaspoon vanilla extract
- 1 Teaspoon nutmeg
- 4 egg white
- whipped cream

Directions:
1. Plan ahead, this recipe requires chill time.
2. Supply your smoker with wood pellets and follow the start-up procedure. Preheat the grill, with the lid closed, to 180° F.
3. Pour the milk and the cream into a baking pan and smoke on the Traeger for 60 minutes. Grill: 180 °F
4. Meanwhile, in the bowl of a stand mixer, beat the egg yolks until they lighten in color. Gradually add 1/3 cup sugar and continue to beat until sugar completely dissolves.
5. After the milk and cream have smoked, add them along with the bourbon, vanilla and nutmeg into the egg mixture and stir to combine.
6. Place the egg whites in the bowl of a stand mixer and beat to soft peaks. When you lift the beaters the whites will make a peak that slightly curls down.
7. With the mixer still running, gradually add 1 tablespoon of sugar and beat until stiff peaks form.
8. Gently fold the egg whites into the cream mixture and then whisk to thoroughly combine.

9. Chill eggnog for a couple hours to let the flavors meld. Garnish with a dash of nutmeg and whipped cream on top. Enjoy!

Traeger Gin & Tonic

Servings: 2
Cooking Time: 45 Minutes

Ingredients:
- 1/2 Cup berries
- 2 orange, sliced
- 4 Tablespoon granulated sugar
- 3 Ounce gin
- 1 Cup tonic water
- 2 Sprig fresh mint, for garnish

Directions:
1. Supply your smoker with wood pellets and follow the start-up procedure. Preheat the grill, with the lid closed, to 180° F.
2. For the Smoked Berries: Spread mixed fresh berries on a sheet pan and place directly on the grill grate. Smoke for 30 minutes then remove from grill. Grill: 180 °F
3. For the Orange Slices: Increase the grill temperature to 450°F and preheat, lid closed for 15 minutes. Grill: 450 °F
4. Toss the orange slices with granulated sugar and place directly on grill grate. Cook for about 5 minutes, turning once or until the slices have developed grill marks. Grill: 450 °F
5. Pour gin into a glass, add ice and berries, then top with tonic water. Garnish with a fresh mint sprig and grilled orange wheel. Enjoy!

Smoke And Bubz Cocktail

Servings: 2
Cooking Time: 45 Minutes

Ingredients:
- 16 Ounce POM Juice
- 2 Cup pomegranate seeds
- 6 Ounce sparkling white wine
- 2 lemon twist, for garnish
- 2 Teaspoon pomegranate seeds

Directions:

1. Supply your smoker with wood pellets and follow the start-up procedure. Preheat the grill, with the lid closed, to 180° F.

2. For the Smoked Pomegranate Juice: Pour POM juice and a cup of pomegranate seeds into a shallow sheet pan. Smoke on the Traeger for 45 minutes. Pull off grill, strain, discard seeds and let sit until chilled. Grill: 180 °F

3. Add 1-1/2 ounces of the smoked pomegranate juice to the bottom of a champagne flute.

4. Add sparkling white wine, a few fresh pomegranate seeds and a lemon twist to garnish. Enjoy!

Smoked Raspberry Bubbler Cocktail

Servings: 2

Cooking Time: 45 Minutes

Ingredients:

- 2 Cup fresh raspberries
- Smoked Simple Syrup
- 8 Ounce sparkling wine

Directions:

1. Supply your smoker with wood pellets and follow the start-up procedure. Preheat the grill, with the lid closed, to 180° F.

2. Smoked Raspberry Syrup: Place 1 cup fresh raspberries on a grill mat and smoke for 30 minutes. Grill: 180 °F

3. After the raspberries have been smoked, set a few aside for garnish. Place the remainder into a shallow sheet pan with Traeger Smoked Simple Syrup. Place back on the grill grate and let smoke for 45 minutes. Remove from heat and allow to cool. Strain and refrigerate until ready to use. Grill: 180 °F

4. Place 1 ounce of the smoked raspberry syrup in the bottom of a champagne flute and top off with sparkling white wine or champagne.

5. Garnish with smoked raspberries. Enjoy!

Smoky Mountain Bramble Cocktail

Servings: 2

Cooking Time: 15 Minutes

Ingredients:

- 16 Ounce blackberries
- 2 Cup sugar
- 10 smoked blackberries
- 3 Ounce vodka
- 1 1/2 Ounce Alpine Distilling Preserve Liqueur
- 1 1/2 Ounce lemon juice
- 1 Ounce smoked blackberry syrup

Directions:

1. Supply your smoker with wood pellets and follow the start-up procedure. Preheat the grill, with the lid closed, to 180° F.

2. To make Smoked Blackberry Simple Syrup: Place blackberries on a grill mat and smoke for 15 to 20 minutes. Grill: 180 °F

3. Combine 1 cup water and sugar in a small sauce pan and warm over medium heat until sugar dissolves. Remove from heat and place 2/3 of blackberries in the simple syrup and macerate.

4. Strain through a fine mesh strainer and store for up to 14 days.

5. To make the cocktail: Muddle 4 to 5 smoked blackberries in a cocktail shaker. Add vodka, Preserve Liqueur, lemon and smoked blackberry syrup. Add ice and shake vigorously. Double strain into an old fashioned glass.

6. Garnish with a smoked blackberry and lemon twist. Enjoy!

BAKING RECIPES

Traeger Baked Protein Bars

Servings: 6
Cooking Time: 25 Minutes

Ingredients:
- 2 Cup Frozen Sweet Cherries
- 1 Cup Apricots, Frozen
- 1 Scoop Vanilla Protein Powder
- 2 Tablespoon honey
- 1 Teaspoon vanilla extract
- 1 Cup rolled oats

Directions:
1. Supply your smoker with wood pellets and follow the start-up procedure. Preheat the grill, with the lid closed, to 350° F.
2. In the bowl of a food processor, add cherries, apricots (revived in hot water for 5 minutes and drained), vanilla protein powder, honey, and vanilla. Pulse about 10 to 15 times, to break the fruit into smaller pieces and to mix all ingredients.
3. In a separate bowl, fold together oats and fruit mixture. Transfer mixture to a loaf pan or silicone mold and place in grill.
4. Bake for approximately 20 to 25 minutes. Grill: 350 °F
5. Let cool completely and cut into 8 pieces. Enjoy!

Vanilla Cheesecake Skillet Brownie

Servings: 2
Cooking Time: 30 Minutes

Ingredients:
- 1 Box Brownie Mix
- 1 Package Cream Cheese
- 2 Egg
- 1/2 Cup Oil
- 1 Can Pie Filling, Blueberry
- 1/2 Cup Sugar
- 1 Tsp Vanilla
- 1/4 Cup Water, Warm

Directions:

1. Combine all brownie ingredients and mix. In a separate bowl, combine cream cheese, sugar, egg and vanilla and mix until smooth. Grease skillets and pour in brownie batter. Top with cheesecake and cherry pie filling, using a knife to blend to give it that marbled look.
2. Supply your smoker with wood pellets and follow the start-up procedure. Preheat the grill, with the lid closed, to 350°F and bake for about 30 minutes.
3. Let cool for about 10 minutes and enjoy!

Sourdough Pizza

Servings: 4
Cooking Time: 12 Minutes

Ingredients:
- 1 1/2 Cup Fresh Sourdough Starter
- 1 Tablespoon olive oil
- 1 Teaspoon Jacobsen Salt Co. Pure Kosher Sea Salt
- 1 1/4 Cup all-purpose flour

Directions:
1. Supply your smoker with wood pellets and follow the start-up procedure. Preheat the grill, with the lid closed, to 450° F.
2. Mix together the fresh sourdough starter, one tablespoon of oil, Jacobsen salt and 1-1/4 cups of flour. Add more flour, a little at a time, as needed to form a pizza dough consistency.
3. Allow the dough to rest for 30 minutes, to allow for easier rolling. Roll the dough out into a circle, using a small amount of flour to prevent sticking.
4. Place on a pizza stone. Bake the crust for approximately 7 minutes Grill: 450 °F
5. Remove the crust from the grill; brush on remaining oil to prevent toppings from soaking into the crust. Add the desired toppings and return pizza to grill; bake until the crust browns and the cheese melts.

Strawberry Basil Daiquiri

Servings: 2

Cooking Time: 20 Minutes

Ingredients:

- 4 strawberries, stemmed
- 6 Tablespoon granulated sugar, divided
- 6 basil leaves
- 3 Ounce white rum
- 2 Ounce lime juice
- 1 Ounce Smoked Simple Syrup
- 2 fresh basil leaves, for garnish
- 2 lime slice, for garnish

Directions:

1. Supply your smoker with wood pellets and follow the start-up procedure. Preheat the grill, with the lid closed, to 375° F.

2. Cut strawberries in half and coat in 2 tablespoons granulated sugar. Place directly on grill grate and cook for 15 to 20 minutes. Remove from heat and cool. Grill: 375 °F

3. Add 1 tablespoon granulated sugar and basil leaves to shaking tin and lightly muddle. Add strawberries and muddle again.

4. Pour in white rum, lime juice and Smoked Simple Syrup. Shake with ice.

5. Strain contents into a chilled glass and garnish with large fresh basil leaf and sliced lime. Enjoy!

Easy Smoked Cornbread

Servings: 4

Cooking Time: 75 Minutes

Ingredients:

- 2 cups self rising flour
- 1 1/2 cups white corn meal
- 2 cups sharp cheddar cheese
- 1/2 cup sour cream
- 1/2 cup sugar
- 1 Tbsp baking powder
- 1 teaspoon sea salt
- 1 12 oz can of evaporated milk
- 1/2 cup vegetable oil
- 2 large eggs beaten

Directions:

1. Mix all ingredients together well and fold into a greased baking pan (such as a round cake Pan).

2. Supply your smoker with wood pellets and follow the start-up procedure. Preheat the grill, with the lid closed, to 375° F. Smoke on 375 °F for 1 hour and 15 minutes or until toothpick comes clean and edges look brown.

3. Rub some butter on top and sprinkle a little Fred's Butt Rub on top before serving.

4. Enjoy!

Baked Chocolate Brownie Cookies With Egg Nog

Servings: 6

Cooking Time: 12 Minutes

Ingredients:

- 16 Ounce Bar bittersweet chocolate, finely chopped
- 4 Tablespoon unsalted butter, room temperature
- 4 eggs
- 1 1/3 Cup granulated sugar
- 1 Teaspoon vanilla extract
- 1 1/2 Cup all-purpose flour
- 1/2 Teaspoon baking powder
- 1 Cup semisweet chocolate chips

Directions:

1. Supply your smoker with wood pellets and follow the start-up procedure. Preheat the grill, with the lid closed, to 350° F.

2. Line two baking sheets with parchment paper.

3. Put the finely chopped chocolate and butter in a heatproof bowl and set over a saucepan of barely simmering water; stir occasionally until chocolate is completely melted and smooth. Set aside and allow to cool to room temperature.

4. Whisk together eggs, sugar and vanilla extract in a medium bowl. Set aside.

5. Sift together the flour and baking powder in a small bowl. Add the melted chocolate mixture to the egg mixture and stir with a rubber spatula until completely combined.

6. Add the flour mixture in three batches, folding gently into the batter with a spatula. Once all of the flour has been incorporated, stir in the chocolate chips.

7. Scoop 1-1/2 tablespoons of dough onto prepared baking sheets. Bake for 10 to 12 minutes or until they are firm on the outside. Do not over bake. Grill:350° F

8. Leave to cool completely on the baking sheets. Enjoy!

Quick Baked Dinner Rolls

Servings: 8
Cooking Time: 30 Minutes

Ingredients:
- 2 Tablespoon quick-rise yeast
- 1 Teaspoon salt
- 1/4 Cup sugar
- 3 1/3 Cup flour
- 1/4 Cup unsalted butter, softened
- 1 egg
- cooking spray
- 1 egg, for egg wash

Directions:
1. Combine yeast and warm water in a small bowl to activate the yeast. Let sit until foamy, about 5-10 minutes.

2. Combine salt, sugar, and flour in the bowl of a stand mixer fitted with the dough hook. Pour water and yeast into the dry ingredients with the machine running on low.

3. Add butter and egg and mix for 10 minutes gradually increasing the speed from low to high.

4. Form the dough into a ball and place in a buttered bowl. Cover with a cloth and let the dough rise for approximately 40 minutes.

5. Transfer the risen dough to a lightly floured surface and divide into 8 pieces forming a ball with each.

6. Lightly spray a cast iron pan with cooking spray and arrange balls in the pan. Cover with a cloth and let rise 20 minutes.

7. Supply your smoker with wood pellets and follow the start-up procedure. Preheat the grill, with the lid closed, to 375° F.

8. Brush rolls with egg wash and then bake for 30 minutes until lightly browned. Serve hot. Enjoy! Grill: 375 °F

Smoker Wheat Bread

Servings: 6
Cooking Time: 60 Minutes

Ingredients:
- As Needed extra-virgin olive oil
- 2 Cup all-purpose flour
- 1 Cup whole wheat flour
- 1 1/4 Ounce Packet, Active Dry Yeast
- 1 1/4 Teaspoon salt
- 1 1/2 Cup water
- As Needed Cornmeal

Directions:
1. Oil a large mixing bowl and set aside. In a second mixing bowl, combine the flours, yeast, and salt.

2. Push your sleeve up to your elbow and form your fingers into a claw. Mix the dry ingredients until well-combined.

3. Add the water and mix until blended. The dough will be wet, shaggy, and somewhat stringy.

4. Tip the dough into the oiled mixing bowl and cover with plastic wrap.

5. Allow the dough to rise at room temperature-- about 70 degrees-- for 2 hours, or until the surface is bubbled.

6. Turn the dough out onto a lightly floured work surface and lightly flour the top. With floured hands, fold the dough over on itself twice. Cover loosely with plastic wrap and allow the dough to rest for 15 minutes.

7. Dust a clean lint-free cotton towel with cornmeal, wheat bran, or flour. With floured hands, gently form the dough into a ball and place it, seam side down, on the towel.

8. Dust the top of the ball with cornmeal, wheat bran, or flour, and cover the dough with a second towel. Let the dough rise until doubled in size; the dough will not spring back when poked with a finger.

9. In the meantime, start the smoker grill and set temperature to 450 F. Preheat, lid closed, for 10-15 minutes.

10. Put a lidded 6- to 8-quart cast iron Dutch oven - preferably one coated with enamel, on the grill grate.

11. When the dough has risen, remove the top towel, slide your hand under the bottom towel to support the dough, then carefully tip the dough, seam side up, into the preheated pot.

12. Remove the towel. Shake the pot a couple of times if the dough looks lopsided: It will straighten out as it bakes.

13. Cover the pot with the lid and bake the bread for 30 minutes. Remove the lid and continue to bake the bread for 15 to 30 minutes more, or until it is nicely browned and sounds hollow when rapped with your knuckles.

14. Turn onto a wire rack to cool. Slice with a serrated knife. Enjoy!

Smoked Lemon Tea

Servings: 6 - 8
Cooking Time: 60 Minutes

Ingredients:
- 8 Black Tea Bags
- 4 Cups Boiling Water
- 2 Cups Ice
- 8 Lemons
- 2 Cups Sugar
- 2 Cups Water

Directions:

1. Place the tea bags in a heat-safe pitcher. Bring 4 Cups of water to a boil and pour over tea bags. Let steep for 5-10 minutes. Remove tea bags and set pitcher aside to cool.

2. Turn on your grill and set to smoke mode. Combine 2 cups of sugar and 2 cups water in a small aluminum pan. Smoke for about 45 minutes, stirring occasionally, or until the mixture reduces to a thick, simple syrup. Remove from the grill and let it cool.

3. Supply your smoker with wood pellets and follow the start-up procedure. Preheat the grill, with the lid closed, to 450° F. If using a charcoal or gas grill, set heat to high.

4. Cut the lemons in half and sear over the flame broiler until charred, about 7 minutes. Remove from grill and set aside to cool.

5. Juice the lemons into a medium bowl. Pour lemon juice through a metal strainer into the tea pitcher to remove seeds and pulp.

6. Pour the cooled simple syrup into pitcher and stir until fully incorporated with tea and lemons. Add 2 cups of ice and refrigerate until serving.

Spiced Carrot Cake

Servings: 10
Cooking Time: 35 Minutes

Ingredients:
- 1/2 Cup Apple Sauce, Unsweetened
- 2 Tsp Baking Powder
- 1 Tsp Baking Soda
- 1 1/2 Cups Brown Sugar
- 1/2 Cup Butter, Room Temp
- 3/4 Cup Canola Oil
- 3 Cups Carrot, Grated
- 1 1/2 Tsp Cinnamon, Ground
- 2 (8-Ounce) Packages Cream Cheese, Room Temperature
- 4 Egg
- 2 Cups Flour, All-Purpose
- 1/2 Tsp Ginger, Ground
- 1/4 Tsp Nutmeg, Ground
- 1/2 Tsp Salt
- 1/2 Cup Sugar
- 3 Cups Sugar, Icing

Directions:

1. Supply your smoker with wood pellets and follow the start-up procedure. Preheat the grill, with the lid closed, to 350° F.

2. Line the bottom of 2 9-inch cake pans with parchment paper and spray the sides with cooking spray. Set aside.

3. In a large bowl, combine flour, baking powder and soda, spices and salt.

4. In a smaller bowl, combine oil, eggs, sugars, and applesauce and whisk together. Add carrots and stir until well combined.

5. Pour the wet ingredients into the dry. Stir until combined but take care not to over mix. Pour the batter evenly between the two cake pans. Bake for about 35

minutes in your Grill, rotating the cake pans halfway between the cook. Remove once a toothpick is inserted in the middle of the cake and comes out clean.

6. While the cake is cooling, prepare the frosting. Beat the cream cheese until smooth with a hand mixer. Add the butter and icing sugar and mix until fully combined.

7. On a clean plate or cake stand, place one half of the cake and top with a good layer of cream cheese frosting. Place the second half on top and cover with the remaining frosting. Icing tip: try not to lift your knife while icing. Instead make long, smooth strokes. Lifting the knife often make cause crumbs to get into your icing. Top with pecans if desired.

Delicious Peanut Butter Cookies

Servings: 24
Cooking Time: 15 Minutes

Ingredients:
- 1 Egg
- 1 Cup Peanut Butter
- 1 Cup Sugar

Directions:

1. Supply your smoker with wood pellets and follow the start-up procedure. Preheat the grill, with the lid closed, to High heat.

2. Combine all ingredients in a bowl. Drop tablespoon amounts of dough on a prepared baking sheet and bake in your Grill for 15-20 minutes. Allow cookies to cool for 5 minutes on the baking sheet before you enjoy!

Caramelized Bourbon Baked Pears

Servings: 4
Cooking Time: 30 Minutes

Ingredients:
- 3 Whole Pears, fresh
- 1/4 Cup brown sugar
- 1/4 Cup bourbon
- 2 Tablespoon butter, melted
- 1 Teaspoon vanilla extract
- 1/2 Teaspoon salt

Directions:

1. Supply your smoker with wood pellets and follow the start-up procedure. Preheat the grill, with the lid closed, to 325° F.

2. Peel and core the pears. Arrange them in a buttered baking dish.

3. In a small bowl, combine the brown sugar, bourbon, butter, vanilla, cinnamon and salt. Pour the bourbon mixture over the pears.

4. Place the baking dish on the grill grate, close the lid and bake for 30-35 minutes or until the pears are fork tender. Grill: 325 °F

5. Transfer to a serving plate and spoon the caramelized bourbon mixture over the pears.

6. Serve warm over vanilla ice cream. Enjoy!

Sweet Cheese Muffins

Servings: 3
Cooking Time: 15 Minutes

Ingredients:
- 1 package butter cake mix
- 1 package Jiffy Corn Muffin Mix
- 1 cup self-rising or cake flour
- 12 tablespoons (1½ sticks) unsalted butter, softened, plus 8 tablespoons (1 stick) melted
- 3½ cups shredded Cheddar cheese
- 2 eggs, beaten, at room temperature
- 2¼ cups buttermilk
- Nonstick cooking spray or butter, for greasing
- ¼ cup packed brown sugar

Directions:

1. Supply your smoker with wood pellets and follow the start-up procedure. Preheat, with the lid closed, to 375°F.

2. In a large mixing bowl, combine the cake mix, corn muffin mix, and flour.

3. Slice the 1½ sticks of softened butter into pieces and cut into the dry ingredients. Add the cheese and mix thoroughly.

4. In a medium bowl, combine the eggs and buttermilk, then add to the dry ingredients, stirring until well blended.

5. Coat three 12-cup mini muffin pans with cooking spray and spoon ¼ cup of batter into each cup.

6. Transfer the pans to the grill, close the lid, and smoke, monitoring closely, for 12 to 15 minutes, or until the muffins are lightly browned.

7. While the muffins are cooking, make the topping: In a small bowl, stir together the remaining 1 stick of melted butter and the brown sugar until well combined.

8. Remove the muffins from the grill. Brush the tops with the sweet butter and serve warm.

Baked Cheesy Parmesan Grits

Servings: 4
Cooking Time: 60 Minutes

Ingredients:
- 4 Cup chicken stock
- 3 Tablespoon butter
- 3/4 Teaspoon salt
- 1 Cup quick grits
- 1 Cup shredded cheddar cheese
- pepper
- 1/2 Cup Monterey Jack cheese, shredded
- 1/2 Cup whole milk
- 2 Large eggs

Directions:
1. Supply your smoker with wood pellets and follow the start-up procedure. Preheat the grill, with the lid closed, to 350° F.
2. Butter an 8" baking dish or a 10" cast iron pan.
3. Bring the chicken stock, butter, and salt to boil in medium saucepan. Gradually whisk in grits.
4. Reduce heat to medium and cook until mixture thickens slightly, stirring often about 8 minutes. Remove from heat.
5. Add cheeses and stir until melted. Season with pepper and salt to taste.
6. Whisk together milk and eggs in small bowl. Gradually whisk mixture into grits.
7. Pour the cheese grits into the buttered cast iron pan. Bake until grits feel firm to touch, about 1 hour. Grill: 350 °F
8. Remove from grill and let stand 10 minutes before serving. Enjoy!

Smoked, Salted Caramel Apple Pie

Servings: 4
Cooking Time: 60 Minutes

Ingredients:
- 1 Cup cream
- 1 Cup brown sugar
- 3/4 Cup Light Corn Syrup
- 6 Tablespoon butter
- 1 Teaspoon sea salt
- 1 Pastry for Double-Crust Pie
- 6 Granny Smith Apples, Cut Into Wedges

Directions:
1. Supply your smoker with wood pellets and follow the start-up procedure. Preheat the grill, with the lid closed, to 180° F.
2. Fill a large pan with ice and water. Pour the cream into a smaller, shallow pan. Place the pan with the cream in the ice bath and place them both on the Traeger to smoke for 15-20 minutes. Grill: 180 °F
3. To make the caramel, combine the sugar and corn syrup in a saucepan and cook over medium heat, stirring constantly until it coats the back of your spoon and starts to turn a copper color, then stir in butter, salt, and smoked cream.
4. To assemble the pie, gather the pie crust, salted caramel, and apples. Place one of the pie crusts into the pie plate and fill with apple slices. Pour caramel over the apples. Lay the top crust over the filling, then crimp the top and bottom crusts together.
5. Make slits in the top crust to release the steam and finish by brushing with egg or cream. Sprinkle with raw sugar and sea salt.
6. When ready to bake, set the Traeger to 375°F and preheat, lid closed for 15 minutes.
7. Place the pie on the grill and bake for 20 minutes. Grill: 375 °F
8. Reduce heat to 325°F and cook for 25 more minutes. When ready, the crust should be golden brown and the filling, bubbly. Grill: 325 °F
9. Remove the pie from the grill and let cool. Serve with vanilla ice cream. Enjoy!

Baked Brie

Servings: 6
Cooking Time: 8 Minutes

Ingredients:

- 16 Ounce (16 oz) brie wheel
- 1/3 Cup honey
- 1/4 Cup pecans
- Crackers
- apple, sliced

Directions:

1. Supply your smoker with wood pellets and follow the start-up procedure. Preheat the grill, with the lid closed, to 350° F.

2. Line a rimmed baking sheet with a piece of parchment or aluminum foil. Using a sharp serrated knife, slice top—the white rind—off the brie. (Le the ave the rind on the sides and bottom intact.)

3. Put the brie, cut side up, on the prepared baking sheet and drizzle with the honey. Sprinkle nuts on top.

4. Bake the brie until it is soft and oozing, but not melting, 8 to 10 minutes. Let it cool for a couple of minutes and transfer to a serving plate. Grill: 350 °F

5. Serve with crackers and sliced apple wedges. Drizzle with more honey, if desired. Enjoy!

Bacon Chocolate Chip Cookies

Servings: 2
Cooking Time: 10-12 Minutes

Ingredients:

- 2¾ cups all-purpose flour
- 1½ teaspoons baking soda
- ½ teaspoon salt
- 12 tablespoons (1½ sticks) unsalted butter, softened
- 1 cup light brown sugar
- 1 cup granulated sugar
- 2 eggs, at room temperature
- 2½ teaspoons apple cider vinegar
- 1 teaspoon vanilla extract
- 2 cups semisweet chocolate chips
- 8 slices bacon, cooked and crumbled

Directions:

1. In a large bowl, combine the flour, baking soda, and salt, and mix well.

2. In a separate large bowl, using an electric mixer on medium speed, cream the butter and sugars. Reduce the speed to low and mix in the eggs, vinegar, and vanilla.

3. With the mixer speed still on low, slowly incorporate the dry ingredients, chocolate chips, and bacon pieces.

4. Supply your smoker with wood pellets and follow the start-up procedure. Preheat, with the lid closed, to 375°F.

5. Line a large baking sheet with parchment paper.

6. Drop rounded teaspoonfuls of cookie batter onto the prepared baking sheet and place on the grill grate. Close the lid and smoke for 10 to 12 minutes, or until the cookies are browned around the edges.

Butternut Squash Macaroni And Cheese

Servings: 2
Cooking Time: 50 Minutes

Ingredients:

- 1 Medium butternut squash
- 2 Cup macaroni, uncooked
- 1 Small yellow onion
- 1/2 Cup chicken broth
- 1 Cup milk
- salt
- pepper
- 1 Cup cheese, grated

Directions:

1. Supply your smoker with wood pellets and follow the start-up procedure. Preheat the grill, with the lid closed, to 225° F.

2. Puncture butternut squash with a fork several times and place on grill grate. Cook until tender, about 40 minutes to an hour. When cooked, scoop out meat and discard seeds. Grill: 225 °F

3. Cook elbow macaroni according to package instructions. Drain and set aside.

4. In a medium skillet, sauté chopped onion until fragrant and golden. Add broth, milk, salt, onions and

butternut squash to a food processor. Puree until smooth and creamy. Add salt and pepper to taste.

5.   Pour pureed sauce over cooked noodles and add the shredded cheese. Stir to melt the cheese and add milk to reach desired consistency. Serve warm. Enjoy!

Pizza Bites

Servings: 6
Cooking Time: 20 Minutes

Ingredients:
- 4 1/2 Cup Bread Flour
- 1 1/2 Tablespoon sugar
- 2 Teaspoon Instant Yeast
- 2 Teaspoon kosher salt
- 3 Tablespoon extra-virgin olive oil
- 15 Fluid Ounce Water, Lukewarm
- 8 Ounce Pepperoni, sliced
- 1 Cup pizza sauce
- 1 Cup mozzarella cheese
- 1 Whole egg, for egg wash
- 1 As Needed salt

Directions:
1.   For the Pizza Dough: Combine flour, sugar, salt, and yeast in food processor. Pulse 3 to 4 times until incorporated evenly. Add olive oil and water. Run food processor until mixture forms ball that rides around the bowl above the blade, about 15 seconds. Continue processing 15 seconds longer.
2.   Transfer dough ball to lightly floured surface and knead once or twice by hand until smooth ball is formed. Divide dough into three even parts and place each into a 1 gallon zip top bag. Place in refrigerator and allow to rise at least one day.
3.   At least two hours before baking, remove dough from refrigerator and shape into balls by gathering dough towards bottom and pinching shut. Flour well and place each one in a separate medium mixing bowl. Cover tightly with plastic wrap and allow to rise at warm room temperature until roughly doubled in volume.
4.   When ready to cook, set the grill temperature to 350°F and preheat, lid closed for 15 minutes.

5.   After the first rise remove the dough from the fridge and let come to room temperature. Roll dough on a flat surface. Cut dough into long strips 3" wide by 18" long.
6.   Slice pepperoni into strips.
7.   In a medium bowl combine the pizza sauce, mozzarella and pepperoni.
8.   Spoon 1 TBSP of the pizza filling onto the pizza dough every two inches, about halfway down the length of the dough. Dip a pastry brush into the egg wash and brush around pizza filling. Fold the half side of the dough (without the pizza filling) over the other the half that contains the pizza filling.
9.   Press down between each pizza bite slightly with your fingers. With a ravioli or pizza cutter, cut around each filling- creating a rectangle shape and sealing the crust in.
10. Transfer each pizza bite onto a parchment lined cookie sheet. Cover with a kitchen towel and let them rise for 30 minutes.
11. When ready to cook, preheat the grill to 350°F with the lid closed for 10-15 minutes.
12. Brush the bites with remaining egg wash, sprinkle with salt and place directly on the sheet tray. Bake 10-15 minutes until the exterior is golden brown.
13. Remove from grill and transfer to a serving dish. Serve with extra pizza sauce for dipping and enjoy!

Zucchini Bread

Servings: 6
Cooking Time: 50 Minutes

Ingredients:
- 1 Cup Walnuts, Chopped
- 2 Large zucchini
- 1 Teaspoon salt
- 1 Teaspoon ground cinnamon
- 1/4 Teaspoon ground cloves
- 1/4 Teaspoon baking powder
- 3 Cup all-purpose flour
- 1 eggs
- 2 Cup sugar
- 1/2 Cup vegetable oil
- 1/2 Cup Yogurt
- 1 1/2 Teaspoon vanilla extract

Directions:

1. Grease and flour two 9- by 5-inch bread pans, preferably nonstick.
2. When ready to cook, set the temperature to 350°F and preheat, lid closed for 15 minutes.
3. Spread the walnuts on a pie plate and toast for 10 minutes, stirring once. Let cool, then coarsely chop. Set aside.
4. Trim the ends off the zucchini, then coarsely grate into a colander set over the sink on a box grater (or use the shredding disk on a food processor). You'll need 2 cups.
5. Sprinkle with the salt and let drain for 30 minutes. Press on the zucchini with paper towels to expel excess water.
6. Sift the flour, baking powder, cinnamon, and cloves in a mixing bowl or on a large sheet of parchment or wax paper.
7. Combine the eggs, sugar, oil, yogurt, and vanilla in a large mixing bowl and mix on medium speed. (You can mix the batter by hand, if desired.) Add half the dry ingredients and mix on low speed; add the remaining dry ingredients and mix until just combined.
8. Stir in the walnuts and zucchini by hand.
9. Divide the batter between the prepared baking pans.
10. Arrange the pans directly on the grill grate and bake for 50 minutes, or until a bamboo skewer inserted in the center of the breads comes out clean.
11. Transfer to a wire rack and let cool for 10 minutes, then remove the breads from the pans. For best results, let the breads cool completely before slicing.

Cheese Mac

Servings: 6 - 10
Cooking Time: 60 Minutes

Ingredients:

- 5 Tbsp All-Purpose Flour
- 4 Strips Bacon
- Black Pepper
- 2 Cups Breadcrumbs
- 4 Oz Brie
- 4 Oz Brie Cheese
- ½ Cup Butter, Melted
- 12 Oz Cheddar Cheese, Grated
- 3 Cloves Garlic, Minced
- 2 Tbsp Extra Virgin Olive Oil
- 1 Tsp Fresh Grated Nutmeg
- 1 Tsp Ground Cayenne
- 8 Oz, Grated Gruyere Cheese
- 1 Cup Heavy Cream
- 1, Minced Jalapeno Pepper
- 4 Oz Mozzarella Cheese, Grated
- 2 Tbsp Parsley, Minced Fresh
- 12 Oz Raclette
- To Taste Salt
- 5 Tbsp Unsalted Butter
- 4 Oz Whole Milk, Warm
- 1 Yellow Onion, Diced

Directions:

1. Supply your smoker with wood pellets and follow the start-up procedure. Preheat the grill, with the lid closed, to 350° F. Bring a large saucepan of water to a boil. Add the pasta and cook according to the package instructions for al dente. Drain.
2. Heat the oil in a large saucepan over medium-high heat.
3. Add the onion and cook for about 5 minutes, stirring often, until lightly colored, then add the garlic and the jalapeño and cook for 2 more minutes.
4. Reduce the heat to medium, add the butter, and stir until melted. Add the flour and cook, stirring often, for 5 minutes to form a light roux.
5. Add the cheeses, the milk, and cream, reduce the heat to medium-low, and cook, stirring often, until the cheese is melted, and a smooth sauce comes together, about 7 minutes.
6. Stir in the cayenne and truffle oil, then add the pasta and stir to fully coat it in the sauce. Season with salt and pepper. Transfer the mixture to a 12-inch cast-iron skillet and cover with aluminum foil.
7. Place on the grill and bake for 20 minutes. Remove the foil and cover the mac and cheese with the breadcrumbs.
8. Return to the grill and bake for another 15 to 20 minutes, until the cheese is bubbling and the breadcrumbs are golden brown. Serve family style right out of the skillet.

Smoky Apple Crepes

Servings: 6
Cooking Time: 60 Minutes

Ingredients:

- 1/2 Cup Apple Juice
- 2 Lbs Apples
- 2 Tbsp Brown Sugar
- 5 Tbsp Butter
- 3 Tbsp Butter, Melted
- Tt Caramel
- 3/4 Tsp Cinnamon, Ground
- Tt Cinnamon-Sugar
- 3/4 Tsp Cornstarch
- 2 Eggs
- 1 Cup Flour
- 2 Tsp Lemon Juice
- Tennessee Apple Butter Seasoning
- 1/2 Cup Water
- 3/4 Cup Milk

Directions:

1. Supply your smoker with wood pellets and follow the start-up procedure. Preheat the grill, with the lid closed, to 225° F. If using a gas or charcoal grill, set it up for low, indirect heat.
2. Peel, halve, and core apples.
3. Season apples with Tennessee Apple Butter then place directly on the grill grate, and smoke for 1 hour.
4. Meanwhile, prepare crêpe batter: combine eggs, milk, water, flour, and 3 tbsp of melted butter in a blender, and blend until smooth.
5. Refrigerate for 30 minutes.
6. Remove apples from grill, cool slightly, then slice thin.
7. Place a cast iron skillet on the grill and melt 3 tbsp butter with brown sugar, cinnamon, cornstarch, apple and lemon juices. Cook for 5 minutes until thick.
8. Add apples and cook for another 3 to 5 minutes, stirring to coat apples in sauce.
9. Remove from grill and set aside.
10. Preheat griddle to medium-low. If using a standard grill, preheat a cast iron skillet on medium-low heat.
11. Melt 1 teaspoon of butter on the griddle.
12. Then add ½ cup of batter, and spread with the bottom of a metal spatula, working quickly, as the batter cooks fast.
13. Cook one minute per side, until edges begin to brown. Remove from griddle, set aside, and repeat with remaining batter.
14. Spoon ¼ cup of apple filling into the center of each crêpe, then quarter-fold into a triangle.
15. Serve warm with additional apple filling, drizzle of warm caramel, and a dusting of cinnamon-sugar.

Green Bean Casserole Circa 1955

Servings: 6
Cooking Time: 30 Minutes

Ingredients:

- 1 1/2 Pound Green Beans, fresh
- 1 Can cream of mushroom soup
- 1/2 Cup milk
- 2 Teaspoon soy sauce
- 1/2 Teaspoon Worcestershire sauce
- 1/2 Teaspoon black pepper
- 1.334 Cup French's Original Crispy Fried Onions
- 1/4 Cup red bell pepper, diced

Directions:

1. In a mixing bowl, combine the beans (trimmed and cooked until tender, or may use 2 16 oz. cans), soup, milk, soy sauce, Worcestershire sauce, black pepper, 2/3 cup of the onion rings, and red pepper, if using. Transfer to a 1-1/2 quart casserole dish.
2. Supply your smoker with wood pellets and follow the start-up procedure. Preheat the grill, with the lid closed, to 375° F.
3. Cook the casserole until the filling is hot and bubbling, 25 to 30 minutes. Top with the remaining onions and cook for 5 to 10 minutes more, or until the onions are crisp and beginning to brown. Grill: 375 °F

Baked Parker House Rolls

Servings: 8
Cooking Time: 15 Minutes

Ingredients:

- 1/2 Ounce (2 packets) active dry yeast
- 6 Tablespoon plus 1 teaspoon cane sugar

- 1 Cup warm water (110°F to 115°F)
- 5 Cup all-purpose flour, plus more as needed
- 2 Teaspoon salt
- 1 Cup warm milk (110°-115°F)
- 1 Large eggs
- oil
- 4 Tablespoon melted butter, divided
- 1 Tablespoon Maldon Sea Salt Flakes
- 2 Tablespoon poppy seeds
- 2 Tablespoon white sesame seeds
- 1 Tablespoon garlic flakes

Directions:

1. Place the yeast, 1 teaspoon of cane sugar and warm water in a mixing bowl or the base of a stand mixer. Stir to combine. Allow the yeast to proof for 5 minutes- it should start to bubble a bit, showing that the yeast is alive.

2. Sprinkle the flour, salt and remaining 6 tablespoons of sugar over the yeast mixture. Using a dough hook or a wooden spoon, stir for 30 seconds. Pour in the warm milk and egg.

3. Knead again on the medium-low setting, or on a floured work surface by hand until the dough is very soft, adding up to one more cup of flour so the dough is soft and smooth and has lost its sticky quality.

4. Coat the bowl with a small film of oil and place the dough in the bowl, turning to coat dough evenly with the oil. Cover the bowl with a clean cloth, place in a warm spot in the kitchen and allow to proof about 45 minutes. The dough will almost double in size.

5. Punch down the dough and place on a floured work surface. Divide the dough in half, then divide each half into 12 equal pieces.

6. Using your hands, tuck in the seams of each piece of dough then place the dough on a lightly floured surface.

7. Place your fingers around the piece of dough, and roll it in a circular motion to create a smooth, even ball. Alternately, roll the dough between your two hands to create a round ball shape. Repeat with the remaining 23 pieces.

8. Butter a 9x13 inch baking pan with a tablespoon of the melted butter. Place the dough balls evenly in the pan, creating rows of 4 pieces of dough across and 6

down. Cover again with a clean towel and allow the dough to rise in a warm spot, about 30 minutes longer.

9. While the dough is proofing, supply your smoker with wood pellets and follow the start-up procedure. Preheat the grill, with the lid closed, to 325° F. Brush the remaining 3 tablespoons of butter on the bread and sprinkle with the flake salt, seeds and garlic flakes.

10. Place the pan on the grill, cover and bake about 15 to 20 minutes, or until rolls are lightly browned on top and cooked through. When done, you should be able to pull apart two pieces and see that the dough is cooked and the bottoms are lightly browned. Grill: 325 °F

Sweet And Spicy Baked Pork Beans

Servings: 20
Cooking Time: 120 Minutes

Ingredients:
- 1 - 21 Oz Apple Pie Filling, Can
- 1 Gallon Baked Beans
- 1 Tbs Chilli, Powder
- 1 Green Bell Pepper, Diced
- 1 10 Oz Drained Jalapeno, Can Diced
- 1 Cup Maple Syrup
- 1 Onion, Diced
- 1 Lb Pork, Pulled

Directions:

1. Supply your smoker with wood pellets and follow the start-up procedure. Preheat the grill, with the lid closed, to 350° F.

2. Place all ingredients in mixing bowl and mix well.

3. Pour bean mixture into foil pans.

4. Bake in grill till bubbling throughout – about 2 hours.

5. Rest at least 15 minutes before serving.

Smoky Pimento Cheese Cornbread

Servings: 4
Cooking Time: 30 Minutes

Ingredients:
- 2 Tsp Baking Powder
- 2 Cups Buttermilk, Low Fat
- 1/2 Cup Cornmeal, Yellow
- 2 Egg

- 1 1/2 Cups Flour, All-Purpose
- 16 Oz Pimento Cheese Spread
- 2 Tbsp Bacon Cheddar Seasoning
- 1/4 Cup Sugar

Directions:

1. Supply your smoker with wood pellets and follow the start-up procedure. Preheat the grill, with the lid closed, to 350° F. Place a cast iron skillet in the grill to preheat.

2. In a bowl, mix together the eggs, buttermilk, Bacon Cheddar Seasoning, and pimento cheese spread. Add in the sugar, baking powder, cornmeal and flour. Mix until well combined.

3. With cooking gloves, carefully remove the cast iron skillet from the grill, grease it, and add the cornbread batter.

4. Grill for 25-30 minutes, or until the cornbread is golden and pulling away from the edges of the skillet.

Smoked Lemon Cheesecake

Servings: 16
Cooking Time: 130 Minutes

Ingredients:

- For the crust
- Vegetable oil, for oiling the pan
- 12 ounces gingersnaps (about 36) or chocolate icebox cookies (about 36)
- 3 tablespoons light brown sugar
- 8 tablespoons (1 stick) unsalted butter, melted
- For the filling
- 4 packages (8 ounces each) cream cheese, at room temperature
- 1 cup firmly packed light brown sugar
- 2 teaspoons pure vanilla extract
- 2 teaspoons finely grated lemon zest
- 1 tablespoon fresh lemon juice
- 2 tablespoons (1/4 stick) unsalted butter, melted
- 5 large eggs
- Burnt Sugar Sauce (recipes follows, optional)

Directions:

1. Supply your smoker with wood pellets and follow the start-up procedure. Preheat the grill, with the lid closed, to 400° F. Lightly oil the springform pan with vegetable oil and wrap a sheet of aluminum foil around the outside.

2. Make the crust: Break the cookies into pieces and grind with the brown sugar to a fine powder in a food processor. You'll want about 1 3/4 cups of crumbs. Add the melted butter and run the processor in short bursts to obtain a crumbly dough. Press the mixture evenly across the bottom and halfway up the sides of the springform pan. Indirect-grill or bake the crust until lightly browned, 5 to 8 minutes. Transfer the pan to a wire rack and let cool.

3. Make the filling: Wipe out the food processor bowl. Add the cream cheese, brown sugar, vanilla, lemon zest, lemon juice, and butter, and process until smooth. Work in the eggs one by one, processing until smooth after each addition. (You can also use a stand mixer, beating the cream cheese mixture until smooth and beating in the eggs one at a time.) Pour the filling into the crust. Gently tap the pan on the countertop a few times to knock out any air bubbles.

4. Supply your smoker with wood pellets and follow the start-up procedure. Preheat the grill, with the lid closed, to 225 °F-250 °F.

5. Place the cheesecake in the smoker. Smoke until the top is bronzed with smoke and the filling is set, 1 1/2 to 2 hours. To test for doneness, gently poke the side of the pan—the filling will jiggle, not ripple. Alternatively, insert a slender metal skewer in the center of the cake; it should come out clean.

6. Transfer the cheesecake in its pan to a wire rack to cool to room temperature. Refrigerate until serving; the cheesecake can be made up to 8 hours ahead. Run a slender knife around the inside of the springform pan. Unclasp and remove the ring. (You'll serve the cheesecake off the bottom of the pan.) Let the cheesecake warm slightly at room temperature before serving.

7. If serving with the sauce, pour some of it over the cheesecake and the rest into a pitcher. Cut into wedges and pass the remaining sauce.

Cake With Smoked Berry Sauce

Servings: 12
Cooking Time: 90 Minutes

Ingredients:

- 12 Oz Blackberries
- 18 Oz Blueberries, Fresh
- 1/4 Cup Brown Sugar
- 2 Tsp Cinnamon, Ground
- 4 Eggs
- 2 Tbsp Flour
- 1 3/4 Cup Granulated Sugar
- 1 Lemon, Juice & Zest
- 1/2 Cup Unsalted Butter
- 3.4 Ounce Box Vanilla Instant Pudding Mix
- 3/4 Cup Vegetable Oil
- 3/4 Cup Water
- 1 Cup White Wine
- 1 Box Yellow Cake Mix

Directions:

1. Fire up your Grill and set to Smoke mode. If using a gas or charcoal grill, set it up for low, indirect heat. Supply your smoker with wood pellets and follow the start-up procedure. Preheat the grill, with the lid closed, to 450° F.

2. Place blueberries and blackberries on a sheet tray, then transfer to upper shelf of smoking cabinet. Make sure that the sear slide and side dampers are open, then preheat the grill, with the lid closed, to 375° F, to ensure the cabinet maintains temperature between 225° F and 250° F. Smoke for 30 to 45 minutes.

3. Place cast iron skillet on grill grate. Add sugar, lemon juice and zest, and wine to skillet. Stir with a wooden spoon until sugar dissolves, then add berries from smoking cabinet.

4. Simmer berries for 15 minutes, then remove sauce from grill to cool.

5. While berries are smoking, prepare cake pans and batter. Grease and flour 2 - 9-inch round cake pans. Set aside.

6. In a large mixing bowl, combine cake mix, brown sugar, granulated sugar, pudding mix, cinnamon, eggs, water, oil, and white wine. Using a hand mixer, mix on low speed for 1 minute, then slowly increase mixing speed to high, and beat an additional 2 to 3 minutes, or until batter is smooth.

7. Evenly distribute batter among cake pans, then place pans on grill shelf and bake at 350° F, for 25 to 30 minutes, or until a toothpick inserted comes out clean. Remove from grill and set aside to cool slightly.

8. While cake is cooling, prepare glaze. Melt butter with sugar in a sauce pot on the grill. Stir for 3 minutes, then add wine. Remove from grill and set aside.

9. Turn out cake onto a sheet tray lined with parchment. Use a toothpick to poke holes in the cake, then slowly pour hot glaze over cake.

10. Spread half of smoked berry sauce on top of one layer, then place second cake layer on top. Pour additional sauce on top of cake and dust with powdered sugar, if desired. Serve warm, or room temperature.

Smoked Blackberry Pie

Servings: 4-6
Cooking Time: 25 Minutes

Ingredients:

- Nonstick cooking spray or butter, for greasing
- 1 box (2 sheets) refrigerated piecrusts
- 8 tablespoons (1 stick) unsalted butter, melted, plus 8 tablespoons (1 stick) cut into pieces
- ½ cup all-purpose flour
- 2 cups sugar, divided
- 2 pints blackberries
- ½ cup milk
- Vanilla ice cream, for serving

Directions:

1. Supply your smoker with wood pellets and follow the start-up procedure. Preheat, with the lid closed, to 375°F.

2. Coat a cast iron skillet with cooking spray.

3. Unroll 1 refrigerated piecrust and place in the bottom and up the side of the skillet. Using a fork, poke holes in the crust in several places.

4. Set the skillet on the grill grate, close the lid, and smoke for 5 minutes, or until lightly browned. Remove from the grill and set aside.

5. In a large bowl, combine the stick of melted butter with the flour and 1½ cups of sugar.

6. Add the blackberries to the flour-sugar mixture and toss until well coated.

7. Spread the berry mixture evenly in the skillet and sprinkle the milk on top. Scatter half of the cut pieces of butter randomly over the mixture.

8. Unroll the remaining piecrust and place it over the top of skillet or slice the dough into even strips and weave it into a lattice. Scatter the remaining pieces of butter along the top of the crust.

9. Sprinkle the remaining ½ cup of sugar on top of the crust and return the skillet to the smoker.

10. Close the lid and smoke for 15 to 20 minutes, or until bubbly and brown on top. It may be necessary to use some aluminum foil around the edges near the end of the cooking time to prevent the crust from burning.

11. Serve the pie hot with vanilla ice cream.

Italian Herb & Parmesan Scones

Servings: 8
Cooking Time: 20 Minutes

Ingredients:
- 2 1/2 Cup all-purpose flour
- 2 Teaspoon baking powder
- 1 Teaspoon baking soda
- 1/2 Teaspoon garlic salt
- 1 Tablespoon Italian Seasoning
- 1 Cup Parmesan cheese, grated
- 2 Large eggs
- 1 1/2 Cup buttermilk
- 1/4 Cup olive oil

Directions:
1. In a large mixing bowl, combine flour, baking powder, baking powder, soda, garlic salt, Italian seasoning, and 1/2 cup of the cheese. Make a well in the center.

2. In a smaller bowl, whisk together eggs, buttermilk, and olive oil.

3. Pour into the well in the dry ingredients, and stir batter just until it's combined. It will appear lumpy.

4. Oil 12 muffin cups, spray with cooking spray, or line with disposable paper liners.

5. Divide the batter evenly between the cups. Sprinkle the tops of the muffins with the remaining Parmesan cheese.

6. Supply your smoker with wood pellets and follow the start-up procedure. Preheat the grill, with the lid closed, to 400° F.

7. Arrange the muffin tin directly on the grill grate and bake the muffins for 20 to 25 minutes, or until a toothpick inserted in the center of the muffin comes out clean.

8. Cool for several minutes before removing from the muffin tin. Serve warm with butter or olive oil. Enjoy!

Mint Butter Chocolate Chip Cookies

Servings: 24
Cooking Time: 12 Minutes

Ingredients:
- 1/2 Cup Butter, Melted
- 1 Package Chocolate Chip Cookie Mix
- 8-10 Drop Food Coloring
- 1/2 Tsp Mint, Extract

Directions:
1. Supply your smoker with wood pellets and follow the start-up procedure. Preheat the grill, with the lid closed, to 350° F.

2. Follow the directions on the back of the Chocolate Chip Cookie mix and also add the mint extract and green food coloring. Mix until combined.

3. On a baking sheet lined with parchment paper, drop balls of dough about 2 tbsp in size onto the pan.

4. Place in your Grill and bake for 10-12 minutes. Let cool for a couple minutes before removing from the pan. Enjoy!

Baked Irish Creme Cake

Servings: 4
Cooking Time: 60 Minutes

Ingredients:
- 1 Cup Pecans, pieces
- 1 Yellow Cake Mix, Boxed
- 1 Vanilla Pudding Mix, Instant Package (3.4oz)
- 4 Large eggs
- 1/2 Cup water

- 1/2 Cup vegetable oil
- 1 Cup Irish Cream Liquor
- 1/2 Cup butter
- 1 Cup sugar

Directions:

1.   Grease and flour a 10" (25 cm) Bundt pan. Sprinkle pecans along the bottom.

2.   In a large bowl, with a mixer, combine yellow cake mix, pudding mix, eggs, water, oil, and Irish Cream liquor. Pour batter over nuts in the pan.

3.   Supply your smoker with wood pellets and follow the start-up procedure. Preheat the grill, with the lid closed, to 325° F.

4.   Place Bundt pan on the Traeger and bake for 1 hour, or until a toothpick comes out clean. Remove from heat, cool for 10 minutes. Grill: 325 °F

5.   While the cake is cooling, combine the butter, water and sugar and bring to a boil. Boil for 5 minutes, stirring constantly. Remove from heat and add Irish cream liquor.

6.   Use a bamboo skewer to poke holes in the cooled cake. Spoon glaze over the cake. Allow cake to absorb the glaze. Enjoy!

Caramel Bourbon Bacon Brownies

Servings: 16
Cooking Time: 60 Minutes

Ingredients:

- 2 Cup All-Purpose Flour
- 1/4 Cup Bourbon
- 1 Cup Brown Sugar
- 1 Cup Canola Oil
- Caramel Sauce
- 1.5 Cup Cocoa Powder
- 1 Tablespoon Hickory Honey Sea Salt
- 2 Tablespoon Instant Coffee
- 6 Large Eggs
- 1/2 Teaspoon Smoked Infused Hickory Honey Sea Salt
- 1 Cup Powdered Sugar
- 6 Slices Bacon, Raw
- 4 Tablespoons Water
- 3 Cups White Sugar

Directions:

1.   Supply your smoker with wood pellets and follow the start-up procedure. Preheat the grill, with the lid closed, to 400° F.

2.   In a large mixing bowl, whisk together the cocoa, powdered sugar, white sugar, instant coffee and flour.

3.   To the flour mixture, add the eggs, oil and water until just combined.

4.   Spray the 9 x 13 pan well with cooking spray.

5.   Pour half the batter in the pan, drizzle with caramel.

6.   Pour other half of batter on top and drizzle with caramel again and add candied bacon to the top.

7.   Bake the brownies in the smoker for 1 hour, or until a toothpick inserted in the center of the pan comes out clean.

8.   Remove from the smoker and allow to cool before slicing.

Cherry Ice Cream Cobbler

Servings: 8
Cooking Time: 45 Minutes

Ingredients:

- 1 Tsp Baking Powder
- 3 Tbsp Butter, Melted
- 1 Cup Flour
- Ice Cream, Prepared
- 1/4 Tsp Salt
- 3/4 Cup Sugar
- 1/2 Cup Milk

Directions:

1.   Supply your smoker with wood pellets and follow the start-up procedure. Preheat the grill, with the lid closed, to 350° F.

2.   In a bowl, combine flour, sugar, baking powder, salt and mix to incorporate. Stir in butter and milk and mix until combined. In a cast iron pan, dump in cherry pie filling and pile on the prepared topping to cover.

3.   Place in your Grill and bake for about 45 minutes, or until the topping is golden brown.

4.   Let cool for a couple minutes and serve with ice cream.

Double Vanilla Chocolate Cake

Servings: 12
Cooking Time: 40 Minutes

Ingredients:

- 1 1/2 Tsp Baking Soda
- 1/2 Cup Butter, Melted
- 1 Cup Buttermilk, Low Fat
- 1 Jar Chocolate Icing, Prepared
- 3/4 Cup Cocoa, Powder
- 1 Cup Coffee, Hot
- 2 Large Egg
- 1 3/4 Cups Flour, All-Purpose
- 3/4 Tsp Salt
- 2 Cups Sugar
- 1 Tbsp Vanilla

Directions:

1. Supply your smoker with wood pellets and follow the start-up procedure. Preheat the grill, with the lid closed, to 350° F.
2. Stir together flour, sugar, cocoa, baking soda and salt in a large bowl. Combine eggs, buttermilk, butter and coffee and mix until smooth. Add in hot coffee and stir until combined and the dough is runny.
3. Pour the batter into two prepared baking pans and bake on the top rack of your for 40 minutes, turning the pans 180 degrees halfway through.
4. Allow to cool and then frost with chocolate icing.

Tarte Tatin

Servings: 6
Cooking Time: 55 Minutes

Ingredients:

- 2 Cup all-purpose flour
- 1 Teaspoon salt
- 1 Cup butter
- 5 Tablespoon cold water
- 1/4 Cup unsalted butter
- 3/4 Cup granulated sugar
- 10 Granny Smith Apples, Cut Into Wedges

Directions:

1. Supply your smoker with wood pellets and follow the start-up procedure. Preheat the grill, with the lid closed, to 350° F.
2. For the crust: Place flour and salt in a food processer and pulse to mix. Add butter a little at a time while pulsing. Once it starts to looks like cornmeal, add the water until dough start to come together. Form a round with the dough, wrap in plastic and let it cool in the refrigerator.
3. While dough cools, place a pie dish or a 10-inch round cake pan on the grill; add butter and sugar to pie dish. Let it caramelize.
4. When the sugar caramelizes and has come to a dark amber color, take off grill. Arrange apple wedges in a fan formation covering the caramel.
5. Roll the pie crust into a circle big enough to cover the pan. Prick the pie dough with a fork and cover the pan with the pie dough. Trim the crust leaving room for shrinkage.
6. Place on the grill and bake for 55 minutes until apples are soft. Let sit for 3 minutes. While pan is still hot, place a plate over pie and flip over. Grill: 350 °F
7. Serve warm, topped with ice cream or whipped cream. Enjoy!

Cast Iron Pineapple Upside Down Cake

Servings: 6
Cooking Time: 40 Minutes

Ingredients:

- 1/4 Cup butter, melted
- 1 Cup brown sugar
- 20 Ounce Pineapple, sliced
- 6 Ounce maraschino cherries
- 1 Whole Yellow Cake Mix, Boxed
- vegetable oil
- eggs

Directions:

1. Supply your smoker with wood pellets and follow the start-up procedure. Preheat the grill, with the lid closed, to 350° F.
2. Pour melted butter into a 12-inch cast iron pan. Sprinkle brown sugar on top of the butter. Arrange

pineapple slices on brown sugar, squeezing in as many slices as possible. Place a cherry in center of each pineapple slice; press gently into brown sugar.

3. Make cake batter as directed on box, substituting pineapple juice mixture for as much of the water as possible, and adding in required oil and eggs. Pour batter into cast iron dish, over pineapple and cherries.

4. Place the cast iron pan on the grill grate and cook for 20 minutes. Rotate the pan a half turn to ensure it cooks evenly. Cook for an additional 20 minutes, or until toothpick inserted in center comes out clean.

5. Immediately run knife around side of pan to loosen cake. Place heatproof serving plate upside down onto pan; turn plate and pan over.

6. Leave pan over cake 5 minutes so brown sugar topping can drizzle over cake. Cool 30 minutes. Enjoy!

S'mores Dip Skillet

Servings: 4-6

Cooking Time: 8 Minutes

Ingredients:

- 2 tablespoons salted butter, melted
- ¼ cup milk
- 12 ounces semisweet chocolate chips
- 16 ounces Jet-Puffed marshmallows
- Graham crackers and apple wedges, for serving

Directions:

1. Supply your smoker with wood pellets and follow the start-up procedure. Preheat, with the lid closed, to 450°F.

2. Place a cast iron skillet on the preheated grill grate and pour in the melted butter and milk, stirring for about 1 minute.

3. Once the mixture starts to heat, top with the chocolate chips in an even layer and arrange the marshmallows standing up to cover all of the chocolate.

4. Close the lid and smoke for 5 to 7 minutes, or until the marshmallows are lightly toasted.

5. Remove from the heat and serve immediately with graham crackers and apple wedges for dipping.

Savory Cheesecake With Bourbon Pecan Topping

Servings: 6

Cooking Time: 75 Minutes

Ingredients:

- Crust
- 12 ounce Oreos
- 6 ounce melted butter
- Filling
- 24 ounces cream cheese - room temperature
- 1 cup granulated sugar
- 3 tbs cornstarch
- 2 large eggs
- 2/3 cup heavy cream
- 1 tbs vanilla
- 1 1/2 tbs bourbon
- Topping
- 3 large eggs beaten
- 1/3 cup granulated sugar
- 1/3 cup brown sugar
- 8 tbsp corn syrup dark corn syrup recommended
- 2 tbsp bourbon
- 1/2 tbsp vanilla
- 1/8 tbsp salt
- 3/4 cup rough chopped pecans (smoked pecans recommended)

Directions:

1. Supply your smoker with wood pellets and follow the start-up procedure. Preheat the grill, with the lid closed, to 350 °F.

2. Wrap foil on the bottom and up the sides of a 9" spring-form pan (outside of pan).

3. Butter the bottom & insides of the pan.

4. Crust

5. Throw ingredients in a food processor until they are finely ground.

6. Spread in 9" cheesecake pan on bottom & about ½ way upsides.

7. Filling

8. Place 8 oz of cream cheese in mixer bowl with 1/3 of sugar & cornstarch.Mix until smooth andcreamy.

9.   Add another 8 oz cream cheese andbeat until smooth, then add remaining cream cheese,beating until smooth.

10. Then mix in the rest of the sugar, bourbon & vanilla.

11. Add eggs one at a time beating well after each one.

12. Add the heavy cream and mix just until smooth. Reminder: Do not over mix.

13. Pour batter into the prepared crust.

14. Topping

15. Mix all together except pecans.

16. Sprinkle pecans on top of cheesecake batter.

17. Pour topping over cheesecake batter.

18. Place in a pan big enough to hold a spring-form pan. Pour boiling water in the roasting pan to come up about ½ way up the spring-form pan.

19. Bake at 350 °F for 75 minutes until the top just barely jiggles. Carefully take the pan out of water-bath and put on cooling rack.

20. Let cool for 2 hours in pan. After 2 hours put in fridge until totally chilled then serve.

Spiced Lemon Cherry Pie

Servings: 6-8

Cooking Time: 60 Minutes

Ingredients:

- 1/2 Teaspoon Cinnamon, Ground
- 1/2 Teaspoon Cloves, Ground
- 1/2 Cup Cornstarch
- 1 Pound Frozen Sweet Dark Cherries, Thawed
- 1 Teaspoon Water (Beaten With Egg) 1 Egg
- 1 Lemon, Juice
- 1 Lemon, Zest
- 2 Prepared Store Bought Or Homemade Pie Crust
- 1 Teaspoon Hickory Honey Sea Salt Seasoning
- 1 Cup Sugar, Granulated
- 1 Teaspoon Vanilla Extract

Directions:

1.   In a large bowl, mix together the thawed cherries and their juices, sugar, cornstarch, lemon zest, lemon juice, cinnamon, clove, vanilla extract and Hickory Honey Sea Salt. Allow to sit for 30 minutes.

2.   Flour a work surface and roll out one of the prepared pie crusts so that it fits a 9 inch pie tin. Fill with the cherry pie filling and refrigerate. When the pie is chilled, roll out the second pie crust, brush the edge of the first pie crust with the egg mixture, top with the second pie crust, crimp the edge with a fork, and chill. Alternatively, cut the second pie crust into strips and form a lattice pattern, attaching the strips with the egg mixture. Chill the pie for 15-30 minutes, or until the dough is very cold and firm. Brush the top of the pie with the remaining egg mixture.

3.   Supply your smoker with wood pellets and follow the start-up procedure. Preheat the grill, with the lid closed, to 350° F and grill for 45 minutes to 1 hour, or until the pie crust is golden and firm and the filling is bubbly. Remove from the grill and allow to cool at room temperature for at least 4 hours to set the filling, then serve and enjoy!

Baked Green Chile Mac & Cheese By Doug Scheiding

Servings: 8

Cooking Time: 120 Minutes

Ingredients:

- 24 Ounce shredded cheddar cheese, divided
- 8 Ounce mozzarella cheese, shredded
- 6 Tablespoon unsalted butter
- 16 Ounce large dry elbow macaroni noodles
- 2 1/2 Cup half-and-half
- 2 Cup heavy whipping cream
- 8 Ounce cream cheese
- 16 Ounce 505 Southwestern Hatch Valley Flame Roasted Green Chile
- 2 Tablespoon Prime Rib Rub

Directions:

1.   Supply your smoker with wood pellets and follow the start-up procedure. Preheat the grill, with the lid closed, to 165° F.

2.   Place 16 ounces of the shredded cheddar and the 8 ounces of shredded mozzarella cheese into a shallow pan or cookie sheet and place the pan directly on the grill grate. Smoke for 30 to 40 minutes. Remove from grill and set aside. Grill: 165 °F

3.   Increase the grill temperature to 300°F and place a large disposable aluminum half pan in the Traeger with

the butter. Remove the pan from the grill after the butter has fully melted. Grill: 300 °F

4. Add the noodles to the pan, along with half-and-half, heavy whipping cream, 16 ounces of the cold smoked cheddar, all of the smoked mozzarella cheese and cream cheese broken into small pieces. Add the green chiles to taste (12 ounces for mild and 16 ounces for spicy) and stir to combine.

5. Place the pan in the grill and bake for 2 hours, stirring every 20 minutes. If macaroni and cheese looks like it is getting dry, add a little more half-and-half and stir to combine. Grill: 300 °F

6. During the last 20 minutes of cooking, sprinkle the remaining (unsmoked) cheddar cheese on top and add a light dusting of Traeger Prime Rib Rub. Serve hot. Enjoy!

Blueberry Bread Pudding

Servings: 4
Cooking Time: 60 Minutes

Ingredients:

- 5 eggs
- 3 Cup sugar
- 2 1/2 Cup milk
- 1 1/2 Teaspoon vanilla
- 1 Teaspoon cinnamon
- 1 Pinch salt
- 5 Cup Bread
- 3 Cup blueberries

Directions:

1. Beat the eggs in a large mixing bowl. Whisk in the sugar, milk, vanilla, cinnamon, and salt.

2. In another large bowl, combine the bread and 2 cups (200 g) of the blueberries.

3. Pour the egg mixture over the bread-blueberry mixture and let sit for 30 minutes. Meanwhile, place muffin liners in a muffin tin.

4. Supply your smoker with wood pellets and follow the start-up procedure. Preheat the grill, with the lid open.

5. Spoon the bread-blueberry mixture into the prepared cups; evenly top each with the remaining cup

of blueberries, pressing them gently into the pudding with the back of a spoon.

6. Dust the top with sugar.

7. Arrange the pan directly on the grill grate and smoke for 30 minutes. Grill:180°F

8. Increase the temperature to 350F (180 C), and bake until the pudding is set and golden brown on top, about 25 minutes. Grill:350°F

9. Let cool slightly, then sift powdered sugar on top. Serve warm with sweetened whipped cream or vanilla ice cream, if desired.

Anzac Coconut Biscuits

Servings: 4
Cooking Time: 30 Minutes

Ingredients:

- This recipe makes a dozen biscuits.
- 1 cup rolled oats
- 3/4 cup raw sugar
- 3/4 cup desiccated coconut
- 1 cup plain flour, sifted
- 125 g butter, melted
- 2 tablespoons Golden Syrup
- 1/2 tsp bicarb soda
- 3 tablespoons boiling water

Directions:

1. Combine and mix thoroughly sifted flour, oats, sugar and coconut in a large bowl.

2. Melt the butter and Golden Syrup over low heat.

3. Add boiling water to the bicarb soda, once dissolved add into the butter/syrup mix, it will bubble/fizz up a bit.

4. Add the liquid into the dry ingredients and mix throughly.

5. Rolls the mix into golf ball size balls and layout on grease proof paper on baking tray and flatten the tops just slightly.

6. Space the balls with about 3 fingers between each ball as they will flatten to about triple the diameter as they cook.

7. Supply your smoker with wood pellets and follow the start-up procedure. Preheat the grill, with the lid closed, to 350° F. Cook for 25-30 minutes until golden brown.

8. Rest on cooling rack until at room temperature then store in air-tight container.

Smokin' Lemon Bars

Servings: 8-12

Cooking Time: 60 Minutes

Ingredients:

- 3/4 Cup lemon juice
- 1 1/2 Cup sugar
- 2 eggs
- 3 Egg Yolk
- 1 1/2 Teaspoon cornstarch
- Pinch sea salt
- 4 Tablespoon unsalted butter
- 1/4 Cup olive oil
- 1/2 Tablespoon lemon zest
- 1 1/4 Cup flour
- 1/4 Cup granulated sugar
- 3 Tablespoon Confectioner's Sugar
- 1 Teaspoon lemon zest
- 1/4 Teaspoon Sea Salt, Fine
- 10 Tablespoon Unsalted Butter, Cut Into Cubes

Directions:

1. When ready to cook, set grill temperature to 180°F and preheat, lid closed for 15 minutes.

2. In a small mixing bowl, whisk together lemon juice, sugar, eggs and yolks, cornstarch and fine sea salt. Pour into a sheet tray or cake pan and place on grill. Smoke for 30 minutes whisking mixture halfway through smoking. Remove from grill and set aside.

3. Pour mixture into a small saucepan. Place on stove top set to medium heat until boiling. Once boiling, boil for 60 seconds. Remove from heat and strain through a mesh strainer into a bowl. Whisk in cold butter, olive oil, and lemon zest.

4. To make a crust, pulse together the flour, granulated sugar, confectioners' sugar, lemon zest and salt in a food processor. Add butter and pulse until just mixed into a crumbly dough. Press dough into a prepared 9" by 9" baking dish lined with parchment paper that is long enough to hang over 2 of the sides.

5. When ready to cook, set the smoker to 350°F and preheat, lid closed for 15 minutes.

6. Bake until crust is very lightly golden brown, about 30 to 35 minutes.

7. Remove from grill and pour the lemon filling over the crust. Return to grill and continue to bake until filling is just set about 15 to 20 minutes.

8. Allow to cool at room temperature, then refrigerate until chilled before slicing into bars. Sprinkle with confectioners' sugar and flaky sea salt right before serving. Enjoy!

Smoked Sweet Beer Bread

Servings: 6

Cooking Time: 60 Minutes

Ingredients:

- 3 cups all-purpose flour, sifted
- 2 tbsp. sugar
- 1 tbsp. baking powder
- 1 tsp. salt
- 1 (12 oz) can or bottle beer (not too dark or bitter)
- 2 tbsp. honey or agave, warmed
- 6 tbsp. butter, melted

Directions:

1. Supply your smoker with wood pellets and follow the start-up procedure. Preheat the grill, with the lid closed, to 350° F.

2. Lightly grease a 9 ×5 inch loaf pan.

3. In a large mixing bowl, put in the flour, sugar, baking powder, and salt. Whisk to combine and aerate, using a wire whisk. Add the beer and honey and stir with a wooden spoon until the batter is properly mixed (Do not over-mix).

4. Pour half of the melted butter into the prepared loaf pan and pour in the batter. Pour the remaining butter over the top of the loaf.

5. Place the loaf pan on the grill grate and bake for 50 to 60 minutes or until the bread is golden brown.

6. Allow the loaf to cool slightly in the pan before removing it from the pan. Leftovers make great toast.

Chocolate Lava Cake With Smoked Whipped Cream

Servings: 4
Cooking Time: 45 Minutes

Ingredients:

- 1 Pint heavy whipping cream
- 9 Tablespoon Butter
- 220 G Semisweet Chocolate
- 1 1/4 Cup powdered sugar
- 2 Large eggs
- 2 egg yolk
- 6 Tablespoon flour
- 1 Tablespoon Bourbon Vanilla
- Powdered Sugar
- cocoa powder

Directions:

1. Supply your smoker with wood pellets and follow the start-up procedure. Preheat the grill, with the lid closed, to 180° F.
2. For the Smoked Whipped Cream: Add cream to a shallow, aluminum baking pan. Place the pan on the grill and smoke for 30 minutes.
3. Pour the smoked cream into a large mixing bowl and refrigerate for later use. Grill: 180 °F
4. Increase the grill temperature to 375°F and preheat. Grill: 375 °F
5. Brush 4 small soufflé cups with 1 tablespoon melted butter.
6. Melt the chocolate and remaining butter in a heatproof bowl over simmering water, stir until smooth.
7. Stir in powdered sugar. Add eggs and egg yolks, stirring continuously. Whisk in flour until blended completely.
8. Pour batter into the prepared soufflé cups. Place them on the Traeger and bake for 13-14 minutes, or until the sides are set. Grill: 375 °F
9. For the Whipped Cream: Remove the chilled smoked cream from the refrigerator, add the bourbon vanilla and whip until airy.
10. Add confectioners sugar and continue whipping until whipped cream forms stiff peaks.
11. Dust lava cakes with confectioners sugar and cocoa, top with a dollop of smoke-infused whipped cream. Enjoy!

Ultimate Baked Garlic Bread

Servings: 4
Cooking Time: 20 Minutes

Ingredients:

- 1 baguette
- 1/2 Cup softened butter
- 1/2 Cup mayonnaise
- 4 Tablespoon chopped Italian parsley
- 6 Clove garlic, minced
- salt
- chile flakes
- 1 Cup mozzarella cheese
- 1/2 Cup Parmesan cheese

Directions:

1. Supply your smoker with wood pellets and follow the start-up procedure. Preheat the grill, with the lid closed, to 375° F.
2. Lay baguette on a cutting board and cut it in half lengthwise.
3. In a bowl, add butter, mayonnaise, parsley, garlic, salt and chile flakes. Mix well.
4. Spread butter mixture on baguette halves and top with mozzarella and Parmesan cheese.
5. Place baguette on the grill (if you like the bread crisp, do not use foil and if you like it soft, wrap with foil). Grill for approximately 15 to 25 minutes. Serve warm. Enjoy! Grill: 375 °F

Dark Chocolate Brownies With Bacon-salted Caramel

Servings: 8
Cooking Time: 40 Minutes

Ingredients:

- 8 Strips bacon
- 1/2 Cup kosher salt
- 1 Whole Brownie Mix
- 1 Jar caramel sauce

Directions:

1. For the bacon salt: Cook a few strips of bacon (6 to 8) until very crisp: 350 degrees for about 25 minutes should do it. Let cool, then pulse in a food processor until finely chopped. Mix with 1/2 cup kosher salt. Store in the refrigerator until ready to use.

2. Supply your smoker with wood pellets and follow the start-up procedure. Preheat the grill, with the lid closed, to 350° F.

3. Mix the brownies according to package directions and pour into a greased pan. Drizzle approximately 2 tablespoons of the caramel sauce over the brownie batter. Sprinkle with approximately 1 teaspoon of the bacon salt. Place directly on the grill grate of your preheated Traeger.

4. Bake the brownies for 20-25 minutes, until the batter has started to set up. Remove from the grill and drizzle with 2 more tablespoons of caramel sauce and sprinkle with more bacon salt. Return to the grill for 20-25 more minutes, or until a toothpick inserted in the middle of the brownies comes out clean.

5. If you like extra caramel, drizzle another layer of caramel on the hot brownies and sprinkle with a final bit of bacon salt. Allow the brownies to cool completely before cutting them into squares. Clean your knife in between each slice to prevent the brownies from sticking to the knife. Enjoy!

Blueberry Sour Cream Muffins

Servings: 8
Cooking Time: 25 Minutes

Ingredients:
- 2 Cup flour
- 1/2 Teaspoon salt
- 1/2 Teaspoon baking soda
- 1/2 Cup butter
- 3/4 Cup sugar, plus more for muffin tops
- 2 Large eggs
- 3/4 Cup sour cream
- 1 1/2 Teaspoon vanilla extract
- 1 1/2 Cup blueberries, fresh or thawed

Directions:
1. In a small mixing bowl, whisk together the flour, salt and baking soda.

2. In another bowl, using a wooden spoon or a mixer, beat the butter and sugar until light-colored and fluffy. Beat in the eggs, one at a time. Stir in sour cream and vanilla.

3. Add the flour mixture gradually and mix just until incorporated. Using a rubber spatula, gently fold in the blueberries.

4. Line a 12-cup muffin tin with the cupcake liners. Using an ice cream scoop or spoon, fill each muffin cup two-thirds full with the batter. Sprinkle sugar evenly over the top of each muffin.

5. Supply your smoker with wood pellets and follow the start-up procedure. Preheat the grill, with the lid closed, to 375° F.

6. Bake the muffins 25 to 30 minutes, or until a toothpick inserted comes out clean. Served warm and with butter. Grill: 375 °F

Baked Bourbon Maple Pumpkin Pie

Servings: 6-8
Cooking Time: 60 Minutes

Ingredients:
- 1/4 Cup Cocoa Powder, Unsweetened
- 1 Tablespoon Cocoa Powder, Unsweetened
- 3 1/2 Tablespoon sugar
- 1 Teaspoon salt
- 1 1/4 Cup all-purpose flour
- 1 Tablespoon all-purpose flour
- 6 Tablespoon butter
- 2 Tablespoon vegetable oil
- 1 Large Egg Yolk
- 1/2 Teaspoon apple cider vinegar
- 1/4 Cup ice water
- 1 Large egg, beaten
- 15 Ounce Pumpkin, canned
- 1/4 Cup sour cream
- 2 Tablespoon bourbon
- 1 Teaspoon ground cinnamon
- 1/2 Teaspoon salt
- 1/4 Teaspoon ground ginger
- 1/4 Teaspoon ground nutmeg
- 1/8 Teaspoon Allspice, ground
- 1/8 Teaspoon Mace, ground

* 3 Large eggs
* 3/4 Cup maple syrup
* 2 Tablespoon sugar
* 1/2 Vanilla Bean, halved
* 1 Cup heavy cream

Directions:

1. For the Chocolate Pie Dough: Pulse cocoa powder, granulated sugar, salt, and 1-1/4 cups plus 1 Tbsp flour in a food processor to combine. Add butter and shortening and pulse until mixture resembles coarse meal with a few pea-sized pieces of butter remaining. Transfer to a large bowl.

2. Whisk together the egg yolk, vinegar, and 1/4 cup ice water in a small bowl. Drizzle half of the egg mixture over flour mixture and, using a fork, mix gently just until combined. Add remaining egg mixture and mix until the dough just comes together (you will have some unincorporated pieces).

3. Turn out dough onto a lightly floured surface, flatten slightly, and cut into quarters. Stack pieces on top of one another. Placing unincorporated dry pieces of dough between layers, and press down to combine. Repeat process twice more (all pieces of dough should be incorporated at this point). Form dough into a 1" thick disk. Wrap in plastic; chill at least 1 hour.

4. Roll out a disk of dough on a lightly floured surface into a 14" round. Transfer to a 9" pie dish. Lift up the edge and allow the dough to slump down into the dish. Trim. Leaving about 1" overhang. Fold overhang under and crimp edge. Chill in freezer 15 minutes.

5. When ready to cook, set the smoker to 350°F and preheat, lid closed for 15 minutes.

6. Line pie with parchment paper or heavy-duty foil, leaving a 1-1/2" overhang. Fill with pie weights or dried beans. Bake until crust is dry around the edge, about 20 minutes.

7. Remove paper and weights and bake until surface of the crust looks dry, 5-10 minutes.

8. Brush bottom and sides of crust with 1 beaten egg. Return to grill and bake until dry and set, about 3 minutes longer.

9. For the Pumpkin Maple Filling: Whisk together pumpkin puree, sour cream, bourbon, cinnamon, salt, ginger, nutmeg, allspice, mace (optional) and remaining 3 eggs in a large bowl; set aside.

10. Pour maple syrup and 2 tbsp sugar in a small saucepan. Scrape in the seeds from vanilla bean (reserve pod for another use) or add vanilla extract and bring syrup to a boil. Reduce heat to medium-high and simmer, stirring occasionally, until mixture is thickened and small puffs of steam start to release about 3 minutes.

11. Remove from heat and add cream in 3 additions, stirring with a wooden spoon after each addition until smooth. Gradually whisk hot maple cream into pumpkin mixture.

12. Place pie dish on a rimmed baking sheet and pour in pumpkin filling. Bake pie, rotating halfway through, until set around edge but center barely jiggles 50-60 minutes.

13. Transfer pie dish to a wire rack and let the pie cool. Slice and serve. Enjoy!

Chocolate Peanut Cookies

Servings: 4
Cooking Time: 12 Minutes

Ingredients:

* 1/2 Tsp Baking Soda
* 1/2 Cup Brown Sugar
* 1/2 Cup + 1 Tbsp Butter, Unsalted
* 1/3 Cup Cocoa Powder, Dark And Unsweetened
* 2 Eggs, Beaten
* 1 1/2 Cups Flour, All-Purpose
* 1/3 Cup Miniature Chocolate Chips
* 2 Cups Peanut Butter Chips, Divided
* 1/4 Tsp Sea Salt
* 1/2 Cup Sugar, Granulated
* 1 Tsp Vanilla Extract

Directions:

1. Supply your smoker with wood pellets and follow the start-up procedure. Preheat the grill, with the lid closed, to medium-low heat. If using a gas or charcoal grill, preheat a cast iron skillet.

2. In a mixing bowl, whisk together the flour, cocoa powder, baking soda, and salt. Set aside.

3. Set a metal saucepan on the griddle, then add ½ cup of butter to melt. Whisk in the sugars and vanilla extract

and cook for 2 minutes. Remove the pan from the griddle, and transfer contents to a large mixing bowl.

4. Slowly pour the beaten eggs into the sugar mixture, whisking constantly to temper the eggs.

5. Add the dry mixture to the wet ingredients until just combined. Fold in 1 cup of peanut butter chips and chocolate chips. Refrigerate mixture for 15 to 30 minutes.

6. Remove the dough from the refrigerator, then add an additional cup of peanut butter chips.

7. Portion dough into 16 to 18 cookie balls.

8. Melt 1 tablespoon of butter on the griddle, then transfer the cookie balls to the griddle. Press down gently on the cookies, then cook for 10 to 12 minutes, flipping halfway.

9. Transfer cookies to a cooling rack for 5 minutes before enjoying.

Lemon Strawberry Rhubarb Pie

Servings: 8
Cooking Time: 30 Minutes

Ingredients:
- 1/3 Cup Flour
- 1 Tbsp Lemon, Zest
- 1 Prepard Pie Shell, Deep
- 3 Stalks Rhubarb
- 2 1/2 Cups Strawberry
- 1 Cup Sugar

Directions:
1. Summer baking never has to stop when you can use your Wood Pellet Grill to bake anything from cookies to pie! In this recipe, we will show you how to bake a delicious barbecued strawberry rhubarb pie without turning your kitchen into an oven.

2. Supply your smoker with wood pellets and follow the start-up procedure. Preheat the grill, with the lid closed, to 400° F.

3. Slice rhubarb and strawberries into bite sized pieces. Combine sugar, flour and lemon zest with rhubarb and strawberries. Pour into prepared pie crust. Cover with top crust.

4. Bake in Grill for 1 hour or until crust is crispy.

5. Serve hot.

Grilled Beer Cheese Dip

Servings: 6
Cooking Time: 20 Minutes

Ingredients:
- 6 Oz Beer, Can
- 8 Oz Cream Cheese
- 1 Tsp Onion Powder
- ½ Tsp Pepper
- ½ Tsp Salt
- 2 Cups Shredded Cheese

Directions:
1. Supply your smoker with wood pellets and follow the start-up procedure. Preheat the grill, with the lid closed, to 350° F. If you're using a gas or charcoal grill, set it up for medium high heat. Preheat with lid closed for 10-15 minutes.

2. In the cast iron pan add cream cheese, shredded cheese, beer, onion powder, salt and pepper. Once grill is at 350°F place cast iron skillet onto the grill and cook for about 10 minutes, stir and cook for another 5-10 minutes.

3. Top with more shredded cheese and fresh parsley. Serve with fresh baked pretzels as well.

The Dan Patrick Show Pull-apart Pesto Bread

Servings: 8
Cooking Time: 25 Minutes

Ingredients:
- 1 Sourdough Bread, loaf
- 1/2 Cup butter, melted
- 1 Cup Pesto Sauce
- 1 1/2 Cup Italian Cheese Blend

Directions:
1. Supply your smoker with wood pellets and follow the start-up procedure. Preheat the grill, with the lid closed, to 350° F.

2. Using a serrated knife, make 1" diagonal cuts through the bread leaving the bottom crust intact. Turn the bread and make diagonal cuts in the opposite direction, creating diamonds.

3. Place the bread on a sheet of foil large enough to wrap around the entire loaf. Pour the melted butter into the cracks in the bread. Using a spoon spread the pesto into the cracks then follow with the cheese stuffing it down into each crack.

4. Fold up the edges of the foil to wrap up the loaf and transfer to a baking sheet. Place the baking sheet directly on the grill grate.

5. Bake for 15 minutes then unwrap the foil and cook for an additional 10 minutes. Remove from the grill and serve. Enjoy! Grill: 350 °F

6. Follow along as we give you a recipe each day this week from The Dan Patrick Show Game Day Recipes eBook.

Smoked Vanilla Apple Pie

Servings: 6
Cooking Time: 45 Minutes

Ingredients:
- 1 1/2 cups of self-raising flour
- 3/4 cup of sugar
- 0.3 lbs of butter melted
- 1 tsp of vanilla extract
- 1 egg
- 0.9-lb tin of pie apples
- sugar & cinnamon for dusting

Directions:
1. Supply your smoker with wood pellets and follow the start-up procedure. Preheat the grill, with the lid closed, to 350° F.

2. Combine the self-raising flour, sugar, melted butter, vanilla, and egg in a large bowl until a golden dough texture is formed.

3. Spread half the mixture in a pie dish and press the bottoms and up the sides of the dish.

4. Pour pie apple tin into the pie and spread out evenly.

5. Sprinkle the remaining mixture over the top of the apple evenly and place in the smoker.

6. Leave for 45 minutes or until the golden crust forms on the top.

7. Dust with cinnamon and a little sugar if desired.

8. Serve warm with custard, ice cream, or both.

Baked Chocolate Coconut Brownies

Servings: 4
Cooking Time: 25 Minutes

Ingredients:
- 1/2 Cup gluten-free or all-purpose flour, such as Bob's Red Mill
- 1/4 Cup unsweetened alkalized cocoa powder
- 1/2 Teaspoon sea salt
- 4 Ounce semisweet chocolate, coarsely chopped
- 3/4 Cup unrefined coconut oil
- 1 Cup raw cane sugar
- 4 eggs
- 1 Teaspoon vanilla extract
- 4 Ounce semisweet chocolate chips, optional

Directions:
1. Supply your smoker with wood pellets and follow the start-up procedure. Preheat the grill, with the lid closed, to 350° F.

2. Grease a 9x9 inch baking pan and line with parchment paper.

3. Combine the flour, cocoa powder and salt in a medium bowl. Set aside.

4. In a double boiler or microwave, melt the chopped chocolate and coconut oil. Let cool slightly.

5. Add the sugar, eggs and vanilla. Whisking until well combined.

6. Whisk in the flour mixture and fold in the chocolate chips. Pour into the prepared pan.

7. Place on the grill and bake until a toothpick inserted in the center of the brownies comes out clean, about 20 to 25 minutes. This will yield a somewhat gooey brownie. Continue to bake for 5 to 10 minutes if you prefer a drier brownie. Grill: 350 °F

8. Let the brownies cool completely, then cut into squares. Store in an airtight container at room temperature for up to 3 days. Enjoy!

Focaccia

Servings: 6
Cooking Time: 40 Minutes

Ingredients:
- 1 Cup warm water (110°F to 115°F)
- 1/2 Ounce Yeast, active

- 1 Teaspoon sugar
- 2 1/2 Cup flour
- 1 Teaspoon salt
- 1/4 Cup extra-virgin olive oil
- 1 1/2 Teaspoon Italian herbs, dried
- 1/8 Teaspoon red pepper flakes
- As Needed coarse sea salt

Directions:

1. Measure the water in a glass-measuring cup. Stir in the yeast and sugar. Let rest for in a warm place. After 5 to 10 minutes, the mixture should be foamy, indicating the yeast is "alive." If it does not foam, discard it and start again.

2. Pour the water/yeast mixture in the bowl of a food processor. Add 1 cup of the flour as well as the salt and 1/4 cup of olive oil. Pulse several times to blend. Add the remaining flour, Italian herbs, and hot pepper flakes.

3. Process the dough until it's smooth and elastic and pulls away from the sides of the bowl, adding small amounts of flour or water through the feed tube if the dough is respectively too wet or too dry.

4. Let the dough rise in the covered food processor bowl in a warm place until doubled in bulk, about 1 hour5. Remove the dough from the food processor (it will deflate) and turn onto a lightly floured surface.

5. Oil two 8- to 9-inch round cake pans generously with olive oil. (Just pour a couple of glugs in and tilt the pan to spread the oil.) Divide the dough into two equal pieces, shape into disks, and put one in each prepared cake pan.

6. Oil the top of each disk with olive oil and dimple the dough with your fingertips. Sprinkle lightly with coarse salt, and if desired, additional dried Italian herbs.

7. Cover the focaccia dough with plastic wrap and let the dough rise in a warm place, about 45 minutes to an hour.

8. When ready to cook, start the smoker grill and set the temperature to 400F and preheat, lid closed, for 10 to 15 minutes.

9. Put the pans with the focaccia dough directly on the grill grate. Bake until the focaccia breads are light golden in color and baked through, 35 to 40 minutes, rotating the pans halfway through the baking time.

10. Let cool slightly before removing from the pans. Cut into wedges for serving.

Baked Molten Chocolate Cake

Servings: 4
Cooking Time: 20 Minutes

Ingredients:
- all-purpose flour
- butter
- 4 Ounce butter
- 6 Ounce Chocolate, Bittersweet
- 2 eggs
- 2 egg yolk
- 1/2 Cup sugar
- 1 Pinch salt

Directions:

1. Supply your smoker with wood pellets and follow the start-up procedure. Preheat the grill, with the lid closed, to 450° F.

2. Butter and flour four (6oz) ramekins. Tap out excess flour. Place ramekins on a baking sheet and reserve.

3. Melt butter and chocolate in a double boiler over simmering water. In a medium bowl, beat eggs and yolks with sugar and salt on high until thick and pale.

4. Whisk in chocolate until smooth and quickly fold into the egg mixture along with flour.

5. Spoon the batter into prepared ramekins and bake for 20 minutes or until sides are firm but centers are soft. Grill: 450 °F

6. Let cool for 1 minute, then cover each with an inverted dessert plate. Carefully turn each over, let stand 10 seconds, then unmold.

7. Serve immediately with Maple Ice Cream with Candied Bacon. Enjoy!

Pretzel Rolls

Servings: 6
Cooking Time: 20 Minutes

Ingredients:
- 2 3/4 Cup Bread Flour
- 1 Quick-Rising Yeast, envelope
- 1 Teaspoon salt
- 1 Teaspoon sugar

- 1/2 Teaspoon celery seed
- 1/2 Teaspoon Caraway Seeds
- 1 Cup hot water
- As Needed Cornmeal
- 8 Cup water
- 1/4 Cup baking soda
- 2 Tablespoon sugar
- 1 Whole Egg White
- Coarse salt

Directions:

1. Combine bread flour, 1 envelope yeast, salt, 1 teaspoon sugar, caraway seeds and celery seeds in food processor or standing mixer with dough hook and blend.

2. With machine running, gradually pour hot water, adding enough water to form smooth elastic dough. Process 1 minute to knead. (You could also knead it by hand for a few minutes.)

3. Grease medium bowl. Add dough to bowl, turning to coat. Cover bowl with plastic wrap, then towel; let dough rise in warm draft-free area until doubled in volume, about 35 minutes.

4. Flour a large baking sheet. Punch dough down and knead on lightly floured surface until smooth. Divide into 8 pieces. Form each dough piece into a ball.

5. Place dough balls on prepared sheet, flattening each slightly. Using serrated knife, cut X in top center of each dough ball. Cover with towel and let dough balls rise until almost doubled in volume, about 20 minutes.

6. When ready to cook, start the smoker on Smoke with the lid open until a fire is established (4-5 minutes). Turn temperature to 375 F (190 C) and preheat, lid closed, for 10 to 15 minutes.

7. Grease another baking sheet and sprinkle with cornmeal. Bring water to boil in large saucepan. Add baking soda and sugar (water will foam up). Add 3 rolls (or however many will fit comfortably in the pot) and cook 30 seconds per side.

8. Using slotted spoon, transfer rolls to prepared sheet, arranging X side up. Repeat with remaining rolls. Brush rolls with egg white glaze. Sprinkle rolls generously with coarse salt.

9. Bake rolls until brown, about 20 to 25 minutes. Transfer to racks and cool 10 minutes. Serve rolls warm or at room temperature. Enjoy!

Chili Cheese Fries

Servings: 6
Cooking Time: 10 Minutes

Ingredients:

- 1 Cup Cheddar Cheese, Shredded
- 1 Cup Chili Con Carne, Prepared
- 1 Bag French Fries
- 1 Tablespoon Olive Oil
- 1 Tablespoon Sweet Heat Rub

Directions:

1. Supply your smoker with wood pellets and follow the start-up procedure. Preheat the grill, with the lid closed, to 350° F. If you're using charcoal or gas, set it up for medium high heat.

2. Bake the fries according to manufacturer's instructions. Once the fries are done, place them in a large bowl and add the olive oil and Sweet Heat Rub. Toss the fries to coat. Once everything is well coated with the oil and seasoning, spread the fries on a baking sheet.

3. Top the fries with the chili and the shredded cheddar cheese. Place the baking sheet on the grill and grill for 7-10 minutes, or until the cheese is melted and bubbly, and the chili is warm all the way through.

4. Remove the baking sheet from the grill and serve the fries immediately.

Carrot Cake

Servings: 4-6
Cooking Time: 60 Minutes

Ingredients:

- 8 carrots, peeled and grated
- 4 eggs, at room temperature
- 1 cup vegetable oil
- ½ cup milk
- 1 teaspoon vanilla extract
- 2 cups sugar
- 2 cups self-rising or cake flour
- 2 teaspoons baking soda
- 1 teaspoon salt
- 1 cup finely chopped pecans
- Nonstick cooking spray or butter, for greasing
- 8 ounces cream cheese

- 1 cup confectioners' sugar
- 8 tablespoons (1 stick) unsalted butter, at room temperature
- 1 teaspoon vanilla extract
- ½ teaspoon salt
- 2 tablespoons to ¼ cup milk

Directions:

1. For the cake:
2. Supply your smoker with wood pellets and follow the start-up procedure. Preheat, with the lid closed, to 350°F.
3. In a food processor or blender, combine the grated carrots, eggs, oil, milk, and vanilla, and process until the carrots are finely minced.
4. In a large mixing bowl, combine the sugar, flour, baking soda, and salt.
5. Add the carrot mixture to the flour mixture and stir until well incorporated. Fold in the chopped pecans.
6. Coat a 9-by-13-inch baking pan with cooking spray.
7. Pour the batter into prepared pan and place on the grill grate. Close the lid and smoke for about 1 hour, or until a toothpick inserted in the center comes out clean.
8. Remove the cake from the grill and let cool completely.
9. For the frosting:
10. Using an electric mixer on low speed, beat the cream cheese, confectioners' sugar, butter, vanilla, and salt, adding 2 tablespoons to ¼ cup of milk to thin the frosting as needed.
11. Frost the cooled cake and slice to serve.

Rosemary Cranberry Apple Sage Stuffing

Servings: 7
Cooking Time: 45 Minutes

Ingredients:

- 10 Cups Day Old Diced Bread, Sliced Loaf
- 2 1/2 Cups Broth, Chicken
- 1 Cup Butter, Unsalted
- 1 Cup Diced Celery, Cut
- 1 1/2 Cups Fresh Cranberries
- 1 Beaten Egg
- 1 Medium Granny Smith Apple, Peel, Core And Dice
- 2 Tbsp Minced Parsley, Fresh
- 1 Tbsp Minced Rosemary, Fresh
- 2 Tbsp Roughly Chopped Sage
- Salt And Pepper
- 1 Tbsp Minced Thyme
- 2 Cups Diced Yellow Onion, Sliced

Directions:

1. Supply your smoker with wood pellets and follow the start-up procedure. Preheat the grill, with the lid closed, to 350° F.
2. Melt butter over medium heat. Add onions then celery and cook until onions start to become translucent.
3. In a large bowl, mix together bread, apples, cranberries, cooked onion and celery mixture, and fresh herbs.
4. Add half of the chicken broth to the mixture and stir.
5. Beat together eggs and the rest of the chicken broth in a small bowl. Pour into the bread mixture and stir until completely combined.
6. Add salt and pepper to taste.
7. Pour stuffing into a cast iron pan or baking dish. Cover with foil and bake on the grill for 30 minutes. Remove the foil and cook for an additional 15 minutes.
8. Serve immediately and enjoy!

Delicious Pellet Grill Cornbread

Servings: 6
Cooking Time: 35 Minutes

Ingredients:

- 1 cup flour
- 1 cup cornmeal
- 2 teaspoons baking powder
- 2 teaspoons salt
- 3/4 cup sugar
- 2 tablespoons honey
- 1/2 cup butter
- 1 cup sour cream
- 3 eggs
- 1 cup milk

Directions:

1. Supply your smoker with wood pellets and follow the start-up procedure. Preheat the grill, with the lid closed, to 350° F.

2. Grease a 12-inch cast iron skillet or an equivalent baking pan.

3. Add flour, cornmeal, baking powder, salt, sugar, honey, butter, sour cream, eggs, and milk into a mixing bowl.

4. Mix well then pour into pan and bake on the grill for 30-35 minutes or until the cornbread is baked through in the center.

Grilled Bourbon Pecan Pie

Servings: 6
Cooking Time: 45 Minutes

Ingredients:

- 2 Tbsp Bourbon
- 1/2 Cup Brown Sugar
- 1/3 Cup Unsalted Butter, Melted
- 1/2 Cup Light, 1/2 Cup Dark Corn Syrup
- 3 Egg
- 1/4 Tsp Hickory Honey Smoked Salt
- Decoration Pecan
- 1 1/4 Cup Chopped Pecans, Coarsely Broken
- 1 Prepared Or Homemade Pie Shell, Deep
- 1/2 Cup Sugar
- 1 Tsp Vanilla Extract

Directions:

1. Supply your smoker with wood pellets and follow the start-up procedure. Preheat the grill, with the lid closed, to 375° F. Meanwhile, prepare your pie crust in a 9 cast iron skillet or heat proof pie plate.

2. In a large bowl, beat the eggs until smooth. Add the brown sugar and white sugar and mix until smooth. Add the light corn syrup, dark corn syrup, vanilla, bourbon, melted butter, and Hickory Honey Salt. Mix until smooth. Stir in your chopped pecans and pour into the pie crust. Top with the whole pecans, if desired.

3. Grill covered for 35-45 minutes, until the pie is just set around the edges but still has a slight jiggle in the center.

4. Allow the pie to cool completely before slicing. Enjoy!

Bananas Rum Foster

Servings: 4
Cooking Time: 10 Minutes

Ingredients:

- 1/3 Cup Banana Nectar
- 4 Bananas, Quartered
- 3/4 Cup Brown Sugar
- 1/4 Cup Butter
- 1/2 Tsp Cinnamon, Ground
- 1/3 Cup Dark Rum
- Vanilla Ice Cream

Directions:

1. Supply your smoker with wood pellets and follow the start-up procedure. Preheat the grill, with the lid closed, to medium heat. If using a gas or charcoal grill, preheat a cast iron skillet.

2. Place a large skillet on the griddle, then melt butter in the skillet. Whisk in brown sugar and cinnamon, stirring until sugar dissolves.

3. Add the banana nectar and bananas. Stir to coat

4. Once the bananas begin to soften and turn brown, add the rum. Stir, then ignite the sauce with a stick lighter. After the flames subside, simmer the sauce for 2 minutes.

5. Divide the bananas among 4 scoops/bowls of vanilla ice cream, then spoon the warm sauce over the top of the ice cream. Serve immediately.

Donut Bread Pudding

Servings: 8
Cooking Time: 40 Minutes

Ingredients:

- 16 Cake Donuts
- 1/2 Cup Raisins, seedless
- 5 eggs
- 3/4 Cup sugar
- 2 Cup heavy cream
- 2 Teaspoon vanilla extract
- 1 Teaspoon ground cinnamon
- 3/4 Cup Butter, melted, cooled slightly
- Ice Cream

Directions:

1. Lightly butter a 9- by 13-inch baking pan. Layer the donuts in an even thickness in the pan. Distribute the raisins over the top, if using. Drizzle evenly with the butter.

2. Make the custard: In a medium bowl, whisk together the sugar, eggs, cream, vanilla, and cinnamon. Whisk in the butter. Pour over the donuts. Let sit for 10 to 15 minutes, periodically pushing the donuts down into the custard. Cover with foil.

3. Supply your smoker with wood pellets and follow the start-up procedure. Preheat the grill, with the lid closed, to 350° F.

4. Bake the bread pudding for 30 to 40 minutes, or until the custard is set. Remove the foil and continue to bake for 10 additional minutes to lightly brown the top. Grill: 350 °F

5. Let cool slightly before cutting into squares. Drizzle with melted ice cream, if desired. Enjoy!

Crescent Rolls

Servings: 8
Cooking Time: 12 Minutes

Ingredients:
- 1 Crescent Dough, Can

Directions:
1. Supply your smoker with wood pellets and follow the start-up procedure. Preheat the grill, with the lid closed, to 375° F.

2. Unroll the dough and separate into triangles. Roll up the triangles and place on an ungreased nonstick cookie sheet. Bake for 10 -12 minutes on your Grill. You will know that they are finished when the rolls are golden brown.

Baked Cast Iron Berry Cobbler

Servings: 6
Cooking Time: 35 Minutes

Ingredients:
- 4 Cup Berries
- 12 Tablespoon sugar
- Cup orange juice
- 2/3 Cup Flour
- 3/4 Teaspoon baking powder

- 1 Pinch salt
- 1/2 Cup butter
- 1 Tablespoon Sugar, raw

Directions:
1. Supply your smoker with wood pellets and follow the start-up procedure. Preheat the grill, with the lid closed, to 350° F.

2. In a 10-inch (25-cm) cast iron or other baking pan, mix together the berries, 4 Tbsp sugar and the orange juice.

3. In a small bowl, mix together the flour, baking powder and salt. Set aside.

4. In a separate bowl, cream together the butter and granulated sugar. Add the egg and vanilla extract and mix to combine. Gradually fold in the flour mixture.

5. Spoon the batter on top of the berries and sprinkle raw sugar on top.

6. Bake the cobbler for approximately 35-45 minutes. Cool slightly and serve with whipped cream. Enjoy! Grill: 350 °F

Pull-apart Dinner Rolls

Servings: 8
Cooking Time: 10 Minutes

Ingredients:
- 1/4 Cup warm water (110°F to 115°F)
- 1/3 Cup vegetable oil
- 2 Tablespoon active dry yeast
- 1/4 Cup sugar
- 1/2 Teaspoon salt
- 1 egg
- 3 1/2 Cup all-purpose flour
- cooking spray

Directions:
1. Supply your smoker with wood pellets and follow the start-up procedure. Preheat the grill, with the lid closed, to 400° F.

2. In the bowl of a stand mixer, combine warm water, oil, yeast and sugar. Let mixture rest for 5 to 10 minutes, or until frothy and bubbly.

3. With a dough hook, mix in salt, egg and 2 cups of flour until combined. Add remaining flour 1/2 cup at a time (dough will be sticky).

4. Prepare a cast iron pan with cooking spray and set aside.

5. Spray your hands with cooking spray and shape the dough into 12 balls.

6. After shaped, place in the prepared cast iron pan and let rest for 10 minutes. Bake in Traeger for about 10 to 12 minutes, or until tops are lightly golden. Enjoy! Grill: 400 °F

Savory Beaver Tails

Servings: 8
Cooking Time: 2 Minutes

Ingredients:
- 2 Tbsp Butter, Melted
- 1 Tbsp Cinnamon, Ground
- 1 Egg
- 2 1/2 Cups Flour, All-Purpose
- 1/2 Cup Milk, Warm
- 1/2 Tsp Salt
- 1 Tsp Sugar
- 1/2 Tsp Vanilla
- 1 L Vegetable Oil
- 1/4 Cup Water, Warm
- 2 1/2 Tsp Active Yeast, Instant

Directions:
1. In a small bowl, combine water, milk, yeast, and sugar. Let it sit for about 10 minutes or until frothy.

2. In another bowl, pour in the flour and make a well in the middle. Pour in butter, sugar, salt, vanilla and egg. Mix everything together until the dough is smooth. Knead for about 5 minutes and set the dough in a greased bowl. Cover with a towel and set aside for about an hour, or until the dough has doubled in size.

3. After one hour, supply your smoker with wood pellets and follow the start-up procedure. Preheat the grill, with the lid open, to 450° F.Pour 1L of vegetable oil into a cast iron pan and place on the grates of your Grill. Keep your flame broiler closed so as to prevent grease flareups. Preheat the oil so that it is 350 degrees F.

4. While you"re waiting for the oil to heat up, punch down the dough and separate into 8 small balls. Shape each piece of dough into a flat circle. Fry the dough in the preheated oil for about 1 minute per side, or until the dough is golden brown.

5. Sprinkle with cinnamon sugar immediately, or top with your desired toppings. Enjoy!

Pound Cake

Servings: 8
Cooking Time: 60 Minutes

Ingredients:
- 1 1/2 Cup butter
- 8 Ounce cream cheese
- 3 Cup sugar
- 6 eggs
- 3 Teaspoon Bourbon Vanilla
- 1 Tablespoon lemon zest
- fresh strawberries
- whipped cream

Directions:
1. In a large bowl, cream the butter, cream cheese, and sugar. Add eggs one at a time, whipping in between. Add vanilla and lemon zest, whip.

2. Pour batter into greased loaf pans, about halfway full to allow cake to rise.

3. Supply your smoker with wood pellets and follow the start-up procedure. Preheat the grill, with the lid closed, to 325° F.

4. Place loaf pans on grill and cook for 1 hour - 1 hour and 15 minutes. Check the cake at 45 minutes, if golden brown, cover loosely with foil and continue to cook until a toothpick inserted comes out clean. Grill: 325 °F

5. Cool loaf in pan for 10 minutes before removing to a wire rack.

6. Cut into 1 inch slices and serve with fresh sliced strawberries, top with smoked whip cream.

Vanilla Chocolate Bacon Cupcakes

Servings: 12

Cooking Time: 120 Minutes

Ingredients:

- 1 Lb Bacon
- 1 1/2 Tsp Baking Powder
- 1 1/2 Tsp Baking Soda
- 1 Cup Cocoa, Powder
- 2 Egg
- 1 3/4 Cups Flour
- 1 Cup Milk, Whole
- 1/2 Cup Oil
- 1 Tsp Salt
- 2 Cups Sugar
- 2 Tsp Vanilla

Directions:

1. Supply your smoker with wood pellets and follow the start-up procedure. Preheat the grill, with the lid closed, to 250° F.

2. Once your grill is preheated, place bacon strips on the grates. Smoke for 1hr-1 ½ hours or until desired crispiness is achieved.

3. Remove the bacon from the grill and set aside.

4. Increase set the temperature to 350°F and preheat.

5. Mix the rest of the ingredients in a bowl with an electric mixer until it is nice and smooth.

6. Pour the mixture into a cupcake tin.

7. Transfer the tin to your grill and bake for about 20 - 25 minutes.

8. Allow the cupcakes to cool on a wire rack. Once cooled, top with your favorite premade icing and a half of strip of the bacon. Serve and enjoy!

SEAFOOD RECIPES

Smoked Mango Shrimp

Servings: 4
Cooking Time: 5 Minutes

Ingredients:
- 2 Tablespoon Olive Oil
- 1 Pound Raw Tail-On, Thawed And Deveined Shrimp, Uncooked

Directions:
1. Supply your smoker with wood pellets and follow the start-up procedure. Preheat the grill, with the lid closed, to 425° F. Rinse shrimp off in sink with cold water. Place in bowl and season generously with Mango Magic seasoning and olive oil. Toss well in bowl.
2. Thread several shrimp onto a skewer, so that they are all just touching each other. Repeat with other skewers and remaining shrimp.
3. Grill shrimp for 2 - 3 minutes on each side, or until pink and opaque all the way through. Remove from grill and serve immediately.

Sweet Mandarin Salmon

Servings: 2
Cooking Time: 10 Minutes

Ingredients:
- 1 Whole lime juice
- 1 Teaspoon sesame oil
- 1 1/2 Cup Mandarin Orange Sauce
- 1 1/2 Tablespoon soy sauce
- 2 Tablespoon cilantro, finely chopped
- Freshly cracked black pepper
- 1 Whole (4 oz) wild salmon fillets

Directions:
1. Supply your smoker with wood pellets and follow the start-up procedure. Preheat the grill, with the lid closed, to 375° F.
2. For the glaze, combine Mandarin orange sauce, lime juice, sesame oil, soy sauce, cilantro and fresh cracked black pepper. Mix together.
3. Cut the salmon into 4 fillets. Brush with glaze and place directly on the grill grate, skin side down.

4. Cook until salmon reaches an internal temperature of 155 degrees F (about 15-20 minutes). Half way through cook time, brush salmon again with the glaze.
5. Remove the salmon from the grill and serve with remaining glaze if desired. Enjoy!

Grilled Artichoke Cheese Salmon

Servings: 12
Cooking Time: 270 Minutes

Ingredients:
- 28 Oz Artichoke Hearts, Whole, Canned
- 1/2 Cup Breadcrumbs
- 1/2 Cup Brown Sugar
- 8 Oz Cream Cheese
- 1 Tbsp Garlic Powder
- 1 Cup Italian Cheese Blend, Shredded
- 1/4 Cup Kosher Salt
- 1 Cup Mayonnaise
- 2 Tsp Olive Oil
- 1 Tbsp Onion Powder
- 1/2 Cup Parmesan Cheese
- 2 Tbsp Parsley, Chopped
- Blackened Sriracha Rub
- 1 1/4 Lbs Salmon, Fillet, Scaled And Deboned
- Sour Cream
- 1/2 Tsp White Pepper, Ground

Directions:
1. In a small mixing bowl, whisk together the brown sugar, salt, garlic powder, onion powder, and white pepper. This will make twice the cure needed, so be sure and place the remaining half in a resealable plastic bag and save for smoking fish at a later date.
2. Lay a sheet of plastic wrap on a sheet tray and sprinkle a thin layer of the cure on it. Place the salmon skin-side down on top of the cure, then sprinkle a couple tablespoons of cure on top. Gently press the cure on top of the salmon flesh, then wrap in plastic wrap.
3. Refrigerate for 8 hours, or overnight.
4. Remove salmon from the refrigerator and wash off the cure in the sink, under cold water.

5.   Blot salmon with a paper towel, then set salmon skin side on a wire rack. Dry at room temperature for two hours, or until a yellowish shimmer appears on the salmon.

6.   Supply your smoker with wood pellets and follow the start-up procedure. Preheat the grill, with the lid closed, to 250° F. If using a gas, charcoal or other grill, set it to low, indirect heat.

7.   Place the salmon in the upper cabinet. Smoke for 2 hours, then increase the grill temperature to 350° F to maintain a cabinet temperature of 225°F and smoke another 1 to 2 hours, until salmon reaches an internal temperature of 145° F.

8.   Remove salmon from the cabinet and set aside to rest for 15 minutes, then flake apart. Reserve ½ cup to top dip after grilling.

9.   While the salmon is resting, drain the artichokes, then skewer onto metal skewers (if using wooden skewers, make sure to soak in water for 1 hour prior to grilling, or you can use a grill basket as well).

10. Season with Blackened Sriracha, then set on the grill. Grill for 2 to 3 minutes, until lightly browned.

11. Remove from the grill, cool slightly, then roughly chop. Set aside.

12. In a mixing bowl, combine shredded Italian cheese, grated parmesan, breadcrumbs and parsley. Set aside.

13. Place cream cheese, mayonnaise, and sour cream in a cast iron skillet. Stir frequently, with a wooden spoon, for about 5 minutes, until the mixture is smooth.

14. Carefully fold in flaked salmon and grilled artichoke hearts, then spread breadcrumb mixture over dip.

15. Drizzle with olive oil, then close the grill lid and bake for 25 to 30 minutes, until dip begins to bubble around the edges, and cheese begins to caramelize on top.

16. Remove dip from the grill, top with reserved salmon and a pinch of parsley. Serve warm with bagel chips, crackers, or crusty bread.

Vodka Brined Smoked Wild Salmon

Servings: 4
Cooking Time: 60 Minutes

Ingredients:

- 1 Cup brown sugar
- 1 Tablespoon black pepper
- 1/2 Cup coarse salt
- 1 Cup vodka
- 1 (1-1/2 to 2 lb) wild caught salmon
- 1 lemon wedges
- capers

Directions:

1.   In a small bowl, whisk together brown sugar, pepper, salt and vodka.

2.   Place the salmon in a large resealable bag. Pour in marinade and massage into the salmon. Refrigerate for 2 to 4 hours.

3.   Remove from bag, rinse and dry with paper towels.

4.   Supply your smoker with wood pellets and follow the start-up procedure. Preheat the grill, with the lid closed, to 180° F.

5.   Smoke the salmon, skin-side down for 30 minutes.

6.   Increase grill temperature to 225°F and continue to cook salmon for an additional 45 to 60 minutes or until the internal temperature in the thickest part of the fish reaches 140°F or the fish flakes easily when pressed with a finger or fork. Grill: 225 °F Probe: 140 °F

7.   Serve with lemons and capers. Enjoy!

Spicy Crab Poppers

Servings: 8
Cooking Time: 30 Minutes

Ingredients:

- 18 Whole jalapeño
- 8 Ounce cream cheese, softened
- 1 Cup Canned Corn, drained
- 1/2 Cup Crab meat, lump
- 1 1/4 Teaspoon Old Bay Seasoning
- 2 Scallions, minced

Directions:

1.   Cut each jalapeño in half lengthwise through the stem and remove the ribs and seeds.

2.   Filling: In a mixing bowl, combine the cream cheese, corn, crab meat, scallions, and Old Bay Seasoning and stir until blended. Stir in the scallions. Spoon the filling into the jalapeño halves, mounding it slightly.

3. Arrange the poppers on a baking sheet covered with foil or parchment paper.

4. Supply your smoker with wood pellets and follow the start-up procedure. Preheat the grill, with the lid closed, to 350° F.

5. Roast the jalapeños for 25 to 30 minutes, or until the peppers have softened and the filling is hot and bubbling.

6. Let cool slightly before serving. Enjoy!

Grilled Garlic Shrimp With Cajun Dip

Servings: 4
Cooking Time: 15 Minutes

Ingredients:
- 1 Grated Garlic Cloves, Peeled
- 1 Tsp Lemon Juice
- ½ Cup Mayonnaise
- 2 Tbsp Olive Oil
- 1 ½ Tbsp Hickory Bacon Rub
- Scallions
- ½ Lb Shelled And Deveined Shrimp
- 1 Cup Sour Cream

Directions:
1. Supply your smoker with wood pellets and follow the start-up procedure. Preheat the grill, with the lid closed, to 350° F. If you're using a gas or charcoal grill, set it to medium heat.

2. In a glass mixing bowl, add mayonnaise, sour cream, Cajun seasoning, garlic, lemon juice, hot sauce, and Hickory Bacon. Whisk together until well combined.

3. Cajun shrimp: In a small bowl, add shrimp, olive oil, Cajun-style seasoning and Hickory Bacon seasoning and toss to combine. Set aside.

4. Transfer dip mixture into cast iron ramekin or small Dutch oven and cover with foil. Place on preheated grill and cook for 10-15 minutes, or until dip begins to bubble along the edges. At the same time, place cast iron pan on grill and add shrimp. Cook for about 3-5 minutes on each side or until shrimp are opaque.

5. Remove dip from grill and top with Cajun shrimp and scallions. Serve warm alongside garlic toast squares and enjoy!

Mango Rice Wine Thai Shrimp

Servings: 4
Cooking Time: 15 Minutes

Ingredients:
- 2 Tablespoons Brown Sugar
- 2 Tablespoons Mango Magic Seasoning
- 1 Pinch (Optional) Red Pepper Flakes
- 1/2 Tablespoons Rice Wine Vinegar
- 1 Pound Raw Tail-On, Thaw And Deveined Shrimp, Uncooked
- 2 Tablespoons Soy Sauce
- 1 Teaspoon Sriracha Hot Sauce
- 1/2 Cup Sweet Chili Sauce

Directions:
1. Supply your smoker with wood pellets and follow the start-up procedure. Preheat the grill, with the lid closed, to 425° F. Rinse shrimp off in sink with cold water. Place in bowl and put in all of the ingredients listed above. Let marinade for 2 - 4 hours.

2. Thread several shrimp onto a skewer, so that they are all just touching each other. Repeat with other skewers and remaining shrimp.

3. Grill shrimp for 2 - 3 minutes on each side, or until pink and opaque all the way through. Remove from grill and serve immediately.

Florentine Shrimp Al Cartoccio

Servings: 4
Cooking Time: 13 Minutes

Ingredients:
- 6 tbsp unsalted butter, melted
- ½ cup heavy whipping cream
- ½ cup grated Parmesan cheese
- 2 garlic cloves, peeled and minced
- 1 cup thinly sliced button mushrooms, cleaned and destemmed
- 1 cup baby spinach leaves
- 2 tbsp chopped sun-dried, oil-packed tomatoes
- ½ tsp dried oregano
- ½ tsp dried basil
- ½ tsp crushed red pepper flakes, plus more
- ½ tsp coarse salt
- ½ tsp freshly ground black pepper

- 20 to 24 jumbo shrimp, about 1lb (450g) total, peeled and deveined
- sprigs of fresh rosemary, basil, thyme, or oregano

Directions:

1. Supply your smoker with wood pellets and follow the start-up procedure. Preheat the grill, with the lid closed, to 400° F.
2. In a large bowl, combine the butter and whipping cream. Stir in the Parmesan, garlic, mushrooms, spinach, tomatoes, oregano, basil, red pepper flakes, and salt and pepper. Add the shrimp and stir gently to coat.
3. Place four 12-inch (30.5cm) sheets of wide heavy-duty aluminum foil on a workspace and pull up the sides. Divide the shrimp mixture evenly between the sheets of foil. Roll and crimp the top and sides of the foil to create sealed packages.
4. Place the packets seam side up on the grate and grill until the shrimp are cooked through, about 10 to 13 minutes. (You can carefully open one package to check on the shrimp.)
5. Transfer the packets to plates. Carefully open the packets to avoid any steam. Scatter fresh herbs over the shrimp before serving.

Cold-smoked Salmon Gravlax

Servings: 6
Cooking Time: 30 Minutes

Ingredients:

- 1 Cup kosher salt
- 1 Cup sugar
- 1 Tablespoon freshly ground black pepper
- 2 Pound Sushi-Grad Salmon Fillet, Skin-on, Pin Bones Removed
- 2 Bunch Dill Weed, fresh
- capers, drained
- red onion, sliced
- cream cheese
- lemons

Directions:

1. In a bowl stir together the salt, sugar and black pepper until thoroughly combined. On a work surface, turn salmon skin side up and sprinkle about half of salt mixture all over and rub in.

2. Arrange half the dill on the bottom of a baking dish large enough to hold the salmon. Set salmon skin side down on bed of dill.
3. Rub remaining salt mixture all over top and sides of salmon, then top with remaining dill. Cover with plastic, then top with a weight on a smaller baking dish or a plate with cans of beans on top, then place in refrigerator and allow to cure for 2 days.
4. Remove salmon from refrigerator, rinse under cold water and pat dry with paper towels. Allow to sit at room temperature on the counter for 1 hour
5. Supply your smoker with wood pellets and follow the start-up procedure. Preheat the grill, with the lid closed, to 180° F. Place salmon onto a baking pan. Fill another baking pan with ice and place baking pan with salmon over ice. Place onto grill and smoke for 30 minutes.
6. Remove from grill and slice thin. Serve with capers, red onion, dill, cream cheese, and lemon. Enjoy!

Prosciutto-wrapped Scallops

Servings: 4
Cooking Time: 10 Minutes

Ingredients:

- 1½lb (680g) jumbo sea or diver scallops (size U-10)
- 8 to 10 thin slices of prosciutto, each halved lengthwise
- coarse salt
- freshly ground black pepper
- for the butter
- 8oz (225g) unsalted butter
- 2 tsp minced fresh curly or flat-leaf parsley
- 1½ tsp finely grated orange zest
- 1 tbsp freshly squeezed orange juice
- 1 tsp finely grated lemon zest
- 1 tsp finely grated lime zest
- ½ tsp coarse salt

Directions:

1. Supply your smoker with wood pellets and follow the start-up procedure. Preheat the grill, with the lid closed, to 450° F.
2. In a small saucepan on the stovetop over medium-low heat, make the citrus butter by melting the butter.

Add the remaining ingredients and simmer for 3 to 5 minutes to blend the flavors. Keep warm.

3. Rinse the scallops under cold running water and dry with paper towels. Place each scallop on its side at the end of a piece of prosciutto and wrap the prosciutto around the scallop. Secure with a toothpick. Season the exposed sides of the scallop with salt and pepper.

4. Place the scallops exposed sides down on the grate and grill until the edges of the prosciutto begin to frizzle and the scallop is warm inside, about 3 to 5 minutes per side.

5. Transfer the scallops to a platter. Brush with some of the warm citrus butter before serving. Serve the remaining butter on the side.

Grilled Garlic Lobster Tails

Servings: 2
Cooking Time: 11 Minutes

Ingredients:
- 4 Lobster Tails (8 oz Each)
- 3 Sticks Unsalted Butter
- 4 Cloves Garlic Minced
- ½ Cup Fresh Parsley Chopped
- Juice of 1 Lemon
- 2 Tablespoons Fresh Lemon Zest
- 2 Teaspoons Crushed Red Pepper
- ¼ Cup Olive Oil
- 1 TBS Kosher Salt
- 1 TBS Cracked Black Pepper

Directions:
1. Supply your smoker with wood pellets and follow the start-up procedure. Preheat the grill, with the lid closed, to 375° F.
2. Split lobster tails in half lengthwise and season with salt, pepper, and olive oil.
3. Place butter in an aluminum pan and put the pan on the hot side of the grill to melt the butter.
4. Add garlic, parsley, lemon zest, lemon juice, and red pepper to butter and simmer for 5 minutes.
5. Place lobster tails meat side down on the grill and cook for 6 minutes. Baste the shell side with the butter mixture.

6. Dunk each tail in the butter mixture and then transfer to the grill, shell side down. Baste meat again with butter mixture.
7. Cook for an additional 5 minutes or until the lobster meat turns opaque and shells are bright pink.
8. Serve with remaining butter mixture, fresh parsley, and lemon wedges.

Smoked Trout

Servings: 6
Cooking Time: 120 Minutes

Ingredients:
- 8 rainbow trout fillets
- 1 Gallon water
- 1/4 Cup salt
- 1/2 Cup brown sugar
- 1 Tablespoon black pepper
- 2 Tablespoon soy sauce

Directions:
1. Clean the fresh fish and butterfly them.
2. For the Brine: Combine one gallon water, brown sugar, soy sauce, salt and pepper and stir until salt and sugar are dissolved. Brine the trout in the refrigerator for 60 minutes.
3. Supply your smoker with wood pellets and follow the start-up procedure. Preheat the grill, with the lid closed, to 225° F.
4. Remove the fish from the brine and pat dry. Place fish directly on grill grate for 1-1/2 to 2 hours, depending on the thickness of the trout. Fish is done when it turns opaque and starts to flake. Serve hot or cold. Enjoy! Grill: 225 °F
5. Fish is done when it turns opaque and starts to flake. Serve hot or cold. Enjoy!

Bbq Roasted Salmon

Servings: 4
Cooking Time: 15 Minutes

Ingredients:
- 1/3 Cup honey
- 3 Tablespoon Mustard, whole-grain
- 1 Cup ketchup
- 1/2 Cup dark brown sugar

- 1 Teaspoon Cider Vinegar
- 1/2 Teaspoon Thyme Leaves, finely chopped
- 1/8 Teaspoon Jacobsen Salt Co. Pure Kosher Sea Salt
- 1/8 Teaspoon freshly ground black pepper
- 4 Whole Salmon Fillets, 6oz each, skin-on

Directions:

1. Combine all sauce ingredients in a large bowl, preferably one day prior to making the salmon.

2. Rub salmon fillets on both sides with sauce. Reserve any extra, unused sauce.

3. Supply your smoker with wood pellets and follow the start-up procedure. Preheat the grill, with the lid closed, to 350° F.

4. Place fillets on grill, skin-side down, and cook for 15 minutes. Grill: 350 °F

5. Let the fish rest for about 3-5 minutes. Serve with extra sauce. Enjoy!

Grilled Blackened Saskatchewan Salmon

Servings: 4
Cooking Time: 30 Minutes

Ingredients:

- 1 salmon fillets
- zesty Italian dressing
- Blackened Saskatchewan Rub
- lemon wedges

Directions:

1. Brush salmon with Italian dressing and season with Traeger Blackened Saskatchewan Rub.

2. Supply your smoker with wood pellets and follow the start-up procedure. Preheat the grill, with the lid closed, to 325° F.

3. Place salmon on the grill and cook for 20 to 30 minutes, until it reaches an internal temperature of 145°F and flakes easily. Remove salmon from grill. Serve with lemon wedges. Enjoy! Grill: 325 °F Probe: 145 °F

Bacon Wrapped Shrimp

Servings: 6

Cooking Time: 20 Minutes

Ingredients:

- 1 1/2 Pound Jumbo Shrimp, Peeled And Deveined
- 10 Strips Bacon
- Cheesy Grits, For Serving
- 1/4 Cup extra-virgin olive oil
- 2 Tablespoon lemon juice
- 1 Teaspoon Fresh Chopped Parsley
- 1 Tablespoon lemon zest
- 1 Teaspoon garlic, minced
- 1 Teaspoon salt
- 1/2 Teaspoon black pepper

Directions:

1. Rinse the shrimp under cold running water and dry thoroughly on paper towels.

2. Transfer to a re-sealable plastic bag or a bowl.

3. For the marinade: Combine the olive oil, lemon juice, lemon zest, garlic, salt, pepper, and parsley in a small jar with a tight-fitting lid and shake vigorously until combined.

4. Pour over the shrimp and refrigerate for 30 minutes to 1 hour.

5. Supply your smoker with wood pellets and follow the start-up procedure. Preheat the grill, with the lid closed, to 400° F.

6. Lay the bacon strips diagonally on the grill grate and grill for 10 to 12 minutes, or until the bacon is partially cooked but still very pliable.

7. Cut each strip in half width-wise. Leave the grill on.

8. Drain the shrimp, discarding the marinade. Wrap a strip of bacon around the body of each shrimp, securing with a toothpick. Grill for 4 minutes per side, turning once. Enjoy! Grill: 400 °F

9. Wrap a strip of bacon around the body of each shrimp, securing with a toothpick.

10. Grill for 4 minutes per side, turning once. Serve over cheesy grits, if desired. Enjoy!

Grilled Lemon Lobster Tails

Servings: 3
Cooking Time: 7 Minutes

Ingredients:

- 6 lobster tails

- 1/4 cup melted butter
- 1/4 cup fresh lemon juice
- 1 tablespoon fresh dill
- 1 teaspoon salt
- 6 lime wedges

Directions:

1. Supply your smoker with wood pellets and follow the start-up procedure. Preheat the grill, with the lid closed, to 375° F.
2. Split the lobster tails in half place then back side down.
3. Cut down through the center to the shell the whole length of each tail.
4. Pull the shell back, exposing the meat.
5. Pat the lobster tails with paper towel to dry.
6. Combine in a small mixing bowl the butter, lemon juice, dill, and salt until the salt has dissolved.
7. Brush the mixture onto the flesh side of each lobster tail.
8. Place the lobster tails onto the grill and cook for 5 to 7 minutes, turning them once during the cooking process. (The shells should turn a bright pink).
9. Remove the heat.
10. Serve with lime wedges!

Barbecued Scallops

Servings: 4
Cooking Time: 10 Minutes

Ingredients:
- 1 pound large scallops
- 2 tablespoons olive oil
- 1 batch Dill Seafood Rub

Directions:

1. Supply your smoker with wood pellets and follow the start-up procedure. Preheat the grill, with the lid closed, to 375°F.
2. Coat the scallops all over with olive oil and season all sides with the rub.
3. Place the scallops directly on the grill grate and grill for 5 minutes per side. Remove the scallops from the grill and serve immediately.

Shrimp Cabbage Tacos With Lime Cream

Servings: 4
Cooking Time: 10 Minutes

Ingredients:
- 1/4 Cabbage, Shredded
- 2 Tsp Cilantro, Chopped
- Corn Tortillas
- 1/2 Lime, Wedges
- 1/4 Cup Mayonnaise
- Blackened Sriracha Rub
- 1/4 Red Bell Pepper, Chopped
- 1 Lb Shrimp, Peeled & Deveined
- 1/4 Cup Sour Cream
- 2 Tsp Vegetable Oil
- 1/2 White Onion, Chopped

Directions:

1. Place shrimp In a medium bowl. Season with Blackened Sriracha Rub, then drizzle with vegetable oil. Toss by hand to coat well then set aside.
2. In a small mixing bowl, stir together mayonnaise, sour cream, and fresh lime juice. Season to taste with Blackened Sriracha. Set aside.
3. In a small mixing bowl, combine jalapeño, onion, red bell pepper, and cilantro. Set aside.
4. Supply your smoker with wood pellets and follow the start-up procedure. Preheat the grill, with the lid closed, till over medium heat. If using a grill, preheat a cast iron skillet over medium-heat.
5. Place tortillas on the griddle to warm each side, then turn off the burner below.
6. Transfer shrimp to the hot griddle, and cook for 4 to 6 minutes, tossing occasionally, until opaque. For spicier shrimp, season with additional Blackened Sriracha.
7. Assemble tacos: shredded cabbage, shrimp, pepper mixture, then drizzle with sauce. Serve warm with fresh lime wedges.

Smoked Fish Chowder

Servings: 4

Cooking Time: 60 Minutes

Ingredients:

- 12 Ounce (1-1/2 to 2 lb) skin-on salmon fillet, preferably wild-caught
- Fin & Feather Rub
- 2 Corn Husks
- 3 Slices Bacon, sliced
- 4 Can Cream of Potato Soup, Condensed
- 3 Cup whole milk
- 8 Ounce cream cheese
- 3 green onions, thinly sliced
- 2 Teaspoon hot sauce

Directions:

1. Supply your smoker with wood pellets and follow the start-up procedure. Preheat the grill, with the lid closed, to 180° F.

2. Sprinkle Traeger Fin & Feather rub as needed on salmon. Arrange the salmon skin-side down on the grill grate. Smoke for 30 minutes. Grill: 180 °F

3. Increase the grill temperature to 350°F. Grill: 350 °F

4. Cook the salmon for 30 minutes, or until the fish flakes easily with a fork. (The exact time will depend on the thickness of the fillet.) There is no need to turn the fish. Using a large thin spatula, transfer the salmon to a wire rack to cool. Remove the skin. (The salmon can be made a day ahead, wrapped in plastic wrap and refrigerated.) Break into flakes and set aside.

5. Arrange the corn and bacon strips on the grill grate. (The salmon will be roasting while you do this.) Roast the corn and the bacon until the corn is cooked through and browned in spots, turning as needed, and the bacon is crisp, about 15 minutes.

6. In the meantime, bring the cream of potato soup and the milk to a simmer over medium heat in a large saucepan or Dutch oven on the stovetop. Gradually stir in the cream cheese and whisk to blend. Chop the bacon into bits and slice the corn off the cobs using long strokes of a chef's knife.

7. Add to the soup along with the green onions. Stir in the salmon. Heat gently for 5 to 10 minutes. Add the hot sauce to taste. If the chowder is too thick, add more milk. Serve at once. Enjoy!

Traeger Jerk Shrimp

Servings: 8

Cooking Time: 10 Minutes

Ingredients:

- 1 Tablespoon brown sugar
- 1 Tablespoon smoked paprika
- 1 Teaspoon garlic powder
- 1/4 Teaspoon Thyme, ground
- 1/4 Teaspoon ground cayenne pepper
- 1 Teaspoon sea salt
- 1 lime zest
- 2 Pound shrimp in shell
- 3 Tablespoon olive oil

Directions:

1. Combine spices, salt, and lime zest in a small bowl and mix. Place shrimp into a large bowl, then drizzle in the olive oil, Add the spice mixture and toss to combine, making sure every shrimp is kissed with deliciousness.

2. Supply your smoker with wood pellets and follow the start-up procedure. Preheat the grill, with the lid closed, to 450° F.

3. Arrange the shrimp on the grill and cook for 2 – 3 minutes per side, until firm, opaque, and cooked through. Grill: 450 °F

4. Serve with lime wedges, fresh cilantro, mint, and Caribbean Hot Pepper Sauce. Enjoy!

Sweet Smoked Salmon Jerky

Servings: 6

Cooking Time: 300 Minutes

Ingredients:

- 2 Quart water
- 3/4 Cup kosher salt
- 1 Cup Morton Tender Quick Home Meat Cure, optional
- 4 Cup dark brown sugar
- 2 Cup maple syrup, divided
- 1 (2-3 lb) wild caught salmon fillet, skinned and pin bones removed

Directions:

1. In a large nonreactive bowl, combine 2 quarts water, salt, curing salt (if using), brown sugar and 1 cup of the maple syrup. Stir with a long-handled spoon to dissolve the salts and sugar.

2. With a sharp, serrated knife, slice the salmon into 1/2 inch thick slices with the short side parallel to you on the cutting board. In other words, make your cuts from the head end to the tail end. (This is considerably easier if the fish is frozen.) Cut each strip crosswise into 4 or 5 inch lengths.

3. Immerse the strips in the brine, weighing down with a plate or a bag of ice. Cover with plastic wrap and refrigerate for 12 hours.

4. Supply your smoker with wood pellets and follow the start-up procedure. Preheat the grill, with the lid closed, to 180° F.

5. Drain the salmon strips and discard the brine. Arrange the salmon strips in a single layer directly on the grill grate. Smoke for several hours (5 to 6), or until the jerky is dry but not rock-hard. You want it to yield when you bite into it. Halfway through the smoking time, mix the remaining cup of maple syrup with 1/4 cup of warm water and brush the salmon strips on all sides with the mixture. Grill: 180 °F

6. Transfer to a resealable bag while the jerky is still warm. Let the jerky rest for an hour at room temperature. Squeeze any air from the bag, and refrigerate the jerky. Enjoy!

Grilled Albacore Tuna With Potato-tomato Casserole

Servings: 8
Cooking Time: 20 Minutes

Ingredients:

- 6 Tuna Steaks, 6oz
- 1 Whole lemon zest
- 1 chile de árbol, thinly sliced
- 1 Tablespoon thyme
- 1 Tablespoon fresh parsley

Directions:

1. To make the fish: Season the fish with the lemon zest, chile, thyme, and parsley. Cover and refrigerate at least 4 hours.

2. Remove fish from the refrigerator 30 minutes before cooking to come to room temperature.

3. Season the fish with salt and pepper on both sides. Grill 2-3 minutes per side (next to the cast iron with the casserole) rotating it once or twice. The tuna should be well seared but still rare.

Charleston Crab Cakes With Remoulade

Servings: 4
Cooking Time: 45 Minutes

Ingredients:

- 1¼ cups mayonnaise
- ¼ cup yellow mustard
- 2 tablespoons sweet pickle relish, with its juices
- 1 tablespoon smoked paprika
- 2 teaspoons Cajun seasoning
- 2 teaspoons prepared horseradish
- 1 teaspoon hot sauce
- 1 garlic clove, finely minced
- 2 pounds fresh lump crabmeat, picked clean
- 20 butter crackers (such as Ritz brand), crushed
- 2 tablespoons Dijon mustard
- 1 cup mayonnaise
- 2 tablespoons freshly squeezed lemon juice
- 1 tablespoon salted butter, melted
- 1 tablespoon Worcestershire sauce
- 1 tablespoon Old Bay seasoning
- 2 teaspoons chopped fresh parsley
- 1 teaspoon ground mustard
- 2 eggs, beaten
- ¼ cup extra-virgin olive oil, divided

Directions:

1. For the remoulade:

2. In a small bowl, combine the mayonnaise, mustard, pickle relish, paprika, Cajun seasoning, horseradish, hot sauce, and garlic.

3. Refrigerate until ready to serve.

4. For the crab cakes:

5. Supply your smoker with wood pellets and follow the start-up procedure. Preheat, with the lid closed, to 375°F.

6. Spread the crabmeat on a foil-lined baking sheet and place over indirect heat on the grill, with the lid closed, for 30 minutes.

7. Remove from the heat and let cool for 15 minutes.

8. While the crab cools, combine the crushed crackers, Dijon mustard, mayonnaise, lemon juice, melted butter, Worcestershire sauce, Old Bay, parsley, ground mustard, and eggs until well incorporated.

9. Fold in the smoked crabmeat, then shape the mixture into 8 (1-inch-thick) crab cakes.

10. In a large skillet or cast-iron pan on the grill, heat 2 tablespoons of olive oil. Add half of the crab cakes, close the lid, and smoke for 4 to 5 minutes on each side, or until crispy and golden brown.

11. Remove the crab cakes from the pan and transfer to a wire rack to drain. Pat them to remove any excess oil.

12. Repeat steps 6 and 7 with the remaining oil and crab cakes.

13. Serve the crab cakes with the remoulade.

Cured Cold-smoked Lox

Servings: 6
Cooking Time: 360 Minutes

Ingredients:
- ¼ cup salt
- ¼ cup sugar
- 1 tablespoon freshly ground black pepper
- 1 bunch dill, chopped
- 1 pound sashimi-grade salmon, skin removed
- 1 avocado, sliced
- 8 bagels
- 4 ounces cream cheese
- 1 bunch alfalfa sprouts
- 1 (3.5-ounce) jar capers

Directions:
1. In a small bowl, combine the salt, sugar, pepper, and fresh dill to make the curing mixture. Set aside.

2. On a smooth surface, lay out a large piece of plastic wrap and spread half of the curing salt mixture in the middle, spreading it out to about the size of the salmon.

3. Place the salmon on top of the curing salt.

4. Top the fish with the remaining curing salt, covering it completely. Wrap the salmon, leaving the ends open to drain.

5. Place the wrapped fish in a rimmed baking pan or dish lined with paper towels to soak up liquid.

6. Place a weight on the salmon evenly, such as a pan with a couple of heavy jars of pickles on top.

7. Put the salmon pan with weights in the refrigerator. Place something (a dishtowel, for example) under the back of the pan in order to slightly tip it down so the liquid drains away from the fish.

8. Leave the salmon to cure in the refrigerator for 24 hours.

9. Place the wood pellets in the smoker, but do not follow the start-up procedure and do not preheat.

10. Remove the salmon from the refrigerator, unwrap it, rinse it off, and pat dry.

11. Put the salmon in the smoker while still cold from the refrigerator to slow down the cooking process. You'll need to use a cold-smoker attachment or enlist the help of a smoker tube to hold the temperature at 80°F and maintain that for 6 hours to absorb smoke and complete the cold-smoking process.

12. Remove the salmon from the smoker, place it in a sealed plastic bag, and refrigerate for 24 hours. The salmon will be translucent all the way through.

13. Thinly slice the lox and serve with sliced avocado, bagels, cream cheese, alfalfa sprouts, and capers.

Cajun Catfish

Servings: 6
Cooking Time: 15 Minutes

Ingredients:
- 2½ pounds catfish fillets
- 2 tablespoons olive oil
- 1 batch Cajun Rub

Directions:
1. Supply your smoker with wood pellets and follow the start-up procedure. Preheat the grill, with the lid closed, to 300°F.

2. Coat the catfish fillets all over with olive oil and season with the rub. Using your hands, work the rub into the flesh.

3. Place the fillets directly on the grill grate and smoke until their internal temperature reaches 145°F. Remove the catfish from the grill and serve immediately

Smoked Crab Legs

Servings: 4
Cooking Time: 30 Minutes

Ingredients:
- 4 Whole crab legs
- 4 Tablespoon butter, melted
- 1/2 Cup Texas Spicy BBQ Sauce
- salt and pepper
- 1 Tablespoon Fin & Feather Rub

Directions:
1. Supply your smoker with wood pellets and follow the start-up procedure. Preheat the grill, with the lid closed, to 250° F.
2. Place the crab legs directly on the grill grate and smoke for 20 minutes. Grill: 250 °F
3. While the crab is smoking, make the sauce. In a medium bowl, combine melted butter, Traeger Texas Spicy BBQ sauce, salt, pepper and Traeger Fin & Feather Rub.
4. After 20 minutes of cooking, brush the crab legs with the BBQ sauce mixture. Continue to cook for another 10 minutes reserving the remaining sauce to serve. Remove crab legs from the grill, and serve with melted butter and BBQ sauce mixture. Enjoy!

Garlic Blackened Salmon

Servings: 4
Cooking Time: 10 Minutes

Ingredients:
- 1 Tablespoon, Optional Cayenne Pepper
- 2 Cloves Garlic, Minced
- 2 Tablespoons Olive Oil
- 4 Tablespoons Sweet Rib Rub
- 2 Pound Salmon, Fillet, Scaled And Deboned

Directions:

1. Supply your smoker with wood pellets and follow the start-up procedure. Preheat the grill, with the lid closed, to 350° F.
2. Remove the skin from the salmon and discard. Brush the salmon on both sides with olive oil, then rub the salmon fillet with the minced garlic, cayenne pepper and Sweet Rib Rub.
3. Grill the salmon for 5 minutes on one side. Flip the salmon and then grill for another 5 minutes, or until the salmon reaches an internal temperature of 145°F. Remove from the grill and serve.

Grilled Maple Syrup Salmon

Servings: 6
Cooking Time: 30 Minutes

Ingredients:
- 1 large salmon fillet (around 3 pounds)
- 1/2 cup salted butter (melted)
- 2 tablespoons soy sauce
- Salt and pepper
- 1/4 cup maple syrup

Directions:
1. Supply your smoker with wood pellets and follow the start-up procedure. Preheat the grill, with the lid closed, to 400° F.
2. Place the salmon fillet in a baking pan lined with parchment paper.
3. Sprinkle the fish with salt and pepper.
4. Add half of the melted butter to the salmon and place the baking pan on the grill.
5. Grill for 15-20 minutes or until fish is roughly 70% cooked. It will feel still gelatinous in the thickest parts of the salmon.
6. Combine the remaining melted butter, soy sauce, and maple syrup and pour over the salmon. It will run off the sides so use a spoon to pour it back over the fish. It's also perfectly fine that some will be left on the sides of the pan.
7. Cook for 5 to 10 additional minutes or until the fish is cooked through. The fish should be firm to the touch but still moist and soft when pressed on, and the ridges will flake or pull apart if pressed on.

Traeger Crab Legs

Servings: 4

Cooking Time: 30 Minutes

Ingredients:
- 3 Pound crab legs, thawed and halved
- 1 Cup butter, melted
- 2 Tablespoon fresh lemon juice
- 2 Clove garlic, minced
- 1 Tablespoon Fin & Feather Rub or Old Bay Seasoning, plus more to taste
- lemon wedges
- Italian Parsley, chopped

Directions:

1. If the crab legs are too long to fit in the roasting pan, break them down at the joints by twisting, or use a heavy knife or cleaver. Split the shells open lengthwise. Transfer to the roasting pan.

2. Combine the butter, lemon juice and garlic; whisk to mix. Pour mixture over the crab legs, turning the legs to coat. Sprinkle the Traeger Fin & Feather Rub or Old Bay Seasoning over the legs.

3. Supply your smoker with wood pellets and follow the start-up procedure. Preheat the grill, with the lid closed, to 350° F.

4. Cook the crab legs, basting once or twice with the butter sauce from the bottom of the pan, for 20 to 30 minutes (depending on the size of the crab legs) or until warmed through. Grill: 350 °F

5. Transfer the crab legs to a large platter and divide the sauce and accumulated juices between 4 dipping bowls. Enjoy!

Swordfish With Sicilian Olive Oil Sauce

Servings: 4

Cooking Time: 10 Minutes

Ingredients:
- 1/2 Cup extra-virgin olive oil, plus 2 tablespoons for oiling the fish
- 1 Whole lemon, juiced
- 2 Clove garlic, minced
- 3 Tablespoon finely chopped fresh parsley
- 1 Tablespoon finely chopped fresh oregano or 1 teaspoon dried oregano
- 1 Tablespoon brined capers, drained (optional)
- 4 (6 to 8 oz) swordfish, halibut, tuna or salmon steaks, 1 inch thick
- salt and pepper

Directions:

1. Put 1/2 cup of olive oil in a small saucepan and warm over low heat.

2. Whisk in lemon juice and 2 tablespoons hot water. Stir in garlic, parsley, oregano, capers (if using), and salt and pepper to taste (go easy on the salt if you're using capers). Keep warm.

3. Supply your smoker with wood pellets and follow the start-up procedure. Preheat the grill, with the lid closed, to 400° F.

4. Brush the fish steaks with 2 tablespoons of olive oil and season with salt and pepper. Grill: 400 °F

5. Arrange on the grill grate and grill until the fish is opaque and flakes easily when pressed with a fork, about 18 minutes. (If you prefer your tuna or salmon on the rare side, cook them for less time.) Grill: 400 °F

6. Transfer the fish steaks to a platter or plates and drizzle with the warm olive oil sauce.

7. Serve the remaining sauce on the side. Enjoy!

Smoke-roasted Halibut With Mixed Herb Vinaigrette

Servings: 4

Cooking Time: 12 Minutes

Ingredients:
- 4 halibut fillets, each about 6 to 8oz (170 to 225g)
- for the vinaigrette
- 2 tbsp white wine vinegar or sherry vinegar, plus more
- ¼ tsp coarse salt, plus more
- ¼ tsp freshly ground black pepper, plus more
- ½ cup extra virgin olive oil
- 2 tbsp minced fresh herbs, such as dill, flat-leaf parsley, or oregano
- for serving
- 4 cups loosely packed baby arugula, spinach, or other mixed greens

- 1 lemon, cut lengthwise into 4 wedges

Directions:

1. Supply your smoker with wood pellets and follow the start-up procedure. Preheat the grill, with the lid closed, to 400° F.

2. In a small bowl, make the vinaigrette by whisking together the vinegar, and salt and pepper. Whisk until the salt dissolves. Continue to whisk while slowly adding the olive oil. Whisk until the vinaigrette is emulsified. Stir in the herbs. Taste, adding vinegar or salt and pepper to taste. Pour 1/3 of the vinaigrette into a separate container. Reserve the remainder.

3. Place the fillets on a rimmed sheet pan. Lightly brush both sides with the smaller portion of vinaigrette. (Dividing the vinaigrette into two containers prevents cross-contamination.) Lightly season with salt and pepper.

4. Place the fillets on the grate at an angle to the bars. Grill until the edges begin to look opaque, about 4 to 6 minutes. Gently turn and grill until the fish is cooked through, about 4 to 6 minutes more. (A fillet will break into clean flakes when pressed with a fork when it's done.)

5. Remove the fish from the grill. Place the greens in a large bowl and toss them with 2 to 3 tablespoons of the reserved vinaigrette (you want the greens lightly coated) and divide between 4 plates. Place a fillet on the greens on each plate. Drizzle a bit more of the vinaigrette over the top. Serve with lemon wedges.

Grilled Oysters With Mignonette

Servings: 2

Cooking Time: 15 Minutes

Ingredients:

- 4 Cup rock salt
- 18 Large oysters
- 4 Tablespoon unsalted butter
- 2 Clove garlic, minced
- kosher salt
- 12 Medium lemon wedges, for serving
- 2 Tablespoon minced shallot
- 1/4 Cup red wine vinegar
- 1/2 Teaspoon freshly ground black pepper

Directions:

1. Choose a shallow serving platter that will hold all of the oysters. Pour the rock salt onto the platter to create a 1/2 inch base. This will steady the oysters for serving.

2. To prepare the oysters, check to ensure they are completely closed. Discard oysters that are not. Wash and lightly scrub the oysters to ensure there is no grit on the surface. This will prevent the grit from entering the oyster once shucked.

3. Using a thick glove or kitchen towel, sturdy the oyster in the hand opposite of the one holding the knife. Using an oyster knife or very sturdy paring knife, locate the "hinge" on each oyster. Place the point of the knife in the hinge, and wiggle the tip of the knife into the oyster until it feels sturdy. Firmly turn the knife to apply a torquing pressure to gently open the oyster.

4. Remove the top shell of the oyster. Using the tip of the knife, loosen the oyster from its shell, leaving the juices intact. Place each loosened oyster on its half shell on a baking sheet.

5. Supply your smoker with wood pellets and follow the start-up procedure. Preheat the grill, with the lid closed, to 450° F.

6. In a small saucepan, melt the butter over medium-low heat. Add the garlic and a generous pinch of salt, and cook until fragrant but not burned, about 1 minute. Remove from the heat. Grill: 450 °F

7. For the Mignonette: Combine the minced shallot, red wine vinegar and 1/2 teaspoon freshly ground black pepper. Set aside.

8. Spoon 1 teaspoon of the garlic butter sauce onto each oyster in its half shell. Carefully place each oyster directly on the grill grates, ensuring they don't slip. Close the lid and allow them to cook for 3 to 4 minutes, until the edges of the oysters have pulled away from the shell. Remove carefully with tongs to keep the juices and butter in the shells. Place directly on the rock salt to balance them. Serve immediately with the mignonette and lemon wedges to squeeze onto the oysters. Enjoy!

Cedar Smoked Garlic Salmon

Servings: 6
Cooking Time: 60 Minutes

Ingredients:
- 1 Tsp Black Pepper
- 3 Cedar Plank, Untreated
- 1 Tsp Garlic, Minced
- 1/3 Cup Olive Oil
- 1 Tsp Onion, Salt
- 1 Tsp Parsley, Minced Fresh
- 1 1/2 Tbsp Rice Vinegar
- 2 Salmon, Fillets (Skin Removed)
- 1 Tsp Sesame Oil
- 1/3 Cup Soy Sauce

Directions:
1. Soak the cedar planks in warm water for an hour or more.
2. In a bowl, mix together the olive oil, rice vinegar, sesame oil, soy sauce, and minced garlic.
3. Add in the salmon and let it marinate for about 30 minutes.
4. Start your grill on smoke with the lid open until a fire is established in the burn pot (3-7 minutes).
5. Supply your smoker with wood pellets and follow the start-up procedure. Preheat the grill, with the lid closed, to 225° F.
6. Place the planks on the grate. Once the boards start to smoke and crackle a little, it's ready for the fish.
7. Remove the fish from the marinade, season it with the onion powder, parsley and black pepper, then discard the marinade.
8. Place the salmon on the planks and grill until it reaches 140°F internal temperature (start checking temp after the salmon has been on the grill for 30 minutes).
9. Remove from the grill, let it rest for 10 minutes, then serve.

Moules Marinières With Garlic Butter Sauce

Servings: 4
Cooking Time: 12 Minutes

Ingredients:
- 3lb (1.4kg) fresh mussels, scrubbed under cold running water and debearded
- lemon wedges
- crusty bread (optional)
- for the sauce
- 6 tbsp unsalted butter
- 3 garlic cloves, peeled and minced
- 1 cup dry white wine or hard cider
- 1 tbsp freshly squeezed lemon juice
- 2 tsp hot sauce, plus more
- coarse salt
- freshly ground black pepper
- 2 tbsp chopped fresh curly parsley or tarragon

Directions:
1. Supply your smoker with wood pellets and follow the start-up procedure. Preheat the grill, with the lid closed, to 450° F.
2. In a small saucepan on the stovetop over medium-low heat, make the sauce by melting the butter. Add the garlic and sauté for 1 to 2 minutes. Add the wine, lemon juice, and hot sauce. Season with salt and pepper to taste. Simmer for 5 minutes. Remove the saucepan from the heat and stir in the parsley. Keep warm.
3. Discard any mussels that are cracked or don't snap shut when tapped. Place the mussels in a large aluminum foil roasting pan and cover tightly with heavy-duty aluminum foil.
4. Place the pan on the grate and steam the mussels until the shells open, about 10 to 12 minutes. Remove the pan from the grill and use long-handled tongs to remove the foil from the pan. (Be careful of escaping steam.) Use the tongs to discard any mussels that don't open.
5. Pour the reserved garlic butter sauce over the mussels. Serve from the pan or transfer the mussels to a shallow serving bowl. Serve immediately with lemon wedges, additional hot sauce, and crusty bread (if using) to sop up the juices.

Oysters Margarita

Servings: 4
Cooking Time: 10minutes

Ingredients:

- 24 fresh oysters in the shell
- 4oz (120ml) freshly squeezed lime juice
- 2oz (60ml) tequila
- 2oz (60ml) orange liqueur, such as triple sec
- 6 tbsp cold butter, cut into 24 cubes
- crunchy salt, such as margarita rimming salt
- lime wedges
- hot sauce (optional)

Directions:

1. Supply your smoker with wood pellets and follow the start-up procedure. Preheat the grill, with the lid closed, to 450° F.
2. Carefully shuck each oyster to remove the top shell. Run your shucking knife under the oyster to release it from the bottom shell, but don't spill the juices. Discard the top shells, but keep the oysters in the bottom shells. Balance each oyster on a wire rack placed on a rimmed sheet pan.
3. Place 1 teaspoon of lime juice, ½ teaspoon of tequila, ½ teaspoon of orange liqueur, and 1 cube of butter on each oyster.
4. Place the pan on the grate and smoke until the butter has melted and the juices are bubbling, about 8 to 10 minutes. (The oysters should be just barely cooked.)
5. Remove the pan from the grill. Sprinkle a pinch of salt on each oyster. Serve immediately with lime wedges and hot sauce (if using).

Honey-soy Garlic Salmon

Servings: 4
Cooking Time: 6 Minutes

Ingredients:

- 1 Tsp Chili Paste
- Chives, Chopped
- 2 Grate Garlic, Cloves
- 2 Tbsp Minced Ginger, Fresh
- 1 Tsp Honey
- 2 Tbsp Lemon, Juice
- 4 Salmon, Fillets (Skin Removed)
- 1 Tsp Sesame Oil
- 2 Tbsp Soy Sauce, Low Sodium

Directions:

1. Supply your smoker with wood pellets and follow the start-up procedure. Preheat the grill, with the lid closed, to 400° F.
2. Take the salmon and place it in a large resealable plastic bag, and then top with all remaining ingredients, except the chives. Seal the plastic bag and toss evenly to coat the salmon. Marinade in the refrigerator for 20 minutes.
3. After the salmon has been marinading for 20 minutes, place salmon on a flat pan or right on the grates and grill for about 3 minutes, and then flip and grill on the second side for about 3 minutes. Turn off the Grill, remove the pan from grill, plate, garnish with chives, and enjoy!

Coconut Shrimp Jalapeño Poppers

Servings: 6
Cooking Time: 55 Minutes

Ingredients:

- 8 Whole shrimp, peeled and deveined
- 1/2 Teaspoon Chicken Rub, plus more as needed
- olive oil
- 6 Whole jalapeños
- 8 Ounce cream cheese, softened
- 2 Tablespoon fresh chopped cilantro
- 1/2 Cup unsweetened coconut flakes
- 12 Slices bacon

Directions:

1. Supply your smoker with wood pellets and follow the start-up procedure. Preheat the grill, with the lid closed, to 425° F.
2. Rinse and season the shrimp with the Traeger Chicken Rub.
3. Drizzle the shrimp with olive oil and cook on the Traeger for about 5 minutes per side, or until the shrimp is opaque. Grill: 425 °F
4. Remove the shrimp and let cool.
5. Reduce Traeger temperature to 350°F. Grill: 350 °F
6. Meanwhile, get those poppers going. Cut the jalapeños in half then remove the stems and seeds.

7. Chop the shrimp. Mix together the softened cream cheese, chopped shrimp, 1/2 teaspoon Traeger Chicken Rub and 2 tablespoons chopped cilantro.

8. Load a generous amount of the filling in each pepper half. Top with a sprinkle of coconut.

9. Wrap each stuffed pepper with a slice of bacon and place on a foil-lined baking sheet.

10. Cook the peppers on the Traeger for about 45 minutes, or until the bacon fat has rendered and the cream cheese is golden. Enjoy! Grill: 350 °F

Smoky Crab Dip

Servings: 6
Cooking Time: 20 Minutes

Ingredients:
- 1/3 Cup mayonnaise
- 3 Ounce sour cream
- 1 Teaspoon smoked paprika
- 1/4 Teaspoon cayenne pepper
- 1 1/2 Pound Crab meat, lump
- salt and pepper
- scallions, chopped
- butter crackers

Directions:
1. Supply your smoker with wood pellets and follow the start-up procedure. Preheat the grill, with the lid closed, to 350° F.

2. Meanwhile, in a large bowl gently stir together all of the ingredients except the crackers, garnish scallions and the crab meat until thoroughly combined. Gently fold in the crab meat, being careful not to break it up too much.

3. Season to taste and transfer to an oven-safe serving dish.

4. Bake for 20 to 25 minutes, until bubbly and golden on top. Grill: 350 °F

5. Garnish with the additional chopped scallions and serve warm with butter crackers. Enjoy!

Wood-fired Halibut

Servings: 4
Cooking Time: 20 Minutes

Ingredients:
- 1 pound halibut fillet
- 1 batch Dill Seafood Rub

Directions:
1. Supply your smoker with wood pellets and follow the start-up procedure. Preheat the grill, with the lid closed, to 325°F.

2. Sprinkle the halibut fillet on all sides with the rub. Using your hands, work the rub into the meat.

3. Place the halibut directly on the grill grate and grill until its internal temperature reaches 145°F. Remove the halibut from the grill and serve immediately.

Lobster Tail

Servings: 2
Cooking Time: 25 Minutes

Ingredients:
- 2 lobster tails
- Salt
- Freshly ground black pepper
- 1 batch Lemon Butter Mop for Seafood

Directions:
1. Supply your smoker with wood pellets and follow the start-up procedure. Preheat the grill, with the lid closed, to 375°F.

2. Using kitchen shears, slit the top of the lobster shells, through the center, nearly to the tail. Once cut, expose as much meat as you can through the cut shell.

3. Season the lobster tails all over with salt and pepper.

4. Place the tails directly on the grill grate and grill until their internal temperature reaches 145°F. Remove the lobster from the grill and serve with the mop on the side for dipping.

Garlic Bacon Wrapped Shrimp

Servings: 4
Cooking Time: 11 Minutes

Ingredients:
- 8 Bacon, Strip
- 1/4 Cup Butter Style Shortening (Melted)
- 1 Clove Garlic, Minced
- 1 Tsp Lemon, Juice
- Pepper

- Salt
- 16 (Peeled And Veined) Shrimp, Jumbo

Directions:

1. Supply your smoker with wood pellets and follow the start-up procedure. Preheat the grill, with the lid closed, to 450° F.

2. Take one slice of bacon, and wrap it around each piece of shrimp, and lock it in place with a wooden toothpick.

3. Place the shortening into a mixing bowl and whisk in the garlic and lemon juice. Brush each shrimp with the sauce on both sides.

4. Place on the grill, and barbecue for 11 minutes.

5. Turn the grill off, remove the shrimp, serve and enjoy!

Alder Smoked Scallops With Citrus & Garlic Butter Sauce

Servings: 4
Cooking Time: 35 Minutes

Ingredients:

- 2 Pound large dry sea scallops
- kosher salt
- freshly ground black pepper
- 8 Tablespoon salted butter, melted
- 1 Clove garlic, minced
- 1 Small orange
- 1/4 Teaspoon Worcestershire sauce
- 1 1/2 Teaspoon fresh chopped parsley or tarragon
- flat-leaf parsley, for serving

Directions:

1. Wash the scallops under cold running water and thoroughly pat dry on paper towels. Remove any tags of abductor muscle tissue you find on the sides of the scallops.

2. Arrange the scallops on a baking sheet fitted with a cooling rack, and season with salt and pepper.

3. Supply your smoker with wood pellets and follow the start-up procedure. Preheat the grill, with the lid closed, to 165° F.

4. Place the baking sheet with the scallops on the grill grate and smoke for 20 minutes.

5. While your scallops are smoking, make your sauce. Melt the butter in a small saucepan over medium-low heat. Add a pinch of salt, garlic, Worcestershire sauce, zest and juice from half of the orange, and parsley. Simmer for 5 minutes. Keep warm.

6. Remove the baking sheet with the scallops from the grill and set aside. Increase the temperature to 400°F and preheat, lid closed. Optional: Place an oyster bed or oyster pan in the grill to preheat. These heavy iron pans are a great way to sear the scallops. Grill: 400 °F

7. Return the baking sheet with the scallops to the grill, brush with the butter sauce, reserving some for serving. Roast until just opaque and tender, 10 to 15 minutes. The time will depend on how thick the scallops are. Do not overcook. If you are using an oyster pan, brush each compartment lightly with olive oil to prevent sticking. Spoon butter sauce on each of the scallops, reserving some for serving.

8. Serve the scallops hot with a little more orange zest, fresh parsley and the the warm citrus and garlic butter sauce. Enjoy!

Grilled Fresh Fish

Servings: 2
Cooking Time: 15 Minutes

Ingredients:

- 1 Whole fillet of firm white fish: sea bass, halibut or cod
- Fin & Feather Rub
- 2 Whole lemons

Directions:

1. Supply your smoker with wood pellets and follow the start-up procedure. Preheat the grill, with the lid closed, to 325° F.

2. Season fish with Traeger Fin & Feather Rub and let sit for 30 minutes. Slice lemons in half.

3. Place the fish and the lemons (cut side down) directly on the grill grates. Cook for 10 to 15 minutes until the fish is flaky and is at least 145°F in the thickest part of fish. Be careful not to over cook.

4. Serve with the grilled lemons. Enjoy!

Mexican Mahi Mahi With Baja Cabbage Slaw

Servings: 4
Cooking Time: 10 Minutes

Ingredients:

- 1½lb (680g) skinless mahi mahi, cod, or other firm white fish fillets
- coarse salt
- freshly ground black pepper
- chili powder
- lime wedges
- for the slaw
- 2 cups finely shredded green cabbage
- 2 cups finely shredded purple cabbage
- 4 tbsp reduced-fat mayo
- 2 tsp hot sauce, plus more
- 2 tsp freshly squeezed lime juice
- ½ tsp coarse salt
- for the marinade
- ¼ cup freshly squeezed orange juice
- ¼ cup freshly squeezed lime juice
- 2 tbsp extra virgin olive oil

Directions:

1. In a medium bowl, make the slaw by combining the ingredients. Stir well. Transfer to a serving bowl. Cover and refrigerate until ready to serve.
2. Place the fish fillets in a baking dish and pour the orange and lime juices and olive oil over them. Turn the fillets to coat thoroughly. Cover and refrigerate for 15 to 20 minutes.
3. Supply your smoker with wood pellets and follow the start-up procedure. Preheat the grill, with the lid closed, to 450° F.
4. Drain the fish and pat dry with paper towels. (Discard the marinade.) Season the fillets on both sides with salt and pepper and chili powder. Place the fillets on the grate and grill until golden brown, about 4 to 5 minutes per side, turning with a thin-bladed spatula.
5. Transfer the fish to a platter. Serve with the slaw and lime wedges.

Bacon Wrapped Scallops

Servings: 8
Cooking Time: 20 Minutes

Ingredients:

- 24 jumbo deep sea diver scallops, dry-packed
- 1/2 Cup butter
- salt
- freshly ground black pepper
- 1 Clove garlic, minced
- 12 Slices thin-cut bacon, cut in half crosswise
- lemon wedges, for serving

Directions:

1. Remove the small, crescent-shaped muscle from the side of each scallop, if still attached. Dry the scallops thoroughly on paper towels, then transfer to a medium bowl.
2. Melt butter in a small saucepan, add garlic and cook for 1 minute. Let cool slightly then pour over the scallops. Season with salt and pepper and gently toss to coat.
3. Wrap a piece of bacon around each scallop and secure with a toothpick.
4. Supply your smoker with wood pellets and follow the start-up procedure. Preheat the grill, with the lid closed, to 400° F.
5. Arrange the scallops directly on the grill grate. Grill for 15 to 20 minutes, or until the scallop is opaque and the bacon has begun to crisp. If desired, you can turn the scallops on their side, bacon-side down, turning occasionally to crisp the bacon. Do not overcook. Grill: 400 °F
6. Transfer the scallops to a platter and serve with lemon wedges.

Lemon Shrimp Scampi

Servings: 3
Cooking Time: 10 Minutes

Ingredients:

- 2 Tsp Blackened Sriracha Rub Seasoning
- 1/2 Cup Butter, Cubed, Divided
- 1/2 Tsp Chili Pepper Flakes
- 3 Garlic Cloves, Minced
- To Taste, Lemon Wedges, For Serving

- 1 Lemon, Juice & Zest
- Linguine, Cooked
- 3 Tbsp Parsley, Chopped
- 1 1/2 Lbs Shrimp, Peeled & Deveined
- Toasted Baguette, For Serving

Directions:

1. Supply your smoker with wood pellets and follow the start-up procedure. Preheat the grill, with the lid closed, to medium-high heat. If using a gas or charcoal grill, set it up for medium-high heat.
2. Add half of the butter to the griddle, then sauté the garlic, Blackened Sriracha, and chili flakes for 1 minute, until fragrant.
3. Add the shrimp, turning occasionally for 2 minutes, until opaque.
4. Add the remaining butter, parsley, lemon zest and juice. Toss the shrimp to coat in lemon butter, then remove from the griddle, and transfer to a serving bowl.
5. Serve immediately, with fresh lemon wedges, and toasted baguette. Serve over linguine, spaghetti or zucchini noodles, if desired.

Thai-style Swordfish Steaks With Peanut Sauce

Servings: 4
Cooking Time: 8 Minutes

Ingredients:
- 4 center-cut swordfish steaks, each about 6oz (170g) and 1 inch (2.5cm) thick
- Peanut Sauce
- lime wedges
- for the marinade
- 1⁄2 cup light Thai-style unsweetened coconut milk
- 2 garlic cloves, peeled and smashed with a chef's knife
- juice and zest of 1 lime
- 1-inch (2.5cm) piece of fresh ginger, peeled and roughly chopped
- ½ Thai bird's eye chili pepper or serrano pepper, deseeded and thinly sliced, plus more
- 2 tbsp fresh cilantro leaves, coarsely chopped
- 1 tbsp Asian fish sauce
- 1 tbsp light soy sauce or liquid aminos

- 1 tbsp light brown sugar or low-carb substitute
- 1 tsp ground coriander
- ½ tsp ground turmeric

Directions:

1. In a medium bowl, make the marinade by whisking together the ingredients. Whisk until the brown sugar dissolves.
2. Place the swordfish steaks in a single layer in a nonreactive baking dish and pour the marinade over them, turning the steaks to coat thoroughly. Refrigerate for 1 hour.
3. Supply your smoker with wood pellets and follow the start-up procedure. Preheat the grill, with the lid closed, to 450° F.
4. Remove the swordfish from the marinade and scrape off any solids. (Discard the marinade.) Place the steaks on the grate and grill until the fish easily flakes when pressed with a fork, about 3 to 4 minutes per side, turning with a thin-bladed spatula.
5. Transfer the swordfish steaks to a platter. Serve with the peanut sauce and lime wedges.

Seared Bluefin Tuna Steaks

Servings: 2
Cooking Time: 5 Minutes

Ingredients:
- 3 Whole Tuna, steak
- olive oil
- salt and pepper
- soy sauce
- Sriracha

Directions:

1. Lightly baste both sides of tuna steaks in olive oil; sprinkle sea salt and ground pepper on each side.
2. Supply your smoker with wood pellets and follow the start-up procedure. Preheat the grill, with the lid closed, to High heat.
3. Grill tuna steaks on each side for 2 to 2-1/2 minutes.
4. Remove tuna from grill and allow to cool slightly.
5. Cut into 1/2 - 3/4" pieces. Serve with a mixture of Soy Sauce and Sriracha. Enjoy!"

Delicious Smoked Trout

Servings: 8
Cooking Time: 120 Minutes

Ingredients:

- 6 rainbow trout fillets
- Brine:
- 2 Tablespoons kosher salt
- 2 Tablespoons brown sugar
- 4 cups cool water

Directions:

1. For the brine, dissolve the kosher salt and brown sugar in water.
2. Place the trout fillets in the brine, skin side up, and brine the fillets for 15 minutes.
3. Supply your smoker with wood pellets and follow the start-up procedure. Preheat the grill, with the lid closed, to 180° F.
4. Remove the trout from the brine and transfer it to the grill grates.
5. Smoke the trout for 1.5 to 2 hours with the lid closed, depending on the thickness of your fillets.
6. Smoke until the trout reaches an internal temperature of 145 °F, or until the trout flakes easily.
7. Remove the trout from the smoker and serve warm, or let it cool completely and serve chilled with your favorite accouterments.

Baked Tuna Noodle Casserole

Servings: 4
Cooking Time: 45 Minutes

Ingredients:

- 1 Whole Wheat Pasta, Box (13.25oz)
- 2 Cup Yogurt
- 1 Cup almond milk
- 1 Teaspoon ground mustard
- 1/2 Teaspoon celery salt
- 1 Cup Button Mushrooms, Sliced
- 10 Ounce Tuna, Cooked
- 1 Cup Peas, canned
- 1 Cup Cheese, Colby/Cheddar

Directions:

1. Bring a large pot of salted water to a boil over high heat. Add pasta and cook according to manufacturer's directions. Drain and set aside.
2. In a medium bowl mix yogurt, milk, ground mustard, and celery salt. Fold in mushrooms, tuna, peas and cooked pasta. Fold in half the cheese.
3. Transfer the mixture to a greased 13" x 9" baking dish and top with remaining cheese.
4. Supply your smoker with wood pellets and follow the start-up procedure. Preheat the grill, with the lid closed, to 350° F.
5. Place casserole dish directly on grill grate and cook for 45 minutes or until warmed through and cheese is melted. Enjoy! Grill: 350 °F

Smoked Sugar Halibut

Servings: 8
Cooking Time: 120 Minutes

Ingredients:

- 1/4 cup granulated sugar
- 1/4 cup brown sugar
- 1/2 cup kosher salt
- 1 tsp ground coriander
- 2 lbs fresh halibut

Directions:

1. In a small bowl, mix the sugars, salt,and coriander together. Season the halibut on all sides.
2. Wrap the halibut in plastic wrap, place on a rimmed sheet pan,and brine in the fridge for 3 hours.
3. Remove the plastic wrap and rinse the fish. Pat it dry. Set it on a drying rack over a sheet pan for 1-2 hours in the fridge.
4. Supply your smoker with wood pellets and follow the start-up procedure. Preheat the grill, with the lid closed, to 200° F. Smoke the fish for 2 hours or until its internal temperature reaches 140 °F.
5. Serve your preferred sauce with the fish.

Oysters In The Shell

Servings: 4
Cooking Time: 20 Minutes

Ingredients:

- 8 medium oysters, unopened, in the shell, rinsed and scrubbed
- 1 batch Lemon Butter Mop for Seafood

Directions:

1. Supply your smoker with wood pellets and follow the start-up procedure. Preheat the grill, with the lid closed, to 375°F.
2. Place the unopened oysters directly on the grill grate and grill for about 20 minutes, or until the oysters are done and their shells open.
3. Discard any oysters that do not open. Shuck the remaining oysters, transfer them to a bowl, and add the mop. Serve immediately.

Dijon-smoked Halibut

Servings: 6
Cooking Time: 120 Minutes

Ingredients:

- 4 (6-ounce) halibut steaks
- ¼ cup extra-virgin olive oil
- 2 teaspoons kosher salt
- 1 teaspoon freshly ground black pepper
- ½ cup mayonnaise
- ½ cup sweet pickle relish
- ¼ cup finely chopped sweet onion
- ¼ cup chopped roasted red pepper
- ¼ cup finely chopped tomato
- ¼ cup finely chopped cucumber
- 2 tablespoons Dijon mustard
- 1 teaspoon minced garlic

Directions:

1. Rub the halibut steaks with the olive oil and season on both sides with the salt and pepper. Transfer to a plate, cover with plastic wrap, and refrigerate for 4 hours.
2. Supply your smoker with wood pellets and follow the start-up procedure. Preheat, with the lid closed, to 200°F.
3. Remove the halibut from the refrigerator and rub with the mayonnaise.
4. Put the fish directly on the grill grate, close the lid, and smoke for 2 hours, or until opaque and an instant-read thermometer inserted in the fish reads 140°F.
5. While the fish is smoking, combine the pickle relish, onion, roasted red pepper, tomato, cucumber, Dijon mustard, and garlic in a medium bowl. Refrigerate the mustard relish until ready to serve.
6. Serve the halibut steaks hot with the mustard relish.

Traeger Smoked Salmon

Servings: 6
Cooking Time: 240 Minutes

Ingredients:

- 1 (2-1/2 to 3 lb) salmon fillet
- 1/2 Cup kosher salt
- 1 Cup brown sugar, firmly packed
- 1 Tablespoon ground black pepper

Directions:

1. Remove all pin bones from salmon.
2. In a small bowl, combine salt, sugar and black pepper. Lay a large piece of plastic wrap on a flat surface that is at least 6 inches longer than the fillet. Spread 1/2 of the mixture on top of the plastic and lay the fillet skin side down on top of the cure. Top with the other 1/2 of the cure spreading it evenly over the top of the fillet. Fold up the edges of the plastic and wrap tightly.
3. Place the wrapped salmon fillet in the bottom of a flat, rectangle baking dish or hotel pan. Place another identical pan on top of the fillet. Place a couple of cans or something heavy inside the top pan to weigh it down making sure the weight is distributed evenly.
4. Transfer the weighted salmon to the refrigerator and cure for 4 to 6 hours.
5. Remove the salmon from the plastic wrap and rinse the cure thoroughly (not rinsing thoroughly will result in a salty finished product). Place skin side down on a wire rack atop a sheet tray and pat dry. Place the sheet tray in the refrigerator and allow the salmon to dry overnight. This allows a tacky film called a pellicle to form on the surface of the salmon. The pellicle helps smoke adhere to the fish.

6. Supply your smoker with wood pellets and follow the start-up procedure. Preheat the grill, with the lid closed, to 180° F.

7. Place the salmon skin side down directly on the grill grate and smoke for 3 to 4 hours or until the internal temperature of the fish registers 140°F . Enjoy warm or chilled. Grill: 180 °F Probe: 140 °F

Smoked Lobster Scampi

Servings: 2
Cooking Time: 30 Minutes

Ingredients:
- 1 Lobster Tail
- 1 Handful Pasta, Angel Hair
- 2 Tablespoon butter
- 1 Teaspoon garlic, minced
- 1/2 Teaspoon lemon juice
- 2 Teaspoon Parmesan cheese, grated
- 2 Tablespoon Sun Dried Tomato Pesto
- fresh parsley

Directions:
1. Supply your smoker with wood pellets and follow the start-up procedure. Preheat the grill, with the lid closed, to 180° F.

2. Use kitchen shears to cut along the top of the lobster on both sides to expose the meat. Place the lobster directly on the grill for 20-25 minutes, depending on the size of the lobster. Grill: 180 °F

3. While lobster smokes, cook pasta according to packaged directions.

4. After 20-25 minutes, take lobster off the grill and remove the meat from the tail. Cut meat into chunks.

5. While the pasta is boiling, melt butter over medium high heat. Once butter starts to brown, add the garlic and lobster chunks. Toss in pan a few times then add lemon and parmesan. Set aside.

6. When pasta has finished, place 1 tbsp of the sun dried tomato pesto on the bottom of a bowl or plate. Top with pasta, then finish with the lobster scampi. Garnish with parsley. Enjoy!

Smoked Salmon Candy

Servings: 4

Cooking Time: 180 Minutes

Ingredients:
- 2 Cup gin
- 1 Cup dark brown sugar
- 1/2 Cup kosher salt
- 1 Cup maple syrup
- 1 Tablespoon black pepper
- 3 Pound salmon
- vegetable oil
- dark brown sugar

Directions:
1. In a large bowl, combine all ingredients for the cure.

2. Cut the salmon into 2 ounce pieces and place in the cure.

3. Cover and refrigerate overnight.

4. Supply your smoker with wood pellets and follow the start-up procedure. Preheat the grill, with the lid closed, to 180° F.

5. Spray foil with vegetable oil. Place salmon on foil and sprinkle with additional brown sugar.

6. Place foil directly on the grill grate. Close the lid and smoke the salmon for 3 to 4 hours or until fully cooked. Grill: 180 °F

7. Serve hot or chilled. Enjoy!

Lemon Lobster Rolls

Servings: 4
Cooking Time: 35 Minutes

Ingredients:
- 1/2 Cup Butter
- 4 Hot Dog Bun(S)
- 1 Lemon, Whole
- 4 Lobster, Tail
- 1/4 Cup Mayo
- Pepper

Directions:
1. Supply your smoker with wood pellets and follow the start-up procedure. Preheat the grill, with the lid closed, to 300° F.

2. Using kitchen shears, cut the shell of the tail and crack in half so that the meat is exposed. Pour in butter and season with pepper. Place the tails meat side up on

the grill and cook until the shell has turned red and the meat is white, about 35 minutes.

3. Remove from the grill and separate the shell from the meat. Place the meat in a bowl with mayo, lemon juice and rind and season with pepper. Stir to combine and evenly distribute into the hot dog buns.

Grilled Lemon Shrimp Scampi

Servings: 4
Cooking Time: 6 Minutes

Ingredients:
- 1 ½ pounds medium shrimp, peeled and deveined
- ¼ cup olive oil
- ¼ cup lemon juice
- 3 tablespoons chopped fresh parsley
- 1 tablespoon minced garlic
- ground black pepper to taste
- ¼ teaspoon crushed red pepper flakes to taste

Directions:
1. In a large, non-reactive bowl, stir together the olive oil, lemon juice, parsley, garlic, and black pepper. Season with crushed red pepper, if desired. Add shrimp, and toss to coat. Marinate in the refrigerator for 30 minutes.
2. Supply your smoker with wood pellets and follow the start-up procedure. Preheat the grill, with the lid closed, to high heat.
3. Thread shrimp onto skewers, piercing once near the tail and once near the head. Discard any remaining marinade.
4. Lightly oil grill grate. Place the shrimp skewers on the grill grates.
5. Grill for 2 to 3 minutes per side, or until opaque.

Mezcal Shrimp With Salsa De Molcajete

Servings: 4
Cooking Time: 14 Minutes

Ingredients:
- 18 to 24 jumbo shrimp, about 1½lb (680g) total, peeled and deveined
- ⅓ cup mezcal
- juice of ½ lime
- 2 tbsp extra virgin olive oil
- 2 tsp coarse salt
- 1 tsp ground cumin
- lime wedges
- for the salsa
- 2 Roma tomatoes
- 2 tomatillos, husked and washed
- 2 garlic cloves, peeled and impaled on a toothpick
- 1 jalapeño or serrano pepper
- 1 small white onion, halved
- ½ tsp coarse salt, plus more
- juice of ½ lime
- ¼ cup loosely packed fresh cilantro leaves

Directions:
1. Supply your smoker with wood pellets and follow the start-up procedure. Preheat the grill, with the lid closed, to 450° F.
2. In a large bowl, combine the shrimp, mezcal, lime juice, olive oil, salt, and ground cumin. Toss with your hands to mix thoroughly. Set aside for 15 minutes and then toss once more.
3. Begin to make the salsa by placing the tomatoes, tomatillos, garlic, jalapeño, and onion on the grate. Grill until they begin to char, about 3 minutes for the garlic and about 6 to 8 minutes for the other vegetables, turning as needed. Transfer the vegetables to a rimmed sheet pan. Remove the skewers from the garlic. Let everything cool. Coarsely chop the vegetables and leave them in separate piles.
4. Place the garlic in the molcajete and add the salt. Mash the garlic to a purée using the temolote. Add the onion and grind it into the garlic paste. Stir in the jalapeño (deseeded for a milder salsa), tomatoes, and tomatillos. Stir in the lime juice and cilantro leaves. Taste, adding salt. (If you don't own a molcajete or temolote, prepare the salsa using a small food processor.)
5. Drain the shrimp and discard the marinade. Thread the shrimp on wood or bamboo skewers. Place the shrimp on the grate and grill until they're white and opaque, about 4 to 6 minutes, tossing with tongs.
6. Transfer the shrimp to a platter. Serve with the salsa and lime wedges.

Tequila & Lime Shrimp With Smoked Tomato Sauce

Servings: 4
Cooking Time: 6 Minutes

Ingredients:

- 24 to 28 jumbo shrimp, about 2lb (1kg) total, peeled and deveined
- 1 lime, quartered
- Smoked Tomato Sauce
- for the marinade
- ½ cup tequila or mezcal
- juice and zest of 1 lime
- 2 garlic cloves, peeled and roughly chopped
- ½ cup freshly squeezed orange juice
- ¼ cup extra virgin olive oil
- 2 tsp agave, light brown sugar, or low-carb substitute
- 2 tsp Mexican hot sauce, plus more
- 1½ tsp coarse salt
- 1 tsp baking soda
- 1 tsp chili powder
- ½ tsp ground cumin

Directions:

1. In a medium bowl, make the marinade by whisking together the ingredients. Whisk until the salt dissolves. Taste for seasoning, adding more hot sauce if desired.

2. Place the shrimp in a resealable plastic bag and pour the marinade over them, turning the bag several times to coat thoroughly. Refrigerate for 30 minutes.

3. Supply your smoker with wood pellets and follow the start-up procedure. Preheat the grill, with the lid closed, to 450° F.

4. Drain the shrimp and discard the marinade. Pat the shrimp dry with paper towels. Thread the shrimp on 4 bamboo skewers (preferably flat ones). Make sure all the shrimp face the same direction. Finish each skewer with a lime wedge.

5. Place the skewers on the grate and grill until the shrimp are white and opaque, about 2 to 3 minutes per side, turning once. (Don't overcook.)

6. Remove the shrimp from the grill. Serve immediately with the warm tomato sauce.

Spicy Lime Shrimp

Servings: 4
Cooking Time: 10 Minutes

Ingredients:

- 2 Tsp Chili Paste
- 1/2 Tsp Cumin
- 2 Cloves Garlic, Minced
- 1 Large Lime, Juiced
- 1/4 Tsp Paprika, Powder
- 1/4 Tsp Red Flakes Pepper
- 1/2 Tsp Salt

Directions:

1. In a bowl, whisk together the lime juice, olive oil, garlic, chili powder, cumin, paprika, salt, pepper, and red pepper flakes.

2. Then pour it into a resealable bag, add the shrimp, toss the coat, let it marinate for 30 minutes.

3. Supply your smoker with wood pellets and follow the start-up procedure. Preheat the grill, with the lid closed, to 400° F.

4. Next place the shrimp on skewers, place on the grill, and grill each side for about two minutes until it's done. One finished, remove the shrimp from the grill and enjoy!

Smoked Cedar Plank Salmon

Servings: 4
Cooking Time: 20 Minutes

Ingredients:

- 1/4 Cup Brown Sugar
- 1/2 Tablespoon Olive Oil
- Competition Smoked Seasoning
- 4 Salmon Fillets, Skin Off

Directions:

1. Soak the untreated cedar plank in water for 24 hours before grilling. When ready to grill, remove and wipe down.

2. Supply your smoker with wood pellets and follow the start-up procedure. Preheat the grill, with the lid closed, to 350° F.

3. In a small bowl, mix the brown sugar, oil, and Lemon Pepper, Garlic, and Herb seasoning. Rub generously over the salmon fillets.

4. Place the plank over indirect heat, then lay the salmon on the plank and grill for 15-20 minutes, or until the salmon is cooked through and flakes easily with a fork. Remove from the heat and serve immediately.

Pacific Northwest Salmon

Servings: 4
Cooking Time: 75 Minutes

Ingredients:

- 1 (2-pound) half salmon fillet
- 1 batch Dill Seafood Rub
- 2 tablespoons butter, cut into 3 or 4 slices

Directions:

1. Supply your smoker with wood pellets and follow the start-up procedure. Preheat the grill, with the lid closed, to 180°F.

2. Season the salmon all over with the rub. Using your hands, work the rub into the flesh.

3. Place the salmon directly on the grill grate, skin-side down, and smoke for 1 hour.

4. Place the butter slices on the salmon, equally spaced. Increase the grill's temperature to 300°F and continue to cook until the salmon's internal temperature reaches 145°F. Remove the salmon from the grill and serve immediately.

Smoked Salt Cured Lox

Servings: 8
Cooking Time: 30 Minutes

Ingredients:

- 1 Cup kosher salt
- 1 Cup sugar
- 1 Tablespoon cracked black pepper
- 1 Whole lemon zest
- 1 Whole orange zest
- 1 Whole Packaged Dill, roughly chopped including stems
- 2 Pound salmon fillet, skin on

Directions:

1. Mix together salt, sugar, black pepper, lemon zest, orange zest, and dill.

2. Slice salmon in half. Coat all flesh of salmon completely with salt sugar mixture. Sandwich the 2 pieces together, flesh to flesh and completely cover with salt sugar mixture.

3. Wrap tightly with plastic wrap and place into a gallon zip top bag. Squeeze out as much air as possible. Place wrapped salmon into a baking dish and place something heavy on top like a pot filled with water or a brick wrapped in foil. Place into the refrigerator for 10 hours. After 10 hours, flip over and put the weight back on top. Refrigerate for another 10 hours.

4. Remove from refrigerator, unwrap and rinse of remaining salt with cold water. Pat dry and leave on counter for 1 hour.

5. Supply your smoker with wood pellets and follow the start-up procedure. Preheat the grill, with the lid closed, to 180° F.

6. Place salmon onto a baking pan. Fill another baking pan with ice and place baking pan with salmon over ice.

7. Place onto grill and smoke for 30 minutes. Remove from grill and slice thin. Grill: 180 °F

8. Serve with bagels, cream cheese, capers, dill, lemon wedges, sliced tomatoes, and red onion. Enjoy!

Citrus-smoked Trout

Servings: 6
Cooking Time: 120 Minutes

Ingredients:

- 6 to 8 skin-on rainbow trout, cleaned and scaled
- 1 gallon orange juice
- ½ cup packed light brown sugar
- ¼ cup salt
- 1 tablespoon freshly ground black pepper
- Nonstick spray, oil, or butter, for greasing
- 1 tablespoon chopped fresh parsley
- 1 lemon, sliced

Directions:

1. Fillet the fish and pat dry with paper towels.

2. Pour the orange juice into a large container with a lid and stir in the brown sugar, salt, and pepper.

3. Place the trout in the brine, cover, and refrigerate for 1 hour.

4. Cover the grill grate with heavy-duty aluminum foil. Poke holes in the foil and spray with cooking spray (see Tip).

5. Supply your smoker with wood pellets and follow the start-up procedure. Preheat, with the lid closed, to 225°F.

6. Remove the trout from the brine and pat dry. Arrange the fish on the foil-covered grill grate, close the lid, and smoke for 1 hour 30 minutes to 2 hours, or until flaky.

7. Remove the fish from the heat. Serve garnished with the fresh parsley and lemon slices.

Garlic Blackened Catfish

Servings: 4
Cooking Time: 10 Minutes

Ingredients:
- ½ Cup Cajun Seasoning
- ¼ Tsp Cayenne Pepper
- 1 Tsp Granulated Garlic
- 1 Tsp Ground Thyme
- 1 Tsp Onion Powder
- 1 Tsp Ground Oregano
- 1 Tsp Pepper
- 4 (5-Oz.) Skinless Catfish Fillets
- 1 Tbsp Smoked Paprika
- 1 Stick Unsalted Butter

Directions:
1. In a small bowl, combine the Cajun seasoning, smoked paprika, onion powder, granulated garlic, ground oregano, ground thyme, pepper and cayenne pepper.

2. Sprinkle fish with salt and let rest for 20 minutes.

3. Supply your smoker with wood pellets and follow the start-up procedure. Preheat the grill, with the lid closed, to 450° F. If you're using a gas or charcoal grill, set it up for medium-high heat. Place cast iron skillet on the grill and let it preheat.

4. While grill is preheating, sprinkle catfish fillets with seasoning mixture, pressing gently to adhere. Add half the butter to preheated cast iron skillet and swirl to coat,

add more butter if needed. Place fillets in hot skillet and cook 3-5 minutes or until a dark crust has been formed. Flip and cook an additional 3-5 minutes or until the fish flakes apart when pressed gently with your finger.

5. Remove fish from grill and sprinkle evenly with fresh parsley. Serve with lemon wedges and enjoy!

Peper Fish Tacos

Servings: 12
Cooking Time: 10 Minutes

Ingredients:
- 1 Tsp Black Pepper
- 1/4 Tsp Cayenne Pepper
- 1 1/2 Lbs Cod Fish
- 1/2 Tsp Cumin
- 1 Tsp Garlic Powder
- 1 Tsp Oregano
- 1 1/2 Tsp Paprika, Smoked
- 1/2 Tsp Salt

Directions:
1. Supply your smoker with wood pellets and follow the start-up procedure. Preheat the grill, with the lid closed, to 350° F.

2. Mix together paprika, garlic powder, oregano, cumin, cayenne, salt and pepper. Sprinkle over cod.

3. Place the cod on your preheated for about 5 minutes per side. Toast tortillas over heat, if desired.

4. Break the cod into pieces, smash the avocado, slice the tomatoes in half and place evenly among the tortillas. Top with red onion, lettuce, jalapenos, sour cream, and cilantro. Spritz with lime juice and enjoy!

Smoked Honey Salmon

Servings: 2
Cooking Time: 25 Minutes

Ingredients:
- 1 lb. salmon fillets
- 1/2 tsp. pepper
- 1/4 tsp. salt
- 2 tbsp. sriracha
- 2 tsp. honey
- 2 tsp. chili sauce
- 1 tsp. lime juice

- 1/2 tsp. fish sauce

Directions:
1. Supply your smoker with wood pellets and follow the start-up procedure. Preheat the grill, with the lid closed, to 350° F.
2. Sprinkle the salmon with salt and pepper.
3. In a bowl, whisk together the sriracha, honey, chili sauce, lime juice, and fish sauce.
4. Once the grill is hot, place the salmon on the grill and leave for 15 minutes.
5. After 15 minutes, brush the salmon with the sriracha chili sauce and keep cooking for 5-10minutes. The salmon should be firm to the touch and crispy on the edges.
6. Serve hot!

Spiced Smoked Swordfish

Servings: 4
Cooking Time: 60 Minutes

Ingredients:
- 4 swordfish fillets (about 4 ounces each)
- For the brine:
- 1 gallon water
- ½ cup kosher salt
- ½ cup brown sugar
- For the rub:
- 1 tablespoon olive oil
- 1 tablespoon kosher salt
- 1 tablespoon coarse ground black pepper
- 1 tablespoon garlic powder
- 1 tablespoon onion powder

Directions:
1. Make the brine by mixing the water, salt,and sugar in a large pot and stir. Add swordfish fillets to the bowl and refrigerate overnight in the mixture.
2. Supply your smoker with wood pellets and follow the start-up procedure. Preheat the grill, with the lid closed, to 225° F.
3. Remove the fillets from the brine, rinse,and blot dry.
4. Brush a coat of olive oil on each fillet and mix salt, pepper, garlic powder,and onion powder in a small bowl for the rub. Apply the rub liberally to each fillet.

5. Put the fillets skin-side down on the smoker and cook for about 1 hour or until the internal temperature in the thickest part of the fillets reaches 145 °F.
6. Enjoy.

Grilled Salmon

Servings: 4
Cooking Time: 25 Minutes

Ingredients:
- 1 (2-pound) half salmon fillet
- 3 tablespoons mayonnaise
- 1 batch Dill Seafood Rub

Directions:
1. Supply your smoker with wood pellets and follow the start-up procedure. Preheat the grill, with the lid closed, to 325°F.
2. Using your hands, rub the salmon fillet all over with the mayonnaise and sprinkle it with the rub.
3. Place the salmon directly on the grill grate, skin-side down, and grill until its internal temperature reaches 145°F. Remove the salmon from the grill and serve immediately.

Barbecued Shrimp

Servings: 4
Cooking Time: 10 Minutes

Ingredients:
- 1 pound peeled and deveined shrimp, with tails on
- 2 tablespoons olive oil
- 1 batch Dill Seafood Rub

Directions:
1. Soak wooden skewers in water for 30 minutes.
2. Supply your smoker with wood pellets and follow the start-up procedure. Preheat the grill, with the lid closed, to 375°F.
3. Thread 4 or 5 shrimp per skewer.
4. Coat the shrimp all over with olive oil and season each side of the skewers with the rub.
5. Place the skewers directly on the grill grate and grill the shrimp for 5 minutes per side. Remove the skewers from the grill and serve immediately.

Kodiak Cakes Candied Bacon Crumble Brownies

Servings: 6
Cooking Time: 45 Minutes

Ingredients:
- 1 Box Big Bear Brownie Mix, Kodiak Cakes
- 2 eggs
- 1 Stick butter, melted
- 2 Tablespoon coconut oil
- 2 Tablespoon water
- 2 Cup cooked bacon
- 1/2 Cup Almonds, chopped
- 1/2 Cup sugar

Directions:
1. Supply your smoker with wood pellets and follow the start-up procedure. Preheat the grill, with the lid closed, to 300° F.
2. Spray an 8" baking pan with non-stick spray.
3. Empty Kodiak Cake brownie mix into a medium-size mixing bowl. Add eggs, melted butter, coconut oil, and water. Gently mix, being careful not to overmix. Pour into prepared pan.
4. Place brownies in center of grill grate; bake for 45 minutes. Grill: 300 °F
5. While the brownies are baking, begin assembling bacon crumble. Add honey or sugar to a medium-size saucepan, over high heat. Add bacon and almonds. Stir for 2-3 minutes, or until sugar has dissolved. Remove from heat and let cool.
6. Remove brownies from grill and cool completely. Sprinkle candied bacon crumble over the top of brownies. Enjoy!

Turkey Stuffing Bacon Balls

Servings: 8
Cooking Time: 25 Minutes

Ingredients:
- 1 Can Cranberry Sauce, Whole Berry (16oz) Can
- 1 jalapeño, diced
- 3 Cup Your Favorite Stuffing, Prepared According to the Package Directions, or Homemade
- 1 Cup Shredded Cooked Turkey
- 6 Slices bacon

Directions:
1. In a small saucepan, combine cranberry sauce and jalapenos. Bring to a boil over medium high heat then reduce the heat to a simmer. Cook for 4-5 minutes then remove from the heat and allow to cool.
2. Supply your smoker with wood pellets and follow the start-up procedure. Preheat the grill, with the lid closed, to 375° F.
3. Start by filling the palm of your hand with approximately 1/4 cup of the stuffing. Use your thumb to create an indentation. Fill the indentation with a heaping tablespoon of the shredded turkey and then close the stuffing all around to form into a ball.
4. Wrap the ball of stuffing with a half a piece of bacon and hold in place with a toothpick, if necessary. Repeat until all of the bombs are made.
5. When ready to cook, place the stuffing balls directly on the grill grate and cook for 25-30 minutes, turning once. The bacon should be crisp. Grill: 375 °F
6. Serve with cranberry jalapeno jelly. Enjoy!

Smoked Bologna

Servings: 4
Cooking Time: 240 Minutes

Ingredients:
- 1 Pound bologna log
- 1/4 Cup brown sugar
- 1 Tablespoon yellow mustard
- 1 Teaspoon soy sauce
- Worcestershire sauce

Directions:
1. Score the bologna log being careful not to cut too deep.
2. Mix brown sugar, mustard, soy sauce and Worcestershire sauce together.
3. Once mixed, rub it all over the bologna.

4. Supply your smoker with wood pellets and follow the start-up procedure. Preheat the grill, with the lid closed, to 225° F.

5. Smoke bologna for 3 to 4 hours. Grill: 225 ℉

6. Remove from grill and let cool.

7. Slice and serve with sandwiches. Enjoy!

Bbq Pork Short Ribs

Servings: 4
Cooking Time: 360 Minutes

Ingredients:
- 2 Pork Short Rib Racks With At Least 1 1/2-2" of Meat On Bone
- Pork & Poultry Rub

Directions:
1. Clean and trim short ribs. Season generously on all sides with Traeger Pork and Poultry rub.
2. Supply your smoker with wood pellets and follow the start-up procedure. Preheat the grill, with the lid closed, to 250° F.
3. Place ribs directly on the grill grate and cook for 4-6 hours or until the internal temperature reaches 202-204℉ when an instant read thermometer is inserted in the thickest part of meat. Spritz with apple juice every hour if desired. Grill: 250 ℉ Probe: 202 ℉
4. Remove from grill and allow to rest 10 minutes before slicing. Cut into individual ribs and serve with your favorite sides. Enjoy!

Baked Beans

Servings: 12
Cooking Time: 180 Minutes

Ingredients:
- 1 Pack Bacon
- 1/2 Cup Brown Sugar
- 1 Coca Cola, Can
- 2 Cans Mixed Beans
- 1/3 Cup Molasses
- 4 Cans Pork And Beans
- 1 Red Onion, Chopped
- 1/3 Cup Yellow Mustard

Directions:

1. Supply your smoker with wood pellets and follow the start-up procedure. Preheat the grill, with the lid closed, to 275° F.

2. Combine all the ingredients and stir until combined.

3. Smoked for 2.5 hours covered. For the last 30 minutes, smoke uncovered.

4. Serve hot. Enjoy!

Double Smoked Apple Spiral Ham

Servings: 12
Cooking Time: 150 Minutes

Ingredients:
- 1 10 lb ham spiral cut
- 1 cup apple jelly
- 1 cup raspberry chipotle BBQ sauce

Directions:
1. Supply your smoker with wood pellets and follow the start-up procedure. Preheat the grill, with the lid closed, to 275° F.
2. Remove ham from all packaging and transfer to a chicken tray, cut-side-down. Then place on a cooking tray and transfer to the smoker. Close the lid and cook for 2 hours.
3. Heat up saucepan over medium heat. Add apple jelly and stir well, until it reaches a liquid consistency.
4. Add raspberry chipotle. Stir in and bring glaze to a simmer. Leave saucepan on warm heat until ham is ready.
5. After two hours, transfer ham to a shallow aluminum pan. Apply the glaze to ham generously using a basting brush. Make sure all cracks on ham surfaceare glazed.
6. Still in a shallow pan, put ham back in smoker. Close the lid and leave to smoke for over 30 minutes.
7. Remove ham from smoker and transfer to a cutting board. Leave to rest for 10 minutes.
8. Cut along the outer seam of the ham, allowing the slices to fall away.

Classic Pulled Pork

Servings: 8-12

Cooking Time: 1200 Minutes

Ingredients:

- 1 (6- to 8-pound) bone-in pork shoulder
- 2 tablespoons yellow mustard
- 1 batch Pork Rub

Directions:

1. Supply your smoker with wood pellets and follow the start-up procedure. Preheat the grill, with the lid closed, to 225°F.

2. Coat the pork shoulder all over with mustard and season it with the rub. Using your hands, work the rub into the meat.

3. Place the shoulder on the grill grate and smoke until its internal temperature reaches 195°F.

4. Pull the shoulder from the grill and wrap it completely in aluminum foil or butcher paper. Place it in a cooler, cover the cooler, and let it rest for 1 or 2 hours.

5. Remove the pork shoulder from the cooler and unwrap it. Remove the shoulder bone and pull the pork apart using just your fingers. Serve immediately as desired. Leftovers are encouraged.

Bbq 3-2-1 St. Louis Ribs

Servings: 6

Cooking Time: 360 Minutes

Ingredients:

- 2 Rack St. Louis-style ribs
- Pork & Poultry Rub
- 1/2 Cup brown sugar, divided
- 1/3 Cup honey, divided
- 1 Cup BBQ Sauce
- BBQ Sauce

Directions:

1. If your butcher has not done so already, remove the thin silverskin membrane from the bone-side of the ribs by working the tip of a butter knife underneath the membrane over a middle bone. Use paper towels to get a firm grip, then tear the membrane off.

2. Season both sides of the ribs generously with Traeger Pork & Poultry Rub.

3. Supply your smoker with wood pellets and follow the start-up procedure. Preheat the grill, with the lid closed, to 180° F.

4. Smoke the ribs, meat-side up for 3 hours. Transfer the ribs to a rimmed baking sheet and increase the grill temperature to 225°F. Preheat the grill with the lid closed. Grill: 225 °F

5. Tear off four long sheets of heavy-duty aluminum foil. Top with a rack of ribs. Sprinkle half the brown sugar on the rack then top with half the honey. Tightly wrap the ribs with the foil to create a leak-proof pouch. Repeat with remaining rack of ribs. Grill: 225 °F

6. Return the foiled ribs to the grill, meat side down and cook for an additional two hours. Grill: 225 °F

7. Carefully remove the foil from the ribs – watch out for hot steam – and brush the ribs on both sides with your favorite Traeger BBQ sauce. Discard the foil. Arrange the ribs directly on the grill grate, bone side down and continue to grill until the sauce tightens, about 30 minutes to 60 minutes more. Let the ribs rest for a few minutes before serving. Enjoy! Grill: 225 °F

Fast Ribs

Servings: 5

Cooking Time: 240 Minutes

Ingredients:

- 1 Rack Baby Back Rib
- 1 Bottle Sweet Rib Rub

Directions:

1. Remove the ribs from their packaging and pat dry. Flip to back of ribs and score the membrane with a knife, then peel off the membrane.

2. Generously sprinkle the ribs with Sweet Rib Rub on both sides of the ribs and rub.

3. Supply your smoker with wood pellets and follow the start-up procedure. Preheat the grill, with the lid open, to 250° F. Once the smoker is ready, add the ribs and smoke for 4 hours, or until the ribs are tender and the meat is pulling away from the bone.

4. Serve and enjoy!

Smoked Stuffed Avocado Recipe

Servings: 8

Cooking Time: 30 Minutes

Ingredients:

- 6 Whole avocados
- 3 Cup leftover pulled pork
- 1 1/2 Cup Monterey Jack cheese, shredded
- 1 Cup Salsa, tomato
- 1/4 Cup cilantro, finely chopped
- 8 Whole Quail Eggs

Directions:

1. Supply your smoker with wood pellets and follow the start-up procedure. Preheat the grill, with the lid closed, to 375° F.
2. Remove the pits from the avocados, removing some avocado from the center if needed.
3. In a bowl, mix together pork, cheese, salsa and cilantro. Place pork mixture on top of avocados and place in grill. Cook for 25 minutes.
4. Take a spoon and make a divot or "nest" for the quail egg. Carefully crack the quail egg into the "nest" and cook for an additional 5 to 8 minutes or until the egg reaches desired doneness.
5. Remove from the grill and serve. Enjoy!

Roasted Pork With Balsamic Strawberry Sauce

Servings: 2

Cooking Time: 35 Minutes

Ingredients:

- 2 Pound pork tenderloin
- salt and pepper
- 2 Tablespoon dried rosemary
- 2 Tablespoon extra-virgin olive oil
- 12 Large fresh strawberries
- 1 Cup balsamic vinegar
- 4 Tablespoon sugar

Directions:

1. Supply your smoker with wood pellets and follow the start-up procedure. Preheat the grill, with the lid closed, to 350° F.
2. Rinse pork and pat dry. Sprinkle both sides with salt, pepper, and rosemary.
3. In a large Dutch oven skillet, heat oil on High until almost smoking. Add the tenderloin and sear on each side until the skin is golden brown, about 2 minutes per side.
4. Set the skillet in the Traeger and cook until pork is no longer pink and internal temperature reaches 150°F, about 20 minutes. Grill: 350 °F Probe: 150 °F
5. Remove from grill and let the pork rest for 5-10 minutes.
6. Add strawberries to the skillet over the stove on medium heat and quickly sear on both sides for less than a minute. Remove berries from the pan.
7. Add balsamic vinegar to the same pan and scrape the browned bits from the bottom.
8. Bring to a boil and then reduce heat to medium low. Add the sugar, stirring frequently. Sauce is ready when it has reduced by half and texture is thick.
9. Slice the pork and place the seared strawberries on top. Serve with a drizzle of the balsamic vinegar sauce. Enjoy!

Apple-smoked Pork Tenderloin

Servings: 4-6

Cooking Time: 300 Minutes

Ingredients:

- 2 (1-pound) pork tenderloins
- 1 batch Pork Rub

Directions:

1. Supply your smoker with wood pellets and follow the start-up procedure. Preheat the grill, with the lid closed, to 180°F.
2. Generously season the tenderloins with the rub. Using your hands, work the rub into the meat.
3. Place the tenderloins directly on the grill grate and smoke for 4 or 5 hours, until their internal temperature reaches 145°F.
4. Remove the tenderloins from the grill and let them rest for 5 to 10 minutes before thinly slicing and serving.

Bbq Pulled Coleslaw Pork Sandwiches

Servings: 12
Cooking Time: 480 Minutes

Ingredients:
- 1 Bottle Bbq Sauce
- Coleslaw, Prepared
- 12 Kaiser Rolls
- 8-10Lbs Pork Butt Roast, Bone-In
- 5 Oz Sugar
- 1 Cup Yellow Mustard

Directions:
1. Supply your smoker with wood pellets and follow the start-up procedure. Preheat the grill, with the lid open, to 225° F. While your grill is heating, remove the pork roast from its packaging and place on a cookie sheet. Rub the pork roast down with yellow mustard.
2. Mix BBQ sauce and sugar in a bowl. Rub the roast down with entire mixture, allowing time for the rub to melt into the meat.
3. Place the roast in the smoker and cook for 6 hours.
4. After 6 hours, remove the roast and double wrap in tin foil. Turn the grill up to 250°F and cook the roast for another 2 hours or until the roast is probe tender (around an internal temperature of 204°F). Let the pork butt rest in the foil for up to an hour before pulling.
5. Cut each Kaiser roll in half, mix pulled pork with some more barbecue sauce and pile on each half of roll. Top with coleslaw and green onions. Don't mix all the pulled pork with barbecue sauce so that you can use the extra pulled pork for different recipes. Serve hot and enjoy!

Stuffed Pork Crown Roast

Servings: 2-4
Cooking Time: 180 Minutes

Ingredients:
- 10 Pound Crown Roast of Pork, 12-14 ribs
- 1 Cup apple juice or cider
- 2 Tablespoon apple cider vinegar
- 2 Tablespoon Dijon mustard
- 1 Tablespoon brown sugar
- 2 Clove garlic, minced
- 2 Tablespoon Thyme or Rosemary, fresh
- 1 Teaspoon salt
- 1 Teaspoon coarse ground black pepper, divided
- 1/2 Cup olive oil
- 8 Cup Your Favorite Stuffing, Prepared According to the Package Directions, or Homemade

Directions:
1. Set the pork on a flat rack in a shallow roasting pan. Cover the end of each bone with a small piece of foil.
2. Make the marinade: Bring the apple cider to a boil over high heat and reduce by half. Remove from the heat, and whisk in the vinegar, mustard, brown sugar, garlic, thyme, and salt and pepper. Slowly whisk in the oil.
3. Using a pastry brush, apply the marinade to the roast, coating all surfaces. Cover it with plastic wrap and allow it to sit until the meat comes to room temperature, about 1 hour.
4. When ready to cook, set grill temperature to High and preheat, lid closed for 15 minutes.
5. Arrange the roasting pan with the pork on the grill grate. Roast for 30 minutes.
6. Reduce the heat to 325°F. Loosely fill the crown with the stuffing, mounding it at the top. Cover the stuffing with foil. (Alternatively, you can bake the stuffing in a separate pan alongside the roast.)
7. Roast the pork for another 1-1/2 hours. Remove the foil from the stuffing and continue to roast until the internal temperature of the meat is 150°F, about 30 minutes to an hour. Make sure the temperature probe doesn't touch bone or you will get a false reading.
8. Remove roast from grill and allow to rest for 15 minutes. Remove the foil covering the bones, but leave the butcher's string on the roast until ready to carve. Transfer to a warm platter.
9. To serve, carve between the bones. Enjoy!

Grilled Lemon Pepper Pork Tenderloin

Servings: 4
Cooking Time: 20 Minutes

Ingredients:

- 2 lemons, zested
- 1 Clove garlic, minced
- 1 Teaspoon freshly minced parsley
- 1 Teaspoon lemon juice
- 1/4 Teaspoon black pepper
- 1/2 Teaspoon kosher salt
- 2 Tablespoon olive oil
- 1 (2 lb) pork tenderloin

Directions:

1. In a small bowl, whisk together everything except the tenderloin.
2. Trim all silverskin and excess fat from the tenderloin.
3. Place pork in a large resealable bag. Pour the marinade over the tenderloin and zip closed. Transfer to the refrigerator and marinate for at least 2 hours but no more than 8.
4. Supply your smoker with wood pellets and follow the start-up procedure. Preheat the grill, with the lid closed, to 375° F.
5. Remove the tenderloin from the bag and discard the marinade.
6. When the grill is hot, place tenderloin directly on the grill grate and cook 15 to 20 minutes, flipping once halfway through until the internal temperature reaches 145°F. Grill: 375 °F Probe: 145 °F
7. Remove from the heat and let rest 5 to 10 minutes before slicing. Enjoy!

Traeger Cajun Broil

Servings: 8
Cooking Time: 60 Minutes

Ingredients:

- 2 Tablespoon olive oil
- 2 Pound red potatoes
- Old Bay Seasoning
- 6 Corn Ears, each cut into thirds
- 2 Pound smoked kielbasa sausage
- 3 Pound large shrimp with tails, deveined
- 2 Tablespoon butter

Directions:

1. Supply your smoker with wood pellets and follow the start-up procedure. Preheat the grill, with the lid closed, to 450° F.
2. Drizzle potatoes with half of the olive oil and lightly season with Old Bay seasoning. Place directly on the grill grate. Roast 20 minutes or until tender. Grill: 450 °F
3. Drizzle corn with remaining olive oil and lightly season with Old Bay seasoning. Place corn and kielbasa directly on the grill grate next to the potatoes. Roast 15 minutes. Grill: 450 °F
4. Season shrimp with Old Bay seasoning. Place shrimp directly on grill grate next to the rest of the items and cook for 10 minutes, or until bright pink and cooked through. Grill: 450 °F
5. Remove everything from the grill and transfer to a large bowl. Add butter and season with more Old Bay seasoning to taste. Toss to coat and serve immediately. Enjoy!

Bbq Pulled Pork Grilled Cheese Sandwich

Servings: 8
Cooking Time: 540 Minutes

Ingredients:

- 1 Pork Butt, bone-in, 8-10 lbs.
- 2 Tablespoon Pork & Poultry Rub
- 1 1/2 Cup apple juice
- 4 Tablespoon brown sugar
- 1 Tablespoon salt
- Sweet & Heat BBQ Sauce
- 16 Pieces White Bread
- cheddar cheese
- butter, softened

Directions:

1. Trim pork butt of all excess fat leaving 1/4-inch of the fat cap attached.

2. Combine 2 Tbsp Traeger Pork & Poultry Rub, apple juice, brown sugar and salt in a small bowl stirring until most of the sugar and salt are dissolved.

3. Inject the pork butt every square inch or so with the apple juice mixture. Season the exterior of the pork butt with remaining rub.

4. Supply your smoker with wood pellets and follow the start-up procedure. Preheat the grill, with the lid closed, to 250° F.

5. Place pork butt directly on the grill grate and cook for about 6 hours or until the internal temperature reaches 160 degrees F. Remove pork butt from grill and wrap in two layers of foil. Pour in 1/2 cup of apple juice. Secure tin foil tightly to contain the apple juice. Grill: 250 °F Probe: 160 °F

6. Increase temperature to 275 degrees F and return to grill in a pan large enough to hold the pork butt in case of leaks. Cook an additional 3 hours or until internal temperature reaches 205 degrees F. Grill: 275 °F Probe: 205 °F

7. Remove from the grill and discard the bone. Shred the pork removing any excess fat or tendons. Season with additional Traeger Pork & Poultry Rub and salt if needed. Add Traeger Sweet & Heat BBQ Sauce and mix to combine. Set pork aside.

8. For the grilled cheese sandwiches: Butter two pieces of bread and place one in a pan warmed over medium heat, butter side down. Place a slice of cheddar cheese on top of the bread and top with pulled pork. Place another slice of cheese on top of pork and finish with the other slice of bread, butter side up.

9. Cook on first side 5-7 minutes until bread is lightly browned. Flip and cook for another 5-7 minutes. Remove from heat and slice in half. Enjoy!

Jalapeño-bacon Pork Tenderloin

Servings: 4-6
Cooking Time: 150 Minutes

Ingredients:
- ¼ cup yellow mustard
- 2 (1-pound) pork tenderloins
- ¼ cup Pork Rub
- 8 ounces cream cheese, softened
- 1 cup grated Cheddar cheese
- 1 tablespoon unsalted butter, melted
- 1 tablespoon minced garlic
- 2 jalapeño peppers, seeded and diced
- 1½ pounds bacon

Directions:
1. Slather the mustard all over the pork tenderloins, then sprinkle generously with the dry rub to coat the meat.

2. Supply your smoker with wood pellets and follow the start-up procedure. Preheat, with the lid closed, to 225°F.

3. Place the tenderloins directly on the grill, close the lid, and smoke for 2 hours.

4. Remove the pork from the grill and increase the temperature to 375°F.

5. In a small bowl, combine the cream cheese, Cheddar cheese, melted butter, garlic, and jalapeños.

6. Starting from the top, slice deeply along the center of each tenderloin end to end, creating a cavity.

7. Spread half of the cream cheese mixture in the cavity of one tenderloin. Repeat with the remaining mixture and the other piece of meat.

8. Securely wrap one tenderloin with half of the bacon. Repeat with the remaining bacon and the other piece of meat.

9. Transfer the bacon-wrapped tenderloins to the grill, close the lid, and smoke for about 30 minutes, or until a meat thermometer inserted in the thickest part of the meat reads 160°F and the bacon is browned and cooked through.

10. Let the tenderloins rest for 5 to 10 minutes before slicing and serving.

Holiday Smoked Cheese Log

Servings: 8
Cooking Time: 60 Minutes

Ingredients:
- 16 Ounce cream cheese
- 3 Cup shredded cheddar cheese
- 1 Tablespoon Worcestershire sauce
- 1 Teaspoon hot sauce
- 8 Slices bacon

- 2 green onion
- 1 Cup coarsely chopped pecans

Directions:

1.   In a mixing bowl, using an electric mixer or large spoon, combine the cream cheese (room temperature) and the cheddar cheese.

2.   Add in the Worcestershire sauce and hot sauce. Mix again.

3.   Add in the cooked and crumbled bacon and chopped green onions. Mix until combined.

4.   Cover the bowl with plastic wrap and refrigerate for 4 hours or until the cheese mixture is firm enough to mold. Shape it into a log and layer the outside with the toasted pecans.

5.   Cover with plastic wrap. Freeze the cheese log overnight to make sure it doesn't get too soft while it's smoking.

6.   The next day supply your smoker with wood pellets and follow the start-up procedure. Preheat the grill, with the lid closed, to 180° F.

7.   Take the cheese log out of the freezer and unwrap. Place on a cooking sheet and smoke for 1 hour. Keep an eye on it to make sure it doesn't get too soft. Grill: 180 °F

8.   Move the cheese log to a serving tray and serve with your favorite crackers. (If the cheese is too soft, throw it in the fridge for an hour or two.)

Grilled Pork Loin

Servings: 4
Cooking Time: 30 Minutes

Ingredients:
- 2 Tablespoons Balsamic Vinegar
- 2 Cups Fresh Washed And Dried Blackberries
- ¼ Cup Seedless Blackberry Preserve
- ½ Teaspoon Dijon Mustard
- Pinch Of Kosher Salt
- 1 Tablespoon Olive Oil
- 1 Pound Silver Skin And Extra Fat Removed Pork Loin
- 2 Tablespoons Sweet Rib Rub
- 1 Tablespoon Worcestershire Sauce

Directions:

1.   Place your pork loin on a flat work surface. Trim the pork loin if necessary. Rub the tenderloin all over with olive oil until it is fully coated. Once the pork loin is completely coated, generously season all over with Sweet Rib Rub until every part of the pork loin is coated. Allow the pork tenderloin to rest at room temperature for 30 minutes.

2.   While the pork loin rests, make the blackberry sauce. In a small bowl, place a metal strainer on top combine the fresh blackberries, seedless blackberry preserves, balsamic vinegar, Worcestershire sauce, Dijon mustard, and Sweet Rib Rub. Mix well and set aside.

3.   Supply your smoker with wood pellets and follow the start-up procedure. Preheat the grill, with the lid open, to 350° F. If you're using a gas or charcoal grill, set it up for medium heat. Insert a temperature probe into the thickest part of the pork loin and smoke at 225°F for 4-5 hours, flipping once, until the pork loin is golden brown and charred in some spots, and reaches an internal temperature of 145°-165°F. Remove the pork loin from the grill and allow it to rest for 5 minutes.

4.   Slice the pork loin thinly and serve with the blackberry sauce.

Anytime Pork Roast

Servings: 6
Cooking Time: 360 Minutes

Ingredients:
- 6 (4-6 lb) pork roast
- Pork & Poultry Rub
- 1/4 Cup apple juice

Directions:

1.   Supply your smoker with wood pellets and follow the start-up procedure. Preheat the grill, with the lid closed, to 180° F.

2.   Sprinkle pork roast with Traeger Pork & Poultry Rub on all sides. Place roast in an aluminum foil pan and pour apple juice on top. Place roast in the grill and smoke the for 1 hour. Grill: 180 °F

3.   Remove roast from grill and increase Traeger temperature to 275°F and preheat, lid closed 15 minutes. Grill: 275 °F

4. Cook roast for an additional 2 hours, uncovered. After two hours, wrap pan with aluminum foil and return to grill to cook for an additional 3 hours or until the internal temperature reaches 205°F. Grill: 275 °F Probe: 205 °F

5. Allow to rest for 10 minutes before serving. Serve with roasted onions, potatoes, carrots and apples. Enjoy!

Bbq Pork Shoulder Roast With Sugar Lips Glaze

Servings: 8
Cooking Time: 540 Minutes

Ingredients:
- 1 (8-10 lb) bone-in pork butt
- 1/4 Cup Pork & Poultry Rub, divided
- 1 1/2 Cup apple juice, divided
- 4 Tablespoon brown sugar
- 1 Tablespoon salt
- 1/2 Cup apple juice
- Sugar Lips Glaze

Directions:
1. Trim pork butt of all excess fat leaving 1/4 inch of the fat cap attached.

2. Combine 2 tablespoons Traeger Pork & Poultry Rub, 1 cup apple juice, brown sugar and salt in a small bowl stirring until most of the sugar and salt are dissolved. Inject the pork butt every square inch or so with the apple juice mixture.

3. Season the exterior of the pork butt with remaining Traeger Pork & Poultry Rub.

4. Supply your smoker with wood pellets and follow the start-up procedure. Preheat the grill, with the lid closed, to 250° F.

5. Place pork butt directly on the grill grate and cook for about 6 hours or until the internal temperature reaches 160°F. Grill: 250 °F Probe: 160 °F

6. Wrap the pork butt in two layers of foil and pour in 1/2 cup of apple juice. Secure tin foil tightly to contain the apple juice.

7. Increase Traeger temperature to 275°F and return wrapped pork butt to grill in a pan large enough to hold the pork butt in case it leaks. Cook an additional 3 hours or until internal temperature reaches 195°F. Grill: 275 °F Probe: 195 °F

8. Remove from the grill and allow to rest 10 to 15 minutes. Slice the pork butt around the bone and top with Traeger Sugar Lips BBQ Sauce. Serve with your favorite sides. Enjoy!

Hickory Smoked Pork Shoulder

Servings: 7
Cooking Time: 420 Minutes

Ingredients:
- 1 Cup Apple Cider Vinegar
- 2 Tbsp Hickory Bacon Seasoning
- 5 - 6 Lbs Pork Shoulder, Bone In
- 1 Tbsp Sugar

Directions:
1. Supply your smoker with wood pellets and follow the start-up procedure. Preheat the grill, with the lid open, to 225° F. If you're using a gas or charcoal, set up your grill for low, indirect heat.

2. Rinse the pork shoulder (aka pork butt) under cold running water and make sure to pat dry the entire surface, including any small cracks and crevices.

3. Place the pork shoulder in the aluminum pan, fat side up, and sprinkle a liberal amount of Hickory Bacon seasoning over the top. You want to be very generous with the outer layer of seasoning here, making sure to coat the meat from end to end.

4. In a large bowl, pour the 1 cup of apple cider vinegar, the 2 tablespoons of Hickory Bacon, and 1 tablespoon of sugar. Mix until the sugars are completely dissolved.

5. Fill your marinade injector with the marinade and inject it deep into the meat. For even flavor, inject the marinade all over the pork shoulder at one-inch intervals. Pressing the syringe slowly will help avoid the marinade squirting out.

6. Tightly wrap aluminum foil over the top of the pan, set it on your grill, and close the lid.

7. Smoke the pork shoulder for 6-8 hours, or until the meat is tender and the internal temperature is 195°F to 200°F.

8. Remove from the grill and let it rest on a cutting board for 20-30 minutes with the aluminum foil loosely tented over the top.

9. When you're ready to serve, shred the pork shoulder, discarding any large pieces of fat.

Home-cured Picnic Ham With Mustard Caviar

Servings: 8
Cooking Time: 420 Minutes

Ingredients:

- 1 pork shoulder roast, about 5lb (2.3kg) total
- 1 cup distilled water, apple cider, or apple juice, plus more
- Mustard Caviar
- for the brine
- 1 cup kosher salt
- 5 tsp pink curing salt #1
- 1 cup light brown sugar or turbinado sugar or low-carb substitute
- ¼ cup molasses or honey
- 1 gallon (3.8 liters) distilled water, divided, plus more

Directions:

1. Trim any excess fat from the pork shoulder, leaving at least ¼ inch. Use a sharp knife to score the skin of the ham in the classic diamond pattern, making the cuts about 1 inch (2.5cm) apart, but don't penetrate the meat. (If you purchased a shoulder without skin, skip this step.)

2. In a stockpot on the stovetop over medium-high heat, make the brine by combining the salts, brown sugar, molasses, and water. Bring the mixture to a boil. Whisk to dissolve the salts and sugar. Remove the stockpot from the stovetop and let the brine cool to room temperature.

3. Submerge the pork shoulder in the brine. If it floats, place a resealable bag of ice on top. Refrigerate for 3 days.

4. Place the ham in a clean container and cover with cold water. Let the ham soak for 30 minutes. Drain and pat dry with paper towels.

5. Supply your smoker with wood pellets and follow the start-up procedure. Preheat the grill, with the lid closed, to 225° F.

6. Place the ham on the grate and grill until the internal temperature in the thickest part of the meat reaches 160°F (71°C), about 4 to 5 hours. Remove the ham from the grill. Let the ham come to room temperature. Cover and refrigerate for up to 3 days. This helps establish the ham's smokiness.

7. Preheat the grill to 325°F (163°C).

8. Transfer the ham to an aluminum foil roasting pan and add the water to the bottom of the pan. Place the pan on the grate and roast the ham until the skin is nicely browned and the internal temperature reaches 145°F (63°C), about 1½ to 2 hours.

9. Remove the ham from the grill and let rest for 10 minutes. Carve the ham and serve with the mustard caviar.

Pickle Brined Grilled Pork Chops

Servings: 4
Cooking Time: 60 Minutes

Ingredients:

- 4 pork chops
- 3 Cup Dill Pickle Brine, jar
- coarse ground black pepper, divided

Directions:

1. Put the pork chops and pickle brine in a resealable plastic bag. Refrigerate for at least 4 hours. Drain well and pat dry with paper towels.

2. Season generously with black pepper.

3. Supply your smoker with wood pellets and follow the start-up procedure. Preheat the grill, with the lid closed, to 300° F.

4. Put the chops directly on the grill grate and grill, turning once, for about 1 hour, or until the internal temperature of the chop is at least 145°F. Grill: 300 °F Probe: 145 °F

5. Let rest for 5 minutes before serving. Enjoy!

Beer Braised Pork Belly And Beef

Servings: 4
Cooking Time: 90 Minutes

Ingredients:

- 1, Dark Beer, Any Brand
- 3 Cups Broth, Beef

- 1 Tablespoon Chinese Cooking Wine (Such As Shaoxing) Or Dry Sherry Wine
- 1 Teaspoon Chinese Five Spice Powder
- 2, Smashed Garlic, Cloves
- 1 Inch Knob Ginger, Peeled And Thinly Sliced
- 1 Onion, Sliced
- 2 Pounds Pork Belly, Cut Into 1 Inch Chunks
- 2 Tablespoons Rice Wine Vinegar
- 2 Tablespoons, Dark Soy Sauce, Low Sodium
- 3 Tablespoons Sugar

Directions:

1. Place a heavy dutch oven on a stovetop over medium high heat. Add the pork belly and brown on all sides, about 5 minutes. Once the pork belly has browned, add in the onion, ginger, and garlic, and stir well.

2. Pour the beer, beef broth, soy sauce, dark soy sauce, sugar, Chinese cooking wine, rice wine vinegar, and Chinese five spice powder into the pan. Place a lid on the pan and bring it to a boil. Once it boils, remove it from the heat.

3. Supply your smoker with wood pellets and follow the start-up procedure. Preheat the grill, with the lid open, to 325° F. Place the pan of pork belly on the grill and braise for 1 ½ hours, or until the pork belly is falling apart tender and glazed.

4. Remove the pork belly from the grill and serve immediately.

Baked Honey Glazed Ham

Servings: 8
Cooking Time: 120 Minutes

Ingredients:

- 1 (6-8 lb) Snake River Farms Kurobuta Half Bone-In Ham
- 20 whole cloves
- 1 Stick butter, softened
- 1/4 Cup dark corn syrup
- 1 Cup honey, room temperature

Directions:

1. Supply your smoker with wood pellets and follow the start-up procedure. Preheat the grill, with the lid closed, to 325° F.

2. Score ham. Smear the entire ham with softened butter and stud with the whole cloves and place ham in foil-lined pan.

3. Combine the dark corn syrup and honey. Warm to combine if needed. Pour 3/4 of the glaze over ham, and bake for 1-1/2 to 2 hours on the grill or until the ham reaches 140°F. Grill: 325 °F Probe: 140 °F

4. Baste ham every 20 minutes with remaining honey glaze. Grill: 325 °F Probe: 140 °F

5. Remove from grill and let rest a few minutes.

6. Slice and serve. Enjoy!

Smoke-roasted Beer-braised Brats

Servings: 8
Cooking Time: 65 Minutes

Ingredients:

- 8 Wisconsin-style bratwursts
- low-carb beer (enough to cover the brats)
- 2 tbsp unsalted butter
- 2 large sweet onions, peeled and sliced crosswise
- 2 garlic cloves, peeled and smashed with a chef's knife
- 8 brat buns (optional)
- coarse ground mustard or German-style mustard

Directions:

1. Supply your smoker with wood pellets and follow the start-up procedure. Preheat the grill, with the lid closed, to 325° F.

2. Place the brats on the grate at a diagonal to the bars. (Don't pierce the brats or the juices will run out.) Grill until the skin is nicely browned, about 40 to 45 minutes.

3. In a Dutch oven on the stovetop over medium-high heat, bring the beer, butter, onions, and garlic to a boil. Transfer the Dutch oven to the grill.

4. Use tongs to transfer the brats to the Dutch oven and let them steep for at least 20 minutes. The brats will stay at serving temperature—160°F (71°C)—for 1 hour or more.

5. Remove the Dutch oven from the grill and serve the brats on buns (if using) with mustard.

Smoked Sausage & Potatoes

Servings: 4

Cooking Time: 50 Minutes

Ingredients:

- 2 Pound Hot Sausage Links
- 2 Pound fingerling potatoes
- 1 Tablespoon fresh thyme
- 4 Tablespoon butter

Directions:

1. Supply your smoker with wood pellets and follow the start-up procedure. Preheat the grill, with the lid closed, to 375° F.

2. Put your sausage links on the grill to get some color. This should take about 3 minutes on each side. Grill: 375 °F

3. While sausage is cooking, cut the potatoes into bite size pieces all about the same size so they cook evenly. Chop the thyme and butter, then combine all the ingredients into a Traeger cast iron skillet.

4. Pull your sausage off the grill, slice into bite size pieces and add to your cast iron.

5. Turn grill down to 275°F and put the cast iron in the grill for 45 minutes to an hour or until the potatoes are fully cooked. Grill: 275 °F

6. After 45 minutes, use a butter knife to test your potatoes by cutting into one to see if its done. To speed up cook time you can cover cast iron will a lid or foil. Serve. Enjoy!

Smoked Rendezvous Ribs

Servings: 4

Cooking Time: 120 Minutes

Ingredients:

- 1/2 Cup apple cider vinegar
- 1/2 Cup water
- 1/2 Cup BBQ Sauce
- 2 Tablespoon Pork & Poultry Rub
- 3 Rack baby back pork ribs, membrane removed
- 1 As Needed Pork & Poultry Rub

Directions:

1. In a mixing bowl, combine vinegar, water, barbecue sauce, and Traeger Pork and Poultry rub. Set the sauce and a barbecue mop or basting brush grill-side.

2. Supply your smoker with wood pellets and follow the start-up procedure. Preheat the grill, with the lid closed, to 325° F.

3. Arrange the ribs on the grill grate, meat-side up.

4. Grill for 30 minutes, then start mopping. Mop every 15 minutes. After 2 hours, check the ribs for doneness. Grill: 325 °F

5. Insert a toothpick between the bones in the center of a rack. If there is little or no resistance, the ribs are done (or close to it). If the ribs are not to your liking, continue to grill them in 30-minute increments, mopping every 15 minutes. Grill: 325 °F

6. When the ribs are done, transfer them to a cutting board and give them a final dose of the mop sauce. Sprinkle lightly with Traeger Pork and Poultry Rub.

7. Let the ribs rest for a few minutes before cutting into half slabs or individual ribs. Enjoy!

Delicious Smoked Bone-in Pork Chops

Servings: 4

Cooking Time: 90 Minutes

Ingredients:

- 1/2 Cup Apple Cider Vinegar
- 4 Pork Butt Roast, Bone-In
- 2 Tbsp Salt
- 1 Tbsp Sugar
- 4 Tablespoons Tennessee Apple Butter Seasoning
- 1/4 Cup Vinegar, Red Wine
- 1/4 Cup Water

Directions:

1. Supply your smoker with wood pellets and follow the start-up procedure. Preheat the grill, with the lid closed, to 250° F.

2. In a large mixing bowl, combine the sugar, red wine vinegar, salt, 2 tablespoons of Tennessee Apple Butter and water to create a brine for the pork chops. Whisk the brine well until the sugar, salt and Tennessee Apple Butter have dissolved.

3. Generously rub the pork chops on all sides with olive oil and season on all sides with the Tennessee Apple Butter. Make sure the meat is coated on all sides.

4. Place the pork chops in the smoker, insert a temperature probe into the thickest part of one of the pork chops, and smoke until the internal temperature reaches 145°F, or about 1 hour 30 minutes. The pork chops should have developed a good color and be juicy, but no longer be pink in the center.

5. Remove the pork chops from the smoker and allow them to rest for 5-10 minutes under tented aluminum foil, then slice along the grain and serve.

Whiskey- & Cider-brined Pork Shoulder

Servings: 8
Cooking Time: 540 Minutes

Ingredients:

- 1 bone-in pork shoulder, about 5 to 7lb (2.3 to 3.2kg)
- fresh coarsely ground black pepper
- granulated garlic
- 1 cup apple juice or apple cider
- low-carb barbecue sauce, warmed
- hamburger buns (optional)
- for the brine
- 1 gallon (3.8 liters) cold distilled water
- 1 cup coarse salt
- 1¼ cup whiskey, divided
- ½ cup light brown sugar or low-carb substitute

Directions:

1. In a large saucepot on the stovetop over medium-high heat, make the brine by bringing the water, salt, 1 cup of whiskey, and brown sugar to a boil. Stir with a long-handled wooden spoon until the salt and sugar dissolve. Let the brine cool to room temperature. Cover and cool completely in the refrigerator.

2. Submerge the pork in the brine. If it floats, place a resealable bag of ice on top. Refrigerate for 24 hours.

3. Supply your smoker with wood pellets and follow the start-up procedure. Preheat the grill, with the lid closed, to 250° F.

4. Remove the pork shoulder from the brine and pat dry with paper towels. (Discard the brine.) Season the pork with pepper and granulated garlic. Place the pork on the grate and smoke until the internal temperature reaches 165°F (74°C), about 5 hours.

5. Transfer the pork to an aluminum foil roasting pan and add the apple juice and the remaining ¼ cup of whiskey. Cover tightly with aluminum foil. Place the pan on the grate and cook the pork until the bone releases easily from the meat and the internal temperature reaches 200°F (93°C), about 3 hours more. (Be careful when lifting a corner of the foil to check on the roast because steam will escape.)

6. Remove the pan from the grill and let the pork rest for 20 minutes. Reserve the juices.

7. Wearing heatproof gloves, pull the pork into chunks. Discard the bone or any large lumps of fat. Pull the meat into shreds and transfer to a clean aluminum foil roasting pan. Moisten with the barbecue sauce or serve the sauce on the side. Stir in some of the drippings—not too much because you don't want the pork to be swimming in its juices. Serve on buns (if using).

Baby Back Ribs

Servings: 12-15
Cooking Time: 360 Minutes

Ingredients:

- 2 full slabs baby back ribs, back membranes removed
- 1 cup prepared table mustard
- 1 cup Pork Rub
- 1 cup apple juice, divided
- 1 cup packed light brown sugar, divided
- 1 cup of The Ultimate BBQ Sauce, divided

Directions:

1. Supply your smoker with wood pellets and follow the start-up procedure. Preheat, with the lid closed, to 150° to 180°F, or to the "Smoke" setting.

2. Coat the ribs with the mustard to help the rub stick and lock in moisture.

3. Generously apply the rub

4. Place the ribs directly on the grill, close the lid, and smoke for 3 hours5. Increase the temperature to 225°F.

5.   Remove the ribs from the grill and wrap each rack individually with aluminum foil, but before sealing tightly, add ½ cup apple juice and ½ cup brown sugar to each package

6.   Return the foil-wrapped ribs to the grill, close the lid, and smoke for 2 more hours.

7.   Carefully unwrap the ribs and remove the foil completely. Coat each slab with ½ cup of barbecue sauce and continue smoking with the lid closed for 30 minutes to 1 hour, or until the meat tightens and has a reddish bark. For the perfect rack, the internal temperature should be 190°F.

Pulled Pork Shoulder And Chicken

Servings: 6 - 8
Cooking Time: 300 Minutes

Ingredients:

- 1/3 Cup Apple Cider Vinegar
- 4 Cups Chicken Broth
- 1/3 Cup Ketchup
- 2 Tbsp Pulled Pork Seasoning
- 4 Lbs. Pork Shoulder, Bone In

Directions:

1.   Supply your smoker with wood pellets and follow the start-up procedure. Preheat the grill, with the lid open, to 350° F. In a bowl, combine the chicken broth, ketchup, apple cider vinegar, and 1 tablespoon of Pulled Pork Seasoning. Whisk well to combine and set aside.

2.   Generously season the pork shoulder with the remaining 3 tablespoons of Pulled Pork Seasoning on all sides of the pork shoulder, then place on the grill and sear on all sides until golden brown, about 10 minutes.

3.   Remove the pork shoulder from the grill and place in the disposable aluminum pan. Pour the chicken broth mixture over the pork shoulder. It should come about 1/3 to ½ way up the side of the pork shoulder. Cover the top of the pan tightly with aluminum foil.

4.   Reduce the temperature of your grill to 250°F. Place the foil pan on the grill and grill for four to five hours, or until the pork is tender and falling off the bone.

5.   Remove the pork from the grill and allow to cool slightly. Drain the liquid from the pan, reserving about a cup, then shred the pork and cover with the reserved liquid. Serve and enjoy!

Smoked Bacon Roses

Servings: 2
Cooking Time: 60 Minutes

Ingredients:

- 1 Pack Bacon, Thick Cut
- 1 Dozen Roses, Fake

Directions:

1.   Supply your smoker with wood pellets and follow the start-up procedure. Preheat the grill, with the lid open, to 225° F.

2.   Roll each piece of bacon tightly, starting on the thicker side of the strip. Take a toothpick and skewer the middle of the bottom of the bacon roll to keep the bacon from unraveling. With a second toothpick, skewer the bacon roll so that the two toothpicks form an "X" at the bottom of the roll of bacon. Do this to every piece of bacon.

3.   Place the bacon rolls directly on the grates of your preheated Grill and smoke for an hour, checking on them every 20 minutes.

4.   While the bacon is smoking, rip the petals of the fake roses off of the steams.

5.   Once the bacon is fully cooked, remove the toothpicks and pierce the bacon in the head of the steam (where the fake flowers once were). If the bacon isn't staying, you can break a toothpick in half and stick it in the tip of the steam, press firmly and try piercing the bacon again.

6.   Place in a nice vase with some babies breath and gift to your Valentine.

Beer-braised Cabbage With Bacon

Servings: 4
Cooking Time: 30 Minutes

Ingredients:

- 1/4 Pound Bacon, bulk unsliced
- 1 Cup yellow onion, diced
- 1 Cup Apple, diced small
- 2 Pound Cabbage, green, sliced
- salt

- ground black pepper
- 12 Ounce Beer, light

Directions:

1. Supply your smoker with wood pellets and follow the start-up procedure. Preheat the grill, with the lid closed, to 325° F.
2. On a stovetop, heat a large heavy pot or Dutch oven over medium heat. Add the bacon and cook until crisp (about 5 mins). Transfer to a plate lined with paper towels.
3. Return the pot to medium heat. Add the onion and cook for 5 minutes, or until golden brown. Add the apple, stir, then add the cabbage. Sprinkle generously with salt and a touch of black pepper and stir for 3 minutes.
4. Pour in the beer and bring to a boil over medium-high heat. Cover and move the pot immediately into the Traeger.
5. Cook at 325 degrees F (160 C) for 10 minutes. Remove lid and cook for an additional 10-15 more minutes, or until cabbage is tender and most of the liquid has evaporated. Grill: 325 °F
6. Add the reserved bacon and stir into the cabbage. Enjoy!

Bangers And Potato Mash

Servings: 6 - 8
Cooking Time: 135 Minutes

Ingredients:

- Bbq Sauce
- ¼ Cup Butter
- 3 Garlic, Cloves
- 1 Onion, Chopped
- 8 Red Potatoes, Medium
- 8 Sausages, Pork
- ½ Cup Milk

Directions:

1. Using a fork, poke holes all over every red potato.
2. Cut a whole bulb of garlic in half and set aside.
3. Supply your smoker with wood pellets and follow the start-up procedure. Preheat the grill, with the lid open, to 300° F.
4. Set the halved garlic bulb and red potatoes on the grill. Cook the garlic for 30 minutes and the potatoes for 75 minutes.
5. Turn your down to 250°F and allow it to settle to that temperature.
6. Peel and mash the potatoes and garlic with butter and milk until the desired smoothness is achieved.
7. Set the sausages on the grill and smoke for 1 hour.
8. Sauté sliced onions in a pan with butter and barbecue sauce to taste.
9. After 1 hour, remove the sausages and turn off the grill. Place the onions on top of the mash potatoes and the sausage on top of the onions. Add more BBQ sauce if you wish.

Triple Threat Pork Fattywith Stuffed Jalapeños

Servings: 10
Cooking Time: 150 Minutes

Ingredients:

- 16 strips of bacon, about 1¼lb (565g) total, not thick cut
- 1½ tsp Tajin seasoning, plus more
- 8oz (225g) light cream cheese, at room temperature
- 3 large jalapeños, decored, destemmed, and deseeded
- 1lb (450g) seasoned breakfast sausage
- 1lb (450g) ground pork
- 6 to 8oz (170 to 225g) thinly sliced pepper Jack cheese

Directions:

1. Supply your smoker with wood pellets and follow the start-up procedure. Preheat the grill, with the lid closed, to 275° F.
2. Moisten a workspace with a damp towel. Place a 15-inch (38cm) rectangle of plastic wrap on the workspace. Place 8 strips of bacon, sides touching, parallel to the edge of the plastic. Fold back the even-numbered strips at the halfway point and place a 9th snugly against the folds (perpendicular to the first 8). Unfold.
3. Fold back the odd-numbered strips and place a 10th snugly against the folds. Unfold. Repeat until the weave

is complete. Place another sheet of plastic over the weave. Use a rolling pin to thin and tighten the weave.

4. In a small bowl, combine the Tajin and cream cheese. Tightly stuff each jalapeño with the mixture. Reserve any extra filling.

5. Place the sausage and pork in a large bowl. Wet your hands with cold water and knead the meats to combine. Transfer to a resealable plastic bag. Use a rolling pin to create a rectangle that's smaller than the dimensions of your bacon weave. (For reference, place the weave alongside the bag.) Slit the sides of the bag to release the meat and then position the bag over the weave and remove the remaining plastic.

6. Cover the meat with the pepper Jack, leaving 1 inch (2.5cm) around the edges. Pipe the reserved cream cheese mixture randomly over the surface. Position the stuffed jalapeños end to end on the long side of the meat. Use the plastic under the weave to tightly roll up the fatty from the side with the jalapeños. Use bamboo skewers to secure the weave. Lightly season the outside with more Tajin seasoning.

7. Place the fatty seam side down on the grate and smoke until the internal temperature reaches 160°F (71°C), about 2 to 2½ hours.

8. Transfer the fatty to a cutting board and let rest for 10 minutes. Use an electric knife to slice the fatty into 1-inch (2.5cm) rounds before serving.

Beer Braised Garlic Bbq Pork Butt

Servings: 6-8
Cooking Time: 300 Minutes

Ingredients:

- One 12Oz Bottle Dark Beer
- 1/2 Cup Brown Sugar
- 2 Tablespoons Granulated Garlic
- 4 Tablespoons Honey
- 1 Cup Ketchup
- 1 Tablespoon Olive Oil
- Pulled Pork Rub
- 1 Pork Butt, Boneless
- 2 Tablespoons Worcestershire Sauce
- 4 Tablespoons Yellow Mustard

Directions:

1. Generously season the pork butt with Pulled Pork Rub, making sure to rub the seasoning in on all surfaces of roast. Place the pork onto a roasting rack inside a 9x13 pan.

2. Pour about half a bottle of dark beer into the bottom of the pan and save the remaining amount of beer, you'll need this later.

3. Supply your smoker with wood pellets and follow the start-up procedure. Preheat the grill, with the lid open, to high heat. If you're using a gas or charcoal, set it up for high direct heat. Place the pan in the center of the grill and grill for 30 minutes until the pork roast is dark in color and charred in some spots.

4. Remove the pork from the grill and decrease the temperature of the grill to 325°F. Set aside and began to make the BBQ sauce.

5. In a medium sized bowl, add ketchup, brown sugar, yellow mustard, honey, Worcestershire, granulated garlic, half bottle of dark beer, and finally 1 tbsp of Pulled Pork Rub. Mix together thoroughly.

6. Take the sauce and pour it over the roast, cover with aluminum foil.

7. Cook the roast for 4 - 6 hours or until the meat is falling apart tender and the bone easily comes away from the meat and reaches an internal temperature of 200°F. Remove the pork from the grill and allow it to rest for 10-15 minutes.

8. Shred the pork with meat claws or forks, discarding any fat or gristle. Toss the shredded pork with the barbecue sauce and serve immediately.

Bbq Brown Sugar Pork Belly

Servings: 8
Cooking Time: 180 Minutes

Ingredients:

- 1 (3-4 lb) pork belly
- 4 Tablespoon brown sugar
- 4 Tablespoon salt

Directions:

1. The night before you plan to cook, take your pork belly out of the fridge and pat dry with paper towels. Score fat with a very sharp knife in a diamond pattern making sure not to cut into the meat.

2. Combine salt and brown sugar and rub pork belly on all sides. Place on a drying rack on a pan and refrigerate uncovered overnight.

3. Thirty minutes before cooking, remove pork belly from fridge. Rinse under cold water and pat very dry with paper towels.

4. Supply your smoker with wood pellets and follow the start-up procedure. Preheat the grill, with the lid closed, to 450° F.

5. Place the pork belly directly on grill grate, fat side up, for 30 minutes. Grill: 500 °F

6. After 30 minutes, reduce the grill temperature to 325°F and cook for 3 hours or until pork is tender and fat is crisp. Grill: 325 °F

7. Remove from grill and allow to rest for 30 minutes before slicing.

8. Serve with baked beans, potato salad, coleslaw, white bread, BBQ sauce, or your favorite BBQ sides. Enjoy!

Fast Bbq Spare Ribs

Servings: 6
Cooking Time: 180 Minutes

Ingredients:
- 1/2 Tsp Black Pepper
- 1/4 Cup Brown Sugar
- 2 Garlic Cloves, Peeled And Smashed
- 1 Tbsp Honey
- 1/4 Cup Ketchup
- 1 Tsp Kosher Salt
- 1 Tbsp Paprika
- 1 Tbsp Parsley, Chopped
- Pulled Pork Rub
- 2 Red Bell Pepper
- 2 Scallions, Chopped
- 10 Lbs Spare Ribs, Rack
- 2 Tbsp Tamari
- 1 Tbsp Tomato Paste

Directions:
1. Supply your smoker with wood pellets and follow the start-up procedure. Preheat the grill, with the lid open, to 325° F, and pull both the side knobs out to ensure the smoking cabinet maintains a temperature of 200°F.

2. Season ribs on both sides with Pulled Pork Rub, then lay on the racks in the smoking cabinet. Smoke for 2 ½ hours.

3. Meanwhile, prepare the sauce: Brush the bell pepper with oil, season with salt, then place directly on the grill grate.

4. Open the sear slide and char over direct flame for 3 minutes, turning often.

5. Remove from the grill, and set aside to cool, then skin and remove seeds.

6. In a food processor, combine peppers, garlic, ketchup, brown sugar, scallions, tamari, honey, tomato paste, parsley, paprika, salt, and pepper.

7. Process for 3 minutes, scraping down sides once or twice. Transfer to a jar and set aside.

8. Lay out 4 large pieces of aluminum foil on a sheet tray. Remove ribs from the smoking cabinet, then lay each rack on 2 overlapping pieces of foil. Spoon sauce over each rack, then tightly close foil around the ribs.

9. Lower temperature to 275°F. Transfer to the lower grill, then cook ribs another 1 to 1 ½ hours, rotating racks half way through cooking.

10. Carefully open foil, place racks directly on grates, and cook for another 10 minutes.

11. Remove ribs from the grill, then rest for 15 minutes, before slicing. Serve warm.

Grilled Lasagna With Cold-smoked Mozzarella

Servings: 8-12
Cooking Time: 70 Minutes

Ingredients:
- 15 Oz. Ricotta Cheese
- 3 Cups Cold-Smoked Mozzarella, Grated Divided
- 2 Eggs
- 6 Garlic Cloves, Chopped
- 1 Tsp Garlic Powder
- 1 Cup Grated Parmesan Cheese, Divided
- 1 Lb. Italian Sausage
- 1 Tbsp Italian Seasoning
- 1 Pkg. "No-Bake" Lasagna Noodles

- 48 Oz. Marinara Sauce
- 1 Lb. Mozzarella Block
- 1 Tbsp Olive Oil
- 1 Tbsp Chopped Oregano
- ¼ Cup Italian Parsley, Chopped
- 1 Yellow Onion, Chopped

Directions:

1. In a glass bowl, mix together the eggs, Italian seasoning, garlic powder, ricotta cheese, ½ cup parmesan cheese, and 1 cup of smoked mozzarella, and 2 tablespoons of parsley. Cover and refrigerate for 1 hour.

2. Supply your smoker with wood pellets and follow the start-up procedure. Preheat the grill, with the lid open, to 400° F. If using a gas or charcoal grill, set it up for medium-high heat. Place a cast iron skillet on the grill grates and allow to preheat.

3. Heat olive oil in skillet, then add Italian sausage and cook for 5 minutes, then add in onion and garlic, and cook an additional 3 minutes. Remove from heat and stir in 1 tablespoon of parsley and dried oregano. Set aside and reduce grill temperature to 350° F.

4. To assemble, begin by covering the bottom of a 9x13 pan with 1 cup of sauce. For the first layer, place a single layer of uncooked noodles over the sauce, followed by ⅓ of the ricotta cheese mixture, half of the Italian sausage, 1 cup of mozzarella cheese, and 1 cup of sauce. Repeat for layer two with a single layer of uncooked lasagna noodles, ⅓ of the ricotta cheese mixture, and 1 ½ cups of sauce. Repeat for layer three with a layer of uncooked lasagna noodles, remaining ricotta mixture, remaining Italian sausage, 1 cup of sauce. For the final layer, add a layer of uncooked lasagna noodles, remaining sauce, and remaining 1 cup mozzarella plus ½ cup parmesan.

5. Transfer lasagna to grill and cook, covered with foil, for 35 minutes. Remove foil and continue cooking for 10 minutes, sprinkle with additional parmesan and parsley, if desired. Remove from grill and let stand 15 minutes before serving.

Everything Pigs In A Blanket

Servings: 4
Cooking Time: 15 Minutes

Ingredients:

- 2 Tablespoon poppy seeds
- 1 Tablespoon dried minced onion
- 2 Teaspoon garlic, minced
- 2 Tablespoon sesame seeds
- 1 Teaspoon salt
- 8 Ounce (8 oz) Can Pillsbury Original Crescent Rolls
- 1/4 Cup Dijon mustard
- 1 Large egg, beaten

Directions:

1. Supply your smoker with wood pellets and follow the start-up procedure. Preheat the grill, with the lid closed, to 350° F.

2. Mix together poppy seeds, dried minced onion, dried minced garlic, salt and sesame seeds. Set aside.

3. Cut each triangle of crescent roll dough into thirds lengthwise, making 3 small strips from each roll.

4. Brush the dough strips lightly with Dijon mustard. Put the mini hot dogs on 1 end of the dough and roll up.

5. Arrange them, seam side down, on a greased baking pan. Brush with egg wash and sprinkle with seasoning mixture.

6. Bake in Traeger until golden brown, about 12 to 15 minutes.

7. Serve with mustard or dipping sauce of your choice. Enjoy!

Braised Pork Carnitas

Servings: 6
Cooking Time: 180 Minutes

Ingredients:
- 2 Tbsp Bacon Fat Or Olive Oil
- 1 Cup Chicken Stock
- Cilantro, Chopped
- Corn Tortillas
- 3 Jalapeno Pepper, Minced
- 1 Lime, Wedges
- 2 Tbsp Pulled Pork Rub
- 3 Lbs Pork Shoulder, Boneless, Cut Into 1 ½ To 2 Inch Cubes
- Queso Fresco, Crumbled
- Red Onion, Minced

Directions:

1. Supply your smoker with wood pellets and follow the start-up procedure. Preheat the grill, with the lid open, to 300° F. If using a gas or charcoal grill, set it up for medium-low heat.

2. Season cubed pork shoulder with Pulled Pork Rub, then transfer to a cast iron Dutch oven, and add chicken stock. Transfer to center of grill with sear slide open. Bring mixture to a boil, then cover and close the sear slide. Simmer pork for 2 ½ hours, until tender.

3. Remove the lid and open the sear slide. Bring to boil and reduce liquid by half, about 15 minutes. Remove from grill and set aside.

4. Heat 1 tablespoon of bacon fat in the skillet, then use a slotted spoon to transfer the pork to the skillet. Fry pork in fat, stirring occasionally, for 8 to 10 minutes, until pork crisps up. Remove from grill.

5. Serve pork carnitas warm in fresh corn tortillas, with cilantro, red onion, jalapeño, queso fresco, and fresh lime.

Lynchburg Bacon

Servings: 4
Cooking Time: 20 Minutes

Ingredients:

- 1 Pound country-style bacon
- 1 Cup Tennessee whiskey, such as Jack Daniel's or apple juice
- 1 Tablespoon Pork & Poultry Rub
- 3/4 Cup all-purpose flour
- 1/3 Cup brown sugar
- 1 Teaspoon freshly ground black pepper

Directions:

1. Separate the bacon slices and place them into a large resealable bag.

2. Stir the Traeger Pork & Poultry Rub into the whiskey (or apple juice). Pour the whiskey over the bacon, massaging the bag to coat all the slices.

3. Set aside for at least 30 minutes.

4. On a piece of wax paper, sift together the flour, brown sugar and black pepper. Transfer to a second resealable bag.

5. Drain the bacon and add to the flour mixture a few slices at a time.

6. Shake the bag to coat each piece evenly, then arrange in a single layer on a baking pan.

7. Supply your smoker with wood pellets and follow the start-up procedure. Preheat the grill, with the lid closed, to 375° F.

8. Bake the bacon until it is golden brown and crisp, about 20 to 25 minutes. Enjoy! Grill: 375 °F

Baked Bacon Caramel Popcorn

Servings: 6
Cooking Time: 30 Minutes

Ingredients:

- 1 Pound bacon
- 1 Cup popcorn kernels
- 2 Stick unsalted butter
- 1/2 Teaspoon salt
- 2 Cup brown sugar, packed
- 1/4 Cup Kentucky bourbon
- 11 Teaspoon baking soda
- 2 Teaspoon vanilla

Directions:

1. Supply your smoker with wood pellets and follow the start-up procedure. Preheat the grill, with the lid closed, to 350° F.

2. Lay bacon strips directly on the grill grate and cook for 15 to 20 minutes or until fat is rendered and bacon is lightly browned. Remove from grill and chop into 1/2 inch pieces. Set aside. Grill: 350 °F

3. While grill is cooling, pop kernels in a popcorn maker. Place popped kernels and bacon in a large bowl and set aside.

4. In a medium saucepan over medium-high heat, combine butter, salt and sugar. Bring the mixture to a boil and cook until an instant-read thermometer reads 275°F. Immediately remove from heat and whisk in bourbon, vanilla and baking powder. Use caution because it will bubble up and release steam.

5. Reduce grill temperature to 225°F and let cool for 10 to 15 minutes. Grill: 225 °F

6. Pour caramel sauce over bacon and popcorn and toss to coat. Spread popcorn out onto a large sheet tray lined with a piece of parchment paper.

7. Place sheet tray directly on the grill grate and cook at 225°F for 15 to 20 minutes, watching closely to make sure the caramel doesn't burn. Grill: 225 °F

8. Remove from grill and pour popcorn on a counter lined with parchment paper. Let cool 30 minutes or until caramel has set. Enjoy!

Baked Pig Candy

Servings: 4
Cooking Time: 60 Minutes

Ingredients:
- 1 Pound thin sliced bacon
- 1/2 Cup maple syrup or corn syrup
- 2 Cup light brown sugar, packed
- 3 Tablespoon chipotle chile powder

Directions:

1. Supply your smoker with wood pellets and follow the start-up procedure. Preheat the grill, with the lid closed, to 250° F.

2. Place the bacon slices in a single layer on a large disposable, perforated aluminum pan. Brush each bacon slice with maple syrup. Sprinkle generously with brown sugar, then chipotle powder.

3. Place the pan on the grill and cook until the bacon has absorbed the brown sugar and is crispy, about 1 hour. Remove the bacon from the pan and place in a single layer on a wire rack set over a rimmed baking sheet. Grill: 250 °F

4. Set aside at room temperature until the surface of the bacon is dry. Refrigerate in an airtight container with parchment paper between the layers and use within 1 week. Enjoy!

Honey Pork Belly Burnt Ends

Servings: 4
Cooking Time: 270 Minutes

Ingredients:
- 2/3 Cup Bbq Sauce
- 2 Tbsp Butter, Melted
- 2 Tbsp Honey
- 2 Tbsp Olive Oil
- Blackened Sriracha Rub
- 3 Lbs Pork Belly, Skin Removed

Directions:

1. Supply your smoker with wood pellets and follow the start-up procedure. Preheat the grill, with the lid open, to 225° F. If using a gas or charcoal grill, set it up for low, indirect heat.

2. Cut pork belly into 2-inch cubes and place into a large mixing bowl.

3. Drizzle olive oil over pork belly, then generously season with Blackened Sriracha.

4. Transfer seasoned pork belly to a wire rack and place on the grill grate. Cook for 3 hours.

5. Remove the pork belly from the wire rack and transfer into a foil-lined aluminum pan or disposable foil pan.

6. Whisk together BBQ sauce, melted butter, and honey, then pour mixture over pork.

7. Toss to coat, then cover the pan with aluminum foil and return to the grill rack.

8. Cook for another 1 to 1 ½ hours, until the internal temperature reaches 200° F.

9. Remove the foil, transfer pork belly to a cast iron skillet and place in the center of the grill.

10. Open the sear slide and continue cooking for another 5 to 7 minutes, turning halfway, to crisp up the pork.

11. Remove pork belly from the grill, and serve warm.

Competition Style Bbq Pulled Pork

Servings: 8
Cooking Time: 600 Minutes

Ingredients:
- 1 (8-10 lb) bone-in pork butt
- 1 Cup Pork & Poultry Rub, divided
- 2 3/4 Cup apple juice, divided
- 1/4 Cup Butcher BBQ Pork Injection
- meat injector

Directions:

1. Supply your smoker with wood pellets and follow the start-up procedure. Preheat the grill, with the lid closed, to 225° F.

2.   While the grill heats up, trim excess fat from pork.

3.   In a small bowl, mix together half the Traeger Pork & Poultry Rub, 2 cups apple juice and butchers pork injection. Thoroughly inject pork butt throughout using an injector.

4.   Season the pork with a layer of Traeger Pork & Poultry Rub. Let pork rest for 20 minutes.

5.   Place pork on the grill and cook for 4-1/2 to 5-1/2 hours. After 4-1/2 hours, check the internal temperature of the pork. It should be between 155-165°F. If not, check again in 30 minutes. Grill: 225 °F Probe: 155 °F

6.   When the temperature reaches 155-165°F, wrap the pork in a double layer of heavy duty aluminum foil. Pour 3/4 cup reserved apple juice in a foil packet with the pork and place back on the grill.

7.   Turn the grill temperature up to 250°F and cook for another 3 to 4 hours. Check the internal temperature after 3 hours. The desired temperature is between 204°F and 206°F in the thickest part of the pork. If the pork is not to temperature, check back every 30 minutes until it reaches 204-206°F. The entire cook time should be between 8-10 hours depending on the size of the pork. Grill: 250 °F Probe: 204 °F

8.   Remove pork from grill and open the foil packet to vent for 10 minutes. Seal back up and let rest for 45 minutes to one hour.

9.   After resting, pour the liquid out of the foil and separate the fat from the broth using a fat separator. Remove the bone and pull the meat. Add 2 cups of the broth to the pulled meat. Add extra broth, if necessary, to achieve desired moisture level. Enjoy!

Pretzel Bun With Pulled Pork

Servings: 4
Cooking Time: 300 Minutes

Ingredients:
- ⅓ Cup Apple Cider Vinegar
- 1 ½ Cups Bbq Sauce, Divided
- 1 Qt. Chicken Stock
- ⅓ Cup Ketchup
- 3 Tbsp Pulled Pork Rub, Divided
- 1, 4 Lb. Pork Shoulder, Bone In
- 4 Pretzel Buns

Directions:
1.   Supply your smoker with wood pellets and follow the start-up procedure. Preheat the grill, with the lid open, to 400° F. If using a gas or charcoal grill, set it up for medium-high heat. In a bowl, combine the apple cider vinegar, chicken stock, ketchup, and 1 tablespoon of Pulled Pork Rub. Whisk well to combine and set aside.

2.   Season the pork shoulder with the remaining 2 tablespoons of Pulled Pork Seasoning on all sides of the pork shoulder, then place on the grill and sear on all sides until golden brown, about 10 minutes.

3.   Remove the pork shoulder from the grill and place in the disposable aluminum pan. Pour the sauce over the pork shoulder. It should come about 1/3 to ½ way up the side of the pork shoulder. Cover the top of the pan tightly with aluminum foil.

4.   Reduce the temperature of your grill to 250°F. Place the foil pan on the grill and cook for 4 to 5 hours, or until the pork is tender and falling off the bone.

5.   Remove the pork from the grill and allow to rest for 15 minutes. Drain the liquid from the pan, reserving about a cup, then shred the pork and cover with the reserved liquid. Set 3 ½ to 4 cups of pulled pork aside for sandwiches, and save the remaining for future use.

6.   While pork is resting, place 1 cup of BBQ sauce in a skillet and heat to simmer. Toss in reserved shredded pork. Divide pork among 4 pretzel buns, spoon additional BBQ sauce over the top and dig in!

Old-fashioned Roasted Glazed Ham

Servings: 8
Cooking Time: 60 Minutes

Ingredients:
- 1 (10 lb) fully cooked bone-in spiral cut ham
- 1 Cup pineapple juice
- 1/2 Cup brown sugar
- 1 cinnamon stick
- 14 whole cloves
- 1 Whole Pineapple, fresh
- 10 Cherries, fresh, sweet

Directions:

1. Supply your smoker with wood pellets and follow the start-up procedure. Preheat the grill, with the lid closed, to 325° F.

2. Rinse ham under cold water and pat dry with paper towel.

3. In a saucepan combine pineapple juice, brown sugar, cinnamon stick and four cloves. Bring to a boil. Reduce heat to medium low and simmer for about 15 minutes or until pineapple juice is reduced by half, thick and syrupy.

4. Brush half of the glaze onto the ham and into the folds of the cut slices. Reserve the other half of the glaze for later.

5. Cut pineapple in desired sized pieces, about 2 inch squares, then place on ham with a cherry and a clove to pin in place, repeating all over ham.

6. Put ham in a deep baking dish with fat side up. Place on the Traeger and cook for about 1-¼ hours. Grill: 325 ˚F

7. Carefully remove from Traeger and brush remaining glaze onto ham.

8. Return ham to Traeger and continue cooking for another 15 to 20 minutes, until internal temperature of ham reaches 160°F. Grill: 325 ˚F Probe: 160 ˚F

9. Allow ham to rest for 15 – 20 minutes before serving. Enjoy!

Chinese Alcoholic Bbq Pork Tenderloin

Servings: 4
Cooking Time: 30 Minutes

Ingredients:

- 14 Cup Bbq Sauce
- 2 Garlic Cloves, Minced
- 14 Cup Hoisin Sauce
- 2 Lbs Pork Tenderloin, Trimmed With Silver Skins Removed
- 1 Tbsp Sugar, Granulated
- 1 Tsp Sweet Rib Rub Seasoning
- 14 Cup Tamari
- 14 Cup White Wine

Directions:

1. In a glass measuring cup, whisk together the hoisin sauce, tamari, wine, garlic, sugar, and Sweet Rib Rub.

2. Place pork tenderloin in a resealable bag, then pour the marinade over the pork and allow to marinate in the refrigerator for 4 to 6 hours.

3. Supply your smoker with wood pellets and follow the start-up procedure. Preheat the grill, with the lid open, to 400° F. If using a gas or charcoal grill, preheat to medium-high heat.

4. Remove the pork from the marinade, then pour the marinade into a grill-safe pan.

5. Place the marinade on the grill and bring to a boil for 3 minutes. Add the BBQ sauce and simmer for 2 minutes. Remove from the grill, and set aside.

6. Place the pork on the grill and cook for 18 to 20 minutes, until an internal temperature of 145° F. Flip and baste the pork with the sauce every 3 to 5 minutes.

7. Remove the pork from the grill and allow it to rest on a cutting board for 10 minutes, prior to serving warm with additional sauce.

Sweet Smoked Country Ribs

Servings: 12-15
Cooking Time: 240 Minutes

Ingredients:

- 2 pounds country-style ribs
- 1 batch Sweet Brown Sugar Rub
- 2 tablespoons light brown sugar
- 1 cup Pepsi or other cola
- ¼ cup The Ultimate BBQ Sauce

Directions:

1. Supply your smoker with wood pellets and follow the start-up procedure. Preheat the grill, with the lid closed, to 180°F.

2. Sprinkle the ribs with the rub and use your hands to work the rub into the meat.

3. Place the ribs directly on the grill grate and smoke for 3 hours.

4. Remove the ribs from the grill and place them on enough aluminum foil to wrap them completely. Dust the brown sugar over the ribs.

5. Increase the grill's temperature to 300°F.

6. Fold in three sides of the foil around the ribs and add the cola. Fold in the last side, completely enclosing the ribs and liquid. Return the ribs to the grill and cook for 45 minutes.

7. Remove the ribs from the foil and place them on the grill grate. Baste all sides of the ribs with barbecue sauce. Cook for 15 minutes more to caramelize the sauce.

8. Remove the ribs from the grill and serve immediately.

Smoked Ham

Servings: 12-15
Cooking Time: 300 Minutes

Ingredients:
- 1 (10-pound) fresh ham, skin removed
- 2 tablespoons olive oil
- 1 batch Rosemary-Garlic Lamb Seasoning

Directions:
1. Supply your smoker with wood pellets and follow the start-up procedure. Preheat the grill, with the lid closed, to 180°F.
2. Rub the ham all over with olive oil and sprinkle it with the seasoning.
3. Place the ham directly on the grill grate and smoke for 3 hours.
4. Increase the grill's temperature to 375°F and continue to smoke the ham until its internal temperature reaches 170°F.
5. Remove the ham from the grill and let it rest for 10 minutes, before carving and serving.

Smoked Pork Spare Ribs

Servings: 8
Cooking Time: 240 Minutes

Ingredients:
- 2 Rack (6 lb) pork spare ribs, trimmed
- 3 Tablespoon Pork & Poultry Rub
- 1 Cup apple juice, cider or beer
- 9 Ounce BBQ Sauce

Directions:

1. Supply your smoker with wood pellets and follow the start-up procedure. Preheat the grill, with the lid closed, to 250° F.
2. If your butcher hasn't done so already, remove the silver-skin on the back of the ribs and trim off any excess fat.
3. Season the ribs on all sides with Traeger Pork & Poultry rub.
4. Arrange the racks of spare ribs on the grill grate, bone-side down and cook for 3 to 4 hours. After the first hour, spray the ribs with apple juice. Continue spraying every hour after that with apple juice. Grill: 250 °F
5. Start checking the temp after 2 hours. The finished internal temperature should be 203°F, about 3 to 4 hours. Grill: 250 °F Probe: 203 °F
6. When the internal temperature registers 203°F, brush the ribs on all sides with Traeger BBQ sauce of your choice. Return ribs to the grill and cook for an additional 30 to 60 minutes to tighten the sauce.
7. To serve, cut each slab in half or into individual ribs and serve with additional BBQ sauce on the side. Enjoy!

Bbq Pork Belly

Servings: 6
Cooking Time: 180 Minutes

Ingredients:
- 1 (3 lb) pork belly, skin removed
- 4 Tablespoon salt
- 1/2 Teaspoon black pepper
- Pork & Poultry Rub

Directions:
1. Supply your smoker with wood pellets and follow the start-up procedure. Preheat the grill, with the lid closed, to 275° F.
2. Meanwhile, season pork belly on both sides with salt, pepper and Traeger Pork & Poultry Rub. Place pork belly directly on the grill grate and cook for 3 to 3-1/2 hours or until the internal temperature reaches 200°F. Grill: 275 °F Probe: 200 °F
3. Remove from grill and let rest 10 to 15 minutes before slicing.
4. Serve in tacos, mac and cheese, nachos or your favorite dish. Enjoy!

Baked Candied Bacon Cinnamon Rolls

Servings: 6
Cooking Time: 35 Minutes

Ingredients:
- 12 Slices Bacon, sliced
- 1/3 Cup brown sugar
- pre-made cinnamon rolls
- 2 Ounce cream cheese

Directions:
1. Supply your smoker with wood pellets and follow the start-up procedure. Preheat the grill, with the lid closed, to 350° F.
2. Dredge 8 of the slices of bacon in brown sugar, making sure to cover both sides of the bacon.
3. Place the brown sugared bacon slices along with the other slices of bacon on a cooling rack placed on top of a large baking sheet.
4. Cook the bacon on the Traeger for 15-20 minutes or until the fat renders but bacon is still pliable. Turn the Traeger down to 325°F.
5. Open and unroll the cinnamon rolls. While bacon is still warm, place 1 slice of the brown sugared bacon on top of 1 of the unrolled rolls and roll back up. Repeat for all the rolls.
6. Place cinnamon rolls in an 8" x 8" baking dish or cake pan that has been sprayed with nonstick cooking spray. Cook the cinnamon rolls at 325°F for 10 to 15 minutes or until golden. Rotate the pan a half turn halfway through cooking time. Grill: 325 °F
7. Meanwhile, take the provided cream cheese frosting and mix in the softened cream cheese. Crumble the cooked bacon and add into the cream cheese frosting.
8. Spread frosting over warm cinnamon rolls. Serve warm, enjoy!

Smoked Rack Of Pork

Servings: 6
Cooking Time: 360 Minutes

Ingredients:
- 4 Bay Leaves
- 2 Jalapeno Peppers
- 1 Six Bone Rack Of Pork
- 1 Cup Salt
- Salt & Freshly Ground Black Pepper
- 2 Tbsp Smokey Apple Chipotle Rub
- 10 Thyme, Fresh Sprigs
- 1 Gallon Water

Directions:
1. To make the rack of pork: Combine the salt, water, bay, thyme and jalapeño in a large stock pot and bring to a boil, let boil for 10 minutes until salt is dissolved.
2. Remove from heat and let cool completely, add pork to the brine and brine overnight. Remove from the brine and rinse. Pat dry and season with Apple Chipotle seasoning and salt and pepper.
3. Supply your smoker with wood pellets and follow the start-up procedure. Preheat the grill, with the lid open, to 140° F. Place the rack of pork on the smoker with a probe inserted and cook for about 5 to 6 hours.
4. Turn the heat up to 450°F and open the heat shield.
5. Sear the pork on all sides, once seared move to a cutting board and tent with foil, rest for 20 minutes then slice in between each bone and serve.
6. To make the pickled fennel: Place the fennel in a bowl. In a small saucepan over medium low heat, add the pickling spice and toast for about 2 minutes or until fragrant.
7. Add the cider vinegar and bring to a boil over high heat. Add the sugar, salt and water and bring to a boil.
8. Cook for 10 minutes over medium high heat to meld the flavors. Strain over the fennel and set aside to cool. Once cool cover and place in the fridge until ready to use.
9. To make the caramelized sweet potato puree: In a large pan add the olive oil over high heat until the oil is shimmering, add the sweet potatoes and cook browning on all sides.
10. Once the sweet potatoes are caramelized add 1 cup of the water and cook until it has evaporated and repeat the process with the remaining water.
11. In a saucepan add the milk and the cream and warm over low heat. Once the sweet potatoes are tender add them to a blender with the milk mixture and blend until smooth but be careful not to over process and turn the potatoes into glue.

12. To make the mustard gravy: Add the olive oil to a large pan over medium high heat, once shimmering, add the shallots and cook until translucent but not browned.

13. Add the bourbon and cooked until almost entirely reduced. Add the heavy cream and the mustard and cook for about 8 to 10 minutes stirring often until the sauce thickens and coats the back of a spoon.

14. Stir in the parsley and season with salt and pepper.

15. To make the fried shallots: Place the shallots in a small bowl and cover them with the milk, let soak in the milk for at least 1 hour.

16. Drain the shallots and transfer them to a large Ziplock bag, add the flour, salt and pepper. Seal the bag and shake well to coat all the shallots in the flour. Remove from the bag shaking off the excess flour.

17. Heat the oil to 350°F in a deep pot. Fry the shallots until golden brown then remove them to a plate lined with paper towels. Season with salt.

18. To put it all together and plate: Spread the puree in a circle in the middle of the plate, place a small handful of the pickled fennel on one side of the puree, Place the pork leaning on the fennel, Spoon over the sauce and top with the fried shallots and the micro arugula.

Prosciutto Wrapped Dates With Marcona Almonds

Servings: 8
Cooking Time: 5 Minutes

Ingredients:

- 24 Whole medjool dates
- 1 Small container Marcona salted almonds
- 8 Ounce prosciutto
- 2 Tablespoon olive oil
- 2 limes, washed and dried for zesting
- honey, for serving
- flake salt, for serving

Directions:

1. Supply your smoker with wood pellets and follow the start-up procedure. Preheat the grill, with the lid closed, to 400° F.

2. Place a large cast iron pan into the grill to preheat. Using a small paring knife, cut a slit lengthwise across the top of each date. Remove the pit. Replace pits with

1 to 2 Marcona almonds, then press the dates back together with your fingers to seal.

3. Cut the prosciutto into 24 pieces lengthwise. To wrap each date, place one at the bottom of a strip of prosciutto, then roll the prosciutto around the date to cover, leaving a little bit of the date showing on each end.

4. Add 2 Tablespoons olive oil to the preheated cast iron pan. Place the dates in the pan and cook, searing the prosciutto on all sides, turning as needed, about 3 to 5 minutes total. When the prosciutto is crispy, carefully remove the pan from the grill.

5. Zest the limes over the pan so the citrus zest is absorbed into the olive oil and onto the dates. Place the dates on a serving platter. Sprinkle with flake salt, an additional drizzle of olive oil, honey and serve. Enjoy!

St Louis Style Bbq Ribs With Texas Spicy Bbq Sauce

Servings: 8
Cooking Time: 300 Minutes

Ingredients:

- 3 Rack St. Louis-style ribs, membrane removed
- 4 Tablespoon Rub
- 6 Tablespoon butter
- 1 1/2 Cup brown sugar
- 1 1/2 Cup agave
- 1 1/2 Cup Texas Spicy BBQ Sauce

Directions:

1. Supply your smoker with wood pellets and follow the start-up procedure. Preheat the grill, with the lid closed, to 250° F.

2. Season ribs with Traeger rub and place directly on grill grate rib side down or in a Traeger rib rack with the bone resting on the rack. Cook for 3 hours. Grill: 250 °F

3. Stack 2 pieces of tin foil on the table large enough to cover one rack of ribs. In the center of the foil place 3 tablespoons butter, 1/2 cup brown sugar, and 1/2 cup agave. Place the rib rack meat side down on top of the brown sugar mixture and wrap tightly. Repeat with remaining 2 racks.

4. Place all ribs directly on the grill grate meat side down and cook an additional 1-1/2 to 2 hours or until

internal temperature reaches 203°F. Grill: 250°F Probe: 203°F

5.   Remove ribs from the grill and cover each rack with 1/2 cup Texas Spicy BBQ sauce.

6.   Rewrap and return to grill an additional 10 minutes allowing sauce to thicken. Grill: 250°F

7.   Remove ribs from the grill, slice and enjoy!

Raspberry Spiral Ham With Glaze

Servings: 12
Cooking Time: 120 Minutes

Ingredients:

- 1 Ham, Spiral (Precooked)
- Raspberry Chipotle Spice Rub
- 1/2 Jar Raspberry Jam
- 1 Quart Raspberry, Fresh
- 1/4 Cup Sugar
- 1/3 Cup Water, Warm

Directions:

1.   Supply your smoker with wood pellets and follow the start-up procedure. Preheat the grill, with the lid open, to 225° F.

2.   Season the ham with Raspberry Chipotle Spice, taking care to season in between each slice. Place in your Grill and smoke for about 2 hours.

3.   Just before you pull the ham, combine glaze ingredients in a saucepan over medium heat until raspberries are no longer whole and the glaze is runny. If you want a smoother glaze, remove the raspberry seeds by draining the glaze through cheesecloth.

4.   Pour glaze over the ham just before serving. Slice and serve hot. Enjoy!

Egg Bacon French Toast Panini

Servings: 2
Cooking Time: 10 Minutes

Ingredients:

- 6 Bacon Slices
- 1 Tbsp Black Pepper
- 4 Brioche Sandwich Slices, Day Old
- 2 Tbsp Butter
- 1 Tbsp Cinnamon-Sugar
- 6 Eggs

- 1 Tbsp Heavy Cream
- 1 Tbsp Maple Syrup
- 1 Tbsp Salt

Directions:

1.   Supply your smoker with wood pellets and follow the start-up procedure. Preheat the grill, with the lid open, to 375° F. If using a gas or charcoal grill, set heat to medium heat. For all other grills, preheat cast iron skillet on grill grates.

2.   Place butter on griddle and spread to coat surface.

3.   In a pie plate, whisk together 2 eggs, heavy cream, and maple syrup.

4.   Soak both sides of bread slices in egg mixture and transfer to griddle. Cook for 2 minutes, flipping halfway until egg mixture is cooked and golden. Set aside.

5.   Lay bacon on the griddle, and cook 3 minutes per side, until golden.

6.   Transfer to lower right-hand corner of griddle to keep warm.

7.   Crack 4 eggs on top of rendered bacon fat. Season with salt and pepper. Cook 1 minute per side, or to desired doneness.

8.   Lay eggs on top of French toast, add bacon, then place the other slice of French Toast on top.

9.   Transfer back to griddle for another minute to warm, sprinkle with extra cinnamon-sugar, then slice in half and serve hot.

Hanging St. Louis-style Grilled Ribs

Servings: 4
Cooking Time: 270 Minutes

Ingredients:

- 1 1/3 Cup Apple Juice
- 1 2/3 Cup BBQ Sauce, Divided
- Pulled Pork Rub
- 4 Half Racks Spare Ribs, St. Louis Style

Directions:

1.   Supply your smoker with wood pellets and follow the start-up procedure. Preheat the grill, with the lid open, to 250° F. If using a gas or charcoal grill, set it up for low, indirect heat.

2.   Using a sharp knife, remove the back membrane from the rib racks and pat dry with paper towel. Cut rib

racks in half, then season generously with Pulled Pork Rub.

3. Insert a hanging hook under the top rib, then transfer racks to the smoking cabinet. Smoke for 2 ½ hours.

4. Remove ribs from the smoking cabinet and set on heavy duty foil. Mix together ⅔ cup BBQ sauce and ⅓ cup apple juice, then brush thinned BBQ sauce on both sides of ribs. Pour ¼ cup of apple juice around each of the ribs. Fold over foil, then transfer to the grill, meat side down. Increase temperature to 300° F and continue cooking for an additional 2 hours.

5. Remove ribs from the grill, baste with BBQ, then return to the grill and cook for another 10 to 15 minutes. Allow to rest for 15 minutes, then slice and serve hot.

Maple Syrup Bacon Wrapped Tenderloin

Servings: 5
Cooking Time: 30 Minutes

Ingredients:
- 1 Package Bacon, Thick Cut
- 1/4 Cup Maple Syrup
- 2 Tbsp Olive Oil
- 3 Tbsp Competition Smoked Rub
- 1 Trimmed With Silver Skin Removed Pork, Tenderloin

Directions:
1. Lay the strips of bacon out flat, with each strip slightly overlapping the other.
2. Sprinkle the pork tenderloin with 1 tablespoon of the Competition Smoked Rub and lay in the center.
3. Wrap with bacon over the tenderloin and tuck in the ends.
4. In a small bowl, mix the olive oil, maple syrup and remaining seasoning together and brush onto the wrapped tenderloin.
5. Supply your smoker with wood pellets and follow the start-up procedure. Preheat the grill, with the lid open, to 350° F.
6. When the grill is ready, place your tenderloin on the grill and cook, turning, for 15 minutes.

7. Increase the grill temperature to 400°F and grill for another 15 minutes or until the internal temperature is 145°F. Serve and enjoy!

Beer Pork Belly Chili Con Carne

Servings: 4
Cooking Time: 120 Minutes

Ingredients:
- Avocado, Diced
- 2 Bay Leaves
- 1 Lbs Beef Stew Meat
- 12 Oz Beef Stock
- 12 Oz Beer, Bottle
- 15 Oz Black Beans, Rinsed And Drained
- 3 Tbsp Chili Powder
- Cilantro, Chopped
- 1 Tsp Coriander, Ground
- 2 Tsp Cumin, Ground
- 1 Tbsp Flour
- 4 Garlic Cloves, Minced
- 2 Tsp Mexican Oregano, Dried
- 2 Tbsp Olive Oil
- 2 Oz Pancetta, Diced
- Pork Belly, Cut Into 1 Inch Chunks
- 2 Red Onion, Chopped
- Rice, Cooked
- To Taste, Salt & Pepper
- Scallion, Sliced Thin
- 1/4 Cup Tomato Purée

Directions:
1. Supply your smoker with wood pellets and follow the start-up procedure. Preheat the grill, with the lid open, to 425° F. If using a gas or charcoal grill, set it up for medium-high heat. Place Dutch oven on grill and allow to preheat.
2. Heat the olive oil in the Dutch oven, then sauté the pancetta until crisp. Add the onions and sauté for 3 minutes, then add the garlic and sauté 1 minute, until fragrant. Remove mixture with a slotted spoon and set aside.
3. Add the pork belly and beef to the pot to brown, then add the chili powder, cumin, oregano, and

coriander. Add the flour and cook for 2 minutes, stirring constantly.

4. Add the beer, beef stock, and tomato purée. Stir well, then return the pancetta mixture to the pot. Add the black beans and bay leaves, then season with salt and pepper.

5. Bring chili to a simmer, then reduce temperature to 325°F and simmer, uncovered, for 2 hours, stirring occasionally, until meat is tender, and sauce has thickened.

6. Remove the chili from the grill, then serve warm with cooked rice, avocado, fresh cilantro, and scallions.

Cocoa-crusted Pork Tenderloin

Servings: 4
Cooking Time: 25 Minutes

Ingredients:
- 1 pork tenderloin
- 1/2 Teaspoon Fennel, ground
- 2 Teaspoon unsweetened cocoa powder
- 1 Teaspoon smoked paprika
- 1/2 Teaspoon kosher salt
- 1/2 Teaspoon black pepper
- 1 Tablespoon extra-virgin olive oil
- 3 green onions, thinly sliced

Directions:
1. With a paring knife, remove the silver skin and connective tissue from the loin. In a small mixing bowl, combine the remaining ingredients, making paste. Rub the paste on the pork loin, and refrigerate for 30 minutes.
2. Supply your smoker with wood pellets and follow the start-up procedure. Preheat the grill, with the lid closed, to 450° F.
3. Place the loin on the front of the grill and sear it on all sides. After it has been seared, reduce the temperature to 350°F and move the pork to the center of the grill. Grill: 350 °F
4. Continue to cook for 10- 15 minutes, or until it has reached an internal meat temp of 145°F for medium to medium well. Probe: 145 °F
5. Once it has cooked, remove it from the grill and let rest for at least 8 to 10 minutes before slicing. Garnish with green onions. Enjoy!

Bacon Weave Smoked Country Sausage

Servings: 4
Cooking Time: 120 Minutes

Ingredients:
- Pound Sausage, Uncooked
- Pork & Poultry Rub
- 8 Slices bacon

Directions:
1. Using your hands, form sausage into a loaf-shape. Season lightly with Traeger Pork and Poultry Shake.
2. Supply your smoker with wood pellets and follow the start-up procedure. Preheat the grill, with the lid closed, to 180° F.
3. Put the sausage loaf directly on the grill grate and smoke for 1-1/2 hours.
4. While sausage is smoking, assemble the bacon weave on a piece of wax paper. First, lay out 4 pieces of bacon so they are touching each other on the wax paper. Next, lay the 5th piece of bacon so it crosses the others. Tuck every other slice under the 5th piece of bacon. Find the two pieces of bacon that were under the 5th piece of bacon and fold them back on top of themselves.
5. Lay down the 6th piece of bacon and unfold the two that were laid back. Continue folding the bacon back that was most recently under the last piece of bacon, two pieces at a time, laying the next piece of bacon on top until your weave is complete. Set aside. After your sausage has smoked for 1-1/2 hours, take it off the grill and increase the heat of your Traeger, lid closed to 350°F and preheat. Grill: 350 °F
6. While the grill is heating, wrap your sausage loaf in the bacon weave. Lay the middle of the weave directly on top of the sausage loaf and press the bacon all around the sausage.
7. Flip the sausage and bacon over to finish the weave on the bottom of the sausage. Alternate the bacon ends across the bottom and tuck the ends around each other.
8. Put your sausage back on the grill and cook for 25-30 minutes until the internal temperature of the sausage reaches 160°F. Enjoy! Probe: 160 °F

Savory Pork Belly Banh Mi

Servings: 4
Cooking Time: 420 Minutes

Ingredients:

- 2 Carrots, Sliced
- 1 Tbsp Cilantro, Minced
- 1 Tbsp Honey
- 2 Kirby Cucumbers, Sliced Thin
- 1 Lime, Zest & Juice
- 2 Tbsp Pickling Spice
- 1 Tbsp Ponzu
- 2 Lbs Pork Belly
- 1 Cup Rice Wine Vinegar
- 2 Tbsp Salt
- 4 Sandwich Buns
- 1 Small Daikon Radish, Sliced Thin
- To Taste, Smoky Salt & Cracked Pepper Rub
- 2 Tbsp Soy Sauce
- 1/2 Cup Sriracha Hot Sauce
- 4 Cloves Star Anise
- 1/2 Cup Sugar
- 1 Cup Water

Directions:

1. 30 minutes before you plan to put the belly on the smoker season liberally with the Smoky Salt and Cracked Pepper rub.

2. Supply your smoker with wood pellets and follow the start-up procedure. Preheat the grill, with the lid open, to 240° F. If using a gas or charcoal grill, set it up for low, indirect heat.

3. Place the belly on the smoker with a tin pan underneath the meat to catch the drippings. Smoke for 7 hours or until you reach an internal temp of 195 degrees. Remove the pork and let rest for 30 minutes.

4. Make the homemade pickles: Place pickling spice and star anise in a small sauce pan and toast. Once fragrant add vinegar and bring to a boil, cook for 3 minutes. Add the water, sugar, and salt and return to a boil, cook for 5 minutes. Strain the liquid and immediately pour over the vegetables, making sure the vegetables are submerged. Set in the fridge once cool.

5. Make the Sriracha Lime Sauce: Combine the sriracha, lime, soy sauce, honey, cilantro and ponzu in a mixing bowl and whisk until combined.

6. Assemble the sandwiches, placing sliced pork belly and homemade pickles on a roll before topping it with the sriracha lime sauce.

Brown Sugar And Bacon Wrapped Lil Smokies

Servings: 6
Cooking Time: 30 Minutes

Ingredients:

- 1 Pound bacon
- 1 (14 oz) cocktail sausages
- 1/2 Cup brown sugar

Directions:

1. Lay strips of bacon out on a clean, flat surface. Roll out bacon strips using a rolling pin, so they are a bit longer with even thickness. Cut bacon strips in half.

2. Wrap each sausage in a 1/2 strip of bacon and secure with a toothpick. Place the bacon-wrapped sausages in a casserole dish in a single layer and cover with brown sugar.

3. Transfer to the fridge and let sit for 30 minutes.

4. Supply your smoker with wood pellets and follow the start-up procedure. Preheat the grill, with the lid closed, to 350° F.

5. Lay the sausages out on a parchment lined sheet tray and place the sheet directly on the grill grate.

6. Cook for 25 to 30 minutes until the bacon is crispy. Enjoy! Grill: 350 °F

Pork Tenderloin

Servings: 2
Cooking Time: 15 Minutes

Ingredients:

- 1 Pound pork tenderloin
- 1/3 Cup Kentucky bourbon or apple juice
- 1/4 Cup low sodium soy sauce
- 1/4 Cup brown sugar, packed
- 2 Tablespoon Dijon mustard
- 2 Teaspoon Worcestershire sauce

- 1 Teaspoon ground black pepper
- 1 Medium onion, chopped
- 2 Clove garlic, minced

Directions:

1. Trim any silverskin from the tenderloins with a sharp knife. Place meat in a large resealable plastic bag.

2. For the marinade: In a small mixing bowl or resealable bag, combine the bourbon, soy sauce, brown sugar, mustard, Worcestershire sauce and pepper, whisk to mix. Stir in the onion and garlic. Pour over the tenderloins and refrigerate for 8 hours or overnight.

3. Supply your smoker with wood pellets and follow the start-up procedure. Preheat the grill, with the lid closed, to 400° F.

4. Remove the pork from the marinade and scrape off any solid ingredients (onion or bits of garlic). Discard the marinade.

5. Arrange the tenderloins on the grill grate and grill for 6 to 8 minutes per side or until the internal temperature is 145°F. The pork will still be slightly pink in the center. If you prefer your pork well-done, cook it to 160°F. Grill: 400 °F Probe: 145 °F

6. Transfer the tenderloins to a cutting board. Let rest for several minutes before carving on a diagonal into 1/2 inch slices. Enjoy!

Bacon Stuffed Onion Rings

Servings: 6
Cooking Time: 120 Minutes

Ingredients:
- 1 Pack Bacon
- 2 White Onions

Directions:

1. Supply your smoker with wood pellets and follow the start-up procedure. Preheat the grill, with the lid open, to 250° F.

2. Peel each onion and cut into thirds, separating the onion slices into rings. Using two slices of bacon, wrap around the onion ring until the ring is fully covered, securing in place with a toothpick. Continue until all the bacon is used up.

3. Place the onion rings on the and smoke until the bacon is cooked, about 120 minutes.

Pickled-pepper Pork Chops

Servings: 4
Cooking Time: 50 Minutes

Ingredients:
- 4 (1-inch-thick) pork chops
- ½ cup pickled jalapeño juice or pickle juice
- ¼ cup chopped pickled (jarred) jalapeño pepper slices
- ¼ cup chopped roasted red peppers
- ¼ cup canned diced tomatoes, well-drained
- ¼ cup chopped scallions
- 2 teaspoons poultry seasoning
- 2 teaspoons salt
- 2 teaspoons freshly ground black pepper

Directions:

1. Pour the jalapeño juice into a large container with a lid. Add the pork chops, cover, and marinate in the refrigerator for at least 4 hours or overnight, supplementing with or substituting pickle juice as desired.

2. In a small bowl, combine the chopped pickled jalapeños, roasted red peppers, tomatoes, scallions, and poultry seasoning to make a relish. Set aside.

3. Remove the pork chops from the marinade and shake off any excess. Discard the marinade. Season both sides of the chops with the salt and pepper.

4. Supply your smoker with wood pellets and follow the start-up procedure. Preheat, with the lid closed, to 325°F.

5. To serve, divide the chops among plates and top with the pickled pepper relish.

VEGETABLES RECIPES

Steak Fries With Horseradish Creme

Servings: 6
Cooking Time: 25 Minutes

Ingredients:
- 5 Potatoes, Baking
- 2 Tablespoon extra-virgin olive oil
- 1 Teaspoon butter
- 3 Clove garlic, crushed
- 1 Teaspoon onion powder
- 2 Teaspoon Jacobsen Salt Co. Pure Kosher Sea Salt
- 1 Teaspoon black pepper

Directions:
1. Wash the potatoes thoroughly, and cut them in eighths, then toss them in the olive oil, butter, crushed garlic, onion powder, salt, and pepper.
2. Supply your smoker with wood pellets and follow the start-up procedure. Preheat the grill, with the lid closed, to 450° F.
3. In order to get great grill marks, line up the wedges on the front of the grill and the back of the grill, turning to get grill marks on all sides.
4. Once they have been seared, move them to the center of the grill and finish cooking about ten more minutes, serve hot with the horseradish mayo. Enjoy!

Grilled Cabbage Steaks With Warm Bacon Vinaigrette

Servings: 4
Cooking Time: 10 Minutes

Ingredients:
- 3 Strips thick-cut lean bacon, cut into 1/4 inch strips
- 1 Large shallot, minced
- 2 Tablespoon sherry vinegar
- 1 Tablespoon whole grain mustard
- 1 Teaspoon chopped thyme
- 2 Tablespoon olive oil, plus more as needed
- 1 Head green cabbage, cut into 3/4 inch thick slices (about 6 steaks)
- salt and pepper

Directions:
1. Supply your smoker with wood pellets and follow the start-up procedure. Preheat the grill, with the lid closed, to 450° F.
2. For the Vinaigrette: In a large skillet, cook the bacon in 2 tablespoons olive oil over medium-high heat until browned and crisp. Remove bacon from heat and stir in the shallot, vinegar, mustard and thyme then set aside.
3. Brush cabbage steaks with olive oil and season with salt and pepper. Place cabbage steaks directly on grill grate and grill for 5 minutes per side. Grill: 450 °F
4. Remove cabbage steaks from grill and drizzle with bacon vinaigrette. Enjoy!

Roasted Pumpkin Seeds

Servings: 8
Cooking Time: 40 Minutes

Ingredients:
- 1 Whole Pumpkin, seeds
- olive oil or vegetable oil
- Jacobsen Salt Co. Pure Kosher Sea Salt

Directions:
1. As soon as possible after removing the seeds from the pumpkin, rinse pumpkin seeds under cold water in a colander and pick out the pulp and strings.
2. Place the pumpkin seeds in a single layer on an oiled baking sheet, stirring to coat. Supply your smoker with wood pellets and follow the start-up procedure. Preheat the grill, with the lid closed, to 180° F.
3. Place the baking sheet with the seeds on the grill grate, close the lid, and smoke for 20 minutes. Grill: 180 °F
4. Sprinkle your seeds with salt and turn the temperature on your grill up to 325°F. Roast the seeds until toasted, about 20 minutes. Check and stir seeds after the first 10 minutes. Grill: 325 °F
5. Seeds will be brown because they were smoked before being roasted. Enjoy!

Traeger Grilled Whole Corn

Servings: 4

Cooking Time: 25 Minutes

Ingredients:

- 3 green onions
- 6 Tablespoon butter, softened
- 1 Teaspoon chile powder
- 1 Teaspoon toasted sesame seeds
- 4 ears corn, in husk

Directions:

1. Supply your smoker with wood pellets and follow the start-up procedure. Preheat the grill, with the lid closed, to 325° F.

2. Place green onions directly on the grill grate and cook 15 minutes until lightly charred. Remove from grill and set aside.

3. Sesame-Chile Butter: Take butter out of fridge and let soften. Chop up charred green onions and add to butter along with chile powder and sesame seeds. Mash all ingredients together.

4. Grill corn, rotating occasionally, until husks are blackened (some will flake and fall off) and kernels are tender with some browned and charred spots, about 25 to 35 minutes. Grill: 325 °F

5. Let corn cool slightly, then shuck. Serve with the Sesame-Chile Butter. Enjoy

Stuffed Jalapenos

Servings: 8

Cooking Time: 60 Minutes

Ingredients:

- 40 Whole jalapeño
- 8 Ounce cream cheese, room temperature
- 1 Cup Sharp Cheddar Grated
- 1 1/2 Teaspoon Pork & Poultry Rub
- 2 Tablespoon sour cream
- 1 Whole (14 oz) cocktail sausages
- 20 Whole Slices of Smoked Bacon, Cut in Half

Directions:

1. Wash and dry the peppers. Cut the stem ends off with a paring knife, and using the same knife or a small metal spoon, carefully scrape the seeds and ribs out of each pepper. Set aside.

2. In a small bowl, combine the cream cheese, grated cheese, Traeger Pork and Poultry Rub, and the sour cream.

3. Transfer the mixture to a sturdy resealable plastic bag and trim 1/2-inch off one of the lower corners with a scissors. Squeeze the cream cheese mixture into each pepper, filling each a little over the halfway point.

4. Stuff one sausage into each pepper. Wrap the outside of each with a piece of bacon, securing with 1 or 2 toothpicks.

5. Arrange the peppers on a foil-lined baking sheet. Supply your smoker with wood pellets and follow the start-up procedure. Preheat the grill, with the lid closed, to 180° F, and smoke the peppers for 1 to 1-1/2 hours.

6. Increase the heat to 350 degrees F and continue to cook for 20 to 30 minutes, or until the bacon begins to render its fat and crisp. Enjoy! Grill: 350 °F

Sicilian Stuffed Mushrooms

Servings: 6

Cooking Time: 25 Minutes

Ingredients:

- 12 Medium Fresh Mushrooms, about 1-1/2 inches in diameter
- 4 Ounce cream cheese, room temperature
- 1/4 Cup Parmesan cheese, grated
- 1/4 Cup shredded mozzarella cheese
- 8 Whole Pimento Stuffed Green Olives, chopped
- 3 Tablespoon Pepperoni, finely diced
- 1 1/2 Tablespoon Sun Dried Tomatoes, drained & minced
- 1/4 Teaspoon freshly ground black pepper

Directions:

1. Dampen a paper towel and wipe the outside of the mushrooms clean. Remove the stem. Using a small spoon, scoop out the inside of the mushroom leaving a shell.

2. Filling: In a small mixing bowl, beat together the cream cheese, Parmesan, and mozzarella. Stir in olives, pepperoni, tomatoes, basil, and pepper.

3. Mound the filling in the mushroom caps. Set each filled cap into the well of a muffin tin.

4. Supply your smoker with wood pellets and follow the start-up procedure. Preheat the grill, with the lid closed, to 350° F.

5. Arrange the muffin tin on the grill grate and bake the mushrooms for 25 to 30 minutes, or until the mushrooms are tender and the filling is beginning to brown.

6. Transfer to a serving plate or platter. Enjoy!

Roasted Tomatoes

Servings: 2
Cooking Time: 180 Minutes

Ingredients:
- 3 Large ripe tomatoes
- 1/2 Tablespoon kosher salt
- 1 Teaspoon coarse ground black pepper
- 1/4 Teaspoon sugar
- 1/4 Teaspoon thyme or basil
- olive oil

Directions:
1. Line a rimmed baking sheet with parchment paper.
2. Supply your smoker with wood pellets and follow the start-up procedure. Preheat the grill, with the lid closed, to 225° F.
3. Remove the stem end from each tomato and cut the tomatoes into 1/2 inch thick slices.
4. Combine the salt, pepper, sugar and thyme or basil in a small bowl and mix.
5. Pour olive oil into the well of a dinner plate.
6. Dip one side of each tomato slice in the olive oil and arrange on the baking sheet. Dust the tomato slices with the seasoning mixture.
7. Arrange the pan directly on the grill grate and roast the tomatoes until the juices stop running and the edges have contracted, about 3 hours. Remove from grill and enjoy!

Carolina Baked Beans

Servings: 12-15
Cooking Time: 180 Minutes

Ingredients:
- 3 (28-ounce) cans baked beans (I like Bush's brand)
- 1 large onion, finely chopped
- 1 cup The Ultimate BBQ Sauce
- ½ cup light brown sugar
- ¼ cup Worcestershire sauce
- 3 tablespoons yellow mustard
- Nonstick cooking spray or butter, for greasing
- 1 large bell pepper, cut into thin rings
- ½ pound thick-cut bacon, partially cooked and cut into quarters

Directions:
1. Supply your smoker with wood pellets and follow the start-up procedure. Preheat, with the lid closed, to 300°F.
2. In a large mixing bowl, stir together the beans, onion, barbecue sauce, brown sugar, Worcestershire sauce, and mustard until well combined
3. Coat a 9-by-13-inch aluminum pan with cooking spray or butter.
4. Pour the beans into the pan and top with the bell pepper rings and bacon pieces, pressing them down slightly into the sauce.
5. Place a layer of heavy-duty foil on the grill grate to catch drips, and place the pan on top of the foil. Close the lid and cook for 2 hours 30 minutes to 3 hours, or until the beans are hot, thick, and bubbly.
6. Let the beans rest for 5 minutes before serving.

Baked Sweet Potatoes

Servings: 8
Cooking Time: 60 Minutes

Ingredients:
- 1 Cup butter, softened
- 1/4 Cup pure maple syrup
- 1/2 Teaspoon ground cinnamon
- 8 Medium sweet potatoes

Directions:
1. Make the Maple-Cinnamon Butter: In a mixing bowl, combine the butter, maple syrup, and cinnamon and whip with a wooden spoon. (Alternatively, blend the ingredients using a hand-held mixer or a stand mixer.) Transfer to a small bowl, cover, and chill until serving time.

2. Supply your smoker with wood pellets and follow the start-up procedure. Preheat the grill, with the lid closed, to 375° F. Arrange the sweet potatoes on the grill grate and bake until soft, 1 to 1-1/2 hours, depending on the size of the potatoes. Make a slit in the side of each, and squeeze the ends gently to fluff.

3. Serve hot with the Maple-Cinnamon Butter. Enjoy!

Traeger Baked Potato Torte

Servings: 6
Cooking Time: 25 Minutes

Ingredients:
- 6 Yukon Gold potatoes, sliced 1/4 inch thick
- 2 Stick butter, melted
- 3 Clove garlic, crushed
- 2 Tablespoon rosemary, chopped
- 1 Cup Parmesan cheese, grated
- salt and pepper

Directions:
1. Supply your smoker with wood pellets and follow the start-up procedure. Preheat the grill, with the lid closed, to 375° F.
2. While the Traeger is heating up, peel and slice the potatoes (make sure to put them in water so they will not oxidize). Melt the butter and combine it with the crushed garlic.
3. Grease a 12" cast iron pan with butter and start to layer the torte. The layers should go as follows, potatoes, butter garlic mixture, rosemary, parmesan, continue layering to the top of the pan, about 4 to 5 layers.
4. Place the pan in the Traeger and bake for 20 to 25 minutes, or until the potatoes are fully cooked. If the top of the torte starts to darken before it is finished cooking, reduce the heat to 325°F. Serve hot and enjoy! Grill: 375 °F

Grilled Asparagus And Spinach Salad

Servings: 8
Cooking Time: 10 Minutes

Ingredients:
- 4 Fluid Ounce apple cider vinegar
- 8 Fluid Ounce Honey Bourbon BBQ Sauce
- 2 Bunch asparagus, ends trimmed
- 3 Fluid Ounce extra-virgin olive oil
- 2 Ounce Beef Rub
- 24 Ounce Spinach, fresh
- 4 Ounce candied pecans
- 4 Ounce feta cheese

Directions:
1. Combine apple cider vinegar and Traeger Apricot BBQ Sauce to create salad dressing.
2. Supply your smoker with wood pellets and follow the start-up procedure. Preheat the grill, with the lid closed, to High heat.
3. Toss the asparagus with Olive Oil and the Beef Shake. Put asparagus in the Traeger Grilling Basket and move the basket to the grill grate.
4. Grill for about 10 minutes. Remove the asparagus once it is cooked. Grill: 350 °F
5. Place the hot asparagus right on top of the bowl of spinach.
6. Add candied pecans, feta cheese & salad dressing then toss and serve. Enjoy!

Baked Loaded Tater Tots

Servings: 6
Cooking Time: 35 Minutes

Ingredients:
- 2 Pound frozen tater tots
- 1 Can Black Beans
- 1 1/2 Cup leftover chili
- 1 Cup leftover queso
- 1 red onion, finely diced
- 1/2 Cup chopped cilantro
- 1/2 Cup sour cream
- 1 jalapeños, sliced

Directions:
1. Supply your smoker with wood pellets and follow the start-up procedure. Preheat the grill, with the lid closed, to 375° F.
2. Spread frozen tots out on a sheet tray and place directly on the grill grate.
3. Cook for 20 to 25 minutes or until tots are crispy. Grill: 375 °F
4. Top with warmed chili, queso and beans. Place back on the grill for 15 minutes. Grill: 375 °F
5. Remove from grill and top with red onion, cilantro, sour cream and jalapeño. Enjoy!

Roasted Garlic Herb Fries

Servings: 4
Cooking Time: 45 Minutes

Ingredients:

- 4 Whole russet potatoes
- 1 Teaspoon salt
- 2 Tablespoon avocado oil
- 1 Teaspoon fresh chopped rosemary
- 1 Teaspoon fresh chopped thyme
- 2 Clove garlic, minced
- 2 Teaspoon flake salt
- 1 Teaspoon chopped parsley, for garnish

Directions:

1. Supply your smoker with wood pellets and follow the start-up procedure. Preheat the grill, with the lid closed, to 425° F.

2. Chop potatoes into fries, (a mandolin works great for this) and place directly into an ice water bath with 1 teaspoon salt for 15 to 30 minutes.

3. Combine oil, rosemary, thyme and garlic in a big bowl. Remove potatoes from ice water and dry thoroughly with paper towels.

4. Toss potatoes in the oil mixture and place them on 2 to 3 parchment-lined baking sheets in a single layer. Sprinkle the flake salt over the fries.

5. Place baking sheets on the grill and roast for 30 minutes, flip the fries, then cook for an additional 15 minutes until golden and crispy. Dust with parsley. Grill: 425 °F

6. Serve with your favorite dipping sauce, side dish or as a nacho base.

Grilled Ratatouille Salad

Servings: 4
Cooking Time: 25 Minutes

Ingredients:

- 1 Whole sweet potatoes
- 1 Whole red onion, diced
- 1 Whole zucchini
- 1 Whole Squash
- 1 Large Tomato, diced
- vegetable oil
- salt and pepper

Directions:

1. Supply your smoker with wood pellets and follow the start-up procedure. Preheat the grill, with the lid closed, to High heat.

2. Slice all vegetables to a ¼ inch thickness.

3. Lightly brush each vegetable with oil and season with Traeger's Veggie Shake or salt and pepper.

4. Place sweet potato, onion, zucchini, and squash on grill grate and grill for 20 minutes or until tender, turn halfway through.

5. Add tomato slices to the grill during the last 5 minutes of cooking time.

6. For presentation, alternate vegetables while layering them vertically. Enjoy!

Baked Sweet Potato Casserole With Marshmallow Fluff

Servings: 6
Cooking Time: 60 Minutes

Ingredients:

- 3 Pound sweet potatoes
- 1/2 Cup milk
- 1 Cup brown sugar
- 3 eggs
- 4 Tablespoon butter
- 1/2 Teaspoon salt
- 3 egg white
- 1 Pinch salt
- 1 Pinch ground cinnamon

Directions:

1. Supply your smoker with wood pellets and follow the start-up procedure. Preheat the grill, with the lid closed, to 375° F.

2. Rinse, dry and pierce the sweet potatoes and place in grill whole. Cook for 45 minutes or until fork tender. Remove from grill and peel. Grill: 375 °F

3. Once peeled, mash the sweet potatoes in a large bowl with the milk, brown sugar, eggs, butter and salt. Place mashed potatoes in a baking dish and cook for 35 minutes. Grill: 375 °F

4. While the potatoes bake, make the fluff. Make a double boiler by bringing a small pot of water to a

simmer, then placing the bowl of your stand mixer or another large stainless steel bowl atop the water.

5.   Add the 3 egg whites, 2/3 cup brown sugar, a pinch of salt and a pinch of cinnamon to the bowl and whisk continuously until the sugar dissolves and the liquid is warm to the touch.

6.   Transfer the bowl from the stovetop to your stand mixer and use the whisk attachment to whip the whites on medium-high speed until it turns glossy with stiff peaks, about 5-8 minutes.

7.   Once the casserole has finished baking, use a rubber spatula to cover the sweet potato mixture with the fluff. Use the back of the spatula to create dramatic peaks.

8.   Return to the grill for 5-7 minutes, or until the fluff starts to turn golden and the peaks are just shy of burnt. Remove from grill and enjoy!

Roasted Fall Vegetables

Servings: 6
Cooking Time: 30 Minutes

Ingredients:
- 1/2 Pound Potatoes, new
- 2 Tablespoon olive oil
- salt and pepper
- 1/2 Pound Butternut Squash, diced
- 1/2 Pound fresh Brussels sprouts
- 1 Pint mushrooms, sliced

Directions:
1.   Supply your smoker with wood pellets and follow the start-up procedure. Preheat the grill, with the lid closed, to 200° F.

2.   Toss potatoes and squash with olive oil, salt and pepper and spread out on a sheet tray.

3.   Place directly on the grill grate and cook for 15 minutes. Add brussels sprouts and mushrooms and toss to coat.

4.   Cook another 15-20 minutes until veggies are lightly browned and cooked through.

5.   Adjust seasoning as needed. Enjoy!

Grilled Fingerling Potato Salad

Servings: 6
Cooking Time: 15 Minutes

Ingredients:
- 10 Whole scallions
- 2/3 Cup extra-virgin olive oil, divided
- 1 1/2 Pound fingerling potatoes, cut in half lengthwise
- pepper
- 2 Teaspoon kosher salt, divided, plus more as needed
- 2 Tablespoon rice vinegar
- 2 Teaspoon lemon juice
- 1 Small jalapeño, sliced

Directions:
1.   Supply your smoker with wood pellets and follow the start-up procedure. Preheat the grill, with the lid closed, to 450° F.

2.   Brush the scallions with oil and place on the grill.

3.   Cook until lightly charred, about 2 to 3 minutes. Remove and let cool. Grill: 450 °F

4.   Once the scallions have cooled, slice and set aside.

5.   Brush the fingerling potatoes with oil (reserving 1/3 cup for later use), then salt and pepper. Place cut-side down on the grill until cooked through, about 4 to 5 minutes. Grill: 450 °F

6.   In a bowl, whisk the remaining 1/3 cup olive oil, 1 teaspoon salt, rice vinegar and lemon juice. Next mix in the scallions, potatoes and sliced jalapeño.

7.   Season with salt and pepper, and serve. Enjoy!

Bacon Wrapped Corn On The Cob

Servings: 4
Cooking Time: 21 Minutes

Ingredients:
- 4 Whole Corn, ears
- 8 Slices bacon
- 1 Teaspoon freshly ground black pepper
- 1 Teaspoon chili powder
- 1 To Taste Parmesan cheese, grated

Directions:
1.   Peel back the corn husks, remove silk strings and rinse corn under cold water.

2.   Wrap 2 pieces of bacon around each ear of corn, securing with toothpicks.

3. Dust each ear of corn with some chili powder and cracked black pepper.

4. Supply your smoker with wood pellets and follow the start-up procedure. Preheat the grill, with the lid closed, to 375° F.

5. Place the ears of corn directly on the Traeger and grill for approximately 20 minutes or until the bacon is cooked crisp. Grill: 375 °F

6. Take the corn off the Traeger. Carefully remove the toothpicks and season with a little more chili powder and a grating of parmesan cheese, if desired. Serve & enjoy!

Broccoli-cauliflower Salad

Servings: 4
Cooking Time: 25 Minutes

Ingredients:
- 1½ cups mayonnaise
- ½ cup sour cream
- ¼ cup sugar
- 1 bunch broccoli, cut into small pieces
- 1 head cauliflower, cut into small pieces
- 1 small red onion, chopped
- 6 slices bacon, cooked and crumbled (precooked bacon works well)
- 1 cup shredded Cheddar cheese

Directions:
1. In a small bowl, whisk together the mayonnaise, sour cream, and sugar to make a dressing.

2. In a large bowl, combine the broccoli, cauliflower, onion, bacon, and Cheddar cheese.

3. Pour the dressing over the vegetable mixture and toss well to coat.

4. Serve the salad chilled.

Grilled Chili-lime Corn

Servings: 8
Cooking Time: 45 Minutes

Ingredients:
- 12 Corn, ears
- 1 Teaspoon chili powder
- 1/2 Teaspoon onion powder
- 1 Teaspoon Leinenkugel's Summer Shandy Rub

- 2 lime, juiced
- 1 Tablespoon lime zest

Directions:
1. Soak the ears of corn, still in their husk, in water for 4 to 8 hours.

2. Supply your smoker with wood pellets and follow the start-up procedure. Preheat the grill, with the lid closed, to 350° F.

3. Place corn directly on grill grates. Turn corn every 15 minutes for 45 minutes total cooking time. Grill: 350 °F

4. Combine chili powder, onion powder, Summer Shandy rub, lime juice, lime zest and butter in an oven safe dish and place in grill for 10 minutes. Remove corn and butter from the grill.

5. Pull corn husk back, but not off and remove corn silk. Using the corn husk as a handle, brush the corn with the melted chili-lime butter. Enjoy!

Baked Garlic Duchess Potatoes

Servings: 8
Cooking Time: 60 Minutes

Ingredients:
- 12 Medium Potatoes, Yukon gold
- salt
- 5 Large Egg Yolk
- 2 Clove garlic, minced
- 1.24 Cup heavy cream
- 3/4 Cup sour cream
- 10 Tablespoon butter, melted
- black pepper

Directions:
1. Place potatoes in a large pot and fill with water. Season with salt. Bring to a boil over medium-high heat.

2. Reduce heat and simmer until a paring knife easily slides through potatoes, about 25 to 35 minutes. Drain and let cool slightly.

3. Supply your smoker with wood pellets and follow the start-up procedure. Preheat the grill, with the lid closed, to 450° F.

4. Whisk together egg yolks, garlic, cream, sour cream, butter, and pepper in a large bowl. Season with salt.

5. Peel potatoes and push flesh through a ricer or a food mill directly into bowl with egg mixture. Fold in the egg mixture being careful not to overmix.

6. Transfer to a 3-quart baking dish and bake until golden brown and slightly puffed, about 30–40 minutes. Enjoy! Grill: 450 °F

Roasted Sweet Potato Steak Fries

Servings: 4
Cooking Time: 40 Minutes

Ingredients:
- 3 Whole sweet potatoes
- 4 Tablespoon extra-virgin olive oil
- salt and pepper
- 2 Tablespoon fresh chopped rosemary

Directions:
1. Supply your smoker with wood pellets and follow the start-up procedure. Preheat the grill, with the lid closed, to 450° F.

2. Cut sweet potatoes into wedges and toss with olive oil, salt, pepper and rosemary. Spread on a parchment lined baking sheet and put in the grill. Cook for 15 minutes then flip and continue to cook until lightly browned and cooked through, about 40 to 45 minutes total. Grill: 450 °F

3. Serve with your favorite dipping sauce. Enjoy! Grill: 450 °F

Skillet Potato Cake

Servings: 4
Cooking Time: 40 Minutes

Ingredients:
- 8 Tablespoon butter, melted
- 2 Pound russet potatoes, peeled and thinly sliced
- 3 Tablespoon kosher salt
- 2 Tablespoon freshly ground black pepper
- thyme

Directions:
1. Supply your smoker with wood pellets and follow the start-up procedure. Preheat the grill, with the lid closed, to 375° F.

2. Brush the bottom of a cast iron skillet with part of the melted butter. Place potato slices vertically around the outer edges then fill in the middle in the same fashion.

3. Pour additional melted butter over the top of the layers and sprinkle with salt and pepper.

4. Place skillet in grill and cook for 35 to 40 minutes or until potatoes are fork tender and golden brown.

5. Garnish with a sprinkle of fresh thyme over the top of the potatoes. Enjoy!

Smoked Pickled Green Beans

Servings: 4
Cooking Time: 45 Minutes

Ingredients:
- 1 Pound Green Beans, blanched
- 1/2 Cup salt
- 1/2 Cup sugar
- 1 Tablespoon red pepper flakes
- 2 Cup white wine vinegar
- 2 Cup ice water

Directions:
1. Supply your smoker with wood pellets and follow the start-up procedure. Preheat the grill, with the lid closed, to 180° F.

2. Place the blanched green beans on a mesh grill mat and place mat directly on the grill grate. Smoke the green beans for 30-45 minutes until they've picked up the desired amount of smoke. Remove from grill and set aside until the brine is ready. Grill: 180 °F

3. In a medium sized saucepan, bring all remaining ingredients, except ice water, to a boil over medium high heat on the stove. Simmer for 5-10 minutes then remove from heat and steep 20 minutes more. Pour brine over ice water to cool.

4. Once brine has cooled, pour over the green beans and weigh them down with a few plates to ensure they are completely submerged. Let sit 24 hours before use. Enjoy!

Parmesan Roasted Cauliflower

Servings: 4

Cooking Time: 40 Minutes

Ingredients:

- 1 Head cauliflower, cut into florets
- 1 Medium onion, sliced
- 4 Clove garlic, unpeeled
- 4 Tablespoon olive oil
- salt
- black pepper
- 1 Teaspoon fresh thyme
- 1/2 Cup Parmesan cheese, grated

Directions:

1. Supply your smoker with wood pellets and follow the start-up procedure. Preheat the grill, with the lid closed, to 400° F.

2. On a baking tray, mix together cauliflower, onion, thyme, garlic, olive oil, salt and pepper.

3. Place tray on preheated grill and cook until cauliflower is firm and almost tender (about 25 minutes). Grill: 400 °F

4. Sprinkle cauliflower with Parmesan cheese and continue to cook on the Traeger for another 10 to 15 minutes. Cauliflower should be tender and the Parmesan crisp. Serve immediately, enjoy!

Baked Sweet And Savory Yams By Bennie Kendrick

Servings: 6

Cooking Time: 60 Minutes

Ingredients:

- 3 Medium Yams
- 3 Tablespoon extra-virgin olive oil
- honey
- Goat Cheese
- 1/2 Cup brown sugar
- 1/2 Cup Pecans, pieces

Directions:

1. Supply your smoker with wood pellets and follow the start-up procedure. Preheat the grill, with the lid closed, to 350° F.

2. While Traeger comes to temperature, wash yams and poke a few holes all over. Wrap yams in foil.

3. Bake for 45-60 minutes or until knife tender. You don't want to overcook and get the yams too soft because you want to be able to cut each yam into rounds.

4. Once yams have cooled to the touch, cut each into 1/4" rounds. Lightly coat each round with oil olive and place on sheet tray.

5. Sprinkle each top with brown sugar. Using a teaspoon, place desired amount of goat cheese on each round. Next top with chopped pecans. Finally, drizzle Bee Local honey over each round.

6. Based on how sweet you like your yams, you can add more brown sugar and honey.

7. After complete, place your sheet tray back in the grill and cook, lid closed, for another 20 minutes. Enjoy!

Grilled Zucchini Squash Spears

Servings: 4

Cooking Time: 10 Minutes

Ingredients:

- 4 Medium zucchini
- 2 Tablespoon olive oil
- 1 Tablespoon sherry vinegar
- 2 thyme, leaves pulled
- salt and pepper

Directions:

1. Clean the zucchini and cut the ends off. Cut each in half lengthwise, then each half into thirds.

2. Combine remaining ingredients in a medium Ziplock bag and add the spears. Toss and mix well to coat the zucchini.

3. Supply your smoker with wood pellets and follow the start-up procedure. Preheat the grill, with the lid closed, to 350° F.

4. Remove the spears from the bag and place directly on the grill grate cut side down.

5. Cook for 3-4 minutes per side, until grill marks appear and zucchini is tender. Grill: 350 °F

6. Remove from grill and finish with more thyme leaves if desired. Enjoy!

Grilled Street Corn

Servings: 6
Cooking Time: 10 Minutes

Ingredients:

- 6 ears corn, husked
- 1 As Needed extra-virgin olive oil
- 1/4 Cup mayonnaise
- 1 Tablespoon ancho or guajillo chile powder
- 1/2 Cup chopped cilantro, plus more for serving
- 1 lime, zested and juiced
- salt
- 1/2 Cup Cotija cheese
- 1 As Needed cilantro, finely chopped

Directions:

1. Supply your smoker with wood pellets and follow the start-up procedure. Preheat the grill, with the lid closed, to 450° F.

2. Brush corn with oil and place on grill, turning occasionally.

3. While corn is on the grill, mix mayonnaise with chile powder, cilantro, lime juice and zest in a bowl. Season with salt.

4. After about 10 minutes corn should be cooked through and slightly charred on the outside. Remove from grill.

5. Top corn with chile mayonnaise then sprinkle on the Cotija cheese and chopped cilantro. Enjoy!

Roasted Jalapeno Cheddar Deviled Eggs

Servings: 6
Cooking Time: 30 Minutes

Ingredients:

- 7 Eggs, hard boiled
- 3 Tablespoon mayonnaise
- 1 Teaspoon brown mustard
- 1 Teaspoon apple cider vinegar
- 1 Dash hot sauce
- 1 jalapeño pepper, seeded and minced
- salt and pepper
- 1/2 Cup shredded cheddar cheese
- paprika

Directions:

1. Supply your smoker with wood pellets and follow the start-up procedure. Preheat the grill, with the lid closed, to 180° F.

2. Place your eggs directly on the grill grate and smoke for 30 minutes.

3. Remove from the grill and allow the eggs to cool. Smoking the eggs will give them a slightly yellowed color, but an intense smoky flavor. If a classic white egg is your preference, then skip this step.

4. Slice the eggs lengthwise and scoop the egg yolks directly into a gallon zip top bag.

5. Add the mayo, mustard, vinegar, hot sauce, roasted jalapeños and salt and pepper to the bag.

6. Zip the bag closed and, using your hands, knead all of the ingredients together in the bag until completely smooth.

7. Squeeze the yolk mixture into one corner of the bag and then cut the corner off. Pipe the yolk mixture into the whites.

8. Sprinkle with the finely shredded cheddar or paprika and chill until you are ready to serve. Enjoy!

Roasted Vegetable Napoleon

Servings: 4
Cooking Time: 30 Minutes

Ingredients:

- 2 Whole sweet potatoes
- 2 Whole zucchini
- 2 Whole Squash
- 1 Whole red onion
- 2 Whole Bell Pepper, Red
- salt and pepper

Directions:

1. Supply your smoker with wood pellets and follow the start-up procedure. Preheat the grill, with the lid closed, to High heat.

2. Salt and pepper all vegetables and grill them on both sides. Begin with the peppers and onions as they will take a little longer to cook. Grill: 450 °F

Red Potato Grilled Lollipops

Servings: 4
Cooking Time: 25 Minutes

Ingredients:

- 8 Large red bliss potatoes, halved
- 2 Clove garlic, minced
- 2 Sprig rosemary, minced
- 2 Tablespoon olive oil
- 1 Teaspoon salt
- 1/2 Teaspoon black pepper
- 5 Wooden Skewers, soaked in water
- 1/4 Cup Parmesan cheese, grated

Directions:

1. Supply your smoker with wood pellets and follow the start-up procedure. Preheat the grill, with the lid closed, to 450° F.
2. Halve potatoes and poke each several times with a fork.
3. Put the potatoes in a large bowl and toss with the minced garlic, rosemary leaves, a few tablespoons of olive oil, kosher salt, and pepper. Microwave the potatoes for 4 minutes. Gently toss potatoes and microwave for another 3 minutes.
4. Skewer potato halves threading about 4 or 5 potato halves on each skewer. Brush potatoes with olive oil.
5. Place the potato skewers on the Traeger, cut side down, and grill until the sides begin to brown (4-7 minutes).
6. Flip and grill skin side down for another 7-10 minutes.
7. They are done when a sharp knife tip easily penetrates the sides. Remove potatoes from grill and top with grated parmesan cheese. Enjoy!

Baked Bacon Green Bean Casserole

Servings: 6
Cooking Time: 50 Minutes

Ingredients:

- 1 1/2 Pound Green Beans, fresh
- 1 Can cream of mushroom soup
- 1/2 Cup milk
- 1/2 Teaspoon Worcestershire sauce
- 1/2 Teaspoon black pepper
- 2/3 Cup French's Original Crispy Fried Onions
- 8 Slices bacon
- 1/4 Cup red bell pepper, diced
- 2/3 French's Original Crispy Fried Onions

Directions:

1. In a mixing bowl, combine beans, soup, milk, Worcestershire sauce, black pepper, 2/3 cup of the onions, 6 of the slices of crumbled bacon, and red bell pepper. Transfer to a 1-1/2 quart casserole dish.
2. Supply your smoker with wood pellets and follow the start-up procedure. Preheat the grill, with the lid closed, to 350° F.
3. Cook casserole until the filling is hot and bubbling, 35 to 40 minutes. Grill: 350 °F
4. Top with remaining onions and the last 2 slices of crumbled bacon and cook for 5 to 10 minutes more, or until the onions are crisp and beginning to brown. Serve, enjoy! Grill: 350 °F

Baked Breakfast Mini Quiches

Servings: 8
Cooking Time: 15 Minutes

Ingredients:

- cooking spray
- 1 Tablespoon extra-virgin olive oil
- 1/2 yellow onion, diced
- 3 Cup Spinach, fresh
- 10 eggs
- 4 Ounce shredded cheddar, mozzarella or Swiss cheese
- 1/4 Cup fresh basil
- 1 Teaspoon kosher salt
- 1/2 Teaspoon black pepper

Directions:

1. Spray a 12-cup muffin tin generously with cooking spray.
2. In a small skillet over medium heat, warm the oil. Add the onion and cook, stirring frequently, until softened, about 7 minutes. Add the spinach and cook until wilted, about 1 minute longer.
3. Transfer to a cutting board to cool, then chop the mixture so the spinach if broken up a little.

4. Supply your smoker with wood pellets and follow the start-up procedure. Preheat the grill, with the lid closed, to 350° F.

5. In a large bowl, whisk the eggs until frothy. Add the cooled onions and spinach, cheese, basil, 1 tsp salt and 1/2 tsp pepper. Stir to combine. Divide egg mixture evenly among the muffin cups.

6. Place tray on the grill and bake until the eggs have puffed up, are set, and are beginning to brown, about 18 to 20 minutes. Grill: 350 °F

7. Serve immediately, or allow to cool on a wire rack, then refrigerate in an air tight container for up to 4 days. Enjoy!

Green Bean Casserole

Servings: 6
Cooking Time: 25 Minutes

Ingredients:
- 1/2 Stick butter
- 1 Small onion
- 1/2 Cup sliced button mushrooms
- 4 Can green beans, drained
- 2 Can cream of mushroom soup
- 1 Teaspoon Lawry's Seasoned Salt
- pepper
- 1 Can French's Original Crispy Fried Onions
- 1 Cup grated sharp cheddar cheese

Directions:
1. Supply your smoker with wood pellets and follow the start-up procedure. Preheat the grill, with the lid closed, to 375° F.

2. Melt butter in a cast iron skillet and add onions and mushrooms, stirring occasionally until softened.

3. Add drained green beans and cream of mushroom soup and stir gently to combine.

4. Season with seasoned salt and pepper and sprinkle the top with grated cheddar cheese and fried onions.

5. Bake for 25 minutes. Serve warm, enjoy! Grill: 375 °F

Roasted Sheet Pan Vegetables

Servings: 4
Cooking Time: 25 Minutes

Ingredients:
- 1 Small head purple cauliflower, stemmed and cut into 2 inch florets
- 1 Small head yellow cauliflower, stemmed and cut into 2 inch florets
- 4 Cup butternut squash
- 2 Cup oyster or shiitake mushrooms, rinsed and sliced
- 3 Tablespoon olive oil
- 2 Teaspoon kosher salt
- freshly ground black pepper
- 1/4 Cup chopped flat-leaf parsley

Directions:
1. Supply your smoker with wood pellets and follow the start-up procedure. Preheat the grill, with the lid closed, to 450° F.

2. In a large mixing bowl, combine all of the vegetables. Drizzle olive oil over the top, along with kosher salt and a generous grinding of black pepper.

3. Using your hands, toss the vegetables until they are evenly coated.

4. Spread out onto 1 or 2 half sheet pans or baking sheets, ensuring there is a little space between the veggies. (If they are too crowded, the vegetables will steam instead of roast and you won't get that crispy texture.)

5. Place the sheet pans on the grill and cook for 15 minutes. Open and stir, then close the lid and continue to cook until the vegetables are brown around the edges, about 5 to 15 minutes longer. Grill: 450 °F

6. Toss with parsley and serve immediately. The vegetables are also delicious at room temperature. Enjoy!

Smoked Macaroni Salad

Servings: 4
Cooking Time: 20 Minutes

Ingredients:
- 1 Pound macaroni, uncooked
- 1/2 Small red onion, diced
- 1 green bell pepper, diced
- 1/2 Cup shredded carrot
- 1 Cup mayonnaise
- 3 Tablespoon white wine vinegar

- 2 Tablespoon sugar
- salt
- black pepper

Directions:

1. Bring a large stock pot of salted water to a boil over medium heat and cook pasta according to package directions. Make sure to cook to al dente, strain, and rinse under cold water.

2. Supply your smoker with wood pellets and follow the start-up procedure. Preheat the grill, with the lid closed, to 225° F.

3. Spread cooked pasta out on a sheet tray and place sheet tray directly on the grill grate. Smoke for 20 minutes, remove from heat, and transfer directly to the refrigerator to cool. Grill: 225 ˚F

4. While the pasta is cooling mix the dressing. Place all ingredients in a medium bowl and whisk to combine.

5. When pasta is cool combine chopped veggies, smoked pasta and dressing in a large bowl.

6. Cover with plastic wrap and place in the fridge for 20 minutes before serving. Enjoy!

Roasted Do-ahead Mashed Potatoes

Servings: 6
Cooking Time: 50 Minutes

Ingredients:

- 5 Pound Yukon Gold or russet potatoes
- 9 Tablespoon butter
- 8 Ounce cream cheese
- 1/2 Cup milk
- salt and pepper

Directions:

1. Peel the potatoes and cut into chunks that are roughly the same size. Cover with cold water and add a teaspoon of salt. Bring to a boil over high heat, then reduce the heat to medium and simmer the potatoes until they are tender.

2. Drain the potatoes and return them to the pot. Stir over low heat for 2 to 3 minutes to evaporate any excess moisture.

3. Mash the potatoes with a hand-held potato masher. (Alternative, rice the potatoes using a ricer.) Incorporate 8 tbsp butter and cream cheese. Add milk until the potatoes are of a good consistency. Stir in salt and pepper to taste.

4. Butter the inside of a casserole dish. Spread the potatoes out in an even layer in the casserole dish, smoothing the top with a spatula. Cool, cover, and refrigerate if not cooking right away. Before cooking, let the potatoes warm to room temperature (about an hour).

5. Supply your smoker with wood pellets and follow the start-up procedure. Preheat the grill, with the lid closed, to 350° F.

6. Bake the potatoes for 45 to 50 minutes, or until hot through. Grill: 350 ˚F

Whole Roasted Cauliflower With Garlic Parmesan Butter

Servings: 4
Cooking Time: 45 Minutes

Ingredients:

- 1 Whole head cauliflower
- 1/4 Cup olive oil
- salt and pepper
- 1/2 Cup butter, melted
- 1/4 Cup shredded Parmesan cheese
- 2 Clove garlic, minced
- 1/2 Tablespoon chopped parsley

Directions:

1. Supply your smoker with wood pellets and follow the start-up procedure. Preheat the grill, with the lid closed, to 450° F.

2. Brush the cauliflower with olive oil and season liberally with salt and pepper.

3. Put cauliflower in a cast iron skillet, place directly on the grill grate and cook for 45 minutes until golden brown and the center is tender.

4. While the cauliflower is cooking, combine the melted butter, parmesan, garlic and parsley in a small bowl.

5. During the last 20 minutes of cooking, baste the cauliflower with the melted butter mixture.

6. Remove the cauliflower from the grill and top with extra parmesan and parsley if desired. Enjoy!

Butternut Squash

Servings: 4

Cooking Time: 45 Minutes

Ingredients:

- 1 Whole butternut squash
- Veggie Rub
- Blackened Saskatchewan Rub
- olive oil

Directions:

1. Cut squash in half and lightly coat with mixture of olive oil, Traeger Veggie Shake, and Traeger Blackened Saskatchewan.

2. Wrap in foil with 1/2 cup (120mL) of water.

3. Supply your smoker with wood pellets and follow the start-up procedure. Preheat the grill, with the lid closed, to 450° F.

4. Place squash on grill for 45 minutes. Remove from grill and unwrap. Enjoy!

Potluck Salad With Smoked Cornbread

Servings: 6

Cooking Time: 45 Minutes

Ingredients:

- 1 cup all-purpose flour
- 1 cup yellow cornmeal
- 1 tablespoon sugar
- 2 teaspoons baking powder
- 1 teaspoon salt
- 1 cup milk
- 1 egg, beaten, at room temperature
- 4 tablespoons (½ stick) unsalted butter, melted and cooled
- Nonstick cooking spray or butter, for greasing
- ½ cup milk
- ½ cup sour cream
- 2 tablespoons dry ranch dressing mix
- 1 pound bacon, cooked and crumbled
- 3 tomatoes, chopped
- 1 bell pepper, chopped
- 1 cucumber, seeded and chopped
- 2 stalks celery, chopped (about 1 cup)
- ½ cup chopped scallions

Directions:

1. For the cornbread:

2. In a medium bowl, combine the flour, cornmeal, sugar, baking powder, and salt.

3. In a small bowl, whisk together the milk and egg. Pour in the butter, then slowly fold this mixture into the dry ingredients.

4. Supply your smoker with wood pellets and follow the start-up procedure. Preheat, with the lid closed, to 375°F.

5. Coat a cast iron skillet with cooking spray or butter.

6. Pour the batter into the skillet, place on the grill grate, close the lid, and smoke for 35 to 45 minutes, or until the cornbread is browned and pulls away from the side of the skillet.

7. Remove the cornbread from the grill and let cool, then coarsely crumble.

8. For the salad:

9. In a small bowl, whisk together the milk, sour cream, and ranch dressing mix.

10. In a medium bowl, combine the crumbled bacon, tomatoes, bell pepper, cucumber, celery, and scallions.

11. In a large serving bowl, layer half of the crumbled cornbread, half of the bacon-veggie mixture, and half of the dressing. Toss lightly.

12. Repeat the layering with the remaining cornbread, bacon-veggie mixture, and dressing. Toss again.

13. Refrigerate the salad for at least 1 hour. Serve cold.

Roasted Red Pepper White Bean Dip

Servings: 4

Cooking Time: 40 Minutes

Ingredients:

- 4 Whole garlic
- 4 Tablespoon extra-virgin olive oil
- 2 Bell Pepper, Red
- 3 Tablespoon Dill Weed, fresh
- 3 Tablespoon chopped flat-leaf parsley
- 2 Can cannellini beans, mashed
- 4 Teaspoon lemon juice
- 1 1/2 Teaspoon salt

Directions:

1. Roasting the garlic and red peppers:

2. Supply your smoker with wood pellets and follow the start-up procedure. Preheat the grill, with the lid closed, to 400° F.

3. Peel away the outside layers of the garlic husk. Cut off the top of the garlic bulb, exposing each of the individual cloves. Drizzle olive oil over the top of the head of garlic and rub it in. Wrap the garlic in foil, completely covering it. Put the head of garlic and the two red peppers (washed and dried) on the Traeger.

4. Roast the garlic for 25-30 minutes and the peppers for about 40 minutes. Rotate the peppers a quarter-turn every 10 minutes until the exterior is blistered and blackened. Grill: 400 °F

5. Pull the peppers off the grill and put them in a bowl. Cover the bowl with plastic wrap and leave them for 15 minutes. The steam will loosen the skins so that they slip off like a drumstick covered in barbecue sauce.

6. Peel off the pepper skin. Cut off the stems and scrape out the seeds and they're ready to use.

7. As for the garlic, let it cool and then pull out the individual cloves as needed.

8. The dip:

9. In a blender put the roasted red peppers, 4 cloves of roasted garlic, dill, parsley, drained and rinsed beans, olive oil, lemon juice and salt.

10. Blend until the dip is smooth and creamy. You may need to scrape down the sides of the blender a couple of times. If it's having difficulty blending or looks too thick add more olive oil or lemon juice. (Add more lemon juice if it tastes like it needs more acid or brightness.) Enjoy!

Tater Tot Bake

Servings: 4
Cooking Time: 15 Minutes

Ingredients:
- 1 Whole frozen tater tots
- salt and pepper
- 1 Cup sour cream
- 1 Cup shredded cheddar cheese, divided
- 1/2 Cup bacon, chopped
- 1/4 Cup green onion, diced

Directions:

1. Supply your smoker with wood pellets and follow the start-up procedure. Preheat the grill, with the lid closed, to 375° F.

2. Line a baking sheet with aluminum foil for easy clean up and spread frozen tater tots onto sheet.

3. Sprinkle with Veggie Shake or salt and pepper to taste.

4. Place the baking sheet on the preheated grill grate and cook the tater tots for 10 minutes.

5. Drizzle sour cream over cooked tater tots.

6. Sprinkle the cheese, bacon bits and green onions on top of the tater tots.

7. Turn heat up to High heat and cook for 5 more minutes until the cheese melts and serve immediately. Enjoy!

Portobello Marinated Mushroom

Servings: 2
Cooking Time: 15 Minutes

Ingredients:
- 1 Teaspoon chopped thyme
- 1 Teaspoon rosemary, chopped
- 1 Teaspoon Oregano, chopped
- 3 Tablespoon extra-virgin olive oil
- 1 To Taste Jacobsen Salt Co. Pure Kosher Sea Salt
- 1 To Taste pepper
- 6 Whole Portobello Mushroom
- 2 Whole russet potatoes

Directions:

1. Supply your smoker with wood pellets and follow the start-up procedure. Preheat the grill, with the lid closed, to 450° F.

2. Mix fresh herbs, olive oil, salt, and pepper together in a bowl. Rub over mushrooms. Grill both sides of mushrooms for approximately 2-3 minutes on each side. Grill: 450 °F

3. Clean the potatoes and slice into long strips.

4. Heat the oil on the Traeger in a sauce pan; drop the potatoes in the hot oil and fry for 7-8 minutes. Let the potatoes cool slightly on a sheet pan. Enjoy! Grill: 450 °F

Grilled Asparagus & Honey-glazed Carrots

Servings: 4
Cooking Time: 35 Minutes

Ingredients:

- 1 Bunch asparagus, woody ends removed
- 1 Pound Carrots, peeled
- 2 Tablespoon olive oil
- sea salt
- 2 Tablespoon honey
- lemon zest

Directions:

1. Rinse all vegetables under cold water. Drizzle asparagus with olive oil and a generous sprinkling of sea salt. Generously drizzle carrots with honey and lightly sprinkle with sea salt.
2. Supply your smoker with wood pellets and follow the start-up procedure. Preheat the grill, with the lid closed, to 350° F.
3. Place carrots on the grill first and cook for 10-15 minutes, then add asparagus and cook both for another 15 to 20 minutes, or until they're done to your liking. Grill: 350 °F
4. Top the asparagus with some fresh lemon zest. Enjoy!

Smoked Parmesan Herb Popcorn

Servings: 2
Cooking Time: 15 Minutes

Ingredients:

- 4 Tablespoon butter
- 2 Teaspoon Italian Seasoning
- 1 Teaspoon garlic powder
- 1 Teaspoon salt
- 1/4 Cup popcorn kernels
- 1/2 Cup Parmesan cheese, grated

Directions:

1. Supply your smoker with wood pellets and follow the start-up procedure. Preheat the grill, with the lid closed, to 250° F.
2. In a small saucepan, melt the butter over medium heat. Add Italian seasoning, garlic powder, and salt and stir to combine. Remove from heat and set aside.
3. Add 1/4 cup of popcorn to a brown paper lunch bag. Fold the top of the bag over twice to close. Place the bag in the microwave and microwave on high for 1 to 2 minutes, or until there are about 5 seconds between pops. Open the bag with care and dump into a large mixing bowl.
4. Pour butter mixture of popcorn in a bowl and toss to combine. Dump popcorn onto a baking sheet and place in grill.
5. Smoke for 10 minutes; remove from grill. Toss with parmesan cheese to serve. Enjoy! Grill: 250 °F

Blt Pasta Salad

Servings: 6
Cooking Time: 45 Minutes

Ingredients:

- 1 pound thick-cut bacon
- 16 ounces bowtie pasta, cooked according to package directions and drained
- 2 tomatoes, chopped
- ½ cup chopped scallions
- ½ cup Italian dressing
- ½ cup ranch dressing
- 1 tablespoon chopped fresh basil
- 1 teaspoon salt
- 1 teaspoon freshly ground black pepper
- 1 teaspoon garlic powder
- 1 head lettuce, cored and torn

Directions:

1. Supply your smoker with wood pellets and follow the start-up procedure. Preheat, with the lid closed, to 225°F.
2. Arrange the bacon slices on the grill grate, close the lid, and cook for 30 to 45 minutes, flipping after 20 minutes, until crisp.
3. Remove the bacon from the grill and chop.
4. In a large bowl, combine the chopped bacon with the cooked pasta, tomatoes, scallions, Italian dressing, ranch dressing, basil, salt, pepper, and garlic powder. Refrigerate until ready to serve.
5. Toss in the lettuce just before serving to keep it from wilting.

Salt Crusted Baked Potatoes

Servings: 4

Cooking Time: 60 Minutes

Ingredients:

- 6 russet potatoes, scrubbed and dried
- 3 Tablespoon canola oil
- 1 Tablespoon kosher salt
- butter
- sour cream
- Chives, fresh
- Bacon Bits
- cheddar cheese

Directions:

1. In a large bowl, coat the potatoes in canola oil and sprinkle heavily with salt.

2. Supply your smoker with wood pellets and follow the start-up procedure. Preheat the grill, with the lid closed, to 450° F.

3. Place the potatoes directly on the grill grate and bake for 30-40 minutes, or until soft in the middle when pricked with a fork. Serve loaded with your favorite toppings. Enjoy! Grill: 450 °F

Roasted Beet & Bacon Salad

Servings: 4

Cooking Time: 45 Minutes

Ingredients:

- 2 Medium raw beets, peeled and thinly sliced
- 8 Slices bacon
- 1/4 Cup raw pecans or walnuts
- 2 Medium ripe pears, sliced
- 2 Large avocados, diced
- 1 Head red leaf lettuce or baby spinach, torn into bite-size pieces
- 1/4 Cup champagne vinaigrette

Directions:

1. Supply your smoker with wood pellets and follow the start-up procedure. Preheat the grill, with the lid closed, to 400° F.

2. Place beets on a foil-lined baking sheet and top with bacon. Place baking sheet directly on the grill grate (while preheating) and cook for 25 minutes. Grill: 400 °F

3. Toss to coat beets in rendered bacon fat.

4. Spread everything out in a single layer and continue to cook for another 15 minutes, or until beets are tender and bacon is crispy. Grill: 400 °F

5. Add pecans or walnuts and roast for 5 more minutes. Spoon out nuts and place on paper towels to drain and cool.

6. Once bacon is cool to the touch, roughly chop into medium pieces.

7. Place bacon, beets, nuts, pears, avocado and lettuce in a large salad bowl. Drizzle with champagne vinaigrette, toss to coat, and serve. Enjoy!

Baked Stuffed Avocados

Servings: 6

Cooking Time: 15 Minutes

Ingredients:

- 4 avocados, halved and pit removed
- 8 eggs
- 2 Cup shredded cheddar cheese
- 1/4 Cup cherry tomatoes, halved
- 4 Slices Bacon, cooked & chopped
- salt and pepper
- 1 scallion, thinly sliced

Directions:

1. Supply your smoker with wood pellets and follow the start-up procedure. Preheat the grill, with the lid closed, to 450° F.

2. After removing the pit from the avocado, scoop out a little of the flesh to make enough room to fit 1 egg per half.

3. Fill the bottom of a cast iron pan with kosher salt and nestle the avocado halves into the salt, cut side up. The salt helps to keep them in place while cooking, like ice with oysters.

4. Crack one egg into each half, top with shredded cheddar cheese, cherry tomatoes and bacon. Season with salt and pepper to taste.

5. Place the cast iron pan directly on the grill grate and bake the avocados for 12 to 15 minutes until the cheese is melted and the egg is just set. Grill: 450 °F

6. Remove from the grill and let rest 5 to 10 minutes. Top with sliced scallions and enjoy!

Grilled Asparagus And Hollandaise Sauce

Servings: 4
Cooking Time: 10 Minutes

Ingredients:

- 1 Pound asparagus
- 2 Teaspoon red pepper flakes
- 2 Tablespoon olive oil
- salt and pepper
- 4 egg yolk
- 1 Tablespoon lemon juice
- 1/2 Cup butter, melted
- cayenne pepper
- salt

Directions:

1. Supply your smoker with wood pellets and follow the start-up procedure. Preheat the grill, with the lid closed, to 375° F.
2. In a large bowl, mix asparagus with olive oil, red pepper flakes and salt. Arrange asparagus on a cooking sheet and take to the grill. Cook for approximately 10 to 15 minutes. Grill: 375 °F
3. In an aluminum bowl, whisk the egg yolks well. Add the lemon juice and whisk until creamy.
4. Place bowl over a double boiler, over low heat, making sure that it does not touches the water.
5. While whisking, add the melted butter slowly. Whisk until it doubles the volume. Take off the heat, still whisking and add the cayenne pepper and salt.
6. Arrange asparagus over a serving plater. Pour hollandaise sauce over asparagus and serve. Enjoy!

Smoked Pico De Gallo

Servings: 4
Cooking Time: 30 Minutes

Ingredients:

- 3 Cup diced Roma tomatoes
- 1 jalapeño, diced
- 1/2 red onion, diced
- 1/2 Bunch cilantro, finely chopped
- 2 lime, juiced
- salt

- olive oil

Directions:

1. Supply your smoker with wood pellets and follow the start-up procedure. Preheat the grill, with the lid closed, to 180° F.
2. Place the diced tomatoes on a small sheet pan spreading them into a thin layer. Place the sheet pan directly on the grill and smoke for 30 minutes. Grill: 180 °F
3. When the tomatoes are finished, toss all ingredients in a medium bowl and finish with lime juice, salt and olive oil to taste. Serve and enjoy!

Baked Kale Chips

Servings: 4
Cooking Time: 20 Minutes

Ingredients:

- 2 Bunch kale, leaves washed and stems removed
- 1 As Needed extra-virgin olive oil
- 1 To Taste sea salt

Directions:

1. Dry the kale leaves well and lay them out on a sheet tray. Drizzle lightly with olive oil and sprinkle with sea salt.
2. Supply your smoker with wood pellets and follow the start-up procedure. Preheat the grill, with the lid closed, to 250° F.
3. Place the sheet tray directly on the grill grate and cook until kale is lightly browned and crispy, about 20 minutes. Enjoy! Grill: 250 °F

Smoked Bbq Onion Brussels Sprout

Servings: 4
Cooking Time: 110 Minutes

Ingredients:

- 4 strip bacon
- 1 onion minced
- 2 cloves garlic minced
- 1 lb brussels sprouts stems trimmed and cut in half
- 1 tbsp BBQ Spice Blend
- 1/2 cup Apple Habanero Bar-B-Que Sauce (or other BBQ sauce)

Directions:

1.   Supply your smoker with wood pellets and follow the start-up procedure. Preheat the grill, with the lid closed, to High heat. Place a cast iron skillet over the highest heat spot and cook the bacon until crisp.

2.   Remove the bacon from pan and drain, reserving the bacon fat in the pan.

3.   Reduce the heat on your smoker to 250°F.

4.   Add the onions, garlic, and brussels to the pan and toss to coat in the bacon drippings. Sprinkle the BBQ spice blend over top.

5.   Cover the lid and allow to smoke for 1 to 1 1/2 hours, until the sprouts are fork tender.

6.   For the last 20 minutes of smoking, toss the brussels sprouts in half of the barbecue sauce.

7.   Remove the sprouts from the smoker.

8.   Chop the bacon and add it and the remaining barbecue sauce to the pan of sprouts, tossing to coat.

9.   Serve hot.

Roasted Hasselback Potatoes By Doug Scheiding

Servings: 6
Cooking Time: 120 Minutes

Ingredients:

- 6 Large russet potatoes
- 1 Pound bacon
- 1/2 Cup butter
- salt
- black pepper
- 1 Cup cheddar cheese
- 3 Whole scallions

Directions:

1.   To cut potatoes, place two wooden spoons on either side of the potato (this prevents your knife from going all the way through). Slice potato into thin chips leaving about 1/4" attached on the bottom.

2.   Freeze bacon slices for about 30 minutes then cut into small pieces about the size of a stamp. Place these in the cracks between every other slice.

3.   Place the potato in a large cast iron skillet. Top the potato with slices of hard butter (you can also place thin slivers of cold butter between the potato slices with the bacon if desired). Season with salt and pepper.

4.   Supply your smoker with wood pellets and follow the start-up procedure. Preheat the grill, with the lid closed, to 350° F.

5.   Place the cast iron directly on the grill grate and cook for two hours. Top potatoes with more butter and baste with melted butter every 30 minutes.

6.   In the last 10 minutes of cooking, sprinkle with cheddar and return to grill to melt.

7.   To finish, top with chives or scallions. Enjoy!

Mashed Red Potatoes

Servings: 4
Cooking Time: 40 Minutes

Ingredients:

- 8 Large red potatoes
- salt
- black pepper
- 1/2 Cup heavy cream
- 1/4 Cup butter

Directions:

1.   Supply your smoker with wood pellets and follow the start-up procedure. Preheat the grill, with the lid closed, to 180° F.

2.   Slice red potatoes in half, lengthwise then cut in half again to make quarters. Season potatoes with salt and pepper.

3.   Increase the heat to High and preheat. Once the grill is hot, set potatoes directly on the grill grate. Grill: 450 °F

4.   Every 15 minutes flip potatoes to ensure all sides get color. Continue to do this until potatoes are fork tender.

5.   When tender, mash potatoes with cream, butter, salt, and pepper to taste. Serve warm, enjoy!

Cast Iron Potatoes

Servings: 4
Cooking Time: 60 Minutes

Ingredients:

- 4 Tablespoon butter, cut into cubes
- 2 1/2 Pound potatoes, peeled and cut into 1/8 inch slices

- 1/2 Large sweet onion, thinly sliced
- salt
- black pepper
- 1 1/2 Cup grated mild cheddar or jack cheese
- 2 Cup milk
- paprika

Directions:

1. Butter the inside of a cast iron skillet and layer half the potato slices on the bottom. Top with half the onions. Season with salt and pepper.

2. Sprinkle 1 cup of the cheese over the potatoes and onions and dot with half the butter. Layer the remaining potatoes and onions on top. Dot with remaining butter.

3. Pour the milk into the skillet. Cover the skillet tightly with aluminum foil.

4. Supply your smoker with wood pellets and follow the start-up procedure. Preheat the grill, with the lid closed, to 350° F.

5. Bake for 1 hour, or until the potatoes are very tender. Grill: 350 ℉

6. Remove the foil and top with the remaining 1/2 cup of cheese. Bake for 30 minutes more (uncovered) until the cheese is lightly browned. Dust the top with paprika and serve immediately.

Traeger Smoked Coleslaw

Servings: 8
Cooking Time: 20 Minutes

Ingredients:

- 1 Head purple cabbage, shredded
- 1 Head green cabbage, shredded
- 1 Cup shredded carrots
- 2 scallions, thinly sliced
- 1 1/2 Cup mayonnaise
- 1/8 Cup white wine vinegar
- 1 Teaspoon celery seed
- 1 Teaspoon sugar
- salt and pepper

Directions:

1. Supply your smoker with wood pellets and follow the start-up procedure. Preheat the grill, with the lid closed, to 180° F.

2. Spread cabbage and carrots out on a sheet tray and place directly on the grill grates. Smoke for 20 to 25 minutes or until cabbage picks up desired amount of smoke. Grill: 180 ℉

3. Remove from grill and transfer to the refrigerator immediately to cool. While cabbage is cooling, make the dressing.

4. For the dressing, combine all ingredients in a small bowl and mix well.

5. Place smoked cabbage and carrots in a large bowl and pour dressing over them. Stir to coat well.

6. Transfer to a serving dish and sprinkle with scallions. Enjoy!

Roasted New Potatoes With Compound Butter

Servings: 4
Cooking Time: 45 Minutes

Ingredients:

- 2 Pound Small Red, White or Purple Potatoes (or Combination of All Three)
- 3 Tablespoon olive oil
- salt and pepper
- 2 Stick Butter, unsalted
- 1 Tablespoon shallot, minced
- 3 Tablespoon Finely Chopped Herbs, Such As Tarragon, Parsley, Basil or Combination
- 2 Teaspoon kosher salt

Directions:

1. Supply your smoker with wood pellets and follow the start-up procedure. Preheat the grill, with the lid closed, to 400° F. Cut the potatoes in half and place in a large mixing bowl. Cover with the olive oil, a teaspoon of salt and generous grinding of pepper.

2. Place on a large baking sheet so there is space between the potatoes. Place on the grill and roast for 45 minutes to 1 hour, until crispy skinned. Toss once during cooking. Grill: 400 ℉

3. To make the butter: Place it in a medium sized shallow mixing bowl. Use a wooden spoon or strong spatula to break it up and soften it even more. Sprinkle the shallot, herbs, and salt over the butter, then use the spoon to combine the ingredients. Taste, adding more

salt or herbs if necessary. Reserve a few tablespoons of the butter to serve on the potatoes.

4. To freeze the butter for future use, place a foot long piece of plastic wrap on the counter. Spread the butter out into a 6" log across the long direction of the plastic wrap towards the bottom. Begin to roll the plastic wrap away from you to roll it into a log, twisting the sides of the plastic wrap like a candy wrapper to secure.

5. Using your hands, shape the log into an even cylinder. Once it's wrapped tightly, place in the freezer. Then when more is needed, simply slice off coins of it to serve over grilled steak, chicken, veggies, or roasted potatoes. The butter holds well in the freezer for up to one month. Enjoy! *Cook times will vary depending on set and ambient temperatures.

Smoked Jalapeño Poppers

Servings: 4
Cooking Time: 60 Minutes

Ingredients:
- 12 Medium jalapeño
- 6 Slices bacon, cut in half
- 8 Ounce cream cheese
- 2 Tablespoon Pork & Poultry Rub
- 1 Cup grated cheese

Directions:
1. Supply your smoker with wood pellets and follow the start-up procedure. Preheat the grill, with the lid closed, to 180° F. For optimal flavor, use Super Smoke if available.
2. Slice the jalapeños in half lengthwise. Scrape out any seeds and ribs with a small spoon or paring knife. Mix softened cream cheese with Traeger Pork & Poultry rub and grated cheese. Spoon mixture onto each jalapeño half. Wrap with bacon and secure with a toothpick.
3. Place the jalapeños on a rimmed baking sheet. Place on grill and smoke for 30 minutes. Grill: 180 °F
4. Increase the grill temperature to 375°F and cook an additional 30 minutes or until bacon is cooked to desired doneness. Serve warm, enjoy! Grill: 375 °F

Grilled Broccoli Rabe

Servings: 4
Cooking Time: 10 Minutes

Ingredients:
- 4 Tablespoon extra-virgin olive oil
- 4 Bunch broccoli rabe or broccolini
- kosher salt
- 1 lemon, halved

Directions:
1. Supply your smoker with wood pellets and follow the start-up procedure. Preheat the grill, with the lid closed, to 450° F.
2. On a platter or in a mixing bowl, drizzle the olive oil over the broccoli rabe. Use your hands to mix thoroughly, coating the vegetables evenly with the oil. Season with sea salt.
3. Place the broccoli rabe in one layer directly on the lowest grill grate. Close the lid and cook for 5 to 10 minutes. You want there to be some color and slight char on the first side. Flip and cook for a few more minutes. Grill: 450 °F
4. Transfer the broccoli rabe to a serving platter and squeeze the juice of half a lemon evenly over the top.
5. Serve with more lemon wedges on the side. Enjoy!

Spicy Asian Brussels Sprouts

Servings: 4
Cooking Time: 10 Minutes

Ingredients:
- 2 Cup fresh Brussels sprouts
- 2 Tablespoon vegetable oil
- 1 Tablespoon Asian BBQ Rub
- 1/4 Cup Thai sweet chile sauce

Directions:
1. Supply your smoker with wood pellets and follow the start-up procedure. Preheat the grill, with the lid closed, to 350° F.
2. Spread the halved brussel sprouts in a single layer on a lined cookie sheet. Drizzle with the oil and toss to coat.

3. Sprinkle the brussel sprouts evenly with an Asian BBQ rub and put the cookie sheet on the grill. Close the lid and cook for 7-8 minutes. Grill: 350 °F

4. Toss the brussels sprouts in the Thai Chili Sauce and return to the grill for an additional 3-4 minutes, or until the sprouts are crisp-tender. Grill: 350 °F

5. Serve immediately. Enjoy!

Smoked Asparagus Soup

Servings: 4
Cooking Time: 40 Minutes

Ingredients:
- Pound Asparagus Spears
- 1 Tablespoon olive oil
- salt and pepper
- 1/2 yellow onion, diced
- 1 Tablespoon butter
- 2 Clove garlic, minced
- 1 1/2 Cup chicken stock
- 1 1/2 Cup cream
- 2 Stalk Raw Asparagus, Shaved

Directions:
1. Supply your smoker with wood pellets and follow the start-up procedure. Preheat the grill, with the lid closed, to 180° F.

2. Drizzle 1 pound of asparagus with olive oil and season with salt and pepper. Place directly on the grill grate and smoke for 20-30 minutes. Taste along the way to assess smoke level pulling earlier if needed. Grill: 180 °F

3. Place 1 Tbsp butter in a saucepan and melt over medium heat. Add onion and garlic and saute for 2-3 minutes or until onion is translucent.

4. Remove asparagus from the grill and cut into 1" pieces. Place asparagus in the pan with the onions and add stock and cream. Bring to a simmer.

5. Remove from heat and puree using a blender or immersion blender until smooth.

6. Season with salt and pepper and serve. Top with fresh shaved asparagus, sprinkle with salt, pepper, and smoked paprika if desired. Enjoy!

Roasted Mashed Potatoes

Servings: 8
Cooking Time: 40 Minutes

Ingredients:
- 5 Pound Yukon Gold potatoes
- 1 1/2 Stick butter, softened
- 1 1/2 Cup heavy whipping cream, room temperature
- kosher salt
- white pepper

Directions:
1. Supply your smoker with wood pellets and follow the start-up procedure. Preheat the grill, with the lid closed, to 300° F.

2. Peel and cut potatoes into 1/2 inch cubes. Place the potatoes in a shallow baking dish with 1/2 cup water and cover. Bake until tender, about 40 minutes. Grill: 300 °F

3. In a medium saucepan, combine cream and butter. Cook over medium heat until butter is melted.

4. Remove potatoes from the grill and drain water.

5. Transfer potatoes to a bowl and mash using a potato masher. Gradually add in cream and butter mixture and mix using the masher. Be careful not to overwork or the potatoes will becomes gluey. Season with salt and pepper to taste. Enjoy!

Smoked & Loaded Baked Potato

Servings: 4
Cooking Time: 60 Minutes

Ingredients:
- 6 Yukon Gold or russet potatoes
- 8 Slices bacon
- 1/2 Cup butter, melted
- 1 Cup sour cream
- 1 1/2 Cup shredded cheddar cheese, divided
- salt and pepper
- 1 Bunch green onions, thinly sliced

Directions:
1. Supply your smoker with wood pellets and follow the start-up procedure. Preheat the grill, with the lid closed, to 375° F.

2. Poke potatoes with a fork, then place straight onto the grill. Cook for 1 hour. Grill: 375 °F

3. At the same time, cook bacon on a baking sheet on the grill for about 20 minutes; remove, cool and crumble. Grill: 375 °F

4. Once potatoes are done, remove and allow to cool for 15 minutes.

5. Cut each potato lengthwise, creating long halves. Use a small spoon to scoop out about 70% of the potato to make a boat, keeping a thick layer of potato near skin.

6. Place excess potato in a bowl and reserve. Lightly mash extra potato with a fork; add butter, sour cream, 1/2 cup cheese and season with salt and pepper.

7. Take the potato skins and fill with potato mixture, then sprinkle with extra cheese and bacon.

8. Place back on grill for about 10 minutes or until warm and cheese has melted. Garnish with green onions and extra sour cream. Enjoy! Grill: 375 °F

Roasted Jalapeño Poppers

Servings: 2
Cooking Time: 30 Minutes

Ingredients:

- 8 Slices Bacon, Center Cut
- 2 Cup cream cheese
- 2 Ounce Cheese, sharp cheddar
- 1/2 Cup green onions, minced
- 2 Teaspoon fresh squeezed lime juice
- 4 Tablespoon Seeded Tomato, Chopped
- 4 Tablespoon cilantro, chopped
- 1/2 Teaspoon kosher salt
- 2 Small garlic clove, minced
- 12 Whole Jalapeños

Directions:

1. Supply your smoker with wood pellets and follow the start-up procedure. Preheat the grill, with the lid closed, to 350° F.

2. Place 2 bacon slices directly on the grill grate and cook 10-15 minutes until cooked through and crispy flipping halfway through. Remove from grill, but leave the grill on. When cool enough to handle, coarsely chop the bacon and reserve. Grill: 350 °F

3. In the bowl of a stand mixer, combine cream cheese, cheddar cheese, green onions, chopped bacon, lime juice, tomatoes, cilantro, salt and garlic. Mix on medium speed with a paddle until combined. Transfer mixture to a piping bag.

4. Cut the tops off the jalapeños and remove the seeds and ribs with a small paring knife.

5. Pipe the filling into each pepper so that the filling comes up a 1/4" over the top of the pepper. Place the tops back on each pepper.

6. With a rolling pin, flatten out the remaining six slices of bacon until they are 1/8" thick. Cut each slice in half. Wrap 1/2 a bacon slice around each pepper and secure with a toothpick.

7. Place the peppers in the Traeger Jalapeno Popper Tray. Place the tray directly on the grill grate and cook for 30-40 minutes until the peppers are tender, bacon is crispy, and cheese is melted. Enjoy! Grill: 350 °F

Smoked Mashed Potatoes

Servings: 6
Cooking Time: 45 Minutes

Ingredients:

- 2 Pound red bliss potatoes, washed and diced medium
- chicken stock or water
- 1/2 Stick salted butter
- 1 Cup whole milk
- 1/2 Cup sour cream
- 1/2 Cup shredded or grated Parmesan cheese
- kosher salt
- freshly ground black pepper
- 1/2 Cup fresh sliced green onions

Directions:

1. Place the diced red potatoes into a small saucepan or stockpot and cover with chicken stock or water.

2. Bring to a boil and cook on a simmer until fork tender, then cook 4 to 5 minutes past that until soft.

3. Supply your smoker with wood pellets and follow the start-up procedure. Preheat the grill, with the lid closed, to 400° F.

4. In a separate ovenproof pan, such as a cast iron skillet, add butter and milk and place in the Traeger

during start up, until melted (approximately 7 to 10 minutes). Grill: 400 °F

5. Carefully remove the butter/milk mixture from the Traeger using heatproof gloves.

6. Drain the potatoes and place into a large bowl. Add the melted butter/milk mixture and slowly mash.

7. Add sour cream, cheese and green onions, then season to taste with salt and pepper.

8. Place into the cast iron skillet, then place the skillet back into the Traeger and cook until the potatoes have a slight crust and are bubbling, about 15 minutes. Grill: 400 °F

9. Carefully remove the mashed potatoes from the Traeger using heatproof gloves. Allow to cool for 5 minutes. Scoop and enjoy!

Christmas Brussel Sprouts

Servings: 6
Cooking Time: 50 Minutes

Ingredients:
- 1/2 Pound thick-cut bacon
- 1 Medium onion, diced
- 2 Pound fresh Brussels sprouts
- 2 Tablespoon olive oil
- salt and pepper

Directions:
1. Supply your smoker with wood pellets and follow the start-up procedure. Preheat the grill, with the lid closed, to 350° F.
2. Place bacon directly on grill grate and cook for 15-20 minutes, or until lightly browned. Remove from grill and set aside on paper towel lined plate.
3. Slice onion in half and then slice into 1/4 inch moons and add to large mixing bowl. Slice brussels sprouts in half lengthwise and add to bowl.
4. Cut reserved bacon into 1/2 inch pieces and add to bowl. Drizzle with olive oil and sprinkle with salt and pepper. Toss to coat and pour into baking pan.
5. Turn the temperature on grill to 375 and place baking pan on grill. Roast for 30 minutes mixing halfway through cooking. Grill: 375 °F

Roasted Tomatoes With Hot Pepper Sauce

Servings: 4
Cooking Time: 60 Minutes

Ingredients:
- 2 Pound fresh Roma tomatoes
- 3 Tablespoon parsley, chopped
- 2 Tablespoon garlic, chopped
- salt and pepper
- 1/2 Cup extra-virgin olive oil
- 1 Pound Spaghetti
- Hot peppers

Directions:
1. Supply your smoker with wood pellets and follow the start-up procedure. Preheat the grill, with the lid closed, to 400° F.
2. Wash tomatoes and cut them in half, lengthwise. Place them in a baking dish cut side up.
3. Sprinkle with chopped parsley, garlic, add salt and black pepper and pour 1/4 cup (100 mL)of olive oil over them.
4. Place on pre-heated grill and bake for 1 1/2 hours. Tomatoes will shrink and the skins will be partly blackened. Grill: 400 °F
5. Remove tomatoes from baking dish and place in a food processor leaving the cooked oil, and puree them.
6. Drop pasta into boiling salted water and cook until tender. Drain and toss immediately with the pureed tomatoes.
7. Add the remaining 1/4 cup (60mL) of raw olive oil and crumbled hot red pepper to taste. Toss and serve. Enjoy!

Roasted Potato Poutine

Servings: 6
Cooking Time: 40 Minutes

Ingredients:
- 4 Large russet potatoes
- Tablespoon olive oil or vegetable oil
- Prime Rib Rub
- Cup chicken or beef gravy (homemade or jarred)
- 1 1/2 Cup white or yellow cheddar cheese curds

- freshly ground black pepper
- 2 Tablespoon scallions

Directions:

1. Supply your smoker with wood pellets and follow the start-up procedure. Preheat the grill, with the lid closed, to 500° F.

2. Scrub the potatoes and slice into fries, wedges or preferred shape.

3. Put potatoes into a large mixing bowl and coat with oil. Season generously with Traeger Prime Rib rub.

4. Tip the potatoes onto a rimmed baking sheet and spread in a single layer, cut sides down.

5. Roast for 20 minutes, then using a spatula, turn the potatoes to the other cut side. Continue to roast until the potatoes are tender and golden brown, about 15 to 20 minutes more.

6. While potatoes cook, warm the gravy on the stovetop or in a heat-proof saucepan on your Traeger.

7. To assemble the poutine, arrange the potatoes in a large shallow bowl or on a serving platter. Distribute the cheese curds on top. Pour the hot gravy evenly over the potatoes and cheese curds.

8. Season with black pepper and garnish with thinly sliced scallions. Serve immediately. Enjoy!

Butter Braised Green Beans

Servings: 6
Cooking Time: 60 Minutes

Ingredients:

- 24 Ounce thin fresh green beans, trimmed or whole frozen green beans, thawed
- 8 Tablespoon butter, melted
- Veggie Rub or coarse salt
- freshly ground black pepper

Directions:

1. Supply your smoker with wood pellets and follow the start-up procedure. Preheat the grill, with the lid closed, to 325° F.

2. Put the green beans in a pile on a rimmed baking sheet and pour the melted butter over them. Using tongs, spread the beans out in the pan and season with Traeger Veggie Rub and black pepper.

3. Roast the beans for about 1 hour, stirring and lifting with tongs every 20 minutes or so. The beans should be very tender, shriveled, and lightly browned in places. Transfer to a serving bowl and serve while hot. Enjoy!

Braised Creamed Green Beans

Servings: 4
Cooking Time: 25 Minutes

Ingredients:

- 6 Tablespoon butter
- 2 Clove garlic, pressed or minced
- 1 shallot, thinly sliced
- 1 Cup heavy cream
- 1 Pinch ground nutmeg
- salt
- 3 Pound mixed greens such as kale, chard or collards; washed, stems removed and torn into bite sized pieces

Directions:

1. Supply your smoker with wood pellets and follow the start-up procedure. Preheat the grill, with the lid closed, to 325° F.

2. In a saucepan, heat 2 tablespoons of the butter over high heat until it foams. Add the garlic and shallot and cook over medium-low heat, stirring, until softened and golden, about 5 minutes.

3. Add the cream, bring to a simmer and cook until slightly thickened, about 10 minutes.

4. Add the nutmeg and salt to taste. Using a hand blender, purée until smooth.

5. In a cast iron pan, heat the remaining 4 tablespoons butter over high heat until it foams.

6. Add the greens and cook until tender but still bright green, about 5 minutes.

7. Sprinkle with salt and add the cream mixture. Cover and transfer to the grill.

8. Braise greens for 15-20 minutes until the cream is bubbling and greens are tender. Grill: 325 °F

9. Season to taste with nutmeg and salt. Serve hot. Enjoy!

Roasted Asparagus

Servings: 4

Cooking Time: 30 Minutes

Ingredients:

- 1 Bunch asparagus
- 2 Tablespoon olive oil, plus more as needed
- Veggie Rub

Directions:

1. Coat asparagus with olive oil and Veggie Rub, stirring to coat all pieces.

2. Supply your smoker with wood pellets and follow the start-up procedure. Preheat the grill, with the lid closed, to 350° F.

3. Place asparagus directly on the grill grate for 15-20 minutes.

4. Remove from grill and enjoy!

POULTRY RECIPES

Chicken Parmesan Sliders With Pesto Mayonnaise

Servings: 4
Cooking Time: 30 Minutes

Ingredients:
- 2 Pound Chicken, ground
- 1 Cup Parmesan cheese
- 1 Tablespoon Worcestershire sauce
- black pepper
- 1 Cup mayonnaise
- 2 Tablespoon Pesto Sauce
- 3 Roma tomatoes
- 1 red onion, sliced
- Baby Spinach

Directions:
1. Line a baking sheet with plastic wrap. In a large mixing bowl, combine the ground chicken, the Parmesan, the Worcestershire, and a few grinds of black pepper. Wet your hands with cold water, and use them to mix the ingredients.
2. Divide the meat mixture in half, then form six 2-inch patties out of each half. Place the patties on the baking sheet, cover with another sheet of plastic wrap, and refrigerate for at least 1 hour.
3. Combine the mayonnaise and pesto in a small bowl and whisk together. Cover and refrigerate until serving time.
4. Supply your smoker with wood pellets and follow the start-up procedure. Preheat the grill, with the lid closed, to 300° F.
5. Arrange the chicken patties on the grill grate and grill, turning once, until the patties are cooked through (165F), about 30 minutes. Grill: 300 °F Probe: 165 °F
6. To serve, put a chicken patty on the bottom of a slider bun and top with a dollop of the pesto mayonnaise. Add tomato, onion, and spinach as desired. Replace the top of the bun and skewer with a frilled toothpick, if desired.

Delicious Smoked Turketta

Servings: 6
Cooking Time: 180 Minutes

Ingredients:
- 1 Shady Brook Farms® Turketta

Directions:
1. Supply your smoker with wood pellets and follow the start-up procedure. Preheat the grill, with the lid closed, to 250° F. If using a gas or charcoal grill, set it up for low, indirect heat.
2. Place the Turketta directly on the grill grate and smoke for 2½ to 3 hours, or until an internal temperature of 165°F is reached.

Smoked Beer Brine Hens

Servings: 4
Cooking Time: 150 Minutes

Ingredients:
- 2 Tbsp Ales Pepper
- 12 Cups Beer Brine
- 2 Cornish Game Hens
- 2 Lemons
- 6 Rosemary Sprigs
- Salt & Freshly Ground Black Pepper
- 12 Thyme Sprigs

Directions:
1. Supply your smoker with wood pellets and follow the start-up procedure. Preheat the grill, with the lid open, to 300° F. (I have found the setting the grill at 300 will keep the top smoker temp between 200°F and 215°F, this could vary depending on the air temp and general weather conditions. You want to keep the upper smoking cabinet between 200°F and 215°F) If you're using a vertical smoker, set temp to 200°F.
2. Stuff your hens with the rosemary, thyme, and lemons. Coat the skin with the ales pepper and freshly ground black pepper.
3. Truss your hens and tie a small loop at the legs so you can hang your birds. Hang them in the smoker and

insert a probe thermometer, cook to an internal temp of 155°F.

4.   Remove the hens to rest. Final temp should be 160°F.

5.   Serve these with some great creamed kale or charred asparagus.

Spatchcocked Turkey

Servings: 10-14
Cooking Time: 120 Minutes

Ingredients:
- 1 whole turkey
- 2 tablespoons olive oil
- 1 batch Chicken Rub

Directions:
1.   Supply your smoker with wood pellets and follow the start-up procedure. Preheat the grill, with the lid closed, to 350°F.
2.   To remove the turkey's backbone, place the turkey on a work surface, on its breast. Using kitchen shears, cut along one side of the turkey's backbone and then the other. Pull out the bone.
3.   Once the backbone is removed, turn the turkey breast-side up and flatten it.
4.   Coat the turkey with olive oil and season it on both sides with the rub. Using your hands, work the rub into the meat and skin.
5.   Place the turkey directly on the grill grate, breast-side up, and cook until its internal temperature reaches 170°F.
6.   Remove the turkey from the grill and let it rest for 10 minutes, before carving and serving.

Apple Bacon Lattice Turkey

Servings: 7
Cooking Time: 180 Minutes

Ingredients:
- 2 Apples
- Bacon
- 2 Celery, Stick
- (Parsley, Rosemary, Thyme) Herb Mix
- 1 Onion, Sliced
- Pepper

- Grills Champion Chicken Seasoning
- 1 Brined Turkey

Directions:
1.   Supply your smoker with wood pellets and follow the start-up procedure. Preheat the grill, with the lid closed, to 300° F.
2.   Be sure all the innards and giblets of the turkey have been removed.
3.   Wash the external and internal parts of the turkey and pat the surface dry with a paper towel.
4.   Slice fruit and veggies into large chunks and stuff inside turkey.
5.   Liberally season the whole Turkey with Champion Chicken Seasoning.
6.   Prep bacon into lattice design on a flexible cutting board. Flip onto top of turkey, covering the breasts.
7.   Season with more Champion Chicken and black pepper
8.   Season with more Champion Chicken and black pepper
9.   Let the turkey rest for 30 minutes.

Roasted Tin Foil Dinners

Servings: 4
Cooking Time: 25 Minutes

Ingredients:
- 4 boneless, skinless chicken breast
- Chicken Rub
- 1/2 Pound new potatoes, quartered
- 8 Ounce cremini mushrooms, cleaned and quartered
- salt and pepper
- 1/2 Pound green beans, ends trimmed
- 1 Medium lemon, cut into 3/4 inch slices

Directions:
1.   Supply your smoker with wood pellets and follow the start-up procedure. Preheat the grill, with the lid closed, to 400° F.
2.   Season chicken breast with salt, pepper and Traeger Chicken Rub. Place the potatoes, mushrooms and chicken in the middle of a large sheet of foil, season with more salt and pepper as needed, and wrap up tightly.

3. Place foil pack directly on the grill grate and cook for 15 minutes. Grill: 400 °F

4. Open up the foil pack and add green beans, lemon and additional salt and pepper, if needed. Wrap back up and return to the Traeger for an additional 10 minutes. Grill: 400 °F

5. Remove from the Traeger, open packet and enjoy!

Smoked Drumsticks

Servings: 2-4
Cooking Time: 25 Minutes

Ingredients:
- 1 pound chicken drumsticks
- 2 tablespoons olive oil
- 1 batch Sweet and Spicy Cinnamon Rub

Directions:
1. Supply your smoker with wood pellets and follow the start-up procedure. Preheat the grill, with the lid closed, to 350°F.
2. Coat the drumsticks all over with olive oil and season with the rub. Using your hands, work the rub into the meat.
3. Place the drumsticks directly on the grill grate and smoke until their internal temperature reaches 170°F. Remove the drumsticks from the grill and serve immediately.

Smoked Boneless Chicken Thighs

Servings: 8 - 10
Cooking Time: 55 Minutes

Ingredients:
- 2 Tbsp Ginger Root, Grated
- 5 Lbs. Boneless Skinless Chicken Thighs
- ⅔ Cup Brown Sugar
- 2 Cups Chicken Broth
- 1 Tsp Chinese Five-Spice Powder
- 5 Garlic Cloves, Minced
- ¼ Cup Honey
- 1 Tbsp Sweet Heat Rub
- ½ Cup Soy Sauce
- 1 Yellow Onion, Minced

Directions:

1. Supply your smoker with wood pellets and follow the start-up procedure. Preheat the grill, with the lid closed, to 225° F. If using a gas or charcoal grill, set it up for low heat.

2. Remove chicken from marinade and place on a metal sheet tray. Using a mesh strainer, strain the marinade directly into a cast iron skillet.

3. Place skillet with marinade and chicken on the grill. Allow chicken to smoke for 10 minutes, then increase grill temperature to 400°F.

4. Grill an additional 15 minutes. Make sure to stir marinade periodically. The sauce will begin to reduce and thicken as it cooks.

5. After 15 minutes, baste chicken thighs with marinade, then flip and baste the other sides. Grill an additional 15 minutes, then baste again.

6. Cook until glaze has caramelized and thickened, then remove from grill and serve hot.

Buffalo Chicken Wraps

Servings: 4
Cooking Time: 20 Minutes

Ingredients:
- 2 teaspoons poultry seasoning
- 1 teaspoon freshly ground black pepper
- 1 teaspoon garlic powder
- 1 to 1½ pounds chicken tenders
- 4 tablespoons (½ stick) unsalted butter, melted
- ½ cup hot sauce (such as Frank's RedHot)
- 4 (10-inch) flour tortillas
- 1 cup shredded lettuce
- ½ cup diced tomato
- ½ cup diced celery
- ½ cup diced red onion
- ½ cup shredded Cheddar cheese
- ¼ cup blue cheese crumbles
- ¼ cup prepared ranch dressing
- 2 tablespoons sliced pickled jalapeño peppers (optional)

Directions:
1. Supply your smoker with wood pellets and follow the start-up procedure. Preheat, with the lid closed, to 350°F.

2. In a small bowl, stir together the poultry seasoning, pepper, and garlic powder to create an all-purpose rub, and season the chicken tenders with it.

3. Arrange the tenders directly on the grill, close the lid, and smoke for 20 minutes, or until a meat thermometer inserted in the thickest part of the meat reads 170°F.

4. In another bowl, stir together the melted butter and hot sauce and coat the smoked chicken with it.

5. To serve, heat the tortillas on the grill for less than a minute on each side and place on a plate.

6. Top each tortilla with some of the lettuce, tomato, celery, red onion, Cheddar cheese, blue cheese crumbles, ranch dressing, and jalapeños (if using).

7. Divide the chicken among the tortillas, close up securely, and serve.

Buffalo Chicken

Servings: 6
Cooking Time: 90 Minutes

Ingredients:
- 1 1/2 Tbsp Apple Cider Vinegar
- 3 Tbsp Bleu Cheese, Crumbled
- 1/4 Cup Buffalo Sauce
- 1/2 Cup Butter, Unsalted, Cubed
- 1/4 Tsp Cayenne Pepper
- 3 Celery Stalks, Cut Into Sticks
- 1 Cup Cheddar Jack Cheese, Shredded
- 1 Lb Chicken Breast, Boneless, Skinless
- 3 Oz Cream Cheese, Softened
- 1/8 Tsp Garlic, Granulated
- 2/3 Cup Hot Pepper Sauce
- 12 Jalapeno Peppers
- Mason Jar(S)
- 1/4 Red Bell Pepper, Chopped
- 2 Scallions, Sliced Thin
- Shredded Chicken
- 3 Tbsp Sour Cream
- To Taste, Sweet Heat Rub
- 1/2 Tsp Sweet Heat Rub (For Sauce)
- 1/4 Tsp Worcestershire Sauce

Directions:

1. Supply your smoker with wood pellets and follow the start-up procedure. Preheat the grill, with the lid open, to 200° F. If using a gas or charcoal grill, set it up for low, indirect heat.

2. Season chicken breasts with Sweet Heat, then place on the grill. Smoke for 1 hour, then remove from the grill, and set aside to rest.

3. While the chicken is resting, prepare the Buffalo sauce: Set a small cast iron pan or saucepan on the grill. Open the sear slide and increase the grill temperature to 350° F. Add the hot pepper sauce, apple cider vinegar, Worcestershire sauce, Sweet Heat, cayenne, and granulated garlic to the skillet, and whisk to combine. When the sauce begins to bubble, remove the skillet from the grill and whisk in butter. Transfer the sauce to a mason jar.

4. Shred the chicken with 2 forks in the sauce skillet. Set aside.

5. Prepare the filling: In a mixing bowl, use a hand mixer to blend cream cheese, bleu cheese, Buffalo sauce and sour cream. Fold in scallions, red bell pepper, and shredded chicken.

6. Prepare the peppers: Cut each jalapeño in half, lengthwise. Use a paring knife or teaspoon to scrape out the seeds and membrane, then place in a cast iron skillet (might need to divide between 2 skillets). Stuff the mixture into the jalapeño halves, then top with shredded cheese.

7. Transfer peppers to the grill, with the sear slide closed. Close the lid and cook for 15 to 20 minutes, until peppers begin to soften and cheese has melted.

8. Remove the peppers from the grill, transfer to a serving board or platter, and serve warm with extra Buffalo sauce.

Smoked Chicken Vermicelli Noodles

Servings: 4 – 6
Cooking Time: 120 Minutes

Ingredients:
- 2 Cup Broccoli
- ¼ Cup Chicken Stock
- 6 - 8 Chicken Thighs, Boneless, Skinless
- 1 Tbsp Chili Flakes

- 1 Tsp Cornstarch
- 4, Chopped Garlic Cloves
- 3 Tbsp Hoisin Sauce, Divided
- Knob Of Fresh Ginger, Grated
- 1, Thin Red Bell Peppers, Sliced
- 1 Tbsp Rice Wine Vinegar
- 8 Scallions, Sliced
- 1 ½ Tbsp Sesame Oil, Divided
- 1 Tbsp, Toasted Sesame Seeds
- 3.5 Oz Shitake Mushrooms, Sliced Thin
- 8 Oz Snow Peas
- 3 Tbsp Soy Sauce
- 2 Tbsp Sweet Chili Sauce
- 3 Tbsp Vegetable Oil
- 1 Lb Vermicelli Noodles, Or Linguini, Cooked And Drained

Directions:

1. In a large bowl, whisk together rice wine vinegar, 1 tablespoon of Hoisin sauce, and 1 tablespoon of sesame oil. Toss chicken to coat and allow to marinate for 1 hour.

2. Supply your smoker with wood pellets and follow the start-up procedure. Preheat the grill, with the lid open, to 225° F. If using a gas or charcoal grill, set it for low, indirect heat. Place chicken directly on the grill grate and smoke for 1 ½ to 2 hours, or until the internal temperature reaches 165° F. Remove it from the smoker, cover with foil, and rest for 10 minutes, then slice thin and set aside.

3. In a glass measuring cup whisk together 2 tablespoons of Hoisin sauce, soy sauce, sweet chili sauce, chicken stock, ½ tablespoon of sesame oil, and cornstarch. Set aside.

4. Preheat griddle to medium flame, then add oil. Working quickly, sauté ginger and garlic for 15 seconds, then add bell pepper and mushrooms and continue cooking for another minute, then add in snow peas and slaw. Toss in cooked pasta, chicken, scallions, and pour sauce over. Cook for one minute until sauce thickens and is well incorporated.

5. Transfer to platter and serve hot. Sprinkle with chili flakes and sesame seeds, if desired.

Smoking Duck With Mandarin Glaze

Servings: 4
Cooking Time: 240 Minutes

Ingredients:

- 1 quart buttermilk
- 1 (5-pound) whole duck
- ¾ cup soy sauce
- ½ cup hoisin sauce
- ½ cup rice wine vinegar
- 2 tablespoons sesame oil
- 1 tablespoon freshly ground black pepper
- 1 tablespoon minced garlic
- Mandarin Glaze, for drizzling

Directions:

1. With a very sharp knife, remove as much fat from the duck as you can. Refrigerate or freeze the fat for later use.

2. Pour the buttermilk into a large container with a lid and submerge the whole duck in it. Cover and let brine in the refrigerator for 4 to 6 hours.

3. Supply your smoker with wood pellets and follow the start-up procedure. Preheat, with the lid closed, to 250°F.

4. Remove the duck from the buttermilk brine, then rinse it and pat dry with paper towels.

5. In a bowl, combine the soy sauce, hoisin sauce, vinegar, sesame oil, pepper, and garlic to form a paste. Reserve ¼ cup for basting.

6. Poke holes in the skin of the duck and rub the remaining paste all over and inside the cavity.

7. Place the duck on the grill breast-side down, close the lid, and smoke for about 4 hours, basting every hour with the reserved paste, until a meat thermometer inserted in the thickest part of the meat reads 165°F. Use aluminum foil to tent the duck in the last 30 minutes or so if it starts to brown too quickly.

8. To finish, drizzle with glaze.

Grilled Whole Chicken Stuffed Sausage And Apple

Servings: 4
Cooking Time: 90 Minutes

Ingredients:

- ¼ Tbsp Black Pepper
- 1 Tbsp Butter, Unsalted
- 1 Celery, Stalk
- ¾ Cup Chicken Broth
- ¼ Tbsp Dried Sage
- 1 ½ Cup Dry Stuffing, Unseasoned
- 1 Granny Smith Apple, Chopped
- 8 Oz. Italian Sausage, Casings Removed
- ½ Tbsp Olive Oil
- 3 Tbsp Tennessee Apple Butter Rub
- ¼ Tbsp Salt
- ¼ White Onion, Chopped
- ½ White Onion, Sliced
- 3-4 Lb. Whole Chicken

Directions:

1. Supply your smoker with wood pellets and follow the start-up procedure. Preheat the grill, with the lid open, to 400° F. If using a gas or charcoal grill, set it up for medium-high heat.

2. Meanwhile, rinse chicken thoroughly and dry with paper towel. Place sliced onion in cast iron pan and set chicken on top. Place stuffing inside chicken cavity. Sprinkle Tennessee Apple Butter seasoning all over chicken and rub into skin. Tuck wings under.

3. Transfer to pellet grill and cook for 45 minutes. Add 1 cup chicken stock to pan, rotate and cook an additional 30 minutes. Remove from grill when internal temperature reaches 165° F and there is even browning. Allow chicken to rest for 15 minutes, then carve and serve.

Grilled Honey Chicken Wings

Servings: 4 - 8
Cooking Time: 30 Minutes

Ingredients:

- 2 Chipotles Chopped In Adobo
- 1 Apple Cider Vinegar
- 2 Tablespoons Balsamic Vinegar
- ¼ Cup Brown Sugar
- 2 ½ Lbs Chicken Wings, Trimmed And Patted Dry
- ¼ Cup Honey
- ½ Cup Ketchup
- ¼ Cup Adobo Sauce
- 2 Tablespoons Sweet Rib Rub
- 2 Teaspoons Worcestershire Sauce

Directions:

1. Supply your smoker with wood pellets and follow the start-up procedure. Preheat the grill, with the lid open, to 350° F. If you're using a charcoal or gas grill, set up the grill for medium high heat.

2. In a large bowl, whisk together the apple cider vinegar, ketchup, brown sugar, honey, chopped chipotle peppers with adobo sauce, balsamic vinegar, Worcestershire sauce, and Sweet Rib Rub. Whisk the glaze until it's well combined.

3. Add the wings to the glaze and place the bowl in the refrigerator. Marinade the chicken wings for up to 12 hours. Once the wings have finished marinating, remove the chicken wings from the marinade and place the chicken wings onto the wing rack.

4. Once all the wings have been placed on the wing rack, place the wing rack on the grill. Insert a temperature probe into the thickest part into one of the wings and grill the wings for 5 minutes, and then rotate the rack 180° and grill for another 5 minutes. Remove the wings once they have an internal temperature of 165°F and the juice from the chicken runs clear.

5. Remove the wings from the grill and serve immediately.

Smoked Turkey Jerky

Servings: 6
Cooking Time: 240 Minutes

Ingredients:

- 1/2 Cup soy sauce
- 1/4 Cup water
- 2 Tablespoon honey
- 2 Tablespoon Asian chili garlic sauce
- 2 Tablespoon lime juice

- 1 Tablespoon Morton Tender Quick Home Meat Cure
- 2 Pound (4-5 lb) boneless turkey breast

Directions:

1. In a mixing bowl, combine the soy sauce, water, honey, chili-garlic paste, lime juice, and curing salt, if using. With a sharp knife, slice the turkey into 1/4" thick slices with the grain, which helps it hold together better as it dries. (This is easier if the meat is partially frozen.) Trim any fat, membrane, or connective tissue.

2. Put the turkey slices in a large resealable plastic bag. Pour the marinade mixture over the turkey, and massage the bag so that all the slices get coated with the marinade. Seal the bag and refrigerate for several hours, or overnight.

3. Supply your smoker with wood pellets and follow the start-up procedure. Preheat the grill, with the lid closed, to 180° F.

4. Remove the turkey from the marinade and discard the marinade. Dry the turkey slices between paper towels. Arrange in a single layer directly on the grill grate.

5. Smoke for 2 to 4 hours, or until the jerky is dry but still chewy and somewhat pliant when you bend a piece. Grill: 180 °F

6. Transfer to a resealable plastic bag while the jerky's still warm. Let the jerky rest for an hour at room temperature. Squeeze any air from the bag, and refrigerate the jerky. It will keep for several weeks. Enjoy!

Cornish Game Hen

Servings: 4
Cooking Time: 180 Minutes

Ingredients:
- 4 Cornish game hens
- Extra-virgin olive oil, for rubbing
- 2 teaspoons salt
- 1 teaspoon freshly ground black pepper
- 1 teaspoon celery seeds

Directions:

1. Supply your smoker with wood pellets and follow the start-up procedure. Preheat, with the lid closed, to 275°F.

2. Rub the game hens over and under the skin with olive oil and season all over with the salt, pepper, and celery seeds.

3. Place the birds directly on the grill grate, close the lid, and smoke for 2 to 3 hours, or until a meat thermometer inserted in each bird reads 170°F.

4. Serve the Cornish game hens hot.

Grilled Honey Garlic Wings

Servings: 4
Cooking Time: 60 Minutes

Ingredients:
- 2 1/2 Pound chicken wings
- Pork & Poultry Rub
- 4 Tablespoon butter
- 3 Clove garlic, minced
- 1/4 Cup honey
- 1/2 Cup hot sauce
- 1 1/2 Cup blue cheese or ranch dressing

Directions:

1. Start by segmenting the wings into three pieces, cutting through the joints. Discard the wing tips or save them to make a stock.

2. Lay out the remaining pieces on a rimmed baking sheet lined with nonstick foil or parchment paper. Season well with Traeger Pork & Poultry Rub.

3. Supply your smoker with wood pellets and follow the start-up procedure. Preheat the grill, with the lid closed, to 350° F.

4. Place the baking sheet with wings directly on the grill grate and cook for 45 to 50 minutes or until they are no longer pink at the bone. Grill: 350 °F

5. To make the sauce: Melt butter in a small saucepan. Add the garlic and sauté for 2 to 3 minutes. Add in the honey and hot sauce and cook for a few minutes until completely combined. Keep sauce warm while the wings are cooking.

6. After 45 minutes, pour the spicy honey-garlic sauce over the wings, turning with tongs to coat.

7. Place wings back on the grill and cook for an additional 10 to 15 minutes to set the sauce. Grill: 350 °F

8. Serve with ranch or blue cheese dressing. Enjoy!

Peanut Butter Chicken Wings

Servings: 4
Cooking Time: 35 Minutes

Ingredients:

- 1 Tsp Black Peppercorns, Ground
- 2 Tbsp Brown Sugar
- 4 Lbs Chicken Wings, Trimmed And Patted Dry
- 2 Tbsp Honey
- 1/4 Cup Peanut Butter
- 10 Oz Peanuts, Whole
- 2 Tsp Sweet Rib Rub
- 1/2 Red Onion, Minced
- 1/2 Cup Strawberry Preserves
- 1 Tbsp Thai Chili Sauce
- 1/4 Cup Worcestershire Sauce

Directions:

1. Place chicken wings in a 9 x13 glass baking dish. Pour mixture over chicken, cover with plastic wrap, and refrigerate for 2 hours.

2. Supply your smoker with wood pellets and follow the start-up procedure. Preheat the grill, with the lid open, to 400° F. Preheat griddle to medium-low flame. If using a gas or charcoal grill, set it to medium-high heat.

3. Place wings directly on grill grate, over indirect heat, and cook for 20 to 25 minutes, rotating wings every 5 minutes.

4. Meanwhile, place shelled peanuts on the griddle, turning occasionally with a metal spatula for 5 to 7 minutes, to lightly roast. Remove from the griddle and set aside to cool.

5. Remove wings from grill and allow to rest for 5 minutes. While wings are resting, shell the peanuts, and transfer to a resealable plastic bag. Use a rolling pin to crush the peanuts, then scatter peanuts on top of the chicken wings. Serve warm.

Spiced Smoked Chicken Quarters

Servings: 4
Cooking Time: 120 Minutes

Ingredients:

- 4 chicken leg quarters
- For the rub:

- 2 tbsp paprika
- 1 tbsp thyme
- 2 tbsp chili powder
- 2 tbsp cayenne pepper
- 1 tbsp garlic powder
- 1 tbsp onion powder
- 1 tbsp kosher/table salt
- 2 tbsp black pepper
- 1 tbsp olive oil

Directions:

1. Supply your smoker with wood pellets and follow the start-up procedure. Preheat the grill, with the lid closed, to 220° F.

2. Pat down chicken pieces with a paper towel to make them dry. Cut off any excess fat that's visible on the outside of the meat.

3. Apply a thin layer of oil to the chicken skin. In a small bowl, combine all the BBQ rub ingredients thoroughly. Apply BBQ rub generously to your chicken thighs, rubbing in firmly and thoroughly.

4. Transfer chicken quarters to your smoker rack.Close the lid.

5. Cook until the quarters reach an internal temperature of 165°F, about 2 hours.

6. Once cooked, increase the grill temperature to medium heat. Cook for just a few minutes, turning regularly, for a crispy skin.

Smoked Cheesy Chicken Quesadilla

Servings: 4-8
Cooking Time: 180 Minutes

Ingredients:

- 2-3 Boneless, Skinless Chicken Breasts
- 1 Jalapeno, Chopped
- 1 Onion, Chopped
- Sweet Heat Rub
- 1, Chopped Red Bell Pepper
- 1-2 Cups Salsa
- 3 Cups Shredded Cheddar Cheese
- 3 Cups Shredded Monterey Or Pepper Jack Cheese
- Taco Sauce
- 20 Taco-Size Tortilla

Directions:

1. Supply your smoker with wood pellets and follow the start-up procedure. Preheat the grill, with the lid closed, to 350° F. If you're using a gas or charcoal grill, set it up for medium heat. Preheat with lid closed for 10-15 minutes.

2. Sprinkle chicken breasts generously in Sweet Heat Rub and rub to coat evenly. Place chicken breasts directly on preheated grill grates and cook for 45 minutes, or until the chicken is completely cooked (165°F internal temperature), tender, and falling apart. Remove from the grill and let cool slightly. Shred with meat claws and set aside. Turn grill up to 375°F.

3. In a large bowl, add the shredded chicken, onion, red bell pepper, jalapeno, and taco sauce. Mix to combine then set aside.

4. Cut each tortilla in half. Add about 2 tablespoons each of the cheddar cheese, Monterey Jack cheese, and chicken mixture to each tortilla half. Roll the tortillas into cones, starting from the cut edge, making sure not to push the ingredients out of the tortilla.

5. Place the small bowl in the center of the pizza plan and begin to stack quesadilla cones in a ring around the bowl. The points of each cone should be in the center just touching the bowl. Sprinkle cheese over the layer and repeat another layer with the remaining cones, finishing with a final sprinkle of cheese.

6. Remove bowl from the center of the ring and place the pizza pan directly on the grill grates. Cook with the lid closed for 15-20 minutes, or until the cheese is melted and the edges are browned and crispy.

7. Fill small bowl with salsa and return to the center of the ring. Serve immediately and enjoy!

Thai Chicken Satays

Servings: 4
Cooking Time: 10 Minutes

Ingredients:
- 1½lb (680g) boneless, skinless chicken breasts
- for the marinade
- ½ cup unsweetened canned light coconut milk
- 2 garlic cloves, peeled and coarsely chopped
- ¼ cup loosely packed fresh cilantro leaves
- 1-inch (2.5cm) piece of fresh ginger, peeled and coarsely chopped
- 2 tbsp light soy sauce
- 1 tbsp Asian fish sauce
- 1 tbsp light brown sugar or low-carb substitute
- 2 tsp sambal oelek (optional)
- 1 tsp Thai-style curry powder
- 1 tsp ground cumin
- 1 tsp ground turmeric
- 1 tsp coarse salt
- 2 tbsp vegetable oil
- for serving
- butter lettuce leaves, washed and dried
- cherry tomatoes
- Peanut Sauce

Directions:
1. Use a sharp knife to slice the chicken breasts lengthwise into strips, each about 1 inch (2.5cm) wide. (If the chicken breasts are unusually thick, butterfly them before cutting them into strips.) Place the breasts in a resealable plastic bag.

2. In a blender, make the marinade by combining the ingredients. Blend until fairly smooth. Pour the marinade over the chicken, turning and massaging the bag to thoroughly coat the chicken. Refrigerate for 2 hours.

3. Supply your smoker with wood pellets and follow the start-up procedure. Preheat the grill, with the lid closed, to 450° F.

4. Remove the chicken from the marinade and let any excess drip off. (Discard the marinade.) Thread each chicken strip on a bamboo skewer, pushing the point in one side of the chicken and out the other as if sewing. Leave very little of the tip exposed because it will burn easily.

5. Place the skewers on the grate perpendicular to the bars. Grill until the chicken has grill marks and is fully cooked, about 3 to 5 minutes per side.

6. Remove the skewers from the grill. Place the lettuce leaves on a platter. Place the satays atop the leaves. Scatter cherry tomatoes over the top. Serve with the peanut sauce.

Mini Turducken Roulade

Servings: 6
Cooking Time: 120 Minutes

Ingredients:

- 1 (16-ounce) boneless turkey breast
- 1 (8-to 10-ounce) boneless duck breast
- 1 (8-ounce) boneless, skinless chicken breast
- Salt
- Freshly ground black pepper
- 2 cups Italian dressing
- 2 tablespoons Cajun seasoning
- 1 cup prepared seasoned stuffing mix
- 8 slices bacon
- Butcher's string

Directions:

1. Butterfly the turkey, duck, and chicken breasts, cover with plastic wrap and, using a mallet, flatten each ½ inch thick.
2. Season all the meat on both sides with a little salt and pepper.
3. In a medium bowl, combine the Italian dressing and Cajun seasoning. Spread one-fourth of the mixture on top of the flattened turkey breast.
4. Place the duck breast on top of the turkey, spread it with one-fourth of the dressing mixture, and top with the stuffing mix.
5. Place the chicken breast on top of the duck and spread with one-fourth of the dressing mixture.
6. Supply your smoker with wood pellets and follow the start-up procedure. Preheat, with the lid closed, to 275°F.
7. Tightly roll up the stack, tie with butcher's string, and slather the whole thing with the remaining dressing mixture.
8. Wrap the bacon slices around the turducken and secure with toothpicks, or try making a bacon weave (see the technique for this in the Jalapeño-Bacon Pork Tenderloin recipe).
9. Place the turducken roulade in a roasting pan. Transfer to the grill, close the lid, and roast for 2 hours, or until a meat thermometer inserted in the turducken reads 165°F. Tent twith aluminum foil in the last 30 minutes, if necessary, to keep from overbrowning.

10. Let the turducken rest for 15 to 20 minutes before carving. Serve warm.

Garlic Sriracha Buffalo Chicken Wings

Servings: 6-8
Cooking Time: 160 Minutes

Ingredients:

- 1 Cup Buffalo Sauce
- 6 Lbs Chicken Wings
- 2 Tbsp Garlic Powder
- 1 Tsp Pepper
- Divided By 2 Tbsp And ½ Tbsp Sweet Heat Rub
- 1 Tsp Salt
- ⅓ Cup, Divided Sriracha Sauce

Directions:

1. In a non-stick sauce pot, add the remaining Sriracha and buffalo sauce. Stir to combine and set aside.
2. Supply your smoker with wood pellets and follow the start-up procedure. Preheat the grill, with the lid open, to 250° F. If using a gas or charcoal grill, set it to low heat with indirect heat. Place marinated wings directly on grill grate and cook (covered) for 1 hour 15 minutes.
3. Flip wings and baste each piece with Sriracha sauce. Season with additional Sweet Heat Rub, cover, and continue to grill for an additional 1 hour 15 minutes.
4. Remove wings from grill and place on sheet tray. Baste with additional sauce, then open Sear Slide and return wings to the grill. Grill for 3-5 minutes, rotating often, until wings begin to char lightly.
5. Transfer wings to a serving tray, baste with remaining sauce and serve!

Apricot Glazed Ham

Servings: 8
Cooking Time: 60 Minutes

Ingredients:

- 1 Cup Apricot Preserves
- 1/2 Cup apricot brandy
- 1/4 Cup honey
- 1/4 Cup brown sugar, firmly packed

- 1/4 Teaspoon ground cloves
- 6 Ounce Apricot Nectar, bottled or ginger ale
- 1 Large ham
- fresh parsley
- apricot, halved

Directions:

1. Supply your smoker with wood pellets and follow the start-up procedure. Preheat the grill, with the lid closed, to 325° F.

2. In a saucepan, stir together the apricot preserves, apricot brandy, honey, brown sugar, cloves, and apricot nectar and simmer over medium heat until the preserves, honey, and brown sugar have melted. Set aside and keep warm.

3. Place ham in large roasting pan lined with aluminum foil. Place pan on grill and cook for 1.5 hours.

4. Open Grill and glaze ham with reserved mixture. Continue cooking for another 30 minutes or until a thermometer is inserted into the thickest part of the meat and reaches an internal temperatures of 135 degrees F. Probe: 135 °F

5. Garnish the platter with the parsley and apricots, if desired. Enjoy!

Savory-sweet Turkey Legs

Servings: 4
Cooking Time: 300 Minutes

Ingredients:

- 1 gallon hot water
- 1 cup curing salt (such as Morton Tender Quick)
- ¼ cup packed light brown sugar
- 1 teaspoon freshly ground black pepper
- 1 teaspoon ground cloves
- 1 bay leaf
- 2 teaspoons liquid smoke
- 4 turkey legs
- Mandarin Glaze, for serving

Directions:

1. In a large container with a lid, stir together the water, curing salt, brown sugar, pepper, cloves, bay leaf, and liquid smoke until the salt and sugar are dissolved; let come to room temperature.

2. Submerge the turkey legs in the seasoned brine, cover, and refrigerate overnight.

3. When ready to smoke, remove the turkey legs from the brine and rinse them; discard the brine.

4. Supply your smoker with wood pellets and follow the start-up procedure. Preheat, with the lid closed, to 225°F.

5. Arrange the turkey legs on the grill, close the lid, and smoke for 4 to 5 hours, or until dark brown and a meat thermometer inserted in the thickest part of the meat reads 165°F.

6. Serve with Mandarin Glaze on the side or drizzled over the turkey legs.

Smoke Roasted Chicken With Herb Butter

Servings: 4
Cooking Time: 60 Minutes

Ingredients:

- 8 Tablespoon butter, room temperature
- 1 Scallions, minced
- 1 Clove garlic, minced
- 2 Tablespoon Fresh Herbs (Thyme, Rosemary, Oregano, Basil, Sage or Parsley, Minced)
- 1 1/2 Tablespoon Chicken Rub
- 1/2 Tablespoon fresh lemon juice
- 1 (4 to 4-1/2 lb) chicken
- Chicken Rub

Directions:

1. In a small bowl, combine butter, scallions, garlic, minced fresh herbs, Traeger Chicken Rub and lemon juice. Blend well with a wooden spoon.

2. Remove any giblets from the cavity of the chicken. Wash the chicken inside and out with cold running water. Dry thoroughly with paper towels.

3. Sprinkle a generous amount of Traeger Chicken Rub into the cavity of the chicken.

4. Gently loosen the skin around the chicken breast and slide in a few tablespoons of the herb butter and cover evenly. Smear the outside of the chicken with the remaining herb butter.

5. Tuck the chicken wings behind the back. Tie the legs together with butcher's twine.

6. Sprinkle the outside of the chicken with more Traeger Chicken Rub and insert sprigs of fresh herbs into the cavity of the chicken if desired.

7. Supply your smoker with wood pellets and follow the start-up procedure. Preheat the grill, with the lid closed, to 400° F.

8. When grill is hot, place chicken directly on the grill grate, breast side up. Cook for 1 to 1-1/4 hours or until the internal temperature registers 165℉. If the chicken is browning too quickly, loosely cover the breast and legs with foil and continue to cook. Grill: 400 ℉ Probe: 165 ℉

9. Remove from the grill and let rest 15 minutes at room temperature before carving. Serve. Enjoy!

Jalapeño- & Cheese-stuffed Chicken

Servings: 4

Cooking Time: 30 Minutes

Ingredients:

- 4 boneless, skinless chicken breasts, each about 6 to 8oz (170 to 225g)
- 8 strips of thin-sliced bacon
- for the filling
- 4oz (110g) light cream cheese, at room temperature
- ⅓ cup shredded pepper Jack or Cheddar cheese
- 2 jalapeños, destemmed, deseeded, and minced
- 2 tbsp reduced-fat mayo
- 1 tsp chili powder
- ½ tsp coarse salt

Directions:

1. Supply your smoker with wood pellets and follow the start-up procedure. Preheat the grill, with the lid closed, to 375° F.

2. In a large bowl, make the filling by combining the ingredients. Mix well.

3. Use a sharp, thin-bladed knife to cut a deep pocket in the side of each chicken breast, angling the knife toward the opposite side. (Don't cut all the way through.) Spoon ¼ of the cheese filling into the pocket of each breast and gently press the edges of the pocket together to enclose. Wrap 2 slices of bacon in a spiral pattern around each breast.

4. Place the chicken on the grate at an angle to the bars. Grill until the chicken is cooked through, the filling melts, and the bacon is golden brown, about 25 to 30 minutes.

5. Transfer the pockets to a platter. Let rest for 2 minutes before serving.

Bbq Pulled Turkey Sandwiches

Servings: 6

Cooking Time: 120 Minutes

Ingredients:

- 6 Whole Turkey Thighs
- Pork & Poultry Rub
- 1 1/2 Cup chicken broth
- 1 Cup 'Que BBQ Sauce
- 6 Whole Kaiser Buns, Split

Directions:

1. Season turkey thighs on both sides with the Traeger Pork & Poultry rub.

2. Supply your smoker with wood pellets and follow the start-up procedure. Preheat the grill, with the lid closed, to 180° F.

3. Arrange the turkey thighs directly on the grill grate and smoke for 30 minutes.

4. Transfer the thighs to a sturdy disposable aluminum foil or roasting pan. Pour the broth around the thighs. Cover the pan with foil or a lid.

5. Increase temperature to 325℉ and preheat, lid closed. Roast the thighs until they reach an internal temperature of 180℉. Grill: 325 ℉ Probe: 180 ℉

6. Remove pan from the grill, but leave grill on. Let the turkey thighs cool slightly until they can be comfortably handled.

7. Pour off the drippings and reserve. Remove the skin and discard.

8. Pull the turkey meat into shreds with your fingers and return the meat to the roasting pan.

9. Add 1 cup or more of your favorite Traeger BBQ Sauce along with some of the drippings.

10. Recover the pan with foil and reheat the BBQ turkey on the Traeger for 20 to 30 minutes.

11. Serve with toasted buns if desired. Enjoy!

Italian Grilled Chicken Saltimbocca

Servings: 4
Cooking Time: 30 Minutes

Ingredients:

- 6 Chicken Breast
- olive oil
- Pork & Poultry Rub
- 6 Slices Prosciutto Slices
- 10 Sage, Leaves
- 1 Cup Parmesan cheese

Directions:

1. Supply your smoker with wood pellets and follow the start-up procedure. Preheat the grill, with the lid closed, to 350° F.

2. Using a sharp knife, carefully butterfly each chicken breast.

3. Oil the outside of each breast and season lightly with Traeger Pork and Poultry rub.

4. Wrap with a slice of prosciutto. Top with fresh sage and Parmesan cheese.

5. Arrange the chicken on a baking sheet or directly on the grill grate at an angle to the bars.

6. Roast until the chicken is cooked through, about 25 to 30 minutes or until it reaches an internal temperature of 165°F (75 C). Grill: 350 °F Probe: 165 °F

7. Let rest for 2 minutes before serving. Top with more fresh sage and parmesan. Enjoy!

Smoked Deviled Eggs

Servings: 4
Cooking Time: 30 Minutes

Ingredients:

- 7 hard boiled eggs, cooked and peeled
- 3 Tablespoon mayonnaise
- 3 Teaspoon diced chives
- 1 Teaspoon brown mustard
- 1 Teaspoon apple cider vinegar
- hot sauce
- salt and pepper
- 2 Tablespoon cooked bacon, crumbled
- paprika

Directions:

1. Supply your smoker with wood pellets and follow the start-up procedure. Preheat the grill, with the lid closed, to 180° F.

2. Place cooked and peeled eggs directly on the grill grate and smoke eggs for 30 minutes. Grill: 180 °F

3. Remove from grill and allow eggs to cool. Slice the eggs lengthwise and scoop the egg yolks into a gallon zip top bag.

4. Add mayonnaise, chives, mustard, vinegar, hot sauce, salt, and pepper to the bag. Zip the bag closed and, using your hands, knead all of the ingredients together until completely smooth.

5. Squeeze the yolk mixture into one corner of the bag and cut a small part of the corner off. Pipe the yolk mixture into the hard boiled egg whites. Top the deviled eggs with crumbled bacon and paprika. Chill until ready to serve. Enjoy!

Delicious Asian Bbq Wings

Servings: 6
Cooking Time: 60 Minutes

Ingredients:

- 2 Lbs Chicken, Wing
- 1 Tsp Garlic, Minced
- 1 Tsp Ginger, Fresh
- 1 Tsp Chopped Green Onion
- 1/2 Cup Hoisin Sauce
- 1 Tsp Honey
- 2 Tsp Rice Vinegar
- 2 Tsp Sesame Oil
- 1 Tsp Sesame Seeds
- 1 Tsp Soy Sauce
- 1 Cup Water, Boiling

Directions:

1. Add all ingredients except wings and sesame seeds to a mixing bowl and whisk to incorporate. Add wings to a resealable plastic bag and pour marinade over. Allow marinating for at least 2 hours up to overnight. Remove wings from bag, reserving marinade.

2. Supply your smoker with wood pellets and follow the start-up procedure. Preheat the grill, with the lid closed, to 300° F. Place wings in a grilling basket and

cook for 1 hour or until they reach an internal temperature of 165°F.

3. While wings are cooking, pour reserved marinade into a small saucepan and add rice wine vinegar. Over high heat, bring to a boil while whisking often, and reduce by 1/3, or about 10 minutes. Set aside.

4. Brush wings with reduced sauce and allow to cook for 5-10 more minutes or until glaze has set. Remove from smoker, sprinkle with sesame seeds, allow to rest for 5 minutes, and serve.

Chicken On A Throne

Servings: 6
Cooking Time: 75 Minutes

Ingredients:
- 1 can of low-carb beer or sugar-free dark-colored soda, about 12oz (350ml)
- 1 whole chicken, about 4lb (1.8kg)
- 3 tbsp barbecue rub, plus more

Directions:
1. Supply your smoker with wood pellets and follow the start-up procedure. Preheat the grill, with the lid closed, to 350° F.
2. Pour half the contents of the can into a glass for drinking. Set the half-full can aside.
3. Blot any juices off the chicken with paper towels. Sprinkle 2 teaspoons of the rub in the body and neck cavities. Sprinkle the remaining rub evenly on the outside. Tuck the wing tips behind the bird's back.
4. Carefully lower the chicken (body cavity side down) over the can. Place the chicken upright on its can on the grate. (For stability, pull the legs forward and rest them on the grate to essentially form a tripod.) Roast the chicken until the internal temperature in the thickest part of a thigh reaches 165°F (74°C), about 1 hour. (Check on your bird periodically to make sure it hasn't tipped over.) If it hasn't yet reached that temperature, continue cooking for about 15 minutes more.
5. Use heavy-duty insulated rubber gloves and tongs to carefully transfer the chicken to the kitchen. Let rest 5 minutes and then carefully ease the chicken off the can. Discard the can and its steaming liquid, being careful not to burn yourself. Carve the chicken and serve.

Chicken Tenders

Servings: 2-4
Cooking Time: 80 Minutes

Ingredients:
- 1 pound boneless, skinless chicken breast tenders
- 1 batch Chicken Rub

Directions:
1. Supply your smoker with wood pellets and follow the start-up procedure. Preheat the grill, with the lid closed, to 180°F.
2. Season the chicken tenders with the rub. Using your hands, work the rub into the meat.
3. Place the tenders directly on the grill grate and smoke for 1 hour.
4. Increase the grill's temperature to 300°F and continue to cook until the tenders' internal temperature reaches 170°F. Remove the tenders from the grill and serve immediately.

Green Goddess Chicken Legs

Servings: 4
Cooking Time: 40 Minutes

Ingredients:
- 2 Pound chicken legs
- 2 Cup Prepared "Green Goddess" Dressing
- 1/4 Cup parsley, chopped
- 1 Tablespoon paprika

Directions:
1. Place the chicken legs in a large resealable plastic bag. Combine the Green Goddess dressing as well as the parsley and paprika. Pour over the chicken legs. Refrigerate for 2 to 8 hours.
2. Supply your smoker with wood pellets and follow the start-up procedure. Preheat the grill, with the lid closed, to 350° F. Drain the chicken legs. Arrange the legs directly on the grill grate and grill, turning once, for 40 to 50 minutes, or until the legs are golden brown and cooked through. Serve at once. Grill: 350 °F

Smoked Beer Garlic Chicken

Servings: 4

Cooking Time: 120 Minutes

Ingredients:

- 1 whole chicken
- 2 tbsp olive oil
- 1 tbsp salt
- 2 tsp thyme
- 2 tsp dill
- 2 tsp garlic powder
- 1 can beer

Directions:

1. Spray or rub olive oil on the outside of the chicken. In a bowl, mix all other ingredients together (except beer).

2. Rub this mixture on the outside of your chicken.

3. Fill the chicken stand with beer(takes about 3/4 of your can of beer).

4. Place chicken on top of the chicken stand. Supply your smoker with wood pellets and follow the start-up procedure. Preheat the grill, with the lid closed, to 350° F. place chicken in the center making sure it is flat and won't tip over(you can lean the chicken against the upper rack).

5. Allow the chicken to cook for 2 hours or until the internal temperature of the chicken reaches at least 165 °F.

6. Remove from the grill and the stand and let rest 5-10 minutes before carving. Serve. Enjoy!

Loaded Chicken Fries

Servings: 4

Cooking Time: 20 Minutes

Ingredients:

- 8 Slices Bacon, Cooked And Diced
- 1 12 Oz Bag Cheese, Shredded
- 1 Bag Fries, Frozen
- 2 Tablespoons Green Onions, Diced
- ¼ Cup White Barbecue Sauce

Directions:

1. Supply your smoker with wood pellets and follow the start-up procedure. Preheat the grill, with the lid open, to 400° F.

2. Bake the fries on the baking sheet in your according to the manufacturer's instructions. Once the fries are done, remove them from the grill and reduce the temperature to 350°F.

3. Top the fries with the cheese, chicken and bacon. Place the fries back on the grill and cook for another 5-7 minutes, or until the chicken is warmed through and the cheese is melted. Remove the fries from the grill.

4. Top the fries with the white barbecue sauce and green onions and serve immediately.

Cheese Chicken Cordon Bleu

Servings: 8

Cooking Time: 75 Minutes

Ingredients:

- 8 Chicken, Boneless/Skinless
- 1 Cup Mozzarella Cheese, Shredded
- Lemon Pepper Garlic Seasoning
- 8 Prosciutto, Sliced

Directions:

1. Supply your smoker with wood pellets and follow the start-up procedure. Preheat the grill, with the lid closed, to 250° F.

2. Pound each chicken breast with a mallet or cast iron pan so that it's about ½ inch thick.

3. On a piece of prosciutto, sprinkle mozzarella cheese and roll up. Place in the middle of a chicken breast and wrap the chicken around the prosciutto roll. Sprinkle with Lemon Pepper seasoning.

4. Smoke for an hour to 75 minutes, or until internal temperature reaches 165 degrees F.

Grilled Cheesy Chicken

Servings: 4

Cooking Time: 45 Minutes

Ingredients:

- 4 Aged Chedder Cheese, Sliced
- 32 Oz Chicken Broth
- 1 Tsp Extra-Virgin Olive Oil
- Sweet Heat Rub And Grill

- 4 Plump Chicken, Boneless/Skinless

Directions:

1. Supply your smoker with wood pellets and follow the start-up procedure. Preheat the grill, with the lid open, to 350° F.

2. Remove the chicken from the brine. Pat the breasts dry and lightly brush olive oil on both sides of the chicken. Take your knife and slice diagonally across the top of each breast. Sprinkle a lit amount of Sweet Heat Rub and Grill on each side.

3. Barbecue your chicken breasts for 30 minutes. Next, place a slice of cheddar cheese on top of each breast.

4. Heat for another 5-10 minutes or until the cheese has fully melted into the incisions you made earlier. Remove and serve for a tender chicken breast with a spicy kick and hot cheesy center. You'll receive too much credit for a recipe this easy.

Duck Breast With Pomegranate Sauce

Servings: 4
Cooking Time: 13 Minutes

Ingredients:

- 4 duck breasts, each about 6oz (170g), skin on
- for the rub
- 2 tsp coarse salt
- 1 tsp ground cumin
- 1 tsp ground coriander
- 1 tsp freshly ground black pepper
- ½ tsp ground cinnamon
- ½ tsp ground fennel
- for the sauce
- 1 shallot, peeled and minced
- 1 cup pomegranate juice
- 1 tbsp sherry vinegar or balsamic vinegar
- 1 tsp cornstarch
- ¼ cup chicken stock or chicken broth
- 1 tbsp chilled unsalted butter, cut into 4 pieces
- ¼ cup fresh pomegranate seeds (optional)
- 1 tbsp minced fresh chives

Directions:

1. Place a cast iron skillet on the grate. Supply your smoker with wood pellets and follow the start-up procedure. Preheat the grill, with the lid closed, to 400° F.

2. In a small bowl, make the rub by combining the ingredients. Use a sharp knife to diagonally score the skin of each duck breast—but don't nick the flesh. Lightly season the scored side of each breast.

3. Place the duck breasts skin side down in the skillet and sear until the skin is crisp and golden brown, about 8 to 10 minutes. Turn the breasts and cook until the internal temperature in the thickest part of a breast reaches 130°F (54°C), about 2 to 3 minutes more. Transfer the breasts to a plate.

4. In a large saucepan on the stovetop over medium heat, make the sauce by heating 1 tablespoon of duck fat from the skillet. (Reserve the remainder for another use.) Add the shallot and sauté until soft, about 2 to 3 minutes.

5. Add the pomegranate juice and bring the mixture to a boil over medium-high heat. Reduce the sauce by half, about 3 to 5 minutes. Add the vinegar and lower the heat to medium low.

6. Whisk together the cornstarch and chicken stock until smooth. Whisk into the sauce and cook until the sauce thickens, about 1 to 2 minutes. Whisk in the butter and stir in the pomegranate seeds (if using).

7. Place the duck breasts on a warm platter. Drizzle the pomegranate sauce over the top. Scatter the chives around the platter before serving.

Smoked Apple Chicken Leg Quarters

Servings: 8
Cooking Time: 120 Minutes

Ingredients:

- 8 leg quarters
- 1 bottle marinade
- Pork & chicken rub
- 1 cup of apple juice or water

Directions:

1. Rinse chicken and pat dry.

2. Marinade chicken in the fridge for at least 30 minutes or overnight (preferred).

3. Once the chicken is marinated, sprinkle both sides with the rub.

4. Supply your smoker with wood pellets and follow the start-up procedure. Preheat the grill, with the lid closed, to 225° F.

5. Place a small stainless steel pot of apple juice or water in the inside corner to help keep moist.

6. Place chicken on your grill, skin side up, with lid closed.

7. Smoke for 2 hours or until the internal temperature in the thickest part of a thigh is 165 °F.

8. Remove chicken from the grill and let it rest for 5 minutes before serving. Enjoy!

Smoke-roasted Chicken Thighs

Servings: 12-15
Cooking Time: 120 Minutes

Ingredients:
- 3 pounds chicken thighs
- 2 teaspoons salt
- 2 teaspoons freshly ground black pepper
- 2 teaspoons garlic powder
- 2 teaspoons onion powder
- 2 cups prepared Italian dressing

Directions:
1. Place the chicken thighs in a shallow dish and sprinkle with the salt, pepper, garlic powder, and onion powder, being sure to get under the skin.

2. Cover with the Italian dressing, coating all sides, and refrigerate for 1 hour.

3. Supply your smoker with wood pellets and follow the start-up procedure. Preheat, with the lid closed, to 250°F.

4. Remove the chicken thighs from the marinade and place directly on the grill, skin-side down. Discard the marinade.

5. Close the lid and roast the chicken for 1 hour 30 minutes to 2 hours, or until a meat thermometer inserted in the thickest part of the thighs reads 165°F. Do not turn the thighs during the smoking process.

Savory Smoked Turkey Legs

Servings: 4
Cooking Time: 150 Minutes

Ingredients:
- 1 Cup Chicken Stock
- 2 Tbsp Blackened Sriracha Rub
- 4 Turkey Legs (Drumsticks)

Directions:
1. Fire up your pellet grill on SMOKE mode. With the lid open, let it run for 10 minutes.

2. Supply your smoker with wood pellets and follow the start-up procedure. Preheat the grill, with the lid closed, to 225° F. If using a gas or charcoal grill, set it up for low, indirect heat.

3. Combine turkey stock with 2 teaspoons of Blackened Sriracha Rub.

4. Place turkey legs on a sheet tray, then inject each with seasoned stock. Season the outside of the legs with remaining Blackened Sriracha.

5. Place turkey legs directly on the grate of the smoking cabinet, and cook for 1 ½ hours.

6. Increase temperature to 325°F, then transfer turkey legs to the bottom grill and cook for another 45 to 60 minutes, until the internal temperature reaches 170°F.

7. Remove turkey from the grill, allow to rest for 10 minutes, then serve warm.

Roasted Whole Chicken

Servings: 6-8
Cooking Time: 120 Minutes

Ingredients:
- 1 whole chicken
- 2 tablespoons olive oil
- 1 batch Chicken Rub

Directions:
1. Supply your smoker with wood pellets and follow the start-up procedure. Preheat the grill, with the lid closed, to 375°F.

2. Coat the chicken all over with olive oil and season it with the rub. Using your hands, work the rub into the meat.

3. Place the chicken directly on the grill grate and smoke until its internal temperature reaches 170°F.

4. Remove the chicken from the grill and let it rest for 10 minutes, before carving and serving.

Smoked Turkey Legs

Servings: 4
Cooking Time: 300 Minutes

Ingredients:

- 1 Cup Rub
- 1/2 Cup Morton Tender Quick Home Meat Cure
- 1/2 Cup brown sugar
- 1 Tablespoon crushed allspice berries, optional
- 1 Tablespoon grains de poivre noir entiers
- 2 bay leaves
- 2 Teaspoon liquid smoke
- 4 turkey legs

Directions:

1. In a large stockpot, combine one gallon of warm water, the rub, curing salt, brown sugar, allspice (if using), peppercorns, bay leaves and liquid smoke.
2. Bring to a boil over high heat to dissolve the salt granules. Cool to room temperature. Add 1/2 gallon cold water and 4 cups ice; chill in the refrigerator.
3. Add the turkey legs, making sure they're completely submerged in the brine. After 24 hours, drain the turkey legs and discard the brine.
4. Rinse the brine off the legs with cold water, then dry thoroughly with paper towels. Brush off any clinging solid spices.
5. Supply your smoker with wood pellets and follow the start-up procedure. Preheat the grill, with the lid closed, to 250° F.
6. Lay the turkey legs directly on the grill grate.
7. Smoke for 4-5 hours, or until the internal temperature reaches 165°F on an instant-read meat thermometer. Make sure the probe doesn't touch bone or you'll get a false reading. Grill: 250 °F Probe: 165 °F
8. The turkey legs should be deeply browned. Don't be alarmed if the meat under the skin is pinkish: that's a chemical reaction to the cure and the smoke.
9. Serve immediately. Enjoy!

Smoked Chicken Leg & Thigh Quarters

Servings: 6
Cooking Time: 120 Minutes

Ingredients:

- 8 chicken legs (thigh and drumstick)
- 3 Tablespoon olive oil
- Pork & Poultry Rub

Directions:

1. Place the chicken pieces in a large mixing bowl. Pour oil over the chicken to coat each piece, then season to taste with the Traeger Pork & Poultry Rub. Massage the chicken pieces to encourage the oil and seasonings get under the skin. Cover and refrigerate for at least 1 to 2 hours.
2. Supply your smoker with wood pellets and follow the start-up procedure. Preheat the grill, with the lid closed, to 180° F.
3. Remove the chicken from the refrigerator, letting any excess oil drip back into the bowl. Grill: 180 °F
4. Arrange the chicken on the grill grate and smoke for 1 hour. Increase Traeger temperature to 350°F and continue to roast the chicken until the internal temperature in the thickest part of a thigh is 165°F or the chicken is golden brown and the juices run clear, about 50 to 60 minutes. Grill: 350 °F Probe: 165 °F
5. Remove from the grill and allow the chicken to rest for 8 to 10 minutes and serve. Enjoy!

Bbq Turkey Breast With Meat Church Holy Cow

Servings: 8
Cooking Time: 180 Minutes

Ingredients:

- 1 Large boneless, skinless turkey breast
- 1/4 Cup Duke's Mayonnaise
- Meat Church Holy Cow BBQ Rub
- 1/2 Cup honey
- 1/4 Cup Dijon mustard
- 2 Tablespoon Meat Church Holy Cow BBQ Rub

Directions:

1. Rinse off the breast and pat dry. Slather it liberally in mayonnaise, this will act as a binder for the seasoning. Apply Meat Church Holy Cow BBQ Rub generously to all sides.

2. Supply your smoker with wood pellets and follow the start-up procedure. Preheat the grill, with the lid closed, to 275° F.

3. Place the breast directly on the grill grate and cook for 2 to 3 hours, or until the internal temperature reaches 160°F in the thickest part. (The breast will continue to cook another 5° or so after it is removed from the grill.) Grill: 275 °F Probe: 160 °F

4. While the turkey is cooking you can go ahead and prepare your glaze (if using). Mix all glaze ingredients in a small saucepan and bring to a simmer. Reduce by 1/3. Remove from the heat and set aside.

5. Drizzle the glaze on the turkey during the last 15 minutes of the cook. I recommend doing this around 158 - 160°F, internal temperature. (This turkey is also delicious as-is, without the optional glaze.)

6. Remove from the grill and let the turkey breast rest 5 to 10 minutes before slicing. Enjoy!

Traditional Smoked Thanksgiving Turkey

Servings: 8
Cooking Time: 240 Minutes

Ingredients:
- 1/2 Pound butter
- 6 Clove garlic, minced
- 8 Sprig fresh thyme
- 1 Sprig fresh rosemary
- 1 Tablespoon cracked black pepper
- 1/2 Tablespoon kosher salt
- 20 Pound Turkey, Whole Birds (18-20 lbs)

Directions:
1. Supply your smoker with wood pellets and follow the start-up procedure. Preheat the grill, with the lid closed, to 300° F.

2. In a small bowl, combine softened butter with minced garlic, thyme leaves, chopped rosemary, black pepper and kosher salt.

3. Prep the turkey by separating the skin from the breast creating a pocket to stuff the butter-herb mixture in. Cover the entire breast with 1/4" thickness of butter mixture.

4. Season the whole turkey with kosher salt and black pepper. Optional: Stuff turkey cavity with Traditional Stuffing recipe. When ready to cook, set the grill temperature to 300°F and preheat, lid closed for 15 minutes.

5. Place turkey on the grill and smoke for 3-4 hours. Check the internal temperature, the desired temperature is 175°F in the thigh next to the bone, and 160°F in the breast. Turkey will continue to cook once taken off grill to reach a final temperature of 165°F in the breast. Grill: 300 °F Probe: 160 °F

6. Let rest for 10-15 minutes before serving. Enjoy!

Smoked Airline Chicken

Servings: 4
Cooking Time: 120 Minutes

Ingredients:
- 2 boneless chicken breasts with drumettes attached
- ½ cup soy sauce
- ½ cup teriyaki sauce
- ¼ cup canola oil
- ¼ cup white vinegar
- 1 tablespoon minced garlic
- ¼ cup chopped scallions
- 2 teaspoons freshly ground black pepper
- 1 teaspoon ground mustard

Directions:
1. Place the chicken in a baking dish.

2. In a bowl, whisk together the soy sauce, teriyaki sauce, canola oil, vinegar, garlic, scallions, pepper and ground mustard, then pour this marinade over the chicken, coating both sides.

3. Refrigerate the chicken in marinade for 4 hours, turning over every hour.

4. When ready to smoke the chicken, supply your smoker with wood pellets and follow the start-up procedure. Preheat, with the lid closed, to 250°F.

5. Remove the chicken from the marinade but do not rinse. Discard the marinade.

6. Arrange the chicken directly on the grill, close the lid, and smoke for 1 hour 30 minutes to 2 hours, or until a meat thermometer inserted in the thickest part of the meat reads 165°F.

7. Let the meat rest for 3 minutes before serving.

Red Onion Chicken Fajita Omelet

Servings: 4

Cooking Time: 12 Minutes

Ingredients:

- 1 Cup Bell Pepper, Sliced Thin
- To Taste, Blackened Sriracha Rub Seasoning
- 2 Tbsp Butter
- 1 Cup Cheddar Jack Cheese, Shredded
- 8 Oz Chicken Breast, Boneless, Skinless, Sliced Thin
- 6 Eggs, Beaten
- 1 Tbsp Heavy Cream
- 1 Jalapeño, Minced
- 1/2 Lime
- 1 Cup Red Onion, Sliced Thinly
- 1/3 Cup Salsa Roja
- 2 Tbsp Sour Cream
- 1 Tbsp Vegetable Oil, Divided

Directions:

1. Supply your smoker with wood pellets and follow the start-up procedure. Preheat the grill, with the lid open, to medium heat. If using a gas or charcoal grill, preheat a cast iron skillet.

2. Drizzle sliced chicken breast with 1 teaspoon oil, then season with Blackened Sriracha.

3. Drizzle the remaining oil on the griddle, then add the chicken. Sauté for 2 minutes, then add the bell peppers and onions. Season with additional Blackened Sriracha and continue to sauté another 2 minutes, then deglaze with fresh squeezed lime juice. Remove mixture from the griddle, set aside.

4. Turn the griddle down to low, then whisk the eggs (3 per omelet) and heavy cream.

5. Melt 1 tablespoon of butter on the griddle. Quickly pour the eggs over the melted butter.

6. Flip the eggs, then add ¼ cup of cheese and divide all but ½ cup of the reserved filling into the middle of each egg. Add additional cheese and some minced jalapeño. Fold the egg over to shape the omelet.

7. Transfer the omelet to a plate and top with additional filling, cheese, salsa, sour cream, and jalapeño. Serve warm.

Chicken Egg Rolls With Buffalo Sauce

Servings: 4

Cooking Time: 75 Minutes

Ingredients:

- 1/4 Cup Bleu Cheese, Crumbled
- 1/4 Cup Buffalo Sauce
- 1 Lb Chicken Breasts - Boneless, Skinless
- 4 Oz Cream Cheese, Softened
- 8 Egg Roll Wrappers
- 1/2 Jalapeno Pepper, Minced
- Pinch Sweet Heat Rub
- 1/4 Red Bell Pepper, Chopped
- 4 Scallion, Sliced Thin
- 1/4 Cup Sour Cream
- 2 Cups Vegetable Oil

Directions:

1. Supply your smoker with wood pellets and follow the start-up procedure. Preheat the grill, with the lid open, to 200° F. If using a gas or charcoal grill, set it up for low, indirect heat.

2. Season chicken breasts with Sweet Heat Rub, then place on the grill. Smoke for 1 hour, then remove from the grill, cool, shred, and set aside.

3. Prepare the filling: In a mixing bowl, use a hand mixer to blend cream cheese, bleu cheese, Buffalo sauce and sour cream.

4. Fold in scallions, jalapeño, red bell pepper, and shredded chicken.

5. Prepare egg rolls: Lay an egg roll wrapper on a flat surface and add 3 tablespoons of filling to the middle.

6. Fold the bottom of the wrapper over the top of the filling, then fold over each side. Brush the top point of the wrapper with warm water, then roll the wrapper tight. Transfer to a tray while filling the remaining wrappers.

7. Increase the temperature of the grill to 425°F, then set a cast iron Dutch oven on the grill. Add vegetable oil and heat for 5 minutes.

8. Place 3 egg rolls in heated oil and fry until golden, 1 to 2 minutes per side.

9. Transfer to a wire rack to cool, then fry the remaining egg rolls, in batches.

10. Cool egg rolls for 2 minutes, then slice in half and serve warm with celery sticks and extra Buffalo sauce for dipping.

Lemon Chicken Breast

Servings: 6

Cooking Time: 15 Minutes

Ingredients:

- 1 Clove garlic, coarsely chopped
- 2 Teaspoon honey
- 2 Teaspoon kosher salt
- 1 Teaspoon freshly ground black pepper
- 2 Sprig fresh thyme leaves
- 1 lemon, zest and juice
- 1/2 Cup high-quality olive oil or vegetable oil
- 6 (6 oz) boneless, skinless chicken breasts
- 1 lemon, cut into wedges, for serving

Directions:

1. To make the marinade, add the garlic, honey, salt, pepper, thyme, lemon juice and zest to a small mixing bowl. Whisk until the salt crystals and honey dissolve. Slowly whisk in the olive oil.

2. Place the chicken breast in a large resealable plastic bag and pour the marinade over them, massaging the bag to distribute the marinade evenly.

3. Refrigerate for 4 hours.

4. Supply your smoker with wood pellets and follow the start-up procedure. Preheat the grill, with the lid closed, to 400° F.

5. Drain the chicken breasts and discard the marinade.

6. Arrange the chicken breasts directly on the grill grate and cook until the internal temperature reaches 165°F. Grill: 400 °F Probe: 165 °F

7. If desired, grill the reserved lemon wedges alongside the chicken, cut sides down, for 15 minutes.

8. Serve the chicken on a platter or plates with the lemon wedges.

Chile Cilantro Lime Chicken Wings

Servings: 4

Cooking Time: 20 Minutes

Ingredients:

- 1 Tsp Ancho Chili Powder
- 2 Tsp Blackened Sriracha Rub Seasoning
- 2 Lbs Chicken Wings, Split
- 2 Tbsp Cilantro, Chopped, Divided
- 1 Tsp Cumin
- 1 Lime, Zest & Juice
- 1 1/2 Tbsp Olive Oil

Directions:

1. In a medium bowl, combine 1 tablespoon of cilantro, lime juice and zest, olive oil, Blackened Sriracha, ancho chili powder, and cumin.

2. Place chicken wings in a resealable gallon bag and add cilantro mixture. Transfer to the refrigerator and marinate for 1 hour, turning occasionally.

3. Supply your smoker with wood pellets and follow the start-up procedure. Preheat the grill, with the lid closed, to 350° F. If using a gas or charcoal grill, set it up for medium heat.

4. Remove chicken wings from the marinade and place on the grill over indirect heat. Grill for 15 to 18 minutes, turning and rotating every 3 to 5 minutes.

5. Remove chicken wings from the grill, garnish with remaining cilantro, and serve warm.

Roasted Rosemary Orange Chicken

Servings: 4

Cooking Time: 45 Minutes

Ingredients:

- 1 (3-4 lb) chicken, backbone removed
- 1/4 Cup olive oil
- 2 oranges, juiced
- 1 orange, zested
- 2 Teaspoon Dijon mustard
- 3 Tablespoon chopped rosemary leaves
- 2 Teaspoon kosher salt

Directions:

1. Rinse the chicken and pat dry with paper towels.

2. For the Marinade: In a medium bowl, combine olive oil, juice from the oranges (about 1/4 cup of freshly squeezed juice), orange zest, Dijon mustard, rosemary and salt. Whisk to combine.

3. Place the chicken in a shallow baking dish large enough for chicken to be fully opened in one piece. Pour marinade over the chicken ensuring it is covered with the marinade.

4. Cover with plastic wrap and refrigerate for a minimum of 2 hours or up to overnight, turning once during the process.

5. Supply your smoker with wood pellets and follow the start-up procedure. Preheat the grill, with the lid closed, to 350° F.

6. Remove the chicken from the marinade and place on the Traeger, skin-side down.

7. Cook for 25 to 30 minutes until the skin is well-browned, then flip. Continue to grill chicken until the internal temperature of the breast reaches 165°F and the thigh reaches 175°F, about 5 to 15 minutes longer. Grill: 350 °F Probe: 165 °F

8. Let rest 10 minutes before carving. Enjoy!

Savory Cajun Bbq Chicken

Servings: 4
Cooking Time: 25 Minutes

Ingredients:
- ½ Cup Barbecue Sauce
- ¼ Cup Beer, Any Brand
- 1 Tablespoon Butter
- 1 Pound Boneless, Skinless Chicken Breasts
- 2 Cloves Garlic Clove, Minced
- ¼ Teaspoon Ground Thyme
- 1 Teaspoon Hot Sauce
- Juice Of 1 Lime
- 1 Tablespoon Olive Oil
- ½ Teaspoon Oregano
- 2 Tablespoons Sweet Heat Rub
- 1 Tablespoon Worcestershire Sauce

Directions:
1. In a small mixing bowl, mix together the Sweet Heat Rub, oregano, and ground thyme.

2. Rub the chicken breasts all over with olive oil, making sure to completely coat the meat. Generously season the chicken breasts on all sides with the Sweet Heat mixture.

3. Supply your smoker with wood pellets and follow the start-up procedure. Preheat the grill, with the lid closed, to 350° F. If you're using a gas or charcoal grill, set it up for medium heat. Insert a temperature probe into the thickest part of one of the chicken breasts and place the meat on the grill. Grill the meat on one side for 10-12 minutes, then flip and grill for another 5-7

minutes, or until the chicken breasts are golden brown and juicy and reaches an internal temperature of 165°F.

4. Remove the chicken from the grill and allow to rest for 10 minutes.

5. While the chicken rests, make the sauce. Combine the butter, barbecue sauce, beer, Worcestershire sauce, lime juice, and minced garlic in a heat proof saucepan and place on the grill. Bring the sauce to a boil. Once it boils, remove it from the heat, whisk it and serve with the chicken.

Roasted Christmas Goose

Servings: 8
Cooking Time: 120 Minutes

Ingredients:
- 5 1/2 Pound Goose
- 2 lemons
- 2 limes
- 2 Teaspoon salt
- 2 thyme sprigs
- 2 sage sprigs
- 1 Medium Apple, green
- 3 Tablespoon honey

Directions:
1. Supply your smoker with wood pellets and follow the start-up procedure. Preheat the grill, with the lid closed, to High heat.

2. Lightly score the breast and leg skin in a criss-cross pattern. This will help the fat to render down more quickly during cooking.

3. Grate the lemon and limes. Mix citrus zest with 2 teaspoons fine sea salt. Cut the lemons and lime into wedges.

4. Season cavity of the goose generously with salt, then rub the citrus mix well into the skin and sprinkle some inside the cavity.

5. Stuff goose with sage, thyme, lemons, limes and apples wedges. Place goose directly on the grill grate and cook for 40 minutes. Brush goose with honey and reduce temperature to 325°F.

6. Cook for 1-1/2 to 2 hours or until an instant read thermometer inserted in the thickest part of the breast reads 160°F. Grill: 325 °F Probe: 160 °F

7. Remove from grill, tent with foil and allow to rest for 30 minutes. Final internal temperature should be 165°F in the thickest part of the breast. Enjoy!

Spicy Bbq Whole Chicken

Servings: 4

Cooking Time: 180 Minutes

Ingredients:

- 6 Thai chiles
- 2 Tablespoon sweet paprika
- 1 Scotch bonnet pepper
- 2 Tablespoon sugar
- 3 Tablespoon salt
- 1 white onion
- 5 Clove garlic
- 4 Cup grapeseed oil
- 1 whole chicken

Directions:

1. In a food processor or blender, puree the Thai chiles, paprika, Scotch bonnet pepper, sugar, salt, onion, garlic and grapeseed oil together until smooth.

2. Smother the chicken with mixture and let rest in fridge overnight.

3. Supply your smoker with wood pellets and follow the start-up procedure. Preheat the grill, with the lid closed, to 300° F.

4. Place chicken on grill, breast side up and smoke for 3 hours, or until it reaches an internal temperature of 165°F in the breast. Grill: 300 °F Probe: 165 °F

5. Remove from grill and allow to rest for 10 to 15 minutes before slicing. Serve with sides of choice. Enjoy!

Hot Turkey Sandwich With Gravy

Servings: 4

Cooking Time: 10 Minutes

Ingredients:

- 8 Slices Bread, Sliced
- 1 Cup Gravy, Prepared
- 2 Cups Leftover Turkey, Shredded

Directions:

1. Supply your smoker with wood pellets and follow the start-up procedure. Preheat the grill, with the lid closed, to 400° F.

2. Place the BBQ Grill Mat on the grates of your preheated grill and lay the shredded turkey evenly across the mat to reheat for about 10 minutes.

3. Prepare or reheat the gravy. You"ll want to have the gravy warmed and ready as soon as the turkey is reheated and the bread is toasted.

4. Hold each slice of bread over the flame broiler to toast to your liking.

5. When all of your ingredients are hot, scoop 1/2 cup of the shredded turkey onto a piece of bread, generously cover with gravy and top with another piece of toasted bread. Serve immediately.

Buttered Thanksgiving Turkey

Servings: 12-14

Cooking Time: 300 Minutes

Ingredients:

- 1 whole turkey (make sure the turkey is not pre-brined)
- 2 batches Garlic Butter Injectable
- 3 tablespoons olive oil
- 1 batch Chicken Rub
- 2 tablespoons butter

Directions:

1. Supply your smoker with wood pellets and follow the start-up procedure. Preheat the grill, with the lid closed, to 180°F.

2. Inject the turkey throughout with the garlic butter injectable. Coat the turkey with olive oil and season it with the rub. Using your hands, work the rub into the meat and skin.

3. Place the turkey directly on the grill grate and smoke for 3 or 4 hours (for an 8- to 12-pound turkey, cook for 3 hours; for a turkey over 12 pounds, cook for 4 hours), basting it with butter every hour.

4. Increase the grill's temperature to 375°F and continue to cook until the turkey's internal temperature reaches 170°F.

5. Remove the turkey from the grill and let it rest for 10 minutes, before carving and serving.

Bbq Chicken Breasts

Servings: 6
Cooking Time: 25 Minutes

Ingredients:

- 6 boneless, skinless chicken breast
- 1 1/2 Cup Sweet & Heat BBQ Sauce
- salt and pepper
- 1 Tablespoon chopped parsley, for garnish

Directions:

1. Place chicken breasts and 1 cup of Traeger Sweet & Heat BBQ Sauce in a resealable bag or large bowl, and gently turn to cover chicken evenly in the sauce. Marinate in the refrigerator overnight.
2. Supply your smoker with wood pellets and follow the start-up procedure. Preheat the grill, with the lid closed, to 450° F.
3. Remove chicken from marinade and season with salt and pepper.
4. Place chicken directly on the grill grate and cook for 10 minutes on each side flipping once or until internal temperature reaches 150°F.
5. Brush on remaining 1/2 cup of Traeger Sweet & Heat BBQ Sauce while chicken is still on the grill, and continue to cook 5 to 10 minutes longer or until a finished internal temperature of 165°F.
6. Remove chicken from grill and let rest 5 minutes before serving. Sprinkle with chopped parsley. Enjoy!

Injected Drunken Smoked Turkey Legs

Servings: 4
Cooking Time: 30 Minutes

Ingredients:

- 1 Bottle Frank's RedHot Sauce
- 1/2 Cup butter
- 1 Cup brown sugar
- 1/2 Cup whiskey or bourbon
- 3 Clove garlic, minced
- 1 Teaspoon Cajun seasoning
- 1/2 Cup chicken stock
- 6 Large turkey legs

Directions:

1. In a large pot, mix together all ingredients except the turkey legs. Bring to a boil. Let cool and pour the marinade into a resealable bag, then add in the turkey legs. Allow them to marinate for 24 hours in the fridge.
2. Remove the turkey legs from the bag, saving the marinade.
3. Bring half of marinade to a boil and reserve for basting.
4. Dilute the other half of marinade with chicken stock. Fill the meat injector with the marinade/chicken stock mixture and insert it into the meaty parts of the turkey leg in several places. Inject turkey legs with marinade until they plump up.
5. Supply your smoker with wood pellets and follow the start-up procedure. Preheat the grill, with the lid closed, to 250° F.
6. Place the turkey legs on the grill grate and cook for 1-1/2 to 3 hours, depending on the thickness of the legs, or until the internal temp registers 165°F on an instant-read thermometer. Baste the legs with the reserved, boiled marinade every 45 minutes. Enjoy! Grill: 250 °F Probe: 165 °F

Texas Style Black Pepper Turkey

Servings: 6
Cooking Time: 240 Minutes

Ingredients:

- 1/2 Cup Coarse Black Pepper
- 1Lb Butter
- 1/2 Cup Salt, Kosher
- 1 Brined Turkey

Directions:

1. Supply your smoker with wood pellets and follow the start-up procedure. Preheat the grill, with the lid closed, to 300° F.
2. Liberally season Turkey with equal parts kosher salt and coarse black pepper.
3. Cook on grill until Internal temp reaches approximately 145°F or the skin has darkened to your liking.
4. Place turkey in a roasting pan topped with a pound of chopped butter and cover.
5. Return to the grill until internal temp of the thigh and breast reaches 165°F
6. Let rest for 30 minutes, carve and serve.

Chicken Nachos

Servings: 6-8
Cooking Time: 10 Minutes

Ingredients:
- 1 Can Black Beans, Rinsed And Drained
- 1 Cup Cheddar Cheese, Shredded
- 2 Cups Chicken, Diced
- (If Desired) Cilantro
- 1 Can Corn Kernels, Drained
- (If Desired) Pickled Jalapeno Peppers
- 1/2 Tablespoon Champion Chicken Seasoning
- 1/2 Red Onion, Diced
- 1/2 Cup Salsa
- 1/4 Cup Sour Cream

Directions:
1. On a large sheet pan, spread out half the tortilla chips, then cover with half the shredded cheese and one cup of chicken. Sprinkle with half of Champion Chicken seasoning. Top with the rest of the tortilla chips, cheese, chicken and remaining seasoning.
2. Supply your smoker with wood pellets and follow the start-up procedure. Preheat the grill, with the lid closed, to 350° F. Grill for 5-7 minutes, or until the cheese is melted and bubbly and everything is warmed all the way through. Remove the pan from the grill.
3. Top the nachos with the black beans, corn, diced red onion, sour cream, cilantro and pickled jalapenos. Serve and enjoy!

Juicy Jerk Chicken Kebabs

Servings: 4
Cooking Time: 12 Minutes

Ingredients:
- 1 Tablespoon All Spice, Ground
- 2 Lbs Chicken, Boneless/Skinless
- 1 Tablespoon Cinnamon, Ground
- 1/4 Cup Extra-Virgin Olive Oil
- 3 Garlic, Cloves
- 2 Inch Piece Ginger, Fresh
- 3 Green Onion
- 1 Lime, Juiced
- 1 Tablespoon Nutmeg, Ground
- 1 Cup Orange Juice, Fresh
- Pepper
- 1 Red Onion, Chopped
- Salt
- Skewers
- 1/4 Cup Soy Sauce
- 1/4 Cup Thyme, Fresh Sprigs

Directions:
1. Soak the bamboo skewers in water for about 30 minutes (the longer the better).
2. In a food processor, combine orange juice, oil, soy sauce, thyme, allspice, nutmeg, cinnamon, garlic, onions, ginger, lime juice, salt and pepper. Puree until smooth.
3. In a large resealable bag, pour all but 1/4 cup of the mixture in along with the sliced up chicken breasts. Seal the bag and marinate in the fridge for 2 - 3 hours.
4. Supply your smoker with wood pellets and follow the start-up procedure. Preheat the grill, with the lid open, to 450° F. Skewer the chicken and grill for about 7 minutes. Flip and continue grilling for about 5 minutes, or until the chicken is cooked through and grill marks appear. Serve with the remaining 1/4 cup of marinade.

Crispy Spiced Chicken Wings

Servings: 10
Cooking Time: 75 Minutes

Ingredients:
- 5 pounds of chicken wings (flats and drumettes)
- 2 1/2 Tablespoons baking powder
- 1 teaspoon salt

Directions:
1. Dry your chicken wings thoroughly on all sides with a paper towel. Place them in a zip-top bag.
2. Add the baking powder and salt to the wings, close the bag, and toss to coat evenly.
3. Supply your smoker with wood pellets and follow the start-up procedure. Preheat the grill, with the lid closed, to 250° F, using your favorite wood. Place the wings directly on the grill grates, close the lid, and smoke for 30 minutes.
4. Increase the heat in your smoker to 425 degrees F and continue cooking for 45 more minutes, or until the internal temperature of the wing reads 175 degrees F.

You can rotate or flip the wings as needed to maintain even cooking and avoid any hot spots on the grill.

5. Remove the wing from the grill and serve. You can serve plain, toss in your favorite BBQ seasoning, or hot sauce.

Bbq Smoked Turkey Jerky

Servings: 4 - 6
Cooking Time: 120 Minutes

Ingredients:
- 2 Tablespoons Apple Cider Vinegar
- 2 Tablespoons (Any Kind) Barbecue Sauce
- 1 Tablespoon Quick Curing Salt
- ½ Cup Soy Sauce
- 4 Tablespoons Sweet Sweet Rib Rub
- 2 Pounds Boneless Skinless Turkey Breast
- ¼ Cup Water

Directions:
1. In a large bowl, combine the soy sauce, water, barbecue sauce, apple cider vinegar, quick curing salt, and 2 tablespoons of the Sweet Rib Rub. Whisk together until well combined and pour into a large, resealable plastic bag.
2. Using a sharp knife, slice the turkey into ¼ inch slices with the grain (this is easier if the meat is partially frozen). Trim off any fat, skin or connective tissue and discard.
3. Place the turkey slices into the plastic bag, seal, and massage the marinade into the turkey. Refrigerate for 24 hours.
4. Once the jerky is ready to go, remove the turkey from the refrigerator, drain the marinade and discard. Pat the turkey dry with paper towels and sprinkle all sides generously with the remaining Sweet Rib Rub.
5. Supply your smoker with wood pellets and follow the start-up procedure. Preheat the grill, with the lid closed, to 180° F. If you're using a sawdust or charcoal smoker, set it up for medium low heat.
6. Place the turkey slices directly onto the smoker grates and smoke for 2-4 hours, or until the jerky is chewy but still bends slightly.
7. Transfer the jerky to a resealable plastic bag while the jerky is still warm and allow it to sit at room temperature for 1 hour. Squeeze any air from the bag and place in the refrigerator. It will keep for several weeks.

Beer Chicken

Servings: 4
Cooking Time: 75 Minutes

Ingredients:
- 1 Beer, Can
- 1 Chicken, Whole
- Lemon Pepper Garlic Seasoning

Directions:
1. Supply your smoker with wood pellets and follow the start-up procedure. Preheat the grill, with the lid open, to 400° F.
2. Season the chicken all over with spices. Open the can of your favorite pop/beer and place the opening of the chicken over the can. Make sure that the chicken can stand upright without falling over. Place on your Grill and barbecue until the internal temperature reaching 165 degrees F (about an hour).
3. Remove from grill, slice and serve hot.

Baked Garlic Parmesan Wings

Servings: 4
Cooking Time: 40 Minutes

Ingredients:
- 3 1/2 Tablespoon Chicken Rub
- 5 Pound chicken wings
- 1 Cup butter
- 10 Clove garlic, minced
- 1/2 Cup unsalted butter
- 10 Clove garlic, finely diced
- 1 Cup shredded Parmesan cheese
- 3 Tablespoon chopped parsley

Directions:
1. Supply your smoker with wood pellets and follow the start-up procedure. Preheat the grill, with the lid closed, to 450° F.
2. In a large bowl, toss the wings with the Traeger Chicken Rub.

3. Place wings directly on the grill grate and cook for 20 minutes. Flip wings and cook for an additional 20 minutes. Grill: 450 °F

4. Check the internal temperature of the wings, finished desired temperature is 165°F to 180°F. Grill: 450 °F Probe: 165 °F

5. To make the Garlic Sauce: While the chicken is cooking, combine butter, garlic and remaining rub in a medium sized saucepan and cook over medium heat on a stove top. Cook sauce for 8 to 10 minutes, stirring occasionally.

6. When wings are finished cooking, remove from grill and place in a large bowl. Toss wings with the garlic sauce, Parmesan cheese and parsley. Enjoy!

Whole Smoked Honey Chicken

Servings: 4
Cooking Time: 40 Minutes

Ingredients:
- 1 Tablespoon Honey
- 1 ½ Lemon
- 4 Tablespoons Champion Chicken Seasoning
- 4 Tablespoons Unsalted Butter
- 1, 4 Pound Chicken, Giblets Removed And Patted Dry

Directions:
1. Supply your smoker with wood pellets and follow the start-up procedure. Preheat the grill, with the lid open, to 225° F.

2. In a small saucepan, melt together the butter and honey over low heat. Squeeze ½ lemon into the honey mixture and remove from the heat.

3. Smoke the chicken, skin side down until the chicken is lightly browned and the skin releases from the grate without ripping, about 6-8 minutes.

4. Turn the chicken over and baste with the honey butter mixture.

5. Continue to smoke the chicken, basting every 45 minutes, until the thickest part of the chicken reaches 160°F.

Roasted Stuffed Turkey Breast

Servings: 6

Cooking Time: 40 Minutes

Ingredients:
- 1 (4-5 lb) boneless turkey breast
- 5 Slices thick-cut bacon, chopped
- 3/4 Cup assorted mushrooms
- 1 Bunch scallions, chopped
- 1/8 Cup white wine
- 3 Tablespoon panko breadcrumbs
- salt
- black pepper

Directions:
1. Supply your smoker with wood pellets and follow the start-up procedure. Preheat the grill, with the lid closed, to 375° F.

2. Slice the turkey breast horizontally, making sure not to slice all the way through. Lay breast open flat.

3. Cook bacon in a skillet over medium heat until crispy. Remove bacon and set aside. Sauté mushrooms in the bacon grease until browned. Add scallions and cook for an additional two minutes. Add white wine and cook down until no wine remains. Stir in breadcrumbs and bacon, adding salt and pepper to taste.

4. Transfer filling to fridge to cool for 15 to 20 minutes. Once chilled, spread the filling onto the turkey breast, pressing lightly to make sure it adheres. Roll the turkey breast tightly and tie with butcher's twine at about 1 inch intervals. Tuck the ends of the turkey breast under and tie with twine lengthwise.

5. Season the outside of the turkey breast with salt and pepper. Place in grill for 40 minutes. Check the internal temperature, desired temperature is 165°F. Once the finished temperature is reached, remove turkey from the grill and let rest for 10 minutes. Slice and serve. Enjoy! Grill: 375 °F Probe: 165 °F

Grilled Chicken Wings

Servings: 6
Cooking Time: 50 Minutes

Ingredients:
- 4 Lbs Chicken Wings, Whole
- 1 Cup Cornmeal
- 2 Eggs
- 1 Cup Flour

- 2 Tbsp Champion Chicken Rub
- 1 Cup Milk

Directions:

1. Supply your smoker with wood pellets and follow the start-up procedure. Preheat the grill, with the lid open, to 300° F. If using a gas or charcoal grill, set it up for medium-low heat.

2. Place chicken wings on a sheet tray, then cut off the tip of each wing with a knife, or scissors. Pat dry with a paper towel.

3. In a mixing bowl, whisk together flour, cornmeal, and Champion Chicken. Set aside.

4. In another mixing bowl, whisk together milk and eggs. Set aside.

5. Form "breading" station: wings, egg wash, seasoned flour, sheet tray. Dunk each wing in egg wash, then coat in seasoned flour. Set aside on a sheet tray, while coating the remaining wings.

6. Place wings directly on the grill rack. Flip/rotate wings every 10 minutes for 45-55 minutes, until golden and "fried crisp."

7. Remove from the grill, rest for 10 minutes, then serve warm.

Smoked Quarters

Servings: 2-4
Cooking Time: 120 Minutes

Ingredients:

- 4 chicken quarters
- 2 tablespoons olive oil
- 1 batch Chicken Rub
- 2 tablespoons butter

Directions:

1. Supply your smoker with wood pellets and follow the start-up procedure. Preheat the grill, with the lid closed, to 180°F.

2. Coat the chicken quarters all over with olive oil and season them with the rub. Using your hands, work the rub into the meat.

3. Place the quarters directly on the grill grate and smoke for 1½ hours.

4. Baste the quarters with the butter and increase the grill's temperature to 375°F. Continue to cook until the chicken's internal temperature reaches 170°F.

5. Remove the quarters from the grill and let them rest for 10 minutes before serving.

Grilled Garlic Chicken Kabobs

Servings: 6
Cooking Time: 15 Minutes

Ingredients:

- 3 (Cut Into 1 Inch Cubes) Chicken Breast, Raw
- 2 Cloves Garlic, Minced
- 2 Tablespoons Honey
- 1 Pound Of Button (Destemmed And Cut In Half) Mushroom
- 1/2 Cup Olive Oil
- 1 Red (Cut Into Quarters And Seperated) Onion
- 1 Green (Cut Into Large Chunks) Bell Pepper
- 2 Tablespoons Competition Smoked Seasoning
- 2 Tablespoons Soy Sauce

Directions:

1. To make the marinade: In a large bowl, combine the olive oil, soy sauce, honey, garlic and Competition Smoked. Add the chicken and mix well. When the chicken is covered completely, allow it to marinate for 2-12 hours.

2. In a large, shallow baking dish, soak the kabob skewers for a minimum of 2 hours and up to 12 hours.

3. Once the chicken has finished marinating and the skewers are finished soaking, drain the water from the skewers and remove the chicken from the marinade.

4. Supply your smoker with wood pellets and follow the start-up procedure. Preheat the grill, with the lid closed, to 350° F.

5. Thread a piece of chicken, followed by a piece of pepper, mushroom, and onion. Repeat until the skewers are full.

6. Grill the kabobs for 5 minutes on one side, then flip and grill for 5 more minutes or until the chicken reaches an internal temperature of 180°F. Remove from the grill and serve.

Chicken Wings With Teriyaki Glaze

Servings: 4
Cooking Time: 50 Minutes

Ingredients:
- 16 large chicken wings, about 3lb (1.4kg) total
- 1 to 1½ tbsp toasted sesame oil
- for the glaze
- ½ cup light soy sauce or tamari
- ¼ cup sake or sugar-free dark-colored soda
- ¼ cup light brown sugar or low-carb substitute
- 2 tbsp mirin or 1 tbsp honey
- 1 garlic clove, peeled, minced or grated
- 2 tsp minced fresh ginger
- 1 tsp cornstarch mixed with 1 tbsp distilled water (optional)
- for serving
- 1 tbsp toasted sesame seeds
- 2 scallions, trimmed, white and green parts sliced sharply diagonally

Directions:
1. Supply your smoker with wood pellets and follow the start-up procedure. Preheat the grill, with the lid closed, to 350° F.
2. Place the chicken wings in a large bowl, add the sesame oil, and turn the wings to coat thoroughly.
3. Place the wings on the grate at an angle to the bars. Grill for 20 minutes and then turn. Continue to cook until the wings are nicely browned and the meat is no longer pink at the bone, about 20 minutes more.
4. To make the glaze, in a saucepan on the stovetop over medium-high heat, combine the ingredients and bring the mixture to a boil. Reduce the glaze by 1/3, about 6 to 8 minutes. If you prefer your glaze to be glossy and thick, add the cornstarch and water mixture to the glaze and cook until it coats the back of a spoon, about 1 to 2 minutes more.
5. Transfer the wings to an aluminum foil roasting pan. Pour the glaze over them, turning to coat thoroughly. Place the pan on the grate and cook the wings until the glaze sets, about 5 to 10 minutes.
6. Transfer the wings to a platter. Scatter the sesame seeds and scallions over the top. Serve with plenty of napkins.

Bacon-wrapped Jalapeño Poppers

Servings: 12
Cooking Time: 30 Minutes

Ingredients:
- 8 ounces cream cheese, softened
- ½ cup shredded Cheddar cheese
- ¼ cup chopped scallions
- 1 teaspoon chipotle chile powder or regular chili powder
- 1 teaspoon garlic powder
- 1 teaspoon salt
- 18 large jalapeño peppers, stemmed, seeded, and halved lengthwise
- 1 pound bacon (precooked works well)

Directions:
1. Supply your smoker with wood pellets and follow the start-up procedure. Preheat, with the lid closed, to 350°F. Line a baking sheet with aluminum foil.
2. In a small bowl, combine the cream cheese, Cheddar cheese, scallions, chipotle powder, garlic powder, and salt.
3. Stuff the jalapeño halves with the cheese mixture.
4. Cut the bacon into pieces big enough to wrap around the stuffed pepper halves.
5. Wrap the bacon around the peppers and place on the prepared baking sheet.
6. Put the baking sheet on the grill grate, close the lid, and smoke the peppers for 30 minutes, or until the cheese is melted and the bacon is cooked through and crisp.
7. Let the jalapeño poppers cool for 3 to 5 minutes. Serve warm.

Bacon Pork Pinwheels (kansas Lollipops)

Servings: 4-6
Cooking Time: 20 Minutes

Ingredients:

- 1 Whole Pork Loin, boneless
- To Taste salt and pepper
- To Taste Greek Seasoning
- 4 Slices bacon
- To Taste The Ultimate BBQ Sauce

Directions:

1. When ready to cook, start the smoker and set temperature to 500F. Preheat, lid closed, for 10 to 15 minutes.

2. Trim pork loin of any unwanted silver skin or fat. Using a sharp knife, cut pork loin length wise, into 4 long strips.

3. Lay pork flat, then season with salt, pepper and Cavender's Greek Seasoning.

4. Flip the pork strips over and layer bacon on unseasoned side. Begin tightly rolling the pork strips, with bacon being rolled up on the inside.

5. Secure a skewer all the way through each pork roll to secure it in place. Set the pork rolls down on grill and cook for 15 minutes.

6. Brush BBQ Sauce over the pork. Turn each skewer over, then coat the other side. Let pork cook for another 5-10 minutes, depending on thickness of your pork. Enjoy!

Bayou Wings With Cajun Rémoulade

Servings: 8
Cooking Time: 40 Minutes

Ingredients:

- 16 large whole chicken wings or 32 drumettes and flats, about 3lb (1.4kg) total
- for the rub
- 1 tbsp kosher salt
- 1 tsp freshly ground black pepper
- 1 tsp paprika
- ½ tsp ground cayenne, plus more
- ½ tsp garlic powder
- ½ tsp celery salt
- ½ tsp dried thyme
- 2 tbsp vegetable oil
- for the rémoulade
- 1¼ cups reduced-fat mayo
- ¼ cup Creole-style or whole grain mustard
- 2 tbsp horseradish
- 2 tbsp pickle relish
- 1 tbsp freshly squeezed lemon juice
- 1 tsp paprika, plus more
- 1 tsp hot sauce, plus more
- 1 tsp Worcestershire sauce
- coarse salt
- for serving
- lemon wedges
- pickled okra (optional)

Directions:

1. Supply your smoker with wood pellets and follow the start-up procedure. Preheat the grill, with the lid closed, to 350° F.

2. If using whole wings, cut through the two joints, separating them into drumettes, flats, and wing tips. (Discard the wing tips or save them for chicken stock.) Alternatively, leave the wings whole. Place the chicken in a resealable plastic bag.

3. In a small bowl, make the rub by combining the ingredients. Mix well. Pour the rub over the wings and toss them to thoroughly coat. Refrigerate for 2 hours.

4. In a small bowl, make the Cajun rémoulade by whisking together the mayo, mustard, horseradish, pickle relish, lemon juice, paprika, hot sauce, and Worcestershire. Season with salt to taste. The mixture should be highly seasoned. Transfer to a serving bowl and lightly dust with paprika. Cover and refrigerate until ready to serve.

5. Remove the wings from the refrigerator and allow the excess marinade to drip off. Place the wings on the grate at an angle to the bars. Grill for 20 minutes and then turn. (They'll brown more evenly but will also have less of a tendency to stick.) Continue to cook until the wings are nicely browned and the meat is no longer pink at the bone, about 20 minutes more.

6. Remove the wings from the grill and pile them on a platter. Serve with the Cajun rémoulade, lemon wedges, and pickled okra (if using).

Pulled Pork Loaded Nachos

Servings: 4
Cooking Time: 10 Minutes

Ingredients:

- 2 cups leftover smoked pulled pork
- 1 small sweet onion, diced
- 1 medium tomato, diced
- 1 jalapeño pepper, seeded and diced
- 1 garlic clove, minced
- 1 teaspoon salt
- 1 teaspoon freshly ground black pepper
- 1 bag tortilla chips
- 1 cup shredded Cheddar cheese
- ½ cup The Ultimate BBQ Sauce, divided
- ½ cup shredded jalapeño Monterey Jack cheese
- Juice of ½ lime
- 1 avocado, halved, pitted, and sliced
- 2 tablespoons sour cream
- 1 tablespoon chopped fresh cilantro

Directions:

1. Supply your smoker with wood pellets and follow the start-up procedure. Preheat, with the lid closed, to 375°F.

2. Heat the pulled pork in the microwave.

3. In a medium bowl, combine the onion, tomato, jalapeño, garlic, salt, and pepper, and set aside.

4. Arrange half of the tortilla chips in a large cast iron skillet. Spread half of the warmed pork on top and cover with the Cheddar cheese. Top with half of the onion-jalapeño mixture, then drizzle with ¼ cup of barbecue sauce.

5. Layer on the remaining tortilla chips, then the remaining pork and the Monterey Jack cheese. Top with the remaining onion-jalapeño mixture and drizzle with the remaining ¼ cup of barbecue sauce.

6. Place the skillet on the grill, close the lid, and smoke for about 10 minutes, or until the cheese is melted and bubbly. (Watch to make sure your chips don't burn!)

7. Squeeze the lime juice over the nachos, top with the avocado slices and sour cream, and garnish with the cilantro before serving hot.

Citrus-infused Marinated Olives

Servings: 6
Cooking Time: 30 Minutes

Ingredients:

- 1½ cups mixed brined olives, with pits
- ½ cup extra virgin olive oil
- 1 tbsp freshly squeezed lemon juice
- 1 garlic clove, peeled and thinly sliced
- 1 tsp smoked Spanish paprika
- 2 sprigs of fresh rosemary
- 2 sprigs of fresh thyme
- 2 bay leaves, fresh or dried
- 1 small dried red chili pepper, deseeded and flesh crumbled, or ¼ tsp crushed red pepper flakes
- 3 strips of orange zest
- 3 strips of lemon zest

Directions:

1. Supply your smoker with wood pellets and follow the start-up procedure. Preheat the grill, with the lid closed, to 180° F.

2. Drain the olives, reserving 1 tablespoon of brine. Spread the olives in a single layer in an aluminum foil roasting pan. Place the pan on the grate and cook the olives for 30 minutes, stirring the olives or shaking the pan once or twice.

3. In a small saucepan on the stovetop over low heat, warm the olive oil. Whisk in the lemon juice and the reserved 1 tablespoon of brine. Stir in the garlic and paprika. Add the rosemary, thyme, bay leaves, chili pepper, and orange and lemon zests. Warm over low heat for 10 minutes. Remove the saucepan from the heat.

4. Transfer the olives and olive oil mixture to a pint jar. Tuck the aromatics around the sides of the jar. Let cool and then cover and refrigerate for up to 5 days. Let the olives come to room temperature before serving.

Chorizo Queso Fundido

Servings: 4-6
Cooking Time: 20 Minutes

Ingredients:

- 1 poblano chile
- 1 cup chopped queso quesadilla or queso Oaxaca
- 1 cup shredded Monterey Jack cheese

- ¼ cup milk
- 1 tablespoon all-purpose flour
- 2 (4-ounce) links Mexican chorizo sausage, casings removed
- ⅓ cup beer
- 1 tablespoon unsalted butter
- 1 small red onion, chopped
- ½ cup whole kernel corn
- 2 serrano chiles or jalapeño peppers, stemmed, seeded, and coarsely chopped
- 1 tablespoon minced garlic
- 1 tablespoon freshly squeezed lime juice
- 1 teaspoon ground cumin
- 1 teaspoon salt
- 1 teaspoon freshly ground black pepper
- 1 tablespoon chopped fresh cilantro
- 1 tablespoon chopped scallions
- Tortilla chips, for serving

Directions:

1. Supply your smoker with wood pellets and follow the start-up procedure. Preheat, with the lid closed, to 350°F.

2. On the smoker or over medium-high heat on the stove top, place the poblano directly on the grate (or burner) to char for 1 to 2 minutes, turning as needed. Remove from heat and place in a closed-up lunch-size paper bag for 2 minutes to sweat and further loosen the skin.

3. Remove the skin and coarsely chop the poblano, removing the seeds; set aside.

4. In a bowl, combine the queso quesadilla, Monterey Jack, milk, and flour; set aside.

5. On the stove top, in a cast iron skillet over medium heat, cook and crumble the chorizo for about 2 minutes.

6. Transfer the cooked chorizo to a small, grill-safe pan and place over indirect heat on the smoker.

7. Place the cast iron skillet on the preheated grill grate. Pour in the beer and simmer for a few minutes, loosening and stirring in any remaining sausage bits from the pan.

8. Add the butter to the pan, then add the cheese mixture a little at a time, stirring constantly.

9. When the cheese is smooth, stir in the onion, corn, serrano chiles, garlic, lime juice, cuvmin, salt, and pepper. Stir in the reserved chopped charred poblano.

10. Close the lid and smoke for 15 to 20 minutes to infuse the queso with smoke flavor and further cook the vegetables.

11. When the cheese is bubbly, top with the chorizo mixture and garnish with the cilantro and scallions.

12. Serve the chorizo queso fundido hot with tortilla chips.

Grilled Guacamole

Servings: 6
Cooking Time: 30 Minutes

Ingredients:

- 3 large avocados, halved and pitted
- 1 lime, halved
- ½ jalapeño, deseeded and deveined
- ½ small white or red onion, peeled
- 2 garlic cloves, peeled and skewered on a toothpick
- 1 tsp coarse salt, plus more
- 1½ tbsp reduced-fat mayo
- 2 tbsp chopped fresh cilantro
- 2 tbsp crumbled queso fresco (optional)
- tortilla chips

Directions:

1. Supply your smoker with wood pellets and follow the start-up procedure. Preheat the grill, with the lid closed, to 225° F.

2. Place the avocados, lime, jalapeño, and onion cut sides down on the grate. Use the toothpicks to balance the garlic cloves between the bars. Smoke for 30 minutes. (You want the vegetables to retain most of their rawness.)

3. Transfer everything to a cutting board. Remove the garlic cloves from the toothpick and roughly chop. Sprinkle with the salt and continue to mince the garlic until it begins to form a paste. Scrape the garlic and salt into a large bowl.

4. Scoop the avocado flesh from the peels into the bowl. Squeeze the juice of ½ lime over the avocado. Mash the avocados but leave them somewhat chunky. Finely dice the jalapeño. Dice 2 tablespoons of onion. (Reserve the remaining onion for another use.) Add the

jalapeño, onion, mayo, and cilantro to the bowl. Stir gently to combine. Taste for seasoning, adding more salt, lime juice, and jalapeño as desired.

5.   Transfer the guacamole to a serving bowl. Top with the queso fresco (if using). Serve with tortilla chips.

Pigs In A Blanket

Servings: 4-6
Cooking Time: 15 Minutes

Ingredients:

- 2 Tablespoon Poppy Seeds
- 1 Tablespoon Dried Minced Onion
- 2 Teaspoon garlic, minced
- 2 Tablespoon Sesame Seeds
- 1 Teaspoon salt
- 8 Ounce Original Crescent Dough
- 1/4 Cup Dijon mustard
- 1 Large egg, beaten

Directions:

1.   When ready to cook, start your smoker at 350 degrees F, and preheat with lid closed, 10 to 15 minutes.
2.   Mix together poppy seeds, dried minced onion, dried minced garlic, salt and sesame seeds. Set aside.
3.   Cut each triangle of crescent roll dough into thirds lengthwise, making 3 small strips from each roll.
4.   Brush the dough strips lightly with Dijon mustard. Put the mini hot dogs on 1 end of the dough and roll up.
5.   Arrange them, seam side down, on a greased baking pan. Brush with egg wash and sprinkle with seasoning mixture.
6.   Bake in smoker until golden brown, about 12 to 15 minutes.
7.   Serve with mustard or dipping sauce of your choice. Enjoy!

Simple Cream Cheese Sausage Balls

Servings: 5
Cooking Time: 30 Minutes

Ingredients:

- 1 pound ground hot sausage, uncooked
- 8 ounces cream cheese, softened
- 1 package mini filo dough shells

Directions:

1.   Supply your smoker with wood pellets and follow the start-up procedure. Preheat, with the lid closed, to 350°F.
2.   In a large bowl, using your hands, thoroughly mix together the sausage and cream cheese until well blended.
3.   Place the filo dough shells on a rimmed perforated pizza pan or into a mini muffin tin.
4.   Roll the sausage and cheese mixture into 1-inch balls and place into the filo shells.
5.   Place the pizza pan or mini muffin tin on the grill, close the lid, and smoke the sausage balls for 30 minutes, or until cooked through and the sausage is no longer pink.
6.   Plate and serve warm.

Deviled Eggs With Smoked Paprika

Servings: 6
Cooking Time: 30 Minutes

Ingredients:

- 6 large eggs
- 3 tbsp reduced-fat mayo, plus more
- 1 tsp Dijon or yellow mustard
- ½ tsp Spanish smoked paprika or regular paprika, plus more
- dash of hot sauce
- coarse salt
- freshly ground black pepper
- for garnishing
- small sprigs of fresh parsley, dill, tarragon, or cilantro
- chopped chives
- minced scallions
- Mustard Caviar
- sliced green or black olives
- celery leaves
- sliced radishes
- diced bell peppers
- sliced cherry tomatoes
- fresh or pickled jalapeños
- sliced or diced pickles
- slivers of sun-dried tomatoes

- bacon crumbles
- smoked salmon
- Hawaiian black salt
- Caviar

Directions:

1. Supply your smoker with wood pellets and follow the start-up procedure. Preheat the grill, with the lid closed, to 180° F.

2. On the stovetop over medium-high heat, bring a saucepan of water to a boil. (Make sure there's enough water in the saucepan to cover the eggs by 1 inch [5cm].) Use a slotted spoon to gently lower the eggs into the water. Lower the heat to maintain a simmer. Set a timer for 13 minutes.

3. Prepare an ice bath by combining ice and cold water in a large bowl. Carefully transfer the eggs to the ice bath when the timer goes off.

4. When the eggs are cool enough to handle, gently tap them all over to crack the shell. Carefully peel the eggs. Rinse under cold running water to remove any clinging bits of shell, but don't dry the eggs. (A damp surface will help the smoke adhere to the egg whites.)

5. Place the eggs on the grate and smoke until the eggs take on a light brown patina from the smoke, about 25 minutes. Transfer the eggs to a cutting board, handling them as little as possible.

6. Slice each egg in half lengthwise with a sharp knife. Wipe any yolk off the blade before slicing the next egg. Gently remove the yolks and place them in a food processor. Pulse to break up the yolks. Add the mayo, mustard, paprika, and hot sauce. Season with salt and pepper to taste. Pulse until the filling is smooth. Add additional mayo 1 teaspoon at a time if the mixture is a little dry. (It shouldn't be too loose either.)

7. Spoon the filling into each egg half or pipe it in using a small resealable plastic bag. You can also use a pastry bag fitted with a fluted tip.

8. Place the eggs on a platter and lightly dust with paprika. Accompany with one or more of the suggested garnishes.

Smoked Cashews

Servings: 6

Cooking Time: 60 Minutes

Ingredients:

- 1 pound roasted, salted cashews

Directions:

1. Supply your smoker with wood pellets and follow the start-up procedure. Preheat the grill, with the lid closed, to 120°F.

2. Pour the cashews onto a rimmed baking sheet and smoke for 1 hour, stirring once about halfway through the smoking time.

3. Remove the cashews from the grill, let cool, and store in an airtight container for as long as you can resist.

Pig Pops (sweet-hot Bacon On A Stick)

Servings: 24

Cooking Time: 30 Minutes

Ingredients:

- Nonstick cooking spray, oil, or butter, for greasing
- 2 pounds thick-cut bacon (24 slices)
- 24 metal skewers
- 1 cup packed light brown sugar
- 2 to 3 teaspoons cayenne pepper
- ½ cup maple syrup, divided

Directions:

1. Supply your smoker with wood pellets and follow the start-up procedure. Preheat, with the lid closed, to 350°F.

2. Coat a disposable aluminum foil baking sheet with cooking spray, oil, or butter.

3. Thread each bacon slice onto a metal skewer and place on the prepared baking sheet.

4. In a medium bowl, stir together the brown sugar and cayenne.

5. Baste the top sides of the bacon with ¼ cup of maple syrup.

6. Sprinkle half of the brown sugar mixture over the bacon.

7. Place the baking sheet on the grill, close the lid, and smoke for 15 to 30 minutes.

8. Using tongs, flip the bacon skewers. Baste with the remaining ¼ cup of maple syrup and top with the remaining brown sugar mixture.

9. Continue smoking with the lid closed for 10 to 15 minutes, or until crispy. You can eyeball the bacon and smoke to your desired doneness, but the actual ideal internal temperature for bacon is 155°F

10. Using tongs, carefully remove the bacon skewers from the grill. Let cool completely before handling.

Chuckwagon Beef Jerky

Servings: 6
Cooking Time: 300 Minutes

Ingredients:

- 2½lb (1.2kg) boneless top or bottom round steak, sirloin tip, flank steak, or venison
- 1 cup sugar-free dark-colored soda
- 1 cup cold brewed coffee
- ½ cup light soy sauce
- ¼ cup Worcestershire sauce
- 2 tbsp whiskey (optional)
- 2 tsp chili powder
- 1½ tsp garlic salt
- 1 tsp onion powder
- 1 tsp pink curing salt

Directions:

1. Slice the meat into ¼-inch-thick (.5cm) strips, trimming off any visible fat or gristle. (Slice against the grain for more tender jerky and with the grain for chewier jerky.) Place the meat in a large resealable plastic bag.

2. In a small bowl, whisk together the soda, coffee, soy sauce, Worcestershire sauce, whiskey (if using), chili powder, garlic salt, onion powder, and curing salt (if using). Whisk until the salt dissolves. Pour the mixture over the meat and reseal the bag. Refrigerate for 24 to 48 hours, turning the bag several times to redistribute the brine.

3. Supply your smoker with wood pellets and follow the start-up procedure. Preheat the grill, with the lid closed, to 150° F.

4. Drain the meat and discard the brine. Place the strips of meat in a single layer on paper towels and blot any excess moisture.

5. Place the meat in a single layer on the grate and smoke for 4 to 5 hours, turning once or twice. (If you're aware of hot spots on your grate, rotate the strips so they smoke evenly.) To test for doneness, bend one or two pieces in the middle. They should be dry but still somewhat pliant. Or simply eat a piece to see if it's done to your liking.

6. For the best texture, when you remove the meat from the grill, place the still-warm jerky in a resealable plastic bag and let rest for 30 minutes. (You might see condensation form on the inside of the bag, but the moisture will be reabsorbed by the meat.) Or let the meat cool completely and then store in a resealable plastic bag or covered container. The jerky will last a few days at room temperature but will last longer (up to 2 weeks) if refrigerated.

Smoked Cheese

Servings: 4
Cooking Time: 150 Minutes

Ingredients:

- 1 (2-pound) block medium Cheddar cheese, or your favorite cheese, quartered lengthwise

Directions:

1. Supply your smoker with wood pellets and follow the start-up procedure. Preheat the grill, with the lid closed, to 90°F.

2. Place the cheese directly on the grill grate and smoke for 2 hours, 30 minutes, checking frequently to be sure it's not melting. If the cheese begins to melt, try flipping it. If that doesn't help, remove it from the grill and refrigerate for about 1 hour and then return it to the cold smoker.

3. Remove the cheese, place it in a zip-top bag, and refrigerate overnight.

4. Slice the cheese and serve with crackers, or grate it and use for making a smoked mac and cheese.

Roasted Red Pepper Dip

Servings: 8
Cooking Time: 45 Minutes

Ingredients:

- 4 red bell peppers, halved, destemmed, and deseeded
- 1 cup English walnuts, divided
- 1 small white onion, peeled and coarsely chopped
- 2 garlic cloves, peeled and smashed with a chef's knife
- ¼ cup extra virgin olive oil, plus more
- 1 tbsp balsamic vinegar or balsamic glaze
- 1 tsp honey (eliminate if using balsamic glaze)
- 1 tsp coarse salt, plus more
- 1 tsp ground cumin
- 1 tsp smoked paprika
- ½ to 1 tsp Aleppo red pepper flakes, plus more
- ¼ cup fresh white breadcrumbs (optional)
- distilled water (optional)
- assorted crudités or wedges of pita bread

Directions:

1. Supply your smoker with wood pellets and follow the start-up procedure. Preheat the grill, with the lid closed, to 400° F.

2. Place the peppers skin side down on the grate and grill until the skins blister and the flesh softens, about 30 minutes. Transfer the peppers to a bowl and cover with plastic wrap. Let cool to room temperature. Remove the skins with a paring knife or your fingers. Coarsely chop or tear the peppers.

3. Place ¾ cup of walnuts in an aluminum foil roasting pan. Place the pan on the grate and toast for 10 to 15 minutes, stirring twice. Remove the pan from the grill and let the walnuts cool.

4. Place the peppers, onion, garlic, and walnuts in a food processor fitted with the chopping blade. Pulse several times. Add the olive oil, balsamic vinegar, honey, salt, cumin, paprika, and red pepper flakes. Process until the mixture is fairly smooth. Taste for seasoning, adding more salt or red pepper flakes (if desired). (If the mixture is too loose, add breadcrumbs until the texture is to your liking. If it's too thick, add olive oil or water 1 tablespoon at a time.)

5. Transfer the dip to a serving bowl. Use the back of a spoon to make a shallow depression in the center. Top with the remaining ¼ cup of walnuts and drizzle olive oil in the depression. Serve with crudités or pita bread.

Delicious Deviled Crab Appetizer

Servings: 30
Cooking Time: 10 Minutes

Ingredients:

- Nonstick cooking spray, oil, or butter, for greasing
- 1 cup panko breadcrumbs, divided
- 1 cup canned corn, drained
- ½ cup chopped scallions, divided
- ½ red bell pepper, finely chopped
- 16 ounces jumbo lump crabmeat
- ¾ cup mayonnaise, divided
- 1 egg, beaten
- 1 teaspoon salt
- 1 teaspoon freshly ground black pepper
- 2 teaspoons cayenne pepper, divided
- Juice of 1 lemon

Directions:

1. Supply your smoker with wood pellets and follow the start-up procedure. Preheat, with the lid closed, to 425°F.

2. Spray three 12-cup mini muffin pans with cooking spray and divide ½ cup of the panko between 30 of the muffin cups, pressing into the bottoms and up the sides. (Work in batches, if necessary, depending on the number of pans you have.)

3. In a medium bowl, combine the corn, ¼ cup of scallions, the bell pepper, crabmeat, half of the mayonnaise, the egg, salt, pepper, and 1 teaspoon of cayenne pepper.

4. Gently fold in the remaining ½ cup of breadcrumbs and divide the mixture between the prepared mini muffin cups.

5. Place the pans on the grill grate, close the lid, and smoke for 10 minutes, or until golden brown.

6. In a small bowl, combine the lemon juice and the remaining mayonnaise, scallions, and cayenne pepper to make a sauce.

7. Brush the tops of the mini crab cakes with the sauce and serve hot.

Smoked Turkey Sandwich

Servings: 1
Cooking Time: 15 Minutes

Ingredients:

- 2 slices sourdough bread
- 2 tablespoons butter, at room temperature
- 2 (1-ounce) slices Swiss cheese
- 4 ounces leftover Smoked Turkey
- 1 teaspoon garlic salt

Directions:

1. Supply your smoker with wood pellets and follow the start-up procedure. Preheat the grill, with the lid closed, to 375°F.
2. Coat one side of each bread slice with 1 tablespoon of butter and sprinkle the buttered sides with garlic salt.
3. Place 1 slice of cheese on each unbuttered side of the bread, and then put the turkey on the cheese.
4. Close the sandwich, buttered sides out, and place it directly on the grill grate. Cook for 5 minutes. Flip the sandwich and cook for 5 minutes more. Remove the sandwich from the grill, cut it in half, and serve.

Sriracha & Maple Cashews

Servings: 10
Cooking Time: 60 Minutes

Ingredients:

- 2 tbsp unsalted butter
- 3 tbsp pure maple syrup
- 1 tbsp sriracha
- 1 tsp coarse salt (use only if nuts are unsalted)
- 2½ cups unsalted cashews

Directions:

1. Supply your smoker with wood pellets and follow the start-up procedure. Preheat the grill, with the lid closed, to 250° F.
2. In a small saucepan on the stovetop over low heat, melt the butter. Add the maple syrup, sriracha, and salt (if using). Stir until combined. Add the nuts and stir gently to coat thoroughly.
3. Spread the nuts in a single layer in an aluminum foil roasting pan coated with cooking spray. Place the pan on the grate and smoke the nuts until they're lightly toasted, about 1 hour, stirring once or twice.
4. Remove the pan from the grill and let the nuts cool for 15 minutes. They'll be sticky at first but will crisp up. Break them up with your fingers and store at room temperature in an airtight container, such as a lidded glass jar.

Jalapeño Poppers With Chipotle Sour Cream

Servings: 8
Cooking Time: 45 Minutes

Ingredients:

- 3 strips of thin-sliced bacon
- 12 large jalapeños, red, green, or a mix
- 8oz (225g) light cream cheese, at room temperature
- 1 cup shredded pepper Jack, Monterey Jack, or Cheddar cheese
- 1 tsp chili powder
- ½ tsp garlic salt
- smoked paprika
- for the sour cream
- 1¼ cups light sour cream
- juice of ½ lime
- ½ to 1 canned chipotle peppers in adobo sauce, finely minced, plus 1 tsp of sauce, plus more
- 1 tbsp minced fresh cilantro leaves
- ½ tsp coarse salt, plus more

Directions:

1. Supply your smoker with wood pellets and follow the start-up procedure. Preheat the grill, with the lid closed, to 375° F.
2. Line a rimmed sheet pan with aluminum foil and place a wire rack on top. Place the bacon in a single layer on the wire rack. Place the pan on the grate and grill until the bacon is crisp and golden brown, about 20 minutes. Transfer the bacon to paper towels to cool and then crumble. Set aside.
3. In a small bowl, make the chipotle sour cream by whisking together the ingredients. Add more salt, chipotle peppers, or adobe sauce to taste. Cover and refrigerate.

4. Slice the jalapeños lengthwise through their stems. Scrape out the veins and seeds with the edge of a small metal spoon.

5. In a small bowl, beat together the cream cheese, shredded cheese, chili powder, and garlic salt. Stir in the crumbled bacon. Mound the cream cheese mixture in the jalapeño halves. Line another rimmed sheet pan with aluminum foil and place a wire rack on top. Place the jalapeños filled side up in a single layer on the wire rack.

6. Place the sheet pan on the grate and roast the jalapeños until the filling has melted and the peppers have softened, about 20 to 25 minutes. (They should no longer look bright in color.) Remove the pan from the grill and let the peppers rest for 5 minutes.

7. Transfer the poppers to a platter and lightly dust with paprika. Serve with the chipotle sour cream.

Cold-smoked Cheese

Servings: 6
Cooking Time: 180 Minutes

Ingredients:
- 2lb (1kg) well-chilled hard or semi-hard cheese, such as:
- Edam
- Gouda
- Cheddar
- Monterey Jack
- pepper Jack
- goat cheese
- fresh mozzarella
- Muenster
- aged Parmigiano-Reggiano
- Gruyère
- blue cheese

Directions:
1. Unwrap the cheese and remove any protective wax or coating. Cut into 4-ounce (110g) portions to increase the surface area.

2. If possible, move your smoker to a shady area. Place 1 resealable plastic bag filled with ice on top of the drip pan. This is especially important on a warm day because you want to keep the interior temperature of the grill between 70 and 90°F (21 and 32°C) or below.

3. Place a grill mat on one side of the grate. Place the cheese on the mat and allow space between each piece.

4. Fill your smoking tube or pellet maze (see Cast Iron Skillets and Grill Pans) with pellets or sawdust and light according to the manufacturer's instructions. Place the smoking tube on the grate near—but not on—the grill mat. When the tube is smoking consistently, close the grill lid.

5. Smoke the cheese for 1 to 3 hours, replacing the pellets or sawdust and ice if necessary. Monitor the temperature and make sure the cheese isn't beginning to melt. Carefully lift the mat with the cheese to a rimmed baking sheet and let the cheese cool completely before handling.

6. Package the smoked cheese in cheese storage paper or bags or vacuum-seal the cheese, labeling each. (While you can wrap the cheese tightly in plastic wrap, the cheese will spoil faster.) Let the cheese rest for at least 2 to 3 days before eating. It will be even better after 2 weeks.

BEEF LAMB AND GAME RECIPES

Grilled Brisket Burger

Servings: 2
Cooking Time: 15 Minutes

Ingredients:

- 2 Pound ground beef brisket
- 2/3 Medium Red Onion, Sliced 1/4" Thick
- 4 Slices cheddar cheese
- 8 Slices cooked bacon
- 2 Whole Burger Buns, Halved
- 6 Ounce Sweet & Heat BBQ Sauce

Directions:

1. Supply your smoker with wood pellets and follow the start-up procedure. Preheat the grill, with the lid closed, to 375° F. Form meat into 6 patties and season with Traeger Beef Rub.
2. Place them directly on the grill grate and cook for 4 minutes, flip patties and cook for 2 more minutes. Grill: 375 °F
3. Place the red onions on the grill next to the burger and cook for 8 minutes total, flipping halfway through. Grill: 375 °F
4. Top burgers with cheese and cook until cheese is melted, about 1–2 minutes. Remove burgers from grill and keep warm.
5. If desired, toast burger buns face side down on the grill for 2 minutes. Assemble as double burgers with the grilled onions, bacon, and Traeger Sweet & Heat BBQ sauce. Enjoy! *Cook times will vary depending on set and ambient temperatures.

Easy Breakfast Cheeseburger

Servings: 2
Cooking Time: 10 Minutes

Ingredients:

- 4 Bacon, Strip
- 6 Ounce Lean Beef, Ground
- 2 Burger Buns
- 2 Cheese, Sliced
- 2 Egg
- Pepper
- Salt

Directions:

1. Supply your smoker with wood pellets and follow the start-up procedure. Preheat the grill, with the lid closed, to 400° F.
2. Take the ground beef and divide it into two thin patties. Brush the grate with oil, then add the patties and grill them on about 2-5 minutes on each side, or until the desired doneness, pressing down to get a good sear.
3. Remove the burgers from the grill, then build your burger. Starting with the bottom bun or bread slice, add the patty, then a slice of American cheese, top with bacon, hash browns, an egg over easy, and finish with the top bun or bread slice. Now it's ready to serve!

Grilled Rosemary Rack Of Lamb

Servings: 8
Cooking Time: 30 Minutes

Ingredients:

- 2 Tablespoons Dijon Mustard
- 1 Tablespoon Fresh Parsley, Chopped
- Chop House Steak Rub
- 2 Chine Bones Removed, And Excess Fat Trimmed Racks Of Lamb
- 1 Teaspoon Rosemary, Finely Chopped

Directions:

1. Place the racks of lamb on a flat work surface, then generously brush the lamb all over with Dijon mustard.
2. Season the meat on all sides with Chophouse Steak seasoning and sprinkle with parsley and rosemary.
3. Supply your smoker with wood pellets and follow the start-up procedure. Preheat the grill, with the lid closed, to 400° F.
4. If you're using a gas or charcoal grill, set it up for high heat.
5. Insert a temperature probe into the thickest part of the rack of lamb and sear the rack, meaty side down for about 6 minutes.
6. Remove the lamb from the grill and turn the temperature down to 300°F.

7. Return the lamb to the grill and lean the two racks against each other so that they stand up, and grill for another 20 minutes, or until the internal temperature reaches 130°F.

8. Remove the racks from the grill and allow to rest for 10 minutes before carving and serving.

Smoked Texas Bbq Brisket

Servings: 8
Cooking Time: 600 Minutes

Ingredients:
- 1 (14-18 lb) whole packer brisket
- Meat Church Holy Cow BBQ Rub
- Meat Church Holy Gospel BBQ Rub

Directions:
1. Trim any hard fat from all sides of the brisket, being careful not to dig too deep into the meat. Trim the sides of any excess or loose fat. Trim the fat side of the brisket to 1/4 inch thick.
2. Season all sides evenly with Meat Church Holy Cow Rub. Optionally add a light layer of Meat Church Holy Gospel Rub. Let the brisket sit in the seasoning at room temp for 20 to 30 minutes.
3. Supply your smoker with wood pellets and follow the start-up procedure. Preheat the grill, with the lid closed, to 275° F.
4. Place the brisket fat side up on the grill grate. Cook until it reaches an internal temperature of 165°F, about 5 to 6 hours
5. Remove brisket and wrap tightly in Traeger Butcher Paper.
6. Place the wrapped brisket back on the grill and cook until it reaches an internal temperature of 204°F, about 3-4 hours. Grill: 275 °F Probe: 204 °F
7. When the brisket reaches 204°F, remove from grill and let rest for 30 minutes. When ready to eat, unwrap brisket and slice against the grain. Enjoy!

Jalapeno Pepper Jack Cheese Bacon Burgers

Servings: 4
Cooking Time: 30 Minutes

Ingredients:
- 4 Slices, Raw Bacon
- 1/2 Cup Prepared Barbecue Sauce
- 1 Pound Ground Beef
- Hickory Bacon Seasoning, Plus More For Sprinkling
- 2 Thinly Sliced Jalapeno Peppers
- 1/2 Cup Olive Oil
- 4 Onion Burger Buns
- Onion, Crispy
- 4 Pepper Jack Cheese, Sliced

Directions:
1. Supply your smoker with wood pellets and follow the start-up procedure. Preheat the grill, with the lid closed, to 350° F. If using a gas or charcoal grill, set it up for medium high heat.
2. Make the burgers: in a large bowl, mix together the ground beef and Hickory Bacon seasoning until the seasoning is well incorporated. Use the Burger Press to make burger patties. Repeat until all the ground beef is gone.
3. In a small bowl, toss the sliced raw jalapenos with the olive oil and place them in the vegetable grill basket. Grill the jalapenos, stirring occasionally, until soft and charred in some spots. Remove from the grill and set aside.
4. Place the bacon on the vegetable grill basket and grill for 5-7 minutes, or until the bacon is crispy and brown. Remove from the grill and set aside.
5. Grill the burgers: place the burger patties on the grill and, if desired, sprinkle more Hickory Bacon seasoning on the patties. Grill the burgers for 5 minutes on one side, then flip and top with a slice of pepper jack cheese and grill for another 5-7 minutes, or until the internal temperature of the burgers is 135-140°F.
6. Remove the burgers from the grill and place on an onion bun. Top with the bacon, grilled jalapenos, crisped onions, and a spoonful of barbecue sauce.

Smoked Elk Loin With Creamy Polenta

Servings: 6
Cooking Time: 120 Minutes

Ingredients:

- 1 1/2 Pound elk loin
- 1 Sprig rosemary, minced
- 1 Clove garlic, minced
- 1 Teaspoon olive oil
- 1/2 Teaspoon salt
- 1/2 Teaspoon pepper
- 1 Cup polenta
- 3 Tablespoon butter
- 1 Tablespoon kosher salt

Directions:

1. Combine rosemary, garlic, olive oil, salt and pepper in a small bowl and rub over elk loin. Marinate for 2 hours.

2. Supply your smoker with wood pellets and follow the start-up procedure. Preheat the grill, with the lid closed, to 165° F.

3. Place the elk loin directly on the grill grate and cook for 1-1/2 to 2 hours, or until it reaches an internal temperature of 100℉. Remove from the grill and increase the temperature to 375℉. Grill: 165 °F Probe: 100 °F

4. When the Traeger is to temperature, place the elk loin back on the grill grate and roast until the internal temperature reaches 120℉. Remove from the grill and let rest 5 to 7 minutes before slicing. Grill: 375 °F Probe: 120 °F

5. For the Polenta: In a heavy-bottomed pot, bring 5-1/2 cups water and kosher salt to a boil over high heat. Add the polenta slowly, whisking continuously. This will look thin at first but as the polenta cooks and the grain swells it will thicken. Grill: 375 °F Probe: 120 °F

6. Turn the heat down to low, and continue cooking for another 20 minutes, whisking often. Add another 1/2 cup water as needed, about every 20 minutes. The flame should be low so that the polenta is barely simmering. Whisk in butter and season to taste.

7. Serve the polenta with the sliced elk loin on top. Enjoy!

Lemon Tomahawk Steak

Servings: 2 – 4
Cooking Time: 215 Minutes

Ingredients:

- Apple Corer Or Metal Spoon
- 3 Lbs Gala Apples
- 1 Lemon
- Chop House Steak Rub
- 1 Tbsp Tennessee Apple Butter Rub
- Sugar
- 4 Cups Water

Directions:

1. Supply your smoker with wood pellets and follow the start-up procedure. Preheat the grill, with the lid closed, to 400° F. If using a gas or charcoal grill, set heat to medium-high heat.

2. Core and halve the apples. Place apples skin-side down on a sheet tray and season with Tennessee Apple Butter and set aside.

3. In a cast iron pot, combine the apple cores with the juice and zest from one lemon. Cover the mixture with water, transfer to the grill and bring to a boil. Reduce heat to 225° F. Place the apples directly on the grill grate (skin-side down) and cook for 1 hour.

4. After 1 hour, remove cast iron pot from the grill. Strain liquid, discard cores, return liquid to pot, and whisk in sugar. Cover with lid and return to grill. Allow to simmer for another hour.

5. Add smoked apples to the pot and continue to simmer for 20 minutes. Remove pot from grill and purée apple mixture in a blender. Pour apple purée back into pot and return to grill. Increase heat to 375° F and simmer for 20 minutes. Remove from grill and allow to cool slightly.

6. Reduce heat on grill to 225° F. Season the tomahawk steak with Chop House Steak Rub on both sides. Place the steak on the grill grates, insert a temperature probe, and grill, undisturbed, for 45 minutes, or until the steak reaches an internal temperature of 120°F

7. Remove steak from grill and set aside. Open the Sear Slide on your and increase temperature to 400°F.

Return tomahawk to grill and sear over open flames, about 2-3 minutes per side.

8. Pull the steak off the grill and allow it to rest for 10 minutes. Ladle reserved apple butter over steak and serve.

Smoked Red Wine Beef Roast

Servings: 8
Cooking Time: 180 Minutes

Ingredients:

- 12 oz beef broth
- 6 lbs eye of round beef roast
- 2 tbsp black pepper
- ½ tbsp celery salt
- ½ tbsp garlic powder
- 2 tbsp kosher salt
- ½ tbsp onion powder
- 2 cups red wine
- 1/3 cup Worcestershire sauce

Directions:

1. Supply your smoker with wood pellets and follow the start-up procedure. Preheat the grill, with the lid closed, to 225 °F.
2. Mix the beef broth, red wine, and Worcestershire sauce in a mixing bowl. Fill your meat injector with the mixture.
3. Mix the seasonings in a spice bottle and apply the rub all over the roast, making sure to coat the whole roast evenly.
4. Place the beef roast in the foil pan, fat side up. Using the meat injector, inject the liquid into all areas of the beef roast. Fill the bottom of the pan with the remaining liquid.
5. Place the pan in the smoker and let it cook for 3 hours, basting with the juices in the pan every hour or so.
6. After 3 hours, start checking the roast for the desired internal temperature (Rare: 135 °F, Medium Rare: 145 °F, Medium: 155 °F, Well Done: 170 °F).
7. Remove from the grill and the pan, and let the roast rest for 20 to 30 minutes before slicing.
8. Slice against the grain and enjoy!

Beer Braised Beef Sandwiches

Servings: 4
Cooking Time: 180 Minutes

Ingredients:

- 12 oz beer, porter or stout
- 1/2 black pepper
- 2 1/2 lbs chuck roast
- 4 hoagie rolls, sliced lengthwise
- 1/4 cup horseradish sauce
- 1 tbsp kosher salt
- 1 tbsp parsley, chopped
- 1 red onion, cut into thick rings
- 1/2 tbsp worcestershire sauce
- 1 yellow onion, cut into thick rings

Directions:

1. Supply your smoker with wood pellets and follow the start-up procedure. Preheat the grill, with the lid open, to 450° F. If using a gas or charcoal grill, set it up for high heat.
2. Set the chuck roast on a sheet tray, then season with salt and pepper. Place onions in a cast iron skillet or Dutch oven with a lid. Set aside.
3. Sear the chuck roast on the grill, 3 minutes per side, then transfer to the skillet set on top of the onions. Add the Worcestershire sauce and beer to the skillet, along the side of the roast. Cover and reduce the temperature to 325°F. Braise the roast for 2 ½ to 3 hours, until tender.
4. Remove the roast from the grill, add parsley, then pull apart and toss in reduced pan jus and onions.
5. Serve warm on hoagie rolls with horseradish sauce.

Bbq Beef Short Ribs

Servings: 8
Cooking Time: 600 Minutes

Ingredients:

- 4 (4 bone) beef short rib racks
- 1/2 Cup Beef Rub
- 1 Cup apple juice

Directions:

1. If your butcher has not already done so, remove the thin papery membrane from the bone-side of the ribs by working the tip of a butter knife underneath the

membrane over a middle bone. Use paper towels to get a firm grip, then tear the membrane off.

2. Season both sides of ribs with Traeger Beef Rub.

3. Supply your smoker with wood pellets and follow the start-up procedure. Preheat the grill, with the lid closed, to 225° F.

4. Arrange the ribs on the grill grate, bone-side down. Grill: 225 °F

5. Cook for 8 to 10 hours, spritzing or mopping with apple juice every 60 minutes until internal temperature reaches 205°F . Grill: 225 °F Probe: 205 °F

6. Slice between ribs and serve immediately. Enjoy!

Savory Reverse Seared Ny Steak

Servings: 4
Cooking Time: 68 Minutes

Ingredients:
- 4 Tbsp Butter
- Steak Seasoning
- 4 - 1 1/2" Steak, New York Strip

Directions:

1. Supply your smoker with wood pellets and follow the start-up procedure. Preheat the grill, with the lid closed, to 250° F.

2. As the grill is preheating to the perfect temperature, spice the steaks with the Chop House steak rub.

3. Lay the steaks on the grill for roughly 60 minutes or until the steaks reach an internal temperature of 105 to 110 degrees F. Remove the steaks and set aside.

4. Crank up the heat to 500°F, open the Flame Broiler plate and let the grill preheat.

5. Place the steaks back on the grill and sear for 4 minutes. Don't forget to add 1 TBSP of butter for flavor to each steak. You know when your steak is done once the internal temperature reaches 130 to 135°F (for medium-rare). Follow the below internal temperature for your cooking preference:

6. Rare: 125°F

7. Medium Rare: 130°F

8. Medium: 140°F

9. Well Done: 160°F

10. Once reached for personal preference, take the steaks off the grill and let them rest for 5 to 10 minutes before eating. ENJOY!

Grilled Tomahawk Steak

Servings: 4
Cooking Time: 60 Minutes

Ingredients:
- 2 Large tomahawk steaks
- 2 Tablespoon kosher salt
- 2 Tablespoon ground black pepper
- 1 Tablespoon paprika
- 1/2 Tablespoon garlic powder
- 1/2 Tablespoon onion powder
- 1/2 Tablespoon brown sugar
- 1 Teaspoon ground mustard
- 1/4 Teaspoon cayenne pepper

Directions:

1. In a small bowl, combine all ingredients for the rub. Season the steaks liberally with the rub and set steaks aside while the grill preheats.

2. Supply your smoker with wood pellets and follow the start-up procedure. Preheat the grill, with the lid closed, to 225° F.

3. Place the steaks directly on the grill grate and smoke for 45 minutes to 1 hour, until the internal temperature reaches 120°F. Grill: 225 °F

4. Remove steaks from the grill and set aside to rest.

5. Increase the grill temperature to 450°F. Grill: 450 °F

6. Place the steaks directly on the grill grate and cook 7 to 10 minutes per side, or until the internal temperature reaches 130°F. Grill: 450 °F Probe: 130 °F

7. Remove from grill and let rest 5 minutes before serving. Enjoy!

Garlic Standing Rib Roast

Servings: 4
Cooking Time: 240 Minutes

Ingredients:
- 1 tbsp cracked black pepper
- 1/2 tbsp granulated garlic
- 1/2 tbsp granulated onion

- 2 tbsp kosher salt
- 1 tbsp olive oil
- 2 tsp oregano, dried
- 1/2 tbsp parsley, dried
- 5 1/2 lbs prime rib roast, bone-in
- 2 tsp smoked paprika

Directions:

1. Place the roast in a glass baking dish. In a small mixing bowl, combine the salt, pepper, granulated garlic, granulated onion, parsley, oregano and smoked paprika. Season the entire roast with the spice blend, then cover and refrigerate overnight.

2. One hour prior to cooking, remove roast from the refrigerator, uncover, and let it sit out at room temperature.

3. Supply your smoker with wood pellets and follow the start-up procedure. Preheat the grill, with the lid closed, to 225° F. If using a gas or charcoal grill, set it up for low, indirect heat.

4. Place seasoned roast on a cast iron skillet, drizzle with olive oil, and transfer to the grill. Smoke the roast for 1 hour 45 minutes, or until internal temperature reaches 120° F. Remove from the grill and allow roast to rest for 15 minutes.

5. Increase the grill temperature to 450 F, then return roast to grill for an additional 10 to 15 minutes. Allow roast to rest for 15 minutes, slice and serve warm.

Wagyu Tri-tip

Servings: 8
Cooking Time: 60 Minutes

Ingredients:
- 2 wagyu beef tri-tip
- 1 Cup Prime Rib Rub

Directions:

1. Supply your smoker with wood pellets and follow the start-up procedure. Preheat the grill, with the lid closed, to 225° F.

2. While grill is preheating, trim any excess fat off of the tri-tip and season with Traeger Prime Rib Rub.

3. Place tri-tip on the Traeger and cook until it reaches an internal temperature of 130°F. This should take 1 to 1-1/2 hours. When the tri-tip reaches 130°F pull off the grill and set aside. Grill: 225 °F Probe: 130 °F

4. Increase the grill temperature to 475°F. After 15 minutes, return the tri-tip to the grill and cook for 3 minutes per side. Pull off and slice. Enjoy! Grill: 475 °F

Smoked Beer Corned Beef

Servings: 6
Cooking Time: 240 Minutes

Ingredients:
- 6 lb corned beef brisket raw
- 2 tbsp black pepper
- 8 oz light beer

Directions:

1. Supply your smoker with wood pellets and follow the start-up procedure. Preheat the grill, with the lid closed, to 275 °F.

2. Cut open packaging of corned beef and drain off liquid. Be sure to grab the spice packet included with the brisket. Gently rinse off corned beef and then pat dry with a paper towel.

3. Open the spice packet included with your corned beef and sprinkle contents over the brisket, then sprinkle a light dusting of black pepper according to your preference.

4. Once pellet grill has reached temperature, insert probes into corned beef brisket pieces. If you only have a single probe, insert that probe in the center of the smallest piece because it will cook the fastest.

5. Smoke for 3 to 4 hours until corned beef reaches an internal temperature of 175 degrees F. Next transfer briskets to an aluminum pan and pour just enough beer in to cover the bottom of the pan. Cover with foil leaving one corner open to let out steam.

6. Continue cooking for another 2-3 hours until internal temperature reaches about 205 degrees F. Use an instant read thermometer and poke different parts of the brisket checking for tenderness. If probe goes into the meat with very little tension than it is done. If not, continue cooking until it becomes tender.

7. Once meat is tender and fully cooked, remove pan from pellet grill and let the corned beef rest for about 30

minutes still covered with one corner open to prevent overcooking.

8.   Slice corned beef into 1/8 inch slices cutting against the grains of the brisket. If brisket crumbles make slices a little thicker.

Cucumber Beef Kefta

Servings: 4
Cooking Time: 10 Minutes

Ingredients:
- bamboo skewers, soaked in warm water
- 1 tbsp blackened saskatchewan rub seasoning
- 3 tbsp cilantro, chopped
- for topping, cucumbers
- 1 tsp cumin
- 2 lbs ground beef
- 1 tsp paprika
- 3 tbsp parsley, chopped
- pitas
- 1 red onion, grated
- for topping, tomatoes
- to taste, tzatziki sauce

Directions:

1.   In a mixing bowl, combine ground beef, onion, Blackened Saskatchewan, cumin, paprika, cilantro, and parsley. Mix well, then cover and refrigerate for 1 hour to allow the flavors to blend.

2.   Supply your smoker with wood pellets and follow the start-up procedure. Preheat the grill, with the lid closed, to 425° F. If using a gas or charcoal grill, set it up for medium-high heat.

3.   Prepare kebabs: take small amounts of ground beef kefta and shape into popsicle-size cylinders. Skewer the meat, squeezing it to mold it to the skewer.

4.   Grill kefta 3 to 5 minutes per side, then remove from the grill and serve warm with pitas, tzatziki sauce, and your favorite fresh veggies.

Bistecca Alla Fiorentina With Mushroom Ragout

Servings: 3
Cooking Time: 25 Minutes

Ingredients:
- 2 sprigs of fresh sage
- 2 sprigs of fresh rosemary
- 2 sprigs of fresh thyme
- 1 porterhouse steak, about 2½lb (1.25kg)
- extra virgin olive oil
- coarse salt
- fresh coarsely ground black pepper
- for the ragout
- 3 tbsp unsalted butter
- 3 shallots or 1 white onion, peeled and chopped
- 2 garlic cloves, peeled and minced
- 2lb (1kg) wild mushrooms, cleaned, destemmed, and sliced or chopped
- coarse salt
- freshly ground black pepper
- 2 tbsp Cognac or brandy
- ½ cup low-salt beef broth, plus more
- 2 tsp light soy sauce
- 2 tsp chopped fresh thyme or 1 tsp dried thyme
- ½ cup heavy whipping cream, plus more
- freshly squeezed lemon juice
- freshly chopped chives

Directions:

1.   Place a cast iron skillet or cast iron griddle on the grate. Supply your smoker with wood pellets and follow the start-up procedure. Preheat the grill, with the lid closed, to 450° F.

2.   In a large skillet on the stovetop over medium heat, begin making the ragout by melting the butter. Add the shallots and sauté until they soften, about 2 to 3 minutes, stirring often. Add the garlic and mushrooms. Season with salt and pepper. Cook until the mushrooms give up their liquid and begin to brown, about 5 minutes. Add the Cognac and cook for 1 minute. Stir in the broth, soy sauce, and thyme. Cook until the liquid reduces slightly, about 5 minutes. Remove the skillet from the stovetop and set aside.

3.   Tie the sprigs of sage, rosemary, and thyme together with butcher's twine. Place the steak on a rimmed sheet pan and use the herb brush to generously brush both sides with olive oil. Season with salt and pepper.

4.   Place the steak on the skillet and grill until the internal temperature reaches 125°F (52°C), about 8 to

10 minutes per side, occasionally using the herb brush to brush the steak with olive oil. If your grill has enough clearance, stand the porterhouse upright, resting on the bone, and continue to cook for a few minutes more.

5. Transfer the meat to a cutting board and brush it one final time with olive oil. Let rest for 5 minutes.

6. Add the cream to the ragout and reheat over medium-high heat until the mixture boils. Taste for seasoning, adding salt and pepper. If the ragout seems dry, add more cream or broth. If the flavors need brightening, stir in 1 or 2 teaspoons of lemon juice. Transfer the ragout to an attractive serving bowl and top with chives.

7. Carve off the strip steak and filet mignon. Slice them on a diagonal, keeping the slices in order. Place the bone on a platter and then place the slices around the bone. Serve immediately with the mushroom ragout.

The Perfect T-bones

Servings: 4
Cooking Time: 30 Minutes

Ingredients:

- 4 (1½- to 2-inch-thick) T-bone steaks
- 2 tablespoons olive oil
- 1 batch Espresso Brisket Rub or Chili-Coffee Rub

Directions:

1. Supply your smoker with wood pellets and follow the start-up procedure. Preheat the grill, with the lid closed, to 500°F.

2. Coat the steaks all over with olive oil and season both sides with the rub. Using your hands, work the rub into the meat.

3. Place the steaks directly on a grill grate and smoke until their internal temperature reaches 135°F for rare, 145°F for medium-rare, and 155°F for well-done. Remove the steaks from the grill and serve hot.

Bbq Sweet Pepper Meatloaf

Servings: 8
Cooking Time: 180 Minutes

Ingredients:

- 5 Pound ground beef, 80% lean
- 2 eggs
- 1 Cup plain panko breadcrumbs
- 1 Tablespoon kosher salt
- 1 Tablespoon black pepper
- 2 Tablespoon Rub
- 1 Cup diced sweet red peppers
- 1 Cup green onion, finely chopped
- 1 Cup ketchup

Directions:

1. Thoroughly mix together the ground beef, eggs, plain panko bread crumbs, kosher salt, black pepper, Traeger Rub, red sweet peppers and green onion.

2. Supply your smoker with wood pellets and follow the start-up procedure. Preheat the grill, with the lid closed, to 225° F.

3. Mold the meat mixture into a loaf and season exterior with the Traeger Rub.

4. Place meatloaf directly on the grill grate and cook for 2 hours and 15 minutes. Grill: 225 °F

5. Increase the grill temperature to 375°F and cook until an internal temperature of 155°F. Grill: 375 °F Probe: 155 °F

6. Glaze the meatloaf with ketchup and cook an additional 15 minutes. Grill: 375 °F

7. Allow to rest for 15 minutes before slicing. Enjoy!

Garlic Parmesan Grilled Filet Mignon

Servings: 2
Cooking Time: 10 Minutes

Ingredients:

- 4 filet mignon steaks
- 1 Teaspoon salt
- 1 Teaspoon black pepper
- 1 Teaspoon garlic salt
- 1 Cup Parmesan cheese
- 4 garlic
- 1 Tablespoon Dijon mustard

Directions:

1. Supply your smoker with wood pellets and follow the start-up procedure. Preheat the grill, with the lid closed, to High heat.

2.   While the grill is heating up, season the filets with salt, pepper, and garlic salt. Also mince your garlic and chop your Parmesan so it's fine, and combine.

3.   When the grill reaches temperature, place filets on the grill and cook for 4 minutes on each side. After 8 minutes total, spread the filets with the Dijon mustard and dip in the minced garlic and Parmesan cheese mixture and place back on the grill for another 1-2 minutes or until the cheese is melted.

4.   Let rest for 5 minutes and serve. Enjoy!

Venison Carne Asada

Servings: 4
Cooking Time: 8 Minutes

Ingredients:
- 1½lb (680g) venison steak, such as sirloin, about ¾ inch (2cm) thick
- southwestern-style rub
- 12 large scallions or spring onions, cleaned and trimmed
- for the marinade
- 2 garlic cloves, peeled and smashed with a chef's knife
- 1 jalapeño or serrano pepper, destemmed and thinly sliced
- juice of 1 orange
- juice of 1 lime
- 1 tbsp distilled white vinegar
- 1 tsp ground cumin
- 1 tsp coarse salt
- ⅓ cup vegetable oil
- ¼ cup chopped fresh cilantro
- for serving
- warmed flour or corn tortillas (optional)
- lime wedges
- sprigs of fresh cilantro
- Salsa de Molcajete or another salsa

Directions:
1.   In a small bowl, make the marinade by combining the garlic, jalapeño, orange juice, lime juice, white vinegar, cumin, and salt. Whisk until the salt dissolves. Whisk in the vegetable oil and stir in the cilantro. Place the venison in a resealable plastic bag and add the marinade, massaging the bag to thoroughly coat the meat. Refrigerate for 2 to 4 hours.

2.   Supply your smoker with wood pellets and follow the start-up procedure. Preheat the grill, with the lid closed, to 450° F.

3.   Drain the venison and remove any solids. (Discard the marinade.) Pat dry with paper towels. Lightly dust on both sides with the rub. Place the venison and scallions on the grate and sear until the internal temperature reaches 135°F (57°C), about 3 to 4 minutes per side. Grill the scallions until the bulbs are browned and tender, about 4 to 6 minutes, turning as needed.

4.   Remove the meat and scallions from the grill. Place the venison on a cutting board and let rest for 3 minutes. Slice thinly on a sharp diagonal. Shingle the meat on a platter. Scatter the scallions and cilantro over the top. Serve with tortillas (if using), lime wedges, cilantro, and salsa.

Salt & Pepper Dinosaur Bones

Servings: 3-4
Cooking Time: 480 Minutes

Ingredients:
- 1 rack of beef plate short ribs, about 4 to 5lb (1.8 to 2.3kg) total, or 3 bones
- coarse kosher salt
- freshly ground black pepper
- granulated garlic
- crushed red pepper flakes (optional)
- 1½ cups sugar-free dark-colored soda, sugar-free root beer, beef broth, or brewed coffee

Directions:
1.   Supply your smoker with wood pellets and follow the start-up procedure. Preheat the grill, with the lid closed, to 250° F.

2.   Place the ribs in an aluminum foil roasting pan. If the rack has a thick cap of fat on the meaty side, trim most of it off because that will impede the formation of a nice bark on the ribs.

3.   Generously season the ribs on all sides with salt, pepper, garlic, and red pepper flakes (if using). Place the ribs bone side down on the grate and smoke for 3 hours.

4. Add the soda to a spray bottle and spritz the ribs. Continue to smoke the ribs until the internal temperature reaches 203°F (95°C), about 4 to 5 hours more, spritzing once an hour. (Insert the probe next to the middle rib, being careful not to touch the bone.) When the ribs are tender, the meat will feel gelatinous and springy and will have shrunk back from the ends of the bones by up to 2 inches (5cm).

5. Transfer the ribs to a clean sheet pan and wrap with heavy-duty aluminum foil. Let rest for 1 hour, preferably in an insulated cooler.

6. Slice the ribs apart or remove the meat from the bones and thinly slice before serving with additional salt and pepper.

Smoked Corned Beef Reuben

Servings: 4

Cooking Time: 255 Minutes

Ingredients:

- aluminum foil
- 1 tbsp butter
- 1 cup chicken stock
- 3 lbs corned beef brisket
- 3 tbsp dijon mustard
- 1/2 cup russian dressing
- 1 cup sauerkraut
- 6 slices sourdough bread
- 6 swiss cheese, sliced
- vegetable oil

Directions:

1. Supply your smoker with wood pellets and follow the start-up procedure. Preheat the grill, with the lid closed, to 250° F. If using a gas or charcoal grill, set it up for low, indirect heat.

2. Coat all sides of corned beef brisket flat generously in mustard. Insert a temperature probe into the middle of the brisket flat, then transfer the brisket flat directly on grill grate, fat cap up, and cook for 2 hours.

3. Remove the brisket from the grill and place it in a pan lined with foil, or a disposable aluminum pan. Add chicken stock, then cover with foil and return to the grill.

4. Increase grill temperature to 300°F, and cook an additional 1 ½ to 2 hours, or until brisket is tender and reaches 190°F.

5. Remove from grill and allow brisket to rest for 15 minutes, then slice thin for Reuben sandwiches.

6. Preheat KC Combo griddle to medium-low flame. If using a gas or charcoal grill, preheat a cast iron skillet on medium-low heat.

7. Grease griddle with butter, then set 4 slices of sourdough on griddle, followed by 2 portions of sliced corned beef brisket. Warm brisket 1 to 2 minutes, then flip. Add sauerkraut and 1 ½ slices of Swiss cheese per portion. Close griddle lid for 2 to 3 minutes to melt cheese and crisp up underside of brisket.

8. Spoon dressing on sourdough, then set brisket on every other slice. Set remaining toasted sourdough on top of cheese to complete the Reuben sandwich.

9. Remove from griddle, then repeat with remaining 2 portions. Slice each sandwich on the bias and serve warm with extra dressing for dipping.

Smoked Rack Of Lamb

Servings: 6

Cooking Time: 360 Minutes

Ingredients:

- 1 (2-pound) rack of lamb
- 1 batch Rosemary-Garlic Lamb Seasoning

Directions:

1. Supply your smoker with wood pellets and follow the start-up procedure. Preheat the grill, with the lid closed, to 225°F.

2. Using a boning knife, score the bottom fat portion of the rib meat.

3. Using your hands, rub the rack of lamb all over with the seasoning, making sure it penetrates into the scored fat.

4. Place the rack directly on the grill grate, fat-side up, and smoke until its internal temperature reaches 145°F.

5. Remove the rack from the grill and let it rest for 20 to 30 minutes, before slicing it into individual ribs to serve.

Jalapeño Beef Jerky

Servings: 8

Cooking Time: 240 Minutes

Ingredients:

- 2 jalapeños, stemmed and seeded (or leave seeds in for a hotter jerky)
- 1/4 Cup lime juice
- 1/4 Cup soy sauce
- 4 Tablespoon brown sugar
- 1 Cup Mexican beer
- 2 Tablespoon Morton Tender Quick Home Meat Cure
- 2 Pound beef top or bottom round, sirloin tip, flank steak or wild game

Directions:

1. In a blender or small food processor, combine the jalapeños, lime juice, soy sauce, curing salt and brown sugar and process until the jalapeño is finely chopped. Set aside.

2. With a sharp knife, trim any fat or connective tissue from the meat. Slice the beef into 1/4 inch thick slices against the grain. (This is easier if the meat is partially frozen.)

3. Place the beef slices in a large resealable bag. Transfer jalapeño mixture to the resealable bag and top with beer. Massage the bag so that all the slices get coated with the marinade. Seal and refrigerate for several hours, or overnight.

4. Supply your smoker with wood pellets and follow the start-up procedure. Preheat the grill, with the lid closed, to 180° F.

5. Remove the beef from the marinade and discard the marinade. Dry the beef slices between paper towels. Arrange the meat in a single layer directly on the grill grate. Grill: 180 ˚F

6. Smoke for 4 to 5 hours, or until the jerky is dry but still chewy and somewhat pliant when you bend a piece. Grill: 180 ˚F

7. Transfer to a cooling rack and rest for an hour at room temperature.

8. Store in a resealable bag. Squeeze any air from the bag, and refrigerate the jerky. It will keep for several weeks in the fridge.

Bourbon-braised Beef Short Ribs

Servings: 4

Cooking Time: 180 Minutes

Ingredients:

- 1/2 Cup yellow mustard
- 2 Tablespoon Worcestershire sauce
- 1 Tablespoon molasses
- 12 beef short ribs, preferably from the chuck or plate
- Prime Rib Rub
- 1 Cup beef broth
- 3 Tablespoon soy sauce or Bragg Liquid Aminos
- 2 Tablespoon bourbon

Directions:

1. Supply your smoker with wood pellets and follow the start-up procedure. Preheat the grill, with the lid closed, to 250° F.

2. In a small mixing bowl, combine mustard, Worcestershire sauce and molasses; whisk to mix.

3. Coat each rib on all sides with the mustard slather sauce. Season with Traeger Prime Rib Rub.

4. Make the mop sauce: Combine the beef broth, soy sauce and bourbon in a food-safe spray bottle.

5. Place the short ribs, bone-side down, directly on the grill grate. Cook for 2 to 2-1/2 hours, or until the internal temperature of each rib is 165°F when read on an instant-read meat thermometer, spraying with the mop sauce every 30 minutes. Grill: 250 ˚F Probe: 165 ˚F

6. Transfer the ribs to a large sheet of heavy-duty aluminum foil. Bring up the edges of the foil and add whatever remains of the mop sauce. Bring the opposite sides of the foil together and fold several times, tightly enclosing the ribs. Return the foil-enclosed ribs to the grill grate.

7. Continue to cook the ribs until the internal temperature is 195°F, about 1 hour more. Grill: 250 ˚F Probe: 195 ˚F

8. Let the ribs rest for 15 minutes, still enclosed in the foil, then open carefully. (Watch out for escaping steam.) Transfer the ribs to a platter or plates, then drizzle with the juices.

Beef Brisket With Chophouse Steak Rub

Servings: 12
Cooking Time: 480 Minutes

Ingredients:
- As Needed, Chop House Steak Rub
- 1, 10 To 12 Lb Whole Beef Brisket

Directions:
1. Supply your smoker with wood pellets and follow the start-up procedure. Preheat the grill, with the lid closed, to 250° F.
2. While the grill is heating up, trim your brisket of excess fat, score the meat against the grain and season with Chop House Steak Rub or your favorite seasoning.
3. Place your brisket on the grates, fat side up and cook for 7-8 hours or until the internal temperature reaches 190°F. If the meat is not probe tender, keep cooking until your temperature probe can easily slide into the meat with little to no resistance.
4. Remove from the grill and allow to rest for 20-30 minutes.
5. Slice against the grain and enjoy!

Grilled Beef Shawarma

Servings: 4
Cooking Time: 10 Minutes

Ingredients:
- arugula
- 1/2 tsp cayenne pepper
- 1/2 tsp cinnamon, ground
- 1/2 tsp cloves, ground
- 1 1/2 tsp coriander, ground
- 1 1/2 lbs flank steak
- 2 garlic cloves, minced
- 2 tsp olive oil
- 1 tsp paprika
- 4 pita
- red onion
- tt salt and pepper
- tahini
- tomatoes
- 1/2 tsp turmeric, powder

Directions:
1. Use a meat mallet to tenderize the steak, then transfer to a glass baking dish and season with salt and pepper. Drizzle with olive oil, then rub minced garlic on steak. Season with spice rub. Cover with plastic wrap and refrigerate overnight.
2. Remove steak from the refrigerator, 1 hour prior to grilling. Supply your smoker with wood pellets and follow the start-up procedure. Preheat the grill, with the lid closed, to 450° F. If using a gas or charcoal grill, set it up for medium-high heat.
3. Grill steak 3 to 5 minutes per side, then remove from grill and rest for 10 minutes. While steak is grilling, place pitas in the upper smoke cabinet of the Lockhart to warm. Slice steak thinly, against the grain and wrap in flatbread or pita with arugula, tomatoes, onion, and tahini.

Bacon Burger

Servings: 8
Cooking Time: 180 Minutes

Ingredients:
- 1 Pack Bacon
- 2 Lbs Beef, Ground
- 1 Fresh Bread, French Loaf
- Condiments (Ketchup, Mustard, Relish, Etc.)
- 2 Egg
- Lettuce
- 2 1/2 Cups Mac And Cheese, Prepared
- 2 Tbsp Mandarin Habanero Spice
- 1/2 Cup Original BBQ Sauce
- 1 Lb Pork, Ground
- Red Onion, Chopped
- Tomato, Sliced

Directions:
1. Place plastic wrap on a clean surface and lay the mac cheese in the middle. Wrap the plastic wrap around the mac cheese so that it becomes a tube. Freeze for 30 minutes or until you're ready to put the burger together.
2. Supply your smoker with wood pellets and follow the start-up procedure. Preheat the grill, with the lid closed, to 250° F.

3. In a large pan or a clean working surface, combine the ground beef, pork, eggs, barbecue sauce, and seasoning. Mix with your hands until everything is combined.

4. Next, you're going to make a bacon weave. There are many strategies for making a bacon weave, so use whatever method you're most comfortable with. Take half of the pack of bacon and lay each strip vertically next to each other. Starting at the top left corner, lay a piece of bacon horizontally on top of the first strip of bacon. Place it under the second piece of bacon and over the third piece. Repeat this pattern until you finish the row. Now, flip the first, third, fifth, and seventh vertical strip of bacon from the end closest to you over the entire bacon weave. Lay another piece of bacon horizontally over the pieces that are still lying flat (the second, fourth, sixth, and eighth piece). Return the odd pieces of bacon back to their original vertical placement. Flip the second, fourth, sixth, and eighth vertical strip of bacon from the end closest to you over the entire bacon weave. Lay another piece of bacon horizontally over the pieces that are still lying flat (the first, third, fifth, and seventh pieceReturn the even pieces of bacon back to their original vertical placement. Continue this pattern until the bacon weave is complete.

5. On top of your bacon weave, spread out the ground beef mixture so that it completely covers the bacon. Remove the mac cheese from the plastic wrap and lay in the middle of the meat spread. Roll the bacon weave and ground beef mixture around the mac cheese tube to form a log. Ensure that the mac cheese is completely surrounded and place on the grill. Smoke for 2 1/2 to 3 hours or until the internal temperature of the meat is 145°F. If you're using a meat probe, make sure that the meat probe is in the center of the MEAT, not in the mac cheese center.

6. Prepare the French loaf by slicing it in half, topping the bottom with lettuce, red onion, tomato and any condiments you prefer. Place the burger directly on to your toppings. Top with the second half of the loaf, cut into slices and enjoy!

Smoked Seed Pastrami

Servings: 16

Cooking Time: 480 Minutes

Ingredients:
- For the brisket and brine:
- 1 beef brisket flat with plenty of fat intact (6 to 8 pounds)
- 2 quarts hot water and 2 quarts ice water
- 2/3 cup coarse salt (sea or kosher)
- 2 teaspoons pink curing salt (Prague Powder No. 1 or Insta Cure No. 1)
- 1 small onion, peeled and cut in half widthwise
- 8 cloves garlic, peeled and cut in half widthwise
- For the spice rub:
- 1/2 cup cracked black peppercorns
- 1/2 cup coriander seeds
- 2 tablespoons mustard seeds
- 1 tablespoon light or dark brown sugar
- 1 teaspoon ground ginger
- Beer (optional)

Directions:
1. Trim the brisket, leaving a fat cap on top at least 1/4 inch thick.

2. Make the brine: Place the hot water, coarse salt, and pink salt in a large bowl or plastic tub and whisk until the salt crystals are dissolved. Stir in the ice water, onion, and garlic. Place the brisket in a jumbo heavy-duty resealable plastic bag. Add the brine and seal the top, squeezing out the air as you go. Place in a second bag and seal, then place in an aluminum foil pan or roasting pan to contain any leaks. Brine the brisket in the refrigerator for 12 days, turning it over once a day.

3. Make the rub: Place the peppercorns, coriander seeds, mustard seeds, brown sugar, and ginger in a spice mill and grind to a coarse powder, running the machine in short bursts, working in batches as needed. The final rub should feel gritty like coarse sand.

4. Drain the brisket, rinse well under cold running water, and blot dry with paper towels. Place it on a rimmed baking sheet or in a roasting pan and thickly crust it on all sides with the rub.

5. Supply your smoker with wood pellets and follow the start-up procedure. Preheat the grill, with the lid closed, to 225 °F-250 °F. Fill an aluminum foil pan with

water or beer to a depth of 3 inches and place it below the rack on which you'll be smoking the ribs.

6. Place the pastrami fat side up in the smoker, directly on the rack. Smoke the pastrami until crusty and black on the outside and cooked to 175 °F on an instant-read thermometer, 7 to 8 hours.

7. Wrap the pastrami in butcher paper. Return it to the smoker. Continue cooking until the internal temperature is 200 °F and the meat is tender enough to pierce with a gloved finger or wooden spoon handle, an additional 1 to 2 hours, or as needed. (You'll need to unwrap it to check it.)

8. Transfer the wrapped pastrami to an insulated cooler and let rest for 1 to 2 hours. Unwrap and slice crosswise (across the grain) for serving.

Roasted Elk Jalapeno Poppers

Servings: 10
Cooking Time: 15 Minutes

Ingredients:
- 4 elk steaks
- 1 Cup Worcestershire sauce
- 1 Cup lime juice
- 1 Cup soy sauce
- 20 jalapeño peppers
- 10 Pieces bacon
- 12 Ounce herb & garlic flavored cream cheese, room temp
- Raw Honey

Directions:
1. Mix the lime juice, Worcestershire, and soy sauce together in a large bowl. Alternatively you can pour the ingredients directly into a large ziplock bag. Add sliced steak, cover and let sit for 4-6 hours to overnight.

2. Supply your smoker with wood pellets and follow the start-up procedure. Preheat the grill, with the lid closed, to 350° F.

3. Remove the steak from the marinade and thinly slice into bite-sized pieces so they are approximately the same width and length as the jalapeños.

4. Cut the jalapeños in half lengthwise; remove seeds and center membrane and set aside.

5. Cut the bacon in half crosswise. Set aside.

6. Spoon cream cheese equally into all jalapeño halves.

7. Lay one slice of marinated elk on top of each jalapeño. Wrap each jalapeño popper with one piece of bacon and secure with a toothpick if needed.

8. Place on grill, cut side up for 10-15 minutes or until elk is cooked and jalapeños are tender and lightly charred.

9. Remove from the grill and optionally drizzle with honey before serving. Enjoy!

Diva Q's Herb-crusted Prime Rib

Servings: 4
Cooking Time: 300 Minutes

Ingredients:
- 1/4 Cup fresh rosemary leaves
- 1/4 Cup fresh flat-leaf parsley leaves
- 1/4 Cup minced garlic
- 1/4 Cup canola oil
- 3 Tablespoon Dijon mustard
- 2 Tablespoon finely ground black pepper
- 2 Tablespoon kosher salt
- 1 (5-7 lb) bone-in prime rib roast

Directions:
1. Combine rosemary, parsley, garlic, canola oil, mustard, salt and pepper in a food processor. Pulse until the herbs are finely chopped and the ingredients are combined.

2. Coat the entire prime rib with the herb mixture. Refrigerate prime rib uncovered, for 4 hours.

3. Supply your smoker with wood pellets and follow the start-up procedure. Preheat the grill, with the lid closed, to 250° F.

4. Place the prime rib bone side down on the grill. Roast meat (allowing 12 to 15 minutes per pound) until the internal temperature in the thickest part of the prime rib reaches 120°F -130°F for rare to medium-rare, about 5 hours. Begin taking the internal temperature every 45 minutes after the 2 hour mark. Grill: 250 °F Probe: 120 °F

5. Remove the prime rib from the grill, tent loosely with foil and let rest for 15 minutes before slicing. Enjoy!

Burnt Beer Beef Brisket

Servings: 10-12

Cooking Time: 1440 Minutes

Ingredients:

- 1 Cup Apple Cider Vinegar
- 1 Jar Barbecue Sauce
- 1/2 (Any Brand) Beer, Can
- Beef And Brisket Rub
- 10 - 12 Pound Whole Beef Brisket
- 2 Tablespoons Worcestershire Sauce

Directions:

1. Remove the brisket from the refrigerator. Trimming a cold brisket is easier than trimming a room temperature brisket. Flip the brisket over so that the pointed end of the meat is facing under. Cut away any silver skin or excess fat from the flat muscle and discard. Next, there will be a large, crescent shaped fat section on the flat of the meat. Trim that fat until it is smooth against the meat so that it looks like a seamless transition between the point and flat. Flip the brisket over and trim the fat cap to ¼ inch thick.

2. Generously season the trimmed brisket on all sides with the Beef and Brisket Seasoning.

3. In a bowl, mix together the beer (for a gluten free brisket, be sure to use GF beer), apple cider vinegar and Worcestershire sauce to make mop sauce.

4. Supply your smoker with wood pellets and follow the start-up procedure. Preheat the grill, with the lid closed, to 225° F. Place the brisket in the smoker, insert a temperature probe, and smoke until the internal temperature reads 165°F, about 8 hours. Baste the brisket with the mop sauce every 2 hours to keep it moist. Once the brisket reaches 165°F, remove from the smoker, wrap in butcher paper, folding the edges over to form a leak proof seal, and return to the smoker seam-side down for another 5-8 hours, or until the brisket reaches 202°F.

5. Remove from the smoker, place in an insulated cooler, and allow to rest for 3 hours. Once the brisket has finished resting, heat your smoker to 275°F. Unwrap the brisket and cut the flat from the point. Re wrap the flat and save for another recipe. Cut the point into chunks, coat in barbecue sauce, and sprinkle with Beef and Brisket seasoning.

6. Smoke the burnt ends for 1 hour, or until deeply burnished and glazed. Serve and enjoy!

The Boss Beef Burger

Servings: 10

Cooking Time: 85 Minutes

Ingredients:

- 4 Lbs Beef, Ground
- 1 Loaf Bread, Sourdough Round
- 1/2 Cup Butter
- Condiments (Ketchup, Mustard, Relish, Etc.)
- Lettuce
- 3 Cups Mushroom
- 3 Onion, Chopped
- Kansas City BBQ Sauce
- Mandarin Habanero Spice
- 1 Lbs Pork, Ground
- Red Onion, Chopped
- 1 Bag Shredded Cheddar Cheese
- Tomato, Sliced

Directions:

1. Supply your smoker with wood pellets and follow the start-up procedure. Preheat the grill, with the lid closed, to 300° F.

2. In a large bowl, mix together the ground beef, ground pork, eggs, barbecue sauce, and seasoning until combined. Do not over mix as this will cause the meat to be tough after cooking. Split the mixture into two equal parts.

3. Melt the butter in a pan over medium heat and sauté the onion mushrooms until golden.

4. In a cast iron pan, flatten one half of the meat mixture into the bottom, taking care to work meat slightly up the sides of the pan. Sprinkle in half of the bag of cheese. Pour in onion mixture and top with the rest of the cheese.

5. On a clean work surface, mold the second half of the meat mixture into a circle and cover the filling to complete the burger. Make sure that the top and bottom meat patties are secured together so that the filling cannot be seen.

6. Place the cast iron pan in the Grill for 1 hour - 1 hour 15 minutes, or until the internal temperature reaches 160°F. Crank up the to "HIGH" and open the flame broiler. Flip the burger out of the cast iron pan onto the grates and sear each side for 5 minutes, to get those beautiful grill marks.

7. To serve: You can make an enormous burger like we did, or you can cut it like a pie into slices to be served on regular hamburger buns with your desired condiments.

Teriyaki Bbq Beef Skewers

Servings: 8
Cooking Time: 8 Minutes

Ingredients:
* 2 Pound Top Round Steak, boneless, cut into 1/4" slices
* 3/4 Cup light brown sugar
* 1/2 Cup soy sauce
* 1/4 Cup Pineapple Juice (optional)
* 1/4 Cup water
* Cup vegetable oil
* 1 Clove Garlic (Large), finely chopped

Directions:
1. Slice the beef into 1-1/2 - 2" wide strips.
2. Whisk brown sugar, soy sauce, pineapple juice, water, vegetable oil, and garlic together.
3. Pour the marinade into a large zip-top bag and drop beef slices into the mixture. Marinate beef in refrigerator for 24 hours.
4. Remove beef from the marinade, shaking to remove any excess liquid. Discard marinade. Thread beef slices in a zig-zag onto the skewers.
5. Supply your smoker with wood pellets and follow the start-up procedure. Preheat the grill, with the lid closed, to 325° F.
6. Cook skewers on preheated grill until the beef is cooked through, about 3 minutes per side. Enjoy! Grill: 325 °F

Standing Venison Rib Roast

Servings: 6
Cooking Time: 30 Minutes

Ingredients:

* 1 (2 To 2-1/2 Lb) 8-Bone Venison Roast
* 1 Tablespoon extra-virgin olive oil
* Prime Rib Rub
* Blackened Saskatchewan Rub
* Coffee Rub

Directions:
1. Supply your smoker with wood pellets and follow the start-up procedure. Preheat the grill, with the lid closed, to 375° F.
2. Rub the olive oil over the roast coating evenly. Then season with Traeger Prime Rib Rub liberally.
3. Place the roast directly on the grill grate bone side down.
4. Cook for 20-25 minutes or until the internal temperature reaches 125°F when an instant read thermometer is inserted into the thickest part of the roast. Grill: 375 °F Probe: 125 °F
5. Remove from the grill and let rest 5-10 minutes before carving. Enjoy!

Bbq Bacon Meatballs

Servings: 4
Cooking Time: 60 Minutes

Ingredients:
* 1 Pound ground beef
* 1 egg
* 1/4 Cup milk
* 1/2 Cup breadcrumbs
* 2 Tablespoon Beef Rub
* 4 Strips bacon, cut in half
* 1/4 Cup Rub
* 1/2 Cup Apricot BBQ Sauce

Directions:
1. Mix beef, egg, milk, breadcrumbs and Traeger Beef Rub in a large bowl by hand. Once well mixed, make 2 ounce meatballs until complete.
2. Wrap each meatball with a half slice of bacon and slide toothpick all the way through.
3. Put Traeger Rub in a small bowl and roll each meatball in the rub until well coated.
4. Supply your smoker with wood pellets and follow the start-up procedure. Preheat the grill, with the lid closed, to 180° F.

5. Place the meatballs on the grate, close the lid and smoke for 1 hour. Grill: 180 °F

6. Increase the Traeger temperature to 350°F and preheat, lid closed for 15 minutes. Cook meatballs for another 20 to 30 minutes or until the internal temperature reaches 160°F to 165°F. Grill: 350 °F Probe: 160 °F

7. About 10 minutes before the meatballs are ready, brush with Traeger Apricot BBQ Sauce and allow it to caramelize.

8. Remove from grill and allow to rest for 5 minutes. Enjoy!

Texas-style Smoked Beef Brisket By Doug Scheiding

Servings: 6
Cooking Time: 1080 Minutes

Ingredients:
- 1 (12-15 lb) brisket
- 2/3 Cup Butcher BBQ Prime Brisket Injection
- 2 Cup water
- 2 Tablespoon canola oil
- 1 1/2 Cup apple juice
- 1 Cup Prime Rib Rub
- 1 Cup Coffee Rub
- 4 Tablespoon ground black pepper

Directions:
1. Trim fat cap off the top of brisket and remove all silverskin. Trim off any brown areas such as on the side of the brisket. Make a long cut with the grain on the flat (thin side) of the brisket and a short cut again on the flat to show direction of cuts after cooking. Trim bottom fat cap to about 1/4 inch thickness.

2. Combine Butcher BBQ Prime Brisket Injection and water. Inject into the brisket with the grain in a checkerboard fashion. Rub entire brisket with canola oil then spritz with apple juice and let sit for 30 minutes.

3. Combine both Traeger rubs and season brisket liberally. Season the top with the black pepper.

4. Supply your smoker with wood pellets and follow the start-up procedure. Preheat the grill, with the lid closed, to 180° F.

5. Place brisket directly on the grill grate and cook 8 to 12 hours fat side down. Spritz with apple juice every 30 to 45 minutes after the first 3 hours. Grill: 180 °F Probe: 160 °F

6. After 8 hours, begin taking the temperature by inserting about two-thirds of the way up into the thickest part. It should register between 150°F to 160°F. Once the brisket registers 160°F, wrap with two sheets of aluminum foil leaving one end open. Pour in remaining brisket injection and seal foil packet. Increase the temperature on the grill to 225°F and place wrapped brisket directly on grill grate. Cook for another 3 to 4 hours until internal temperature registers 204°F. Grill: 225 °F Probe: 204 °F

7. Remove from the grill and place in a cooler wrapped in a towel to rest for at least 2 hours. When ready to serve, cut slices about the thickness of a pencil against the grain. If desired, separate cooking liquid from fat and pour juices over cut slices of brisket. Enjoy!

Santa Maria Tri-tip With Pico De Gallo

Servings: 4
Cooking Time: 68 Minutes

Ingredients:
- 1 tri-tip roast, about 2 to 2½lb (1 to 1.2kg)
- coarse salt
- freshly ground black pepper
- granulated garlic or garlic powder
- for the pico de gallo
- 8 Roma tomatoes, decored, deseeded, and diced
- 1 white onion, peeled and diced
- 1 serrano pepper, destemmed, deseeded, and minced, plus more
- 1 garlic clove, peeled and minced
- juice of 1 lime
- ½ cup loosely packed cilantro leaves, chopped
- 1 tsp coarse salt

Directions:
1. In a medium bowl, make the pico de gallo by combining the tomatoes, onion, serrano, garlic, lime juice, and cilantro. Stir gently with a rubber spatula and

season with salt to taste. Cover and refrigerate for 2 hours.

2. Approximately 45 minutes before you're ready to cook, season the roast on all sides with salt and pepper and granulated garlic.

3. Supply your smoker with wood pellets and follow the start-up procedure. Preheat the grill, with the lid closed, to 180° F.

4. Place the roast on the grate and smoke until the internal temperature in the thickest part of the roast reaches 115°F (46°C), about 45 minutes to 1 hour. Transfer the roast to a plate.

5. Raise the temperature to 450°F (232°C). Place the roast on the grate and sear until the internal temperature in the thickest part of the roast reaches 130 to 135°F (54 to 57°C), about 3 to 4 minutes per side. For best results, don't cook beyond medium rare. (The thinner tail should satisfy any diner who prefers beef to be more well done.)

6. Remove the roast from the grill and thinly slice on a sharp diagonal against the grain. Serve with the pico de gallo.

Bistro Steaks With Avocado Relish

Servings: 4

Cooking Time: 34 Minutes

Ingredients:
- 2lb (1kg) bistro steaks
- extra virgin olive oil
- liquid aminos
- for the rub
- 2 tsp coarse salt
- 2 tsp fresh coarsely ground black pepper
- 2 tsp light brown sugar or low-carb substitute
- 2 tsp chili powder
- 2 tsp ground cumin
- 2 tsp granulated garlic
- 2 tsp sweet or smoked paprika
- for the relish
- 2 avocados
- 1½ tbsp freshly squeezed lime juice, plus more
- 2 garlic cloves, peeled and finely minced
- 1 Roma tomato, decored, deseeded, and diced
- 1 jalapeño, destemmed, deseeded, and finely diced
- ¼ cup coarsely chopped fresh cilantro leaves
- 2 tbsp diced red onion
- 1 tbsp mayo
- 1 tsp hot sauce
- coarse salt

Directions:
1. Supply your smoker with wood pellets and follow the start-up procedure. Preheat the grill, with the lid closed, to 180° F.

2. In a small bowl, make the rub by combining the ingredients.

3. Trim any silver skin from the steaks and place them on a rimmed sheet pan. Coat with olive oil. Dust with the rub, patting it on with your fingertips.

4. Place the steaks on the grate and grill until the internal temperature reaches 110 to 115°F (43 to 46°C), about 30 minutes. Pour some liquid aminos into a small spray bottle and spritz the steaks before wrapping them in heavy-duty aluminum foil. Let the steaks rest.

5. Cut the avocados in half and then pit, peel, and dice them. In a medium bowl, make the relish by combining the avocado and lime juice. Add the remaining ingredients and season with salt to taste. Use a rubber spatula to gently mix. Transfer to an attractive serving bowl. Cover and refrigerate. (The relish is best if not made more than 1 hour ahead.)

6. Raise the temperature to 450°F (232°C). Remove the steaks from the foil and place them on the grate. Sear until they're browned and the internal temperature reaches 130 to 135°F (54 to 57°C), about 2 minutes per side, turning with tongs.

7. Transfer the steaks to a cutting board and let rest for 3 minutes. Slice them crosswise on a diagonal into 3/8-inch (1cm) slices. Shingle the slices on a platter and pour any juices remaining on the cutting board over the meat. Serve with the avocado relish.

Cheesy French Dip Sliders

Servings: 8 - 12

Cooking Time: 60 Minutes

Ingredients:

- 1 ¾ cup beef stock
- 3 lbs. beef top round roast, boneless
- 1 tbsp olive oil
- 2 tbsp chop house steak rub
- 1 8 oz. block of provolone cheese
- 1 red onion, sliced thinly
- ¼ cup sherry
- 1 dozen slider rolls, sliced

Directions:

1. Supply your smoker with wood pellets and follow the start-up procedure. Preheat the grill, with the lid closed, to 400° F.If using a gas or charcoal grill, set it up for medium-high heat.

2. Rub roast with olive oil, then season with Chop House Steak Rub.

3. Place red onion in the bottom of a cast iron skillet and set roast on top. Transfer to grill and roast for 15 minutes. Reduce grill temperature to 325°F then add beef stock and sherry, and continue to cook another 30 minutes, or until 125 to 130°F internal temperature is reached.

4. Remove from grill and allow the roast to rest for 10 minutes, then slice thinly.

5. Assemble sliders on sheet tray by placing sliced beef on the bottom half of each roll. Top with onion and provolone cheese, then place top half of roll on top of cheese. Transfer jus into a metal gravy boat or porcelain ramekin and reserve for serving.

6. Transfer rolls back into cast iron skillet and return to grill for 5 minutes, until cheese melts. Serve hot with jus for dipping

Blackened Saskatchewan Tomahawk Steaks

Servings: 4

Cooking Time: 45 Minutes

Ingredients:

- 2 Whole tomahawk steaks
- 4 Tablespoon Blackened Saskatchewan Rub
- 2 Tablespoon butter

Directions:

1. Supply your smoker with wood pellets and follow the start-up procedure. Preheat the grill, with the lid closed, to 225° F.

2. Cover cold steaks in the Blackened Saskatchewan Rub. Let rest 10 minutes for the seasoning to adhere.

3. Place steaks directly on grill grates and smoke for about 40 minutes, or until an internal temp reaches 119°F. Remove from grill and wrap tightly in foil to rest.

4. Turn up temperature on the grill to 400°F - with a cast iron pan or griddle inside. When the pan is hot, add 2 Tbsp of butter and sear the first steak, about 2-4 minutes per side, or until the internal temperature reads 125°F - 130°F. Repeat with the other Tomahawk. Rest, slice, serve. Enjoy!

Bbq Brisket Breakfast Tacos

Servings: 6

Cooking Time: 30 Minutes

Ingredients:

- 4 Pound leftover beef brisket
- 1/2 Teaspoon extra-virgin olive oil
- 1 green bell pepper, diced
- 1 Yellow Bell Pepper, diced
- 10 eggs
- 1/2 Cup milk
- salt and pepper
- 2 Cup shredded cheddar cheese
- flour tortillas

Directions:

1. Supply your smoker with wood pellets and follow the start-up procedure. Preheat the grill, with the lid closed, to 375° F.

2. Place leftover brisket in a double layer of foil and warm in grill. Grill: 375 °F

3. Coat the inside of a cast iron skillet with oil and preheat the skillet in the grill for 10 minutes. When skillet is hot, sauté diced peppers, stirring every few minutes until desired doneness.

4. While peppers are cooking, whisk together the eggs, milk, salt and pepper to taste. Add the beaten eggs to

the skillet and scramble. Add cheese to the skillet when the eggs are almost done.

5. Remove eggs and heated brisket from grill. Serve eggs in a tortilla topped with brisket. Top with salsa or guacamole if desired. Enjoy!

Smoked Beef Ribs

Servings: 4-8
Cooking Time: 360 Minutes

Ingredients:

- 2 (2- or 3-pound) racks beef ribs
- 2 tablespoons yellow mustard
- 1 batch Sweet and Spicy Cinnamon Rub

Directions:

1. Supply your smoker with wood pellets and follow the start-up procedure. Preheat the grill, with the lid closed, to 225°F.
2. Remove the membrane from the backside of the ribs. This can be done by cutting just through the membrane in an X pattern and working a paper towel between the membrane and the ribs to pull it off.
3. Coat the ribs all over with mustard and season them with the rub. Using your hands, work the rub into the meat.
4. Place the ribs directly on the grill grate and smoke until their internal temperature reaches between 190°F and 200°F.
5. Remove the racks from the grill and cut them into individual ribs. Serve immediately.

Teriyaki Deer Jerky

Servings: 4
Cooking Time: 240 Minutes

Ingredients:

- 1/2 Cup soy sauce
- 1/4 Cup mirin
- 2 Tablespoon sugar
- 3 coins fresh ginger, each ¼ inch thick
- 1 Clove garlic, crushed
- 1/2 Teaspoon onion powder
- 1/2 Teaspoon black pepper
- 2 Pound venison, trimmed

Directions:

1. In a mixing bowl, combine the soy sauce, mirin, sugar, ginger, garlic, onion powder and pepper.
2. With a sharp knife, slice the venison into 1/4 inch thick slices. Trim any fat or connective tissue.
3. Put the meat slices in a large resealable plastic bag. Pour the marinade mixture over the venison and massage the bag so that all the slices get coated with the marinade. Seal the bag and refrigerate for several hours, or overnight.
4. Supply your smoker with wood pellets and follow the start-up procedure. Preheat the grill, with the lid closed, to 180° F. Remove the venison from the marinade; discard marinade. Dry the meat slices between paper towels.
5. Arrange the meat in a single layer directly on the grill grate. Smoke for 3 hours or until the jerky is dry but still chewy and somewhat pliant when you bend a piece. Grill: 180 °F
6. Transfer to a resealable plastic bag while the jerky is still warm leaving the top open. Let the jerky rest for an hour at room temperature.
7. Squeeze any air from the bag and refrigerate the jerky. It will keep for several weeks. Enjoy!

Smoked Roast Beef

Servings: 5-8
Cooking Time: 840 Minutes

Ingredients:

- 1 (4-pound) top round roast
- 1 batch Espresso Brisket Rub
- 1 tablespoon butter

Directions:

1. Supply your smoker with wood pellets and follow the start-up procedure. Preheat the grill, with the lid closed, to 180°F.
2. Season the top round roast with the rub. Using your hands, work the rub into the meat.
3. Place the roast directly on the grill grate and smoke until its internal temperature reaches 140°F. Remove the roast from the grill.
4. Place a cast-iron skillet on the grill grate and increase the grill's temperature to 450°F. Place the roast

in the skillet, add the butter, and cook until its internal temperature reaches 145°F, flipping once after about 3 minutes.

5.   Remove the roast from the grill and let it rest for 10 to 15 minutes, before slicing and serving.

Carrot Elk Burgers

Servings: 4
Cooking Time: 15 Minutes

Ingredients:
- To Taste, Blackened Sriracha Rub Seasoning
- 1/2 Tbsp Butter
- To Taste, Cilantro Mayonnaise
- 4 Pieces Green Leaf Lettuce
- 2 Lbs Ground Elk
- 4 Hamburger Buns
- 1 Jalepeno, Sliced
- 4 Pickled Carrots

Directions:
1.   Place ground elk in a mixing bowl and season with Blackened Sriracha. Divide into 4 portions, then form into large patties.
2.   Supply your smoker with wood pellets and follow the start-up procedure. Preheat the grill, with the lid open, to medium heat. If using a gas or charcoal grill, set it up for medium heat and use a cast iron skillet.
3.   Place butter on the left side of the griddle and let melt. Place buns on the left side (on melted butter), and burger patties on the right side.
4.   Toast the buns, then turn off the burner, keeping the buns in place to keep warm. Cook the burgers 2 to 3 minutes per side, then remove from the griddle and allow to rest for 5 minutes.
5.   Assemble burger: bottom bun, cilantro mayonnaise, lettuce, burger, pickled carrots, sliced jalapeño, cilantro mayonnaise on top bun.

Crusted Prime Rib With Rosemary

Servings: 4-6
Cooking Time: 180 Minutes

Ingredients:
- 4-6 garlic, cloves
- 1/3 cup olive oil
- chop house steak seasoning
- 7 pound, boned tied and rolled prime rib roast
- 3 tablespoon rosemary, fresh
- 3 tablespoon thyme, fresh sprigs

Directions:
1.   In a food processor, blend together the garlic, rosemary, thyme, sage, and oil until a rough paste forms. Place the prime rib on a sheet pan over a wire rack and rub the prime rib generously with the herb paste on all sides.
2.   Season the prime rib with Chop House Steak Seasoning generously on all sides, then chill uncovered in the refrigerator overnight, or for 12 hours.
3.   Once the prime rib has chilled for 12 hours, supply your smoker with wood pellets and follow the start-up procedure. Preheat the grill, with the lid closed, to 250° F, and grill for 2 hours or until the internal temperature of the roast reaches 110°F, then increase the temperature to 400 and grill for an additional 15-30 minutes, or until the internal temperature reaches 125 - 140°F.
4.   Remove the prime rib from the grill, cover tightly in foil and allow to rest for 30 minutes. The final temperature of the prime rib should be 125 - 140°F after resting. Serve and enjoy!

Smoked Duck Breast Bacon

Servings: 6
Cooking Time: 30 Minutes

Ingredients:
- 4 Cup water
- 2 Cup freshly brewed strong coffee
- 1 Cup kosher salt
- 1/2 Cup dark brown sugar
- 2 1/2 Tablespoon curing salt
- 1/4 Cup molasses
- 3 Cup ice
- 3 Pound skin-on duck breasts

Directions:
1.   Stir together 4 cups water with coffee, kosher salt, brown sugar, and curing salt in a container with a lid. Mix until solids are dissolved. Add the molasses and stir until completely dissolved. Add 3 cups ice and stir until cure is cold. (It's ok if all the ice doesn't melt completely.)

2. Add duck breasts to cure and weigh them down with a large plate to keep submerged. Place covered container in refrigerator for a minimum of 6 hours.

3. Remove from refrigerator, take breasts out of brine and discard brine. Rinse duck breasts under cold running water and pat dry.

4. Supply your smoker with wood pellets and follow the start-up procedure. Preheat the grill, with the lid closed, to 165° F.

5. Place duck breasts on grill grate and smoke for 2 hours. Grill: 165 °F

6. Cool duck completely, wrap in plastic wrap and place in refrigerator until ready to use.

7. To cook, slice breast thinly and fry in a pan just like you would pork bacon. Or slice breast thinly, place on Traeger set to 350°F and cook for 10 minutes per side. Enjoy! Grill: 350 °F

Salt & Pepper Beer-braised Beef Ribs

Servings: 4
Cooking Time: 180 Minutes

Ingredients:
- 2 Rack meaty beef back ribs
- coarse kosher or sea salt
- freshly ground black pepper
- granulated garlic
- 1 1/2 Cup beer or beef stock
- 'Que BBQ Sauce

Directions:

1. If your butcher has not already done so, remove the thin papery membrane from the bone-side of the ribs by working the tip of a butter knife or a screwdriver underneath the membrane over a middle bone. Use paper towels to get a firm grip, then tear the membrane off.

2. About an hour before cooking, put the ribs in a foil pan, meat-side up, and season the ribs on both sides with the salt, pepper and granulated garlic.

3. Supply your smoker with wood pellets and follow the start-up procedure. Preheat the grill, with the lid closed, to 165° F.

4. Arrange the pan of ribs on the grill grate and smoke for 1 hour. Pour the beer into the bottom of the pan (be careful not to wash the seasonings off the ribs). Cover the pan tightly with foil. Grill: 165 °F

5. Increase Traeger temperature to 250°F and continue to cook the ribs until the meat is meltingly tender, about 2 to 3 hours more. Grill: 250 °F

6. Carefully remove the foil. Discard the braising liquid and serve the ribs with Traeger 'Que BBQ Sauce. (You can brush the sauce on the ribs and sizzle them on the grill, or you can serve the sauce on the side.) Enjoy!

Savory Smoked Brisket

Servings: 10
Cooking Time: 600 Minutes

Ingredients:
- 4 Tbsp Apple Cider Vinegar
- 10Lb Trimmed Brisket
- 2 Cups Broth, Beef
- Sweet Heat Rub
- 2 Tbsp Worcestershire Sauce

Directions:

1. Trim the fat cap from your brisket, leaving enough fat to baste the meat during the smoke process.

2. Generously coat the brisket with Sweet Heat rub, and massage into the brisket.

3. In a bowl, whisk together the apple cider vinegar, Worcestershire sauce and beef broth, then pour into a clean spray bottle.

4. Supply your smoker with wood pellets and follow the start-up procedure. Preheat the grill, with the lid closed, to 225° F. Once the smoker is up to temperature, place the brisket inside and insert the temperature probe. Smoke for 10 to 12 hours, or until the internal temperature of the brisket reaches 200°F at the thickest part. Once an hour, spray the brisket with the mop sauce to baste it.

5. Once the brisket is done, remove from the smoker, allow to rest for 30 minutes under tin foil, then slice and enjoy!

Garlic Beef Meatballs

Servings: 6
Cooking Time: 15 Minutes

Ingredients:

- 1 1/2 Pounds Beef, Ground Round
- 1/2 Cup Breadcrumb, Dry
- 2 Cloves Garlic, Crushed
- 3/4 Tsp Italian Seasoning, Dried
- 1 Tsp Mustard, Dry
- 1/4 Cup Parmesan Cheese, Shredded
- 1/3 Cup Parsley, Minced Fresh
- 1/4 Tsp Crushed Red Red Bell Peppers
- 1/4 Tsp Salt
- 1/4 Cup Tomato Sauce

Directions:

1. Start your Grill on "smoke" with the lid open until a fire is established in the burn pot (3-7 minutes).
2. Supply your smoker with wood pellets and follow the start-up procedure. Preheat the grill, with the lid closed, to 400° F.
3. Place all ingredients in a bowl, combine them and stir well. Shape the mixture into 30 meatballs (1 ½ inches in width).
4. Spray a broiler pan with cooking spray, place on the grill, and bake for 15 minutes until fully cooked and browned.
5. Remove from grill, cool for 5 minutes, and serve.

Spiced Smoked Kielbasa Dogs

Servings: 12
Cooking Time: 300 Minutes

Ingredients:

- 1 tsp all spice, ground
- 2 tsp black peppercorns, ground
- 3 tbsp brown sugar
- 1 cup distilled ice water, divided
- 1 1/2 tsp garlic powder
- 1 1/2 lbs ground beef
- 5 lbs ground pork
- 32 - 35 hog casings
- 2 tbsp kosher salt
- 2 tsp marjoram, dried
- 1 1/2 tsp paprika
- 1 1/4 tsp speed cure, pink salt curing

Directions:

1. In a glass bowl or measuring cup, cover hog casings in warm water and let soak for 1 hour.
2. In a small bowl, whisk together brown sugar, salt, black pepper, marjoram, garlic powder, paprika, allspice, and speed cure.
3. In a large tub, combine ground pork and ground beef. Mix together by hand, then add seasoning and distilled ice water. Mix mixture by hand for 1 minute, until seasoning is incorporated throughout.
4. Prepare the sausage stuffer, and fit one hog casing over a 1 to 1 ¼ inch horn. Place a sheet tray, with a bit of water on it, underneath the nozzle of the stuffer and start filling the casings.
5. Once the casings are filled, twist off into desired lengths, and refrigerate overnight.
6. Hang the links with S-hooks from the top rack of your Grill or Smoker. Smoke on SMOKE mode for 3 hours. Supply your smoker with wood pellets and follow the start-up procedure. Preheat the grill, with the lid closed, to 300° F, which will raise the temperature of the smoking cabinet to 170°F. If using a vertical smoker, keep smoking on SMOKE mode. Continue smoking the sausage for another 1 to 2 hours, until the internal temperature of the sausage reaches 155° F.
7. Remove sausage from the smoking cabinet and either enjoy hot with your favorite toppings, or place in an ice water bath for 15 minutes, dry at room temperature and refrigerate or freeze for future use.

Spiced Lamb Burgers With Tzatziki

Servings: 4
Cooking Time: 10 Minutes

Ingredients:

- 1½lb (680g) ground lamb or a mixture of lamb and beef, well chilled
- ⅓ cup grated red onion
- 1 to 2 garlic cloves, peeled and minced
- 2 tbsp chopped fresh dill or fresh mint
- 1 tsp ground cumin
- ½ tsp ground cinnamon
- ½ tsp crushed red pepper flakes (optional)

- extra virgin olive oil
- coarse salt
- freshly ground black pepper
- for the tzatziki
- 1⁄3 hothouse cucumber, unpeeled and coarsely grated
- coarse salt
- 1½ cups plain Greek yogurt, drained
- 1 to 2 garlic cloves, peeled
- 1 tbsp freshly squeezed lemon juice or white distilled vinegar
- 1½ tbsp extra virgin olive oil
- 1 tbsp chopped fresh dill or fresh mint

Directions:

1. Supply your smoker with wood pellets and follow the start-up procedure. Preheat the grill, with the lid closed, to 450° F.

2. Make the tzatziki by placing the cucumber in a sieve and lightly sprinkle with salt. After 15 minutes, rinse with cold running water. Drain and then squeeze the cucumber dry with paper towels. Transfer the cucumber to a large bowl. Add the yogurt, garlic, and lemon juice. Stir to mix. Season with salt to taste. Transfer to a serving bowl. Set aside. Just before serving, drizzle with the olive oil and scatter the fresh dill over the top.

3. In a large bowl, combine the lamb, red onion, garlic, dill, cumin, cinnamon, and red pepper flakes (if using). Wet your hands with cold water and mix thoroughly but gently. (Try not to overhandle the meat.) Form the meat into 4 patties of equal size, each about ¾ inch (2cm) thick. Use your thumbs to make a shallow depression in the top of each burger. Lightly oil the outsides of the burgers with olive oil. Season with salt and pepper.

4. Place the burgers on the grate and grill until the internal temperature reaches 160°F (71°C), about 4 to 5 minutes per side, turning once.

5. Transfer the burgers to a platter. On a separate platter, place thinly sliced red onions, thinly sliced tomatoes, thinly sliced cucumbers, crumbled feta, and Kalamata olives. Serve with the tzatziki and pita bread.

Smoked Peppered Beef Tenderloin

Servings: 4

Cooking Time: 60 Minutes

Ingredients:

- 1 (2 to 2-1/2 lb) Snake River Farms Beef Tenderloin Roast, trimmed
- 1/2 Cup Dijon mustard
- 2 Clove garlic, minced to a paste
- 2 Tablespoon bourbon or strong cold coffee
- Jacobsen Salt Co. Pure Kosher Sea Salt
- coarse ground black and green peppercorns

Directions:

1. Lay the tenderloin on a large piece of plastic wrap.

2. Combine the mustard, garlic and bourbon in a small bowl. Slather the mixture evenly all over the tenderloin. Wrap in plastic and allow to sit at room temperature for 1 hour.

3. Unwrap the plastic wrap and generously season the tenderloin on all sides with the salt and ground black and green peppercorns.

4. Supply your smoker with wood pellets and follow the start-up procedure. Preheat the grill, with the lid closed, to 180° F.

5. Place the tenderloin directly on the grill grate and smoke for 60 minutes. Grill: 180 °F

6. Remove the tenderloin from the grill and set aside. Increase the grill temperature to 400°F. Once the grill is hot, place the tenderloin back on the grill. Roast until the internal temperature reaches 130°F, about 20 to 30 minutes depending on the thickness of the tenderloin. Do not overcook. Grill: 400 °F Probe: 130 °F

7. Let rest for 10 minutes before slicing. Enjoy!

Smoked Brisket

Servings: 8

Cooking Time: 720 Minutes

Ingredients:

- 2 Tablespoon garlic powder
- 2 Tablespoon onion powder
- 2 Tablespoon paprika
- 2 Teaspoon chile powder
- 1/3 Cup Jacobsen Salt or kosher salt
- 1/3 Cup coarse ground black pepper, divided
- 1 (12-14 lb) whole packer brisket, trimmed
- 1 1/2 Cup beef broth

Directions:

1. Supply your smoker with wood pellets and follow the start-up procedure. Preheat the grill, with the lid closed, to 225° F.

2. For the Rub: Mix together garlic powder, onion powder, paprika, chili pepper, kosher salt and pepper in a small bowl.

3. Season the brisket on all sides with the rub.

4. Place brisket, fat side down on grill grate. Cook brisket until it reaches an internal temperature of 160°F, about 5 to 6 hours. When brisket reaches internal temperature of 160°F, remove from grill. Probe: 160 °F

5. Double wrap meat in aluminum foil and add the beef broth to the foil packet. Return brisket to grill and cook until it reaches an internal temperature of 204°F, about 3 hours more. Probe: 204 °F

6. Once finished, remove from grill, unwrap from foil and let rest for 15 minutes. Slice against the grain and serve.

Smoked Spiced Rump Roast

Servings: 8
Cooking Time: 60 Minutes

Ingredients:

- 3 pounds rump roast (or bottom round roast)
- 1 ½ teaspoons coarse ground pepper
- 1 teaspoon kosher salt
- ¼ teaspoon garlic powder
- ¼ teaspoon onion powder

Directions:

1. Supply your smoker with wood pellets and follow the start-up procedure. Preheat the grill, with the lid closed, to 250 °F.

2. Combine the seasonings in a small bowl and coat the rump roast evenly with seasonings on all sides.

3. Place roast into the smoker.

4. Cook for 1 hour and 45 minutes, or until the internal temperature reaches 135 degrees (or your desired level of doneness; rare: 135 °F, medium rare: 145 °F, medium: 155 °F, well done: 170 °F)

5. Remove rump roast from the smoker and let it rest for 10 minutesbefore slicing.

6. Slice thinly and serve.

Herb Chipotle Lamb

Servings: 6
Cooking Time: 120 Minutes

Ingredients:

- Black Pepper
- 1 Tbsp Chipotle Peppers, Crushed
- 3/4 Cup Extra-Virgin Olive Oil
- 3 Garlic, Cloves
- 2 Tbsp Italian Parsley
- 1 Rack Lamb Ribs
- ¼ Cup Applewood Bacon Rub
- 2 Tbsp Rosemary, Fresh
- 2 Tbsp Sage, Fresh
- 2 Tbsp Thyme, Fresh Sprigs

Directions:

1. For the dry rub: baste the lamb ribs with olive oil and season with the chipotle powder and black pepper. Let the lamb ribs rest for at least 15 minutes in the refrigerator.

2. Supply your smoker with wood pellets and follow the start-up procedure. Preheat the grill, with the lid closed, to 275° F.

3. For the wet rub: Blend rosemary, cilantro, Italian parsley, sage, thyme, and oregano with ¼ cup Extra Virgin Olive Oil, ¼ cup of Smoke Infused Applewood Bacon and 2-3 garlic cloves.

4. Apply the wet rub all over the lamb ribs.

5. Lay your lamb ribs bone side down on the grill and smoke until they reach an internal temp of 120-125°F.

6. Turn your grill temp up to 425°F and sear until it of 135-145°F.

7. Rest 10-15 minutes. Carve and enjoy!

Cheeseburger Hand Pies

Servings: 4
Cooking Time: 10 Minutes

Ingredients:

- ½ pound lean ground beef
- 1 tablespoon minced onion
- 1 tablespoon steak seasoning
- 1 cup shredded Monterey Jack and Colby cheese blend
- 8 slices white American cheese, divided

- 2 (14-ounce) refrigerated prepared pizza dough sheets, divided
- 2 eggs, beaten with 2 tablespoons water (egg wash), divided
- 24 hamburger dill pickle chips
- 2 tablespoons sesame seeds
- 6 slices tomato, for garnish
- Ketchup and mustard, for serving

Directions:

1. Supply your smoker with wood pellets and follow the start-up procedure. Preheat, with the lid closed, to 325°F.

2. On your stove top, in a medium sauté pan over medium-high heat, brown the ground beef for 4 to 5 minutes, or until cooked through. Add the minced onion and steak seasoning.

3. Toss in the shredded cheese blend and 2 slices of American cheese, and stir until melted and fully incorporated.

4. Remove the cheeseburger mixture from the heat and set aside.

5. Make sure the dough is well chilled for easier handling. Working quickly, roll out one prepared pizza crust on parchment paper and brush with half of the egg wash.

6. Arrange the remaining 6 slices of American cheese on the dough to outline 6 hand pies.

7. Top each cheese slice with ¼ cup of the cheeseburger mixture, spreading slightly inside the imaginary lines of the hand pies.

8. Place 4 pickle slices on top of the filling for each pie.

9. Top the whole thing with the other prepared pizza crust and cut between the cheese slices to create 6 hand pies.

10. Using kitchen scissors, cut the parchment to further separate the pies, but leave them on the paper.

11. Using a fork dipped in egg wash, seal the edges of the pies on all sides. Baste the tops of the pies with the remaining egg wash and sprinkle with the sesame seeds.

12. Remove the pies from the parchment paper and gently place on the grill grate. Close the lid and smoke for 5 minutes, then carefully flip and smoke with the lid closed for 5 more minutes, or until browned.

13. Top with the sliced tomato and serve with ketchup and mustard.

Garlic Prime Rib Roast

Servings: 8
Cooking Time: 30 Minutes

Ingredients:
- 2 tsps black pepper
- 10 cloves garlic, minced
- steak seasoning
- 2 lbs prime rib roast
- 2 tsps salt

Directions:

1. Supply your smoker with wood pellets and follow the start-up procedure. Preheat the grill, with the lid closed, to 400° F.

2. Rub roast garlic, salt, pepper and some Chop House Steak Rub.

3. Insert meat thermometer sideways into the center of the roast so that the shaft is not visible, avoiding fat and bone.

4. Cook in a closed grill, maintaining constant heat, until the thermometer reads 145°F(63°C) for medium-rare for about 50 minutes, or cook until desired doneness.

5. Remove roast to cutting board; tent with foil for 5 to 10 minutes. Serve with mashed potatoes and asparagus on the side.

Savory Whiskey Grilled Elk Steaks

Servings: 4
Cooking Time: 10 Minutes

Ingredients:
- ¼ Cup Brown Sugar
- 1 Tbsp Chop House Steak Seasoning
- 1 Tbsp Coarse Ground Pepper
- 4 Elk Steaks
- ½ Cup Olive Oil
- ½ Cup Soy Sauce
- ½ Cup Whiskey, Such As Jack Daniel'S
- ¼ Cup Yellow Mustard

Directions:

1. In a large mixing bowl, add the whiskey, soy sauce, olive oil, brown sugar, yellow mustard, and Chophouse Steak seasoning to a large mixing bowl and whisk until everything is well combined. Pour the marinade into a large, resealable plastic bag or glass baking dish, then add the elk steaks. Seal the bag and turn the steaks once to coat. Place the bag in the refrigerator and marinate for 4-12 hours.

2. Supply your smoker with wood pellets and follow the start-up procedure. Preheat the grill, with the lid open, to 425° F. If you're using a gas or charcoal grill, set it up for medium heat. Remove the elk steaks from the bag and discard the excess marinade. Insert a temperature probe into one of the elk steaks and place on the grill.

3. Grill the steaks for 7-10 minutes per side, or until the steaks reach an internal temperature of 135°F. Remove the steaks from the grill and allow the steaks to rest for 10 minutes before serving.

Savory Bacon Wrapped Hot Dogs

Servings: 6
Cooking Time: 10 Minutes

Ingredients:
- 1 - 2 Green Bell Pepper, Diced
- 1 Per Hot Dog Bacon, Strip
- 6 - 8 Hot Dog Bun(S)
- 6 - 8 Hot Dog(S)
- Smoke Infused Applewood Bacon Rub
- 2 Tbsp Vegetable Oil

Directions:
1. Supply your smoker with wood pellets and follow the start-up procedure. Preheat the grill, with the lid closed, to 400° F. Before placing anything on the grill, generously oil the cooking grids, using a cloth and vegetable oil.

2. Heat your grill to medium-high heat.

3. Lay a slice of bacon on a cutting board.

4. Roll the bacon and hot dog around until the bacon covers the whole hot dog. Secure with a toothpick on each end.

5. Repeat steps 3 and 4 again, by wrapping each hot dog with one strip of bacon, and secure with a toothpick on each end.

6. Cook the bacon wrapped hot dogs on the grill. When the bacon is lightly crisp, remove from the heat. This takes about 4-6 minutes.

7. Toast the buns by turning the grill up to high. Open the flame broiler. Place bun face down on cooking grids. Toast until desired done.

8. As soon as the hot dogs are done, place them on a toasted bun, pile on the chopped green peppers, and serve.

Sweet Heat Burnt Ends

Servings: 8-10
Cooking Time: 360 Minutes

Ingredients:
- 1 (6-pound) brisket point
- 2 tablespoons yellow mustard
- 1 batch Sweet Brown Sugar Rub
- 2 tablespoons honey
- 1 cup barbecue sauce
- 2 tablespoons light brown sugar

Directions:
1. Supply your smoker with wood pellets and follow the start-up procedure. Preheat the grill, with the lid closed, to 225°F.

2. Using a boning knife, carefully remove all but about ½ inch of the large layer of fat covering one side of your brisket point.

3. Coat the point all over with mustard and season it with the rub. Using your hands, work the rub into the meat.

4. Place the point directly on the grill grate and smoke until its internal temperature reaches 165°F.

5. Pull the brisket from the grill and wrap it completely in aluminum foil or butcher paper.

6. Increase the grill's temperature to 350°F and return the wrapped brisket to it. Continue to cook until its internal temperature reaches 185°F.

7. Remove the point from the grill, unwrap it, and cut the meat into 1-inch cubes. Place the cubes in an

aluminum pan and stir in the honey, barbecue sauce, and brown sugar.

8. Place the pan in the grill and smoke the beef cubes for 1 hour more, uncovered. Remove the burnt ends from the grill and serve immediately.

Texas Hill Country Brisket With Mustard Barbecue Sauce

Servings: 10-12
Cooking Time: 660 Minutes

Ingredients:

- 1 whole packer brisket, about 12 to 14lb (5.4 to 6.4kg)
- for the sauce
- ½ cup yellow mustard
- ½ cup brown mustard
- ½ cup apple cider vinegar
- ¼ cup light brown sugar or low-carb substitute, plus more
- 1 tbsp ketchup
- 1 tbsp Worcestershire sauce
- 1 tbsp hot sauce
- 1 tsp beef bouillon granules
- 1 tsp granulated garlic
- 1 tsp coarse salt, plus more
- ½ tsp freshly ground black pepper
- for the rub
- ¼ cup coarse salt
- ¼ cup fresh coarsely ground black pepper
- 1 tbsp granulated garlic
- 1 tbsp chili powder

Directions:

1. Place a pan of water on the grate.Supply your smoker with wood pellets and follow the start-up procedure. Preheat the grill, with the lid closed, to 250° F.

2. In a medium saucepan on the stovetop over medium-low heat, make the sauce by whisking together the ingredients. Bring the mixture to a simmer, stirring occasionally. Simmer for 10 minutes. Taste, adding brown sugar or salt. Transfer the sauce to a covered jar and refrigerate until ready to use.

3. In a small bowl, make the rub by combining the ingredients. Trim some of the excess exterior fat off the brisket, leaving a cap of at least ¼ inch (.5cm). Place the brisket on a rimmed baking sheet. Evenly but conservatively season the meat on all sides with the rub.

4. Place the brisket fat side down on the grate and smoke until the internal temperature reaches 165°F (74°C), about 5 to 6 hours.

5. Remove the brisket from the grill and wrap it fat side up in unlined butcher paper, crimping the seams. (You can also use aluminum foil—many well-known Texas pitmasters do—but it's not as porous.) Return the brisket seam side up to the grate. Continue to cook until the internal temperature reaches 203°F (95°C), about 6 to 8 hours more. The meat should be very tender, with the melted collagen making it almost jiggly.

6. Transfer the brisket to an insulated cooler lined with clean towels or a thick layer of newspapers. Let the meat rest for 1 to 2 hours.

7. Place the brisket on a cutting board and unwrap it. Separate the point from the flat following the seam of fat that runs between them. Use a serrated knife to slice the meat against the grain into pencil-thick pieces. (The grain in the point runs perpendicular to the grain in the flat.)

8. Shingle the meat on a platter. Drizzle with any meat juices from the cutting board. Serve with the barbecue sauce.

Fajita Style Mexican Hot Dogs

Servings: 4
Cooking Time: 10 Minutes

Ingredients:

- 1 Green Bell Pepper, Sliced
- 1 Package Hot Dog Bun(S)
- 1 Package High Quality Ballpark Hot Dog(S)
- 1 Tbsp Olive Oil
- 1 Tsp Beef And Brisket Rub
- 1 Yellow Bell Pepper, Sliced
- 1 Yellow Onion, Sliced

Directions:

1. Supply your smoker with wood pellets and follow the start-up procedure. Preheat the grill, with the lid closed, to 350° F.

2. In a large bowl, toss the peppers and onions with the olive oil and Beef and Brisket Rub. Place the vegetables on the mesh grilling basket.

3. Remove from the grill and assemble the hot dogs. Top the buns with a hot dog and a generous scoop of the onion and pepper mixture. Serve immediately.

Cheesy Skillet Shepherd's Pie

Servings: 4 - 6

Cooking Time: 40 Minutes

Ingredients:

- 2 Tbsp All-Purpose Flour
- 1 Cup Beef Broth
- ½ Tsp Black Pepper
- 2 Tbsp Butter
- 1 Cup Cheddar Cheese, Grated
- 4 Oz. Cream Cheese
- 3 Garlic Cloves, Minced
- 1 Lb. Ground Beef
- 1 Tbsp Italian Parsley
- 1 Tbsp Kosher Salt
- 1 Tbsp Olive Oil
- ½ Cup Minced Onion
- 1 ½ Cup Peas, Frozen
- 2 Tsp Pulled Pork Rub
- 1 Tsp Rosemary, Finely Chopped
- 1 ½ Lbs. Russet Potatoes, Peeled And Quartered

Directions:

1. Supply your smoker with wood pellets and follow the start-up procedure. Preheat the grill, with the lid closed, to 400° F. If using a gas or charcoal grill, set the temp to medium-high heat.

2. In a cast iron Dutch oven, bring potatoes and just enough water to cover to a boil. Add salt and cook until tender, 12 to 15 minutes. Drain potatoes, and return to pot. Add cream cheese, butter, ½ teaspoon salt, ½ teaspoon black pepper, and mash until smooth. Set aside.

3. Place cast iron skillet on grill and heat oil. Add onion and sauté 2 minutes, then add garlic and sauté until fragrant. Add ground beef, Pulled Pork Rub, and

rosemary, and cook, stirring occasionally, breaking up the meat until browned.

4. Sprinkle flour over beef and stir until combined. Add the broth and cook, stirring until thickened, about 3 minutes.

5. Add a layer of peas over beef and sprinkle with parsley. Dollop mashed potatoes on top of peas and spread evenly.

6. Increase temperature to 450° F. Cover and cook for 5 minutes, then top with grated cheese. Cover and cook and additional 5 to 7 minutes, until cheese is melted, and edges of potatoes begin to brown. Serve hot.

Smoked Brisket With Traeger Coffee Rub

Servings: 8

Cooking Time: 540 Minutes

Ingredients:

- 1 (15 lb) beef brisket
- 1/4 Cup Coffee Rub, divided
- 15 Ounce beef broth
- 4 Tablespoon salt, divided

Directions:

1. Supply your smoker with wood pellets and follow the start-up procedure. Preheat the grill, with the lid closed, to 225° F.

2. Trim brisket of all excess fat.

3. To make the beef broth injection, combine 2 tablespoons Traeger Coffee Rub, beef broth and 2 tablespoons salt in a small bowl, stirring until the salt is dissolved. Inject the brisket by inserting the needle parallel to the grain about 1 inch apart in a checker pattern over the entire brisket. Pull it back out as you press the plunger. Inject in a high-sided aluminum pan or bus tub and hold your hand over where you are injecting to contain the mess.

4. Season the exterior of the brisket with remaining rub and remaining salt.

5. Place brisket directly on the grill grate and cook for about 6 hours or until the internal temperature reaches 160℉. Grill: 225 ℉ Probe: 160 ℉

6. Wrap the brisket tightly in two layers of foil or butcher paper. Return to grill.

7. Cook an additional 3 hours or until the internal temperature reaches 204°F. Remove brisket from the grill and make a small opening in the foil to let steam escape. Grill: 225 °F Probe: 204 °F

8. Close the opening after 10 minutes and allow meat to rest 60 minutes before slicing. Slice and enjoy!

Grilled Skirt Steak Quesadillas

Servings: 4
Cooking Time: 15 Minutes

Ingredients:

- 2 Tablespoon chili powder
- 2 Teaspoon kosher salt
- 1 Teaspoon ground cumin
- 1/2 Teaspoon Chipotle Chili Powder
- 1/2 Teaspoon cayenne pepper
- 1 Teaspoon lime zest
- 1 1/2 Pound skirt steak
- 12 Whole Corn Tortillas, 6 inch
- 1 vegetable oil
- 1/2 Cup shredded pepper jack cheese

Directions:

1. For the skirt steak, combine the chili powder, salt, cumin, chipotle powder, cayenne and lime zest in a small bowl.

2. Rub the spice mixture over entire skirt steak and let marinate in a zip-top bag at least 20 to 25 minutes.

3. Supply your smoker with wood pellets and follow the start-up procedure. Preheat the grill, with the lid closed, to 400° F.

4. Place skirt steak on grill 3-4 minutes per side. Let rest for 20 minutes before cutting into bite sized pieces. Grill: 400 °F

5. For the quesadillas, take the tortillas and fill with cheese and grilled skirt steak. Cook on a grill pan or in a sauté pan with extra oil to prevent burning.

6. Serve with guacamole, sour cream or salsa. Enjoy!

Grilled Double Burgers With Texas Spicy Bbq Sauce

Servings: 4
Cooking Time: 30 Minutes

Ingredients:

- 3 Pound ground beef
- 4 Tablespoon Beef Rub
- 1/2 Pound bacon
- 8 Slices cheddar cheese
- 4 Whole burger buns, for serving
- 1 Cup Texas Spicy BBQ Sauce
- sliced pickles, for serving

Directions:

1. Form ground beef into eight 1/3 pound patties. Season each patty on both sides with Traeger Beef Rub.

2. Supply your smoker with wood pellets and follow the start-up procedure. Preheat the grill, with the lid closed, to 350° F.

3. For the Bacon: Place bacon slices directly on grill grate and cook for 15 to 20 minutes, or until crispy. Grill: 350 °F

4. Increase the Traeger temperature to 450°F and preheat. Grill: 450 °F

5. Place burger patties directly on grill grate and cook for 4 minutes on each side, or to desired doneness. Grill: 450 °F

6. Top each patty with a slice of cheddar cheese and cook, lid closed, until cheese melts.

7. To serve, spread the Traeger Texas Spicy BBQ Sauce onto each bottom bun and top with the pickles and patty, then repeat with BBQ sauce, pickles, patty, BBQ sauce, and finally the bacon. Top with top bun. Enjoy!

Cheddar Bacon Beef Burgers

Servings: 12
Cooking Time: 30 Minutes

Ingredients:

- Bacon Cheddar Burger Seasoning
- 3/4 Cup Bacon, Chopped
- 3 Lbs Beef, Ground
- 1 Jalapeno, Chopped
- Pepper
- 1/2 Cup Ranch Dressing
- Salt
- 1 1/2 Cups Shredded Cheddar Cheese

Directions:

1. Supply your smoker with wood pellets and follow the start-up procedure. Preheat the grill, with the lid closed, to 350° F.

2. In a small bowl, combine cheese, bacon, jalapeno and ranch dressing.

3. In a clean, large bowl, combine ground beef with enough salt and pepper to taste.

4. Form meat into patties and place on a pan. A good rule of thumb is for each patty to be about the size of the palm of your hand.

5. Using a clean glass, press into each patty, leaving the imprint of the bottom of the glass in the patty. Stuff the filling into the indent. Grill for 25 minutes or until the ground beef reaches an internal temperature of 160°F. Serve hot.

Hickory Smoked Prime Rib

Servings: 6

Cooking Time: 240 Minutes

Ingredients:

- 1 (8-10 lb) 4-bone prime rib roast
- 3 Tablespoon Dijon mustard
- 2 Tablespoon Worcestershire sauce
- 4 Clove garlic, mashed to a paste
- 2 Teaspoon dried thyme
- 2 Teaspoon dried rosemary
- Prime Rib Rub or coarse salt and freshly ground black pepper
- prepared horseradish, for serving

Directions:

1. If the roast has a fat cap more than 1/4 inch thick, trim it with a sharp knife or ask your butcher to do it for you. Tie the roast between the bones with butcher's twine. This discourages the eye of the meat from separating from the cap.

2. In a small bowl, whisk together the Dijon mustard, Worcestershire sauce, garlic, thyme and rosemary. If the dried rosemary needles are long, finely chop them before adding.

3. Slather the outside of the roast with the mustard paste and season generously with Traeger Prime Rib Rub on all sides. Refrigerate uncovered for up to 8 hours.

4. Supply your smoker with wood pellets and follow the start-up procedure. Preheat the grill, with the lid closed, to 250° F.Place the prime rib directly on the grill grate, fat-side up. Roast for 3-1/2 to 4 hours, or until the internal temperature of the meat (the tip of the temperature probe should be in the center of the meat) reaches 125°F to 130°F for rare or for medium-rare, 135°F. Grill: 250 °F Probe: 125 °F

5. Transfer meat to a cutting board, preferably one with a deep well so you don't lose the juices, and loosely tent the meat with foil. Allow meat to rest for 30 minutes. Grill: 250 °F Probe: 135 °F

6. To carve, remove the twine. Use a sharp knife to remove the rack of bone following the curvature of the meat. Carve the meat across the grain into 1/2 inch thick slices. Serve with horseradish, if desired. Enjoy!

RECIPE INDEX

Roasted Tomatoes 132
Roasted Tomatoes With Hot Pepper Sauce 153
Roasted Vegetable Napoleon 139
Roasted Whole Chicken 172
Rosemary Cranberry Apple Sage Stuffing 68
Ryes And Shine Cocktail 26

S

S'mores Dip Skillet 57
Salt & Pepper Beer-braised Beef Ribs 215
Salt & Pepper Dinosaur Bones 202
Salt Crusted Baked Potatoes 146
Santa Maria Tri-tip With Pico De Gallo 210
Savory Bacon Wrapped Hot Dogs 220
Savory Beaver Tails 71
Savory Cajun Bbq Chicken 177
Savory Cheesecake With Bourbon Pecan Topping 57
Savory Pork Belly Banh Mi 128
Savory Reverse Seared Ny Steak 198
Savory Smoked Brisket 215
Savory Smoked Turkey Legs 172
Savory Whiskey Grilled Elk Steaks 219
Savory-sweet Turkey Legs 166
Seared Bluefin Tuna Steaks 91
Shrimp Cabbage Tacos With Lime Cream 79
Sicilian Stuffed Mushrooms 131
Simple Cream Cheese Sausage Balls 188
Skillet Potato Cake 137
Smoke And Bubz Cocktail 39
Smoke Roasted Chicken With Herb Butter 166
Smoked & Loaded Baked Potato 151
Smoked Airline Chicken 174
Smoked Apple Chicken Leg Quarters 171
Smoked Apple Cider 25
Smoked Asparagus Soup 151
Smoked Bacon Roses 113
Smoked Barnburner Cocktail 34
Smoked Bbq Onion Brussels Sprout 147
Smoked Beef Ribs 213
Smoked Beer Brine Hens 156
Smoked Beer Corned Beef 199
Smoked Beer Garlic Chicken 170
Smoked Berry Cocktail 24
Smoked Blackberry Pie 53

Smoked Bologna 100
Smoked Boneless Chicken Thighs 158
Smoked Brisket 217
Smoked Brisket With Traeger Coffee Rub 222
Smoked Cashews 189
Smoked Cedar Plank Salmon 96
Smoked Cheese 190
Smoked Cheesy Chicken Quesadilla 163
Smoked Chicken Leg & Thigh Quarters 173
Smoked Chicken Vermicelli Noodles 159
Smoked Cold Brew Coffee 32
Smoked Corned Beef Reuben 203
Smoked Crab Legs 83
Smoked Deviled Eggs 168
Smoked Drumsticks 158
Smoked Duck Breast Bacon 214
Smoked Eggnog 39
Smoked Elk Loin With Creamy Polenta 196
Smoked Fish Chowder 80
Smoked Grape Lime Rickey 37
Smoked Ham 122
Smoked Hibiscus Sparkler 33
Smoked Honey Salmon 98
Smoked Hot Buttered Rum 27
Smoked Ice Mojito Slurpee 29
Smoked Irish Coffee 35
Smoked Jacobsen Salt Margarita 33
Smoked Jalapeño Poppers 150
Smoked Lemon Cheesecake 52
Smoked Lemon Tea 44
Smoked Lobster Scampi 94
Smoked Macaroni Salad 141
Smoked Mango Shrimp 73
Smoked Mashed Potatoes 152
Smoked Mulled Wine 28
Smoked Parmesan Herb Popcorn 145
Smoked Peppered Beef Tenderloin 217
Smoked Pickled Green Beans 137
Smoked Pico De Gallo 147
Smoked Pineapple Hotel Nacional Cocktail 34
Smoked Plum And Thyme Fizz Cocktail 38
Smoked Pomegranate Lemonade Cocktail 28
Smoked Pork Spare Ribs 122
Smoked Pumpkin Spice Latte 30